Gladstone aged thirty-three. *Drawing by George Richmond (1843) for the series commissioned by Grillion's Club*

GLADSTONE

*

1809–1874

H. C. G. MATTHEW

Fellow and Tutor in Modern History at St. Hugh's
College. Lecturer in Gladstone Studies at Christ Church,
Oxford, and editor of *The Gladstone Diaries*.

Oxford   New York
OXFORD UNIVERSITY PRESS
1988

941·0810924 MAT

Oxford University Press, Walton Street, Oxford OX2 6DP

Oxford New York Toronto
Delhi Bombay Calcutta Madras Karachi
Petaling Jaya Singapore Hong Kong Tokyo
Nairobi Dar es Salaam Cape Town
Melbourne Auckland

and associated companies in
Beirut Berlin Ibadan Nicosia

Oxford is a trade mark of Oxford University Press

British Library Cataloguing in Publication Data
Matthew, H. C. G.
Gladstone 1809–1874.—(Oxford lives).
1. Gladstone, W. E. 2. Prime ministers—
Great Britain—Biography
I. Title
941.081′092′4   DA563.4
ISBN 0–19–282122–9

Library of Congress Cataloging in Publication Data
Matthew, H. C. G. (Henry Colin Gray)
Gladstone, 1809–1874.
Bibliography: p.
Includes index.
1. Gladstone, W. E. (William Ewart), 1809–1898.
2. Prime ministers—Great Britain—Biography. 3. Great
Britain—Politics and government—1837–1901. I. Title.
DA563.4.M38 1988   941.081′092′4 [B] 87–28164
ISBN 0–19–282122–9 (pbk.)

Printed in Great Britain by
Richard Clay Ltd.
Bungay, Suffolk

TO SUE

Preface

WILLIAM EWART GLADSTONE was elected to the Commons in 1832, was first in office in 1834, ended his fourth term as Prime Minister in 1894 and retired from the Commons in 1895. It is as if, in our own times, a man first in office in Ramsay MacDonald's National Government had been fairly constantly in Cabinet since 1941 and was still, in late 1985, to serve a further two separate terms as Prime Minister and another decade in the Commons. Throughout this huge career, Gladstone spoke constantly, wrote books and articles copiously, and kept most of his enormous correspondence, as well as writing almost 26,000 daily entries in his diary. Consequently, it would not have been difficult, indeed it would have been much easier, to have made this book twice or five times its present length.

The book is an introduction to Gladstone, an extended biographical essay; it makes no claim to be exhaustive or definitive. Indeed, such a claim with respect to so Protean a person as Gladstone would be silly. All but two of the book's chapters have been available for some years in the form of the Introductions I have written to those volumes of *The Gladstone Diaries with Cabinet Minutes and Prime-Ministerial Correspondence* which cover the years from 1840 onwards. The first two chapters have been written for this book. The *Diaries'* Introductions have been extensively used by scholars, but they have, hitherto, been printed together with the diary text in volumes only affordable by libraries. I hope it may be convenient to general readers and to students of the nineteenth century to have them available first hand, and in a gathered form. Some alterations and additions have been made to suit them for this book. Details of the correlation between the chapters of this book and the printed Introductions are given at the back of this volume.

I have chosen to stop for the time being at 1874. This is a natural break in Gladstone's career, for by the end of that year, following his first government's defeat in the General Election of 1874 and his resignation as Prime Minister, he had retired from leadership of the Liberal Party and was preparing for the sale of his London house. This was the end of what was, in retrospect, his first political career. His return to politics in 1876 and his remaining three premierships will be dealt with later as the editing of the *Diaries* reaches its conclusion (the period to the end of 1880 is already available: as Volume IX, with an Introduction).

It is a pleasure to have this opportunity to acknowledge debts and to express gratitude. My family has now lived with Gladstone for some time and my children—David, Lucy, and Oliver—have grown up with him. On the whole, like me, they have grown rather to like him. I am obliged to them for their tolerance and support. Sir William Gladstone has helped in a variety of ways, as have Christopher Williams of the Clwyd Record Office, Geoffrey Bill of Lambeth Palace Library, and Ivon Asquith of the Oxford University Press. Michael Foot supervised my early work on the *Diaries*; I thank him for inducting me into their complexities. Writing the Introductions has involved frequent importunity, acknowledged in their various Prefaces; Robert Blake, Peter Ghosh, Boyd Hilton, Ross McKibbin, Francis Phillips, and A. F. Thompson have been kind enough, over the years, to comment on all, or most, of the series. I am also obliged to the Gladstone Diaries Committee, which gave me my chance.

I would like especially to thank in this Preface those who introduced me to Victorian history: my grandparents who in their various ways showed me how Victorians lived and thought; Andrew Morgan and Ivan Christopherson, my history masters at Sedbergh School; Charles Stuart, my tutor for the modern period at Christ Church; and Pat Thompson, my supervisor. These taught me Victorian history; my pupils at Old Moshi School, Christ Church, and St Hugh's required me to learn it.

Coming to terms with an historical personality, especially a personality as powerful and wide-ranging as Gladstone, is not easy. The Victorian period seems close because it is close chronologically. But it was a phase, and a phase that has passed. We live with its consequences, but we do not live with it itself. Our distance from it is a loss and a gain; what we gain in perspective, we lose in understanding. I have tried to understand Gladstone, and to be fair. But it is good to sense the distance and also to keep in mind his own view and that of one of his 'four Doctors':

Every secret which is disclosed, every discovery which is made, every new effect which is brought to view, serves to convince us of numberless more which remain concealed.   (Butler, 'Upon the Ignorance of Man')

There is scarcely a single moral action of a single man of which other men can have such a knowledge, in its ultimate grounds, its surrounding incidents, and the real determining causes of its merits, as to warrant their pronouncing a conclusive judgment upon it.   (Gladstone on Leopardi)

Oxford   COLIN MATTHEW
December 1985

Contents

Illustrations

*

Thanks for permission to reproduce these illustrations are due, respectively, to Sir Richard Acland, Sir William Gladstone, the Archbishop of Canterbury, B.B.C. Hulton Picture Library, Clwyd Record Office, the Trustees of the British Library, the British Museum, the Wallace Collection, the National Portrait Gallery, and the Scottish National Portrait Gallery.

Prologue

'MEN make their own history, but not of their own free will; not under circumstances they themselves have chosen but under the given and inherited circumstances with which they are directly confronted.' Of few can Marx's truism be truer than of William Ewart Gladstone. His epic public career—first in office in 1834, last in 1894—confronted the prime of Britain as the first industrial nation. The agenda of free trade and imperialism was dictated by forces far beyond the control of individuals acting as such. Yet the interpretation and execution of the agenda was achieved by the decisions and actions of individuals and explained through their speeches and writings. In this interpretation, execution, and explanation, Gladstone's career holds a central place. In the process through which the British governing class came to terms with its new commercial and industrial destiny, Gladstone was a vital agent.

Forged by an education essentially pre-industrial, Gladstone mirrored his times in adapting politically, religiously, and socially to new circumstances. 'He'll shape his old course in a country new' (*King Lear*) was the motto he placed on the cover of his 1865 *Speeches and Addresses*, and it fairly describes what came to be his intentions and his actions. A radical conservatism, which fused at times with an advanced liberalism, was Gladstone's method. It was a method which deeply perplexed Conservatives, and often disappointed Liberals. For the former, it was almost always too much, too soon; for the latter, it was sometimes too little, too late. But it came to give Gladstone a curious position of great power in the centre of British politics, the power of surprise, of resource, of stability, and of an appeal, after the 1830s, that history and time were on his side.

Allied to this was an intuitive appreciation of the requirements and possibilities of modern politics, of the availability to the politician of a whole new forum of public debate made possible by the development of the public meeting and the national exchange of debate fostered by an integrated London and provincial press. In this process of directly addressing the people in great meetings, Gladstone confronted the popular politics of his day, but he also to an extent directed and controlled them. He was both their creature and creator.

In all this, the fixed point for Gladstone was his Christian faith, the preservation of the Church and the triumph of Christian values. Christianity gave Gladstone a powerful sense of his destiny, both in general and in particular situations. A man of intense temper and sexuality, he used his Christianity to maintain self-control. He also was required by it to be

truthful. Truthfulness in representative government is never an easy business: as he wrote in 1896 in almost the last entry of his lifelong journal, 'It is
so easy to write, but to write honestly nearly impossible.' Gladstone tried to
meet the problem of honesty in public life first, by not telling untruths, and,
second, by living for the record. Nobody has more assiduously compiled
materials for the benefit of history, including the careful preservation of a
private journal intended to show its author to be 'the chief of sinners'.
Gladstone had high standards and expectations of himself, and so have had
historians, always eager for a slip or an inconsistency. On the whole, he has
proved an awkward fellow to catch out. 'Terrible in the rebound' was Lord
Aberdeen's comment on his *protégé*, and, like contemporaries, historians
have often found the same.

As a chief representative of the Victorian age, Gladstone's career
displays the strengths and weaknesses of a liberal democracy at the height
of its self-confidence. The powerful individualism, the executive competence, the capacity for a sense of history, a feel for 'ripeness' and for
national development; against these may be balanced, for all the introspection, a curious lack of self-awareness.

This book describes Gladstone's attempts to explain and to justify his
age and its place in history to himself and to his contemporaries; his efforts
to help it to prune and to consolidate, to adapt and to reform itself politically, administratively, ecclesiastically, and intellectually; and his strivings
to harness his will and his passions to the service of God.

CHAPTER I

Liverpool, Eton, and Oxford

Family and Fortune—An Evangelical Family—An Eton Boy—
A House Man

My [twenty-first] birthday. Surely to me a day of pain in as far as it was a day of reflection: to others perhaps (God bless them) of joy. As to *idleness* one of my great foes, there has been *less* of it thank God during the past year: but the only redeeming portion was the Long Vacation—and then it was owing to my close contact with industrious persons.

This has been my Debating Society year: now I fancy done with. Politics are fascinating to me. perhaps too fascinating. . . .

I have thank God enjoyed much in Society. But as to real progress in religion: that is in the practical part of religion—the subjugation of the will & affections—I see no progress: though I may have clearer notions perhaps: which if so increase guilt.—

May God keep me during the coming year & from day to day may I approach more a practical belief that *he* is my friend, I mine enemy.

Family and Fortune

The earliest document in the Gladstone family papers is dated 1550; none the less, John Gladstone, the Prime Minister's father, was a self-made man. His career epitomized the entrepreneurial drive which made British commerce the dominant influence in world trade in the first half of the nineteenth century. His father, Thomas Gladstones, was a middle-ranking corn dealer in Edinburgh and Leith, the family having moved to the capital from the village of Biggar in the Scottish Borders. John Gladstone, born in Leith in 1764, soon saw the limitations of east coast trade, and moved west. Ignoring the difficulties of the French and American wars, and indeed turning those difficulties to advantage by surefooted anticipation of shortages, he assembled a huge fortune, travelling widely in North America and the Baltic in pursuit of purchases. On the basis of the transatlantic grain trade, which fed the rapidly growing population of Lancashire, and of diversification into property, shipping and West Indian sugar, cotton and slavery, his fortune rose from about £15,900 in 1795, to £40,700 in 1799, £333,600 in 1820, £502,550 in 1828.[1] In 1860 Samuel Smiles told William Gladstone, then Chancellor of the Exchequer, that he hoped to write John Gladstone's biography. Though William encouraged Smiles, nothing came of the proposal because of a dispute within the Gladstone family about it.[2] This was unfortunate, for John Gladstone was a classic Smilesian character, mixing duty, probity, and religion with materialism, initiative, and a strong drive for worldly success.

Of Lowland Scottish Presbyterian stock, John Gladstone made his way from Leith to Liverpool, from Whig to Tory, and from the Church of Scotland to the Church of England, dropping the 's' at the end of his name on the way. By his second marriage, to Anne Mackenzie Robertson—his first wife, Jane, died childless in 1798—he linked himself with a minor line of Highland gentry, William Gladstone recalling his grandmother as 'stoutly Episcopalian and Jacobite'.[3] He began to translate his money into social prestige through land, buying the Seaforth estate by Sefton then in the countryside outside Liverpool, and, in 1830, when his six children's education was nearing completion, buying the house and estate of Fasque, in the Mearns between Aberdeen and Montrose on the east coast of Scotland. In 1846, on the fall of the Peel government, he became Sir John Gladstone, baronet, of Fasque and Balfour. Sir Thomas Gladstone, the Prime Minister's elder brother, inherited the title and the estate of Fasque, but took no significant part in commerce.

John Gladstone also attempted to use his money politically, sitting in the Commons from 1818 to 1827 for a series of corrupt boroughs: Lancaster from 1818–20, Woodstock 1820–6 (bought cheaply from the Duke of Marlborough), Berwick-on-Tweed 1826–7 (unseated on petition). He was, therefore, one of those representatives of the new commercial class in the north of England who paid their way into the unreformed House of Commons. He was the sort of man who, in the eyes of the Canningites—the following of George Canning, Foreign Secretary and MP for Liverpool—demonstrated that the Constitution needed no reform since it was capable of representing new interests in an old system, or, alternatively, the sort of man who in the eyes of the ultra-Tories—the extreme defenders of the Protestant constitution—represented the corruption of the constitution by money. John Gladstone had thrived in unreformed Britain. His desire for continuing social stability, his distrust of speculative thought, and his respect for established religion, made him a natural supporter of the administrations of Lord Liverpool in the 1820s, and especially of the style of modest fiscal and administrative reform pursued by Canning, Huskisson, and Peel which justified by works the anomalies of the British representative system.

Thus, in brief, was forged the family context in which the fifth child, and fourth son, William Ewart Gladstone, was raised. His brothers and sisters were of very varied character. Anne, the first child, born in 1802, was an invalid like her mother and died unmarried at the age of 26. Her important religious influence on her brother will be discussed later. Tom, the oldest of the boys, tried hard to carry the burden of expectation which his father placed upon him, and preceded William at Eton and Christ Church, Oxford. He lacked the ability to capitalize on his advantages and never rose beyond the level of a Tory backbench MP. Robertson, born in 1805, was taken from Eton by his father and moved into the family business. A huge fat man when in his prime, he was for most of his life an able businessman, active in radical Liverpool politics, becoming Mayor of Liverpool and President of the Financial Reform Association before disintegrating mentally in his later years. John Neilson, the third son, refused to accept his father's wishes and with great character followed the naval career on which he was determined. He was for a time a Conservative MP and ended as High Sheriff for Wiltshire, the county in which he settled. Next came William Ewart, named from John Gladstone's political friend in Liverpool (the families quarrelled over the Ewarts' increasing radicalism in the 1831 election[4]), and last, Helen Jane, born in 1814. Like her sister and mother she was as a child often ill, but lived till 1880. A woman of high intelligence, she enjoyed a period of considerable intimacy with her brother William in the late 1820s and early 1830s. Her subsequent tragic life will punctuate the chapters of this book.

This was, then, a family of character, variety, and strong personalities. It was clearly upwardly-mobile and politically ambitious, but its huge correspondence for all the members wrote regularly to each other, sometimes even when in the same house—is characterized by gentility. The code of the English gentleman—the assumptions of honour, of duty, of charity, and of an easy acceptance of a social superiority which it would be bad manners to assert—was quickly assimilated by the male Gladstone children; the corresponding role of the pure but supine woman was exemplified by the mother and Anne, but not by Helen Jane, whose life was to be a series of rebellions.

Money, clearly, was never a problem. In the dangerous world of speculation, slumps, and gluts which characterized Regency Britain, John Gladstone moved adroitly and successfully. The bankruptcies which so shook the families of John Henry Newman and Henry Edward Manning, unsettling their confidence in the social arrangements of English society, did not disturb the Gladstones, and as a young man William Gladstone never had to consider money seriously. There was, however, a certain social uncertainty about the Gladstone household. In Britain money tempered by gentility could buy status, and in John Gladstone's case it certainly did, but it could not altogether buy recognition. In most obvious senses the career of John Gladstone represented a classic demonstration of the openness of the British ruling élite. But there was, none the less, a certain restlessness about his position, compounded by the chronic illnesses of his wife and daughters, which from the mid-1820s prevented entertaining and required frequent peregrinations to watering-places: a rather isolated residence in Leamington Spa was not really a fitting reward for a merchant prince. His political disappointments, and especially his inability to gain selection as Canning's running-mate in the two-member constituency of Liverpool, rankled personally, and the move to the then remote estate at Fasque constituted an exile from the mainstream of British public life from which John Gladstone never returned, active though he remained in correspondence to the press, in commerce, and in local affairs.

An Evangelical Family

When William Ewart Gladstone was born on 29 December 1809 in Rodney Street, Liverpool, his father was forty-six and his mother thirty-eight. The atmosphere of the home was moderately Evangelical, with the Evangelicals' strong emphasis on the reading of the Bible and on personal duty, family obligation, sin and atonement. Religion brought joy to the Gladstone women, but it weighed heavily upon the men, and especially upon William. William's mother believed that he had been 'truly converted to God' when he was about ten.[5] But there is little direct evidence of this: certainly it was not a vivid transformation such as that experienced by J. H. Newman, who kept the anniversary of his conversion to the end of his life. Indeed, as we shall see, the question of conversion came to preoccupy William in his student days.

Strong paternalism was a characteristic of evangelical families, and in the Gladstones' case this was reinforced by the contrast of the rude vigour of the tall, dark-suited husband with the sickliness of the mother and her elder daughter. An innate respect for male authority, and for the institutions that reflected it, was thus inherent in both a moral and a physical sense in William Gladstone's upbringing. The physical helplessness of the two Anne Gladstones made a permanent impression on the young William, who throughout his life saw women essentially as potentially noble creatures to be helped and lifted to a moral state as pure as that of his mother and his elder sister. When his mother died in 1835, Gladstone wrote of her:

Sin was the object of her hatred—and she can now sin no more. Sin is the cause of all the sorrow in the world: she can now no more add to the sin nor to the sorrow.... She departed in seraphic peace, like the gentleness of her own disposition.... She was eminent in the discharge of every duty: she sorrowed for sin: she trusted in the atonement of Christ. But this was not all: these elementary sentiments of religion were matured in her by the power of God, and she was made partaker of the nature and very life of the Redeemer, and her will conformed to his. Therefore, being, like Him, perfected through suffering, she had no new thing to learn, no fresh character to assume, upon translation to the world of spirits.... Two only have been taken from our family: and both are angels in heaven.[6]

He annually marked the birthday of the other 'angel in heaven', his sister Anne, who was also his godmother, remembering it as a special day of religious observance, rather in the manner that Newman remembered his experience of conversion. For Gladstone, the memory of his sister's 'ascendancy to Heaven' served almost as a vicarious conversion. His mother and sister, in fact, possessed that Evangelical religious assurance, repose, and sense of grace which Gladstone never throughout his life gained. For him, awareness of sin—certainly one of the Evangelical attributes—was always uppermost, never its atoning opposite. His mother and his sister represented to him, therefore, a quality of holiness which both inspired him and intensified his sense of inadequacy. Despite this, however, his extensive early writings on religion do not show any particular personal awareness or fear of hell of the sort exemplified for his generation by Thomas Chalmers, the Scottish presbyterian Evangelical and a family friend.

Another aspect of the Evangelical home was its very powerful emphasis on retribution for particular actions—the lazy moment, the naughty thought, the small, cheating trick—each must be marked, atoned for, and the appropriate lesson for the future learned. And not only this: such sins must inwardly be continually sought for, searched out, even when perhaps they were non-existent. This sense of permanent accountability, this searching oneself for sin, this acute awareness of God's immanence in watching for a chance for retribution, became a deep, perhaps the most profound, element in Gladstone's character. This inward searching, leading to a developed awareness of sin, led many Evangelicals to keep journals, and it was in this spirit that William Gladstone continued the journal which he began at Eton in 1824 or 1825—the date of the first surviving entry is 16 July 1825—as a simple, very brief record of work and events. He maintained it daily in over 25,000 entries with only the odd break until almost the end of his life. William Wilberforce, the archetypal lay Evangelical, noted of his own journal: 'I put these things down, that I may fix and ascertain, and re-consider my own corruptions and the deceitful working of my mind and passions.' Similarly Gladstone wrote his to 'tell, amidst the recounting of numberless mercies, . . . a melancholy tale of my own inward life'.[7]

But if Evangelicalism was the dominant ethos in the Gladstone home, it was not the exclusive influence. Gladstone's mother's Episcopalian background naturally linked her once she had come to Liverpool to the Church of England, and William Gladstone was baptized an Anglican. Though the two churches built by the Gladstones increased the Evangelical presence in the Liverpool area from one to three, their membership of the Church of England linked them with various wider and differing traditions, and both the Anne Gladstones—and especially the daughter—were familiar with the 'standard divines of the English Church',[8] including Richard Hooker's *Ecclesiastical Polity*. More importantly, from the point of view of William

Gladstone's later development, his family's membership of the Church of England meant that their Evangelicalism was nurtured in the context of an episcopal form of church government, very different from the democratic presbyterianism of John Gladstone's youth. Evangelicals generally took a somewhat 'low' view of episcopacy and of the national and established role of the Church of England; none the less their continuing membership—a deliberate choice in that many Evangelicals left it—meant a self-conscious association with a national church whose bishops were appointed by the Prime Minister and whose governing body, as far as it had one, was the Crown in Parliament. Membership of the Church of England, for an Evangelical, represented an integrative political act as well as a set of religious beliefs.

Politics no doubt played a part of some importance in John Gladstone's Church of Englandism. Like the Wilberforce family, the young Gladstones were brought up in an atmosphere of close interest in national politics, politicians, and the commercial world. As William Gladstone later remembered, 'the Evangelical movement . . . in lay life . . . did not ally itself with literature, art and general cultivation; but it harmonized very well with the money-getting pursuits'. Accompanying his father on business expeditions, the young Gladstone gained a very early experience of British geography. Despite the difficulty of movement in the pre-railway age—he was almost always sick in the coach—by the time he was eleven William Gladstone not only knew Lancashire well, but had visited Dingwall, Edinburgh, Cambridge, and London. It was in Edinburgh that he heard, as he later recalled, the 'rattling of the windows when the guns were fired on some great occasion, probably the abdication of Napoleon'.[9]*

From the start, Gladstone was familiar with the great, and ready to argue with them. One of his earliest memories was, at the age of two, being taken into the dining-room of his father's house when George Canning was a guest. Dressed in a red frock, 'I was set up on one of the chairs, standing, and directed to say to the company: "Ladies and gentlemen". I am sorry to add that I remember showing in boyhood an uncivilised nature by contending that it ought to be "gentlemen and ladies"'.[10] As a boy in Liverpool he was acquainted with the great political figures of the town, especially those in Tory circles, and on several occasions the family spent the

---

* Gladstone had what he called an excellent 'local memory' (i.e. for places) and the fragments—extensively used by Morley and now printed in *The Prime Minister's Papers* series—which he wrote in the 1890s on his early life in preparation for an autobiography were, considering the length of time which had elapsed and the extraordinary range of his public activities, unusually accurate. Gladstone had the chronology of his career very accurately in his head and when recalling a political event in conversation or on paper he was rarely more than a week or so out. None the less, an accurate factual memory is not necessarily a completely reliable guide to opinion and these 'autobiographica', as Gladstone called them, must be used with caution, the more so as they so often quite closely *approximate* to what can be shown from other contemporary sources to have been his opinion as expressed at the time.

parliamentary sessions in London. John Gladstone intended that as many of his sons as possible should consolidate this acquaintance with the political world, and so he sent them to Eton and to Christ Church, Oxford; their education would thus be that of George Canning.

An Eton Boy

When sent to Eton in 1821, at the age of eleven (rather older than was the custom), William Gladstone brought with him a curious intellectual and emotional baggage: a mixture of worldly experience through his father and from his mother a degree of religious separateness which, as we have seen, was not as sternly Evangelical as it could have been but which none the less set him apart from other boys. This blend was to stand him in good stead as he met the world of affairs which Eton represented. Gladstone came to Eton with little in the way of learning. He had been taught at the rather carefree school run by William Rawson on the sands at Bootle on the Mersey. Rawson was a moderate Evangelical brought to the Liverpool area by John Gladstone on the advice of Charles Simeon, the famous Cambridge preacher. At his school, Gladstone 'shirked my work as much as I could. I went to Eton in 1821 after a pretty long spell in a very middling state of preparation, and wholly without any knowledge or other enthusiasm, unless it were a priggish love of argument which I had begun to develop.'[11] This lack of preparation was not any great disadvantage. The formal education at Eton was largely mechanical: Latin and Greek—but mainly Latin—grammar, translation, and construing. 'Gladstone *mi*.'—for his brother Tom, for whom he fagged, was already at the school had, with his control of detail and his excellent memory, little difficulty in mastering the system. Such stimulation beyond the technical competence required for such exercises came from the weekly 'Verses', a composition in Latin on an original subject but with little advice or assistance. Gladstone kept his fair copies of many of these; they are largely uncorrected by the schoolmaster, but have a laconic 'Well' (or sometimes 'Very Well') written at the end in the master's hand.[12]

In addition to classics, some modern languages were taught, and Gladstone clearly benefited considerably from M. Berthomier, his French instructor, who introduced him to French drama and especially Molière, an unusual interest for the time (shared incidentally with Disraeli) and one which he maintained throughout his life. Though Gladstone at the end of his life stated that the 'system was without merit', on reflection he believed that 'in one point it was admirable. I mean its rigid, inflexible, and relentless accuracy . . . it has been my habit to say that at Eton in my day a boy might if he chose learn something, or might if he chose learn nothing, but that one thing he could not do, and that was to learn anything inaccurately.'[13]

John Gladstone had not sent his son to Eton to acquire proficiency in the hexameter. Attending Eton was a confirmation of the Gladstones' arrival in the upper echelon of British society and was also the means of penetration to its centre, the House of Commons, and the London professions. The curious structure of Eton, with its College and its Oppidans, its self-employed housemasters, its private tutors and its Dames, was a microcosm of the British ruling élite: at first glance a fairly clearly identifiable body of people, at second glance an extraordinarily complex organism with rules and conventions known fully only to those brought up within it, and only very rarely penetrated successfully from outside (as, for example, by Disraeli).* It was to be brought up in these ways of thinking, and to be part of the class that thought that way, that John Gladstone sent three of his sons (Tom, Robertson (briefly), and William) to Eton.

The absence of general education at the school assisted this process, if a boy had character and ability. Such boys made their own education, and William Gladstone quite quickly found a place among them. In 1825 he was elected to the Eton Society (also known as the 'Literati' and later as 'Pop'), founded in 1811 by Charles Fox Townshend to give the boys an organization in which intellectual discussion and debate could develop. The success of the society, after a poor period about 1820, meant that by Gladstone's day membership was one of the chief glittering prizes which the school had to offer and the blackballing election system—mirroring the London political clubs—was taken most seriously. The society was small, self-electing, and wholly independent of the masters. Former pupils of the school continued for a time to be members, and in Gladstone's day the membership included eight MPs.[14] It also included, unbeknown at the time to him, his future brother-in-law and his best man, Stephen Glynne and Francis Doyle. Members read papers for discussion, and debated motions on aesthetic and political topics; 'Our Society men are great politicians in a small way'.[15] A 'fifty year rule' excluded motions on contemporary politics, but this could be got around, Catholic Emancipation, for example, being debated in 1826 in the form of a motion on the right of the former Polish government to exclude Protestants from the civil service. As the political tension rose in the 1820s with the gradual disintegration of Liverpool's Tory Party, private debates, ancillary to the Society, became common, Catholic emancipation and political reform being naturally among the topics. The effect of the 'fifty year rule' was to encourage historical knowledge and an identification with the parties and factions of pre-industrial Britain, for many of the

---

* Eton's complex structure contrasted markedly with that of the reformed public schools later in the century where the emphasis was on a simple, authoritarian structure based on school and house prefects and with clear lines of demarcation of authority.

motions involving Britain were on Reformation or Civil War topics, the rest being mainly on classical issues. The terms in which these youths learned to discuss politics were therefore those of the Greek–Roman period and those of the making of the Protestant constitution and nation-state in what would now be called the early-modern period. The atmosphere within the Society was both friendly and competitive, with an especial emphasis on prowess of presentation of argument.

Gladstone formed two friendships of particular importance, as well as a wide circle of acquaintances many of which relationships he maintained by letter, despite political differences, until the death of the correspondent (for he outlived them all). James Milnes Gaskell was, Gladstone wrote at the time, 'a very clever fellow ... [with] by far the most extensive political knowledge and intimate acquaintance with English history of any boy that I ever saw'; he recalled him seventy-two years later as 'that rare and most precious thing, an enthusiast'.[16] Gaskell's enthusiasm was for the minutiae of politics, the division lists, the journals, the details of the conventions: he 'inoculated us all with a love for politics'.[17] That mastery of the detail of debating procedures, so formidable a weapon throughout his career in the Commons, Gladstone learned with the enthusiastic Gaskell. For Gaskell, politics was a process justified in its own terms, an endless game in which knowing the rules was more important than winning. When Gladstone later referred to politics as being both a game and a high art,[18] he referred to a sport whose rules he had learnt very early.

The chief love of Gladstone's schooldays was Arthur Henry Hallam, son of the Whig historian and subject of Tennyson's great elegy, *In Memoriam*. This relationship with Arthur Hallam was certainly not the usual 'crush' developed between boarding-school boys living in close proximity, for Hallam was tutored by F. C. Hawtrey, while Gladstone's tutor was H. H. Knapp, and 'messing' (i.e. eating) between boys in different houses was most unusual.[19] None the less the relationship was intense, though not directly sexual, and prefigured several such relationships, with both sexes, in Gladstone's later life. It developed chiefly within the Eton Society where competition for affection as well as for superiority was often overt as well as covert. Hallam wrote to his sister in 1826: 'walking out a good deal, & running the changes on Rogers, Gladstone, Farr and Hanmer'.[20] What heartaches for the others lie buried in that simple phrase, 'running the changes'! It shows Hallam to have had a cool edge to his brilliant personality. Despite this, he certainly captivated Gladstone emotionally, though not intellectually, in the way we shall see Manning and James Hope doing in later years. Hallam was, like his father, a steadfast Whig: he put the case for political reform to Gladstone in a letter of astonishing maturity, but he did not convince him.[21] In 1829, when Hallam was at Cambridge with Tennyson and Gladstone was at Oxford, the latter noted a brief history of his relationship with Hallam:

The history of my connection with [Hallam] is as follows.
It began late in 1824, more at his seeking than mine.
It slackened soon: more on my account than his.
It recommenced in 1825, late, more at my seeking than his.
It ripened much from the early part of 1826 to the middle.
In the middle, [Farr?] *rather* took my place.
In the latter end [of 1826], it became closer & stronger than ever.
Through 1827, it flourished most happily, to my very great enjoyment.
Beginning of 1828, [Hallam] having been absent since he left Eton, it varied but very slightly.
Middle of 1828, [Hallam] returned, and thought me cold. (I did not increase my *rate* of letters as under the circumstances I ought to have done.)
Early in 1829, there was friendly expostulation (unconnected with the matter last alluded to) and affectionate reply.
Illness in [spring and summer of 1829].
At present, almost an uncertainty, very painful, whether I may call [Hallam] my friend or not.

Clearly, for Gladstone 1827 was the best year. In 1828, Gaskell and Hallam were both in Italy, and both fell in love with Anna Wintour. Gladstone indirectly came to know of the affair, but almost certainly not of the depth of the passion in both men.[22] How far this upset the delicate balance of his friendship with Hallam can probably not now be known. From Hallam, Gladstone not only gained a direct and intimate confrontation with Whig arguments, but also encouragement towards a powerful aesthetic sense, for it was in aesthetics and Italian literature that Hallam's real interests came to lie; and he had little interest or ability in the feats of memory required to produce accurate Greek and Latin verse and prose.[23] Gladstone brought to Hallam, clearly a rather sophisticated youth, a quality of innocence blended with intellect which Hallam, writing in May 1829 when the height of the friendship's intensity had passed, captured in a powerful line:

... the father of good
On my early spring one perfect gem bestowed.[24]

The Eton Society also gave the stimulus to the *Eton Miscellany*, jointly edited by Gladstone as 'Bartholomew Bouverie' and George Selwyn, later the tractarian Bishop of New Zealand. Like most schoolboy journalism, there was a good deal of wrangling about late entries, and some of the result was rather precious. None the less, the various numbers, which were collected into a volume, have a natural authority about them. As with the contributors' correspondence, a reader coming across it unawares would probably not realize it was written by schoolboys.

In the debates with his friends, Gladstone on the whole took a Tory line, but, as in his Oxford days and in the early 1830s, his conservatism had some unusual elements to it. Predictably enough, he spoke for the Norman Conquest against Hallam, but he voted at first, somewhat indecisively, and perhaps reflecting his mother's influence, for the 'Stewarts' in the 1745 Rebellion, which most Liverpool Conservatives in the 1820s would have regarded as merely quixotic and irresponsible romanticism, wedded as they had become to the Hanoverian constitution. Further study and conversation led to his 'getting a new light on subject of Stuarts, 1745 &c.' He was undecided whether it could be said that the Whigs in the reign of Anne had deserved well of their country, and initial hostility and a vote against that greatest of the Whigs, Sir Robert Walpole, changed to a favourable vote, with the comment: 'there were surely considerable blots,—but nothing to *over*-balance, or to equal, the great merit of being the bulwark of the Protestant Succession—and his commercial measures—& (*in general*) his Pacific Policy'.[25]

These positions were not lightly taken. Though high-spirited, the members of the Eton Society were fully aware of their political destinies, and flippancy in debate was severely disapproved of, by none more so than Gladstone, later remembered by Francis Doyle in his poem 'The Poetaster's plea: a familiar epistle to W. E. Gladstone, Esq., M.P.':

> To one I turn—the monarch of debate,
> President Minos of our little state,
> Who, when we met to give the world the law
> About Confucius, Caesar or Jack Straw,
> Saw with grave face the unremitting flow
> Of puffs and jellies from the shop below;
> At the right moment called us to forsake
> Intrusive fruit, and unattending cake;
> And if unheeded, on the stroke of four,
> With rigid hand closed the still-opening door.[26]

'To give the world the law' was a fair description of the Eton Society's members' ambition and expectation. They had an innate awareness of their natural membership of 'the clerisy', the phrase coined at this time by Coleridge to describe what would now in Gramsci's terminology be called the hegemonic class.

One law much in contention because of its abolition's potential effect on the Anglican nature of that clerisy—indeed its abolition in 1829 was the stimulant to Coleridge's definition—was the law excluding Roman Catholics from full British citizenship, and especially from holding public office. Gladstone seems to have been consistently in favour of Catholic Emancipation, in contrast with many Tories, but in harmony with his father and George Canning. In 1827 he noted: 'Received the horrid news of the defeat of [Burdett's motion in the Commons on] the Catholics. I trust it is all for the best; but the prospect is awful.'[27] This last phrase suggests it was the prospect of disorder which concerned William Gladstone, at this stage following his father in seeing 'emancipation' in the light of prudence rather than of right.

Tory though Gladstone saw himself to be, his experience at Eton was essentially Whiggish, in the sense that it taught him to see society in terms of politics, and to see the history of Britain in terms of development and of the centrality to that development of constitutional politics rather narrowly defined. The framework of discussion, even for those in disagreement with aspects of it, was determined by the Whig view of history. For what was the constitution so steadfastly maintained by the Tories of the 1820s, but the Whig settlement of 1688? Ready to abandon the Tory settlement of the 1660s by repealing the Test and Corporation Acts and the acts restricting Roman Catholics, the Tories regathered to defend the parliamentary constitution of the late seventeenth and early eighteenth century Whigs. Catholic Emancipation passed shortly after Gladstone left Eton, and its passing opened a new political era, the reforming decade of the thirties in which the young Gladstone attempted to forge his Toryism into a doctrine.

We have seen the social and political influences of Eton on him: what of the intellectual and religious?

Gladstone read widely at school, ranging far outside the required texts. He began his life-long practice of noting all his reading (except newspapers) in his daily journal entry. He read much modern British history—Clarendon, Burnet, Coxe's *Walpole*, Tomline's *Pitt*—he read most of the plays of Shakespeare, and he read Scott. In this, perhaps, he built on an earlier enthusiasm for Ossian (in an early letter home from Eton he requested the sending on of his Ossian, and he continued to be interested in the controversy). For it was the Scottish works of Scott that attracted him as a schoolboy—*Waverley* (read for the second time when he was sixteen), *Old Mortality* ('in the first rank of Waverley Novels, me judice'), *Heart of Midlothian*, *Legend of Montrose*, *Rob Roy*, *Chronicles of the Canongate*, and *Tales of a Grandfather*. For the rest of his life Scott was to be 'a treat', not written about or analysed, but absorbed. Gladstone can hardly have been unaffected by the central theme of Scott's Scottish novels, how society progresses in an irreversible direction and how those individuals who fail to progress with it, while particularly attractive and fascinating, are ultimately quaint. Not to have met Scott before he died in 1832—there was a chance in Rome in April 1832 'but we could not find him out'—was one of the regrets of Gladstone's life.

Important parts of Gladstone's schoolboy reading were prompted by the topics chosen for debate in the Eton Society. Debating preparation launched him on Milton, Clarendon, and Hume. In each case he continued his reading after the context of the debate and its subsequent discussions had passed.

Gibbon was begun in November 1825, returned to for a debate in 1827, and then completed. Not surprisingly, Gladstone thought the 'style . . . beautiful, but much sneering at Christian religion, partially disguised',[28] but his general view of the work was more favourable than might have been expected from one of his background. He made one of his detailed 'Epitomes' (a digest of the argument written on long thin strips of paper). He found 'Gibbon's style diffuse; sometimes very beautiful, sometimes too highly ornamented'. He preferred David Hume's *History of England*, of which he also made an Epitome: 'Hume *me judice* a greater historian', and 'Finished Gibbon. Elegant and acute as he is, he seems to me not so clear, so able, nor so attractive as Hume: does not impress my mind so much.' This enthusiasm for Hume ('a delightful history—barring the religious principles'[29]) was important in conditioning Gladstone's youthful view of the lack of a correlation between liberty and democracy.

Gladstone discounted the scepticism of Gibbon and Hume without much difficulty. He read many other works at school which might have surprised his mother: 'read [on a Sunday] . . . a little Locke on Toleration, but found much Repetition, so began [his] Reasonableness of Christianity'.[30] The whole of his Eton experience built upon the outward-looking aspects of his family's religion, but usually in a secular way. At Eton, Gladstone's religion was privately practised. He learned to observe his religion regardless of a largely indifferent surrounding, and without making a fuss. This was a valuable lesson. Throughout his life he was to be able to exist in close and happy relationship in male society with those—like Lord Granville—who shared none of his religiosity. He does not seem to have behaved in the school or in the Eton Society as in any way an overt Evangelical; he did not try to convert his friends, and his letters to them attempt to match the jocular tone of Hallam and Gaskell. He sometimes argued about religion with them ('stiff arguments with Hallam, as usual on Sundays, about Articles, Creeds &c.') but this was probably on their legal and political role, rather than as questions of faith. In such discussions he took a Cavalier's view of the seventeenth century church, defending Charles I for 'saving our religion', and relying on the authority of Clarendon's *History of the Rebellion*: 'it is astonishing how your Cavalier spirit runs away with you' complained the strongly Parliamentarian Hallam.[31]

Privately, however, in the manner of his family, Gladstone read the Bible daily and extensively on Sundays, sometimes in Greek; in his last year he read through the Gospels using the High-Church commentary by D'Oyly and Mant.[32] He was also an avid sermon-reader. Some of his choices—the sermons of the moderate Evangelical J. B. Sumner and the sermons and discourses of Thomas Chalmers, the Scottish Evangelical and a family friend—were predictable. But he also made a prolonged study of the sermons of the moderate Presbyterian Hugh Blair, a prominent figure in the Scottish Enlightenment and a friend of Adam Smith and David Hume. Gladstone found him, eventually, 'more flowery than solid', hardly a strong reaction to the Enlightenment.[33] This, and his voluntary reading of William Paley's *Evidences of Christianity* with its argument from Design, suggests, when taken together with Mant's commentary, a considerable eclecticism and a curiosity to move well beyond the simplicities of Biblical evangelicalism, together with an embryonic High-Churchmanship as yet historical in form and only partially integrated into his developing religious persona.

To describe Gladstone at Eton simply as an Evangelical would therefore be at the least an over-simplification. The most surprising item in his religious studies at Eton is his Sunday reading of 'the Roman Catholic Prayer Book' in 1826:[34] in the Evangelical world of Gladstone's upbringing, knowledge of and interest in the details of the bishop of Rome's church was regarded as little short of Satanism.

In his last year at Eton, after a brief preparation, Gladstone was confirmed 'according to the apostolical rite preserved in the Church of England',[35] a turn of phrase pointing quite clearly to the developments of the 1830s. As in most Anglican churches in the 1820s, the Sacrament was not often celebrated at Eton, but by the end of the year Gladstone had communicated six times.

He left Eton at the end of 1827, a noted figure among a notable coterie, 'no ordinary individual', as Milnes Gaskell observed.[36] His time there was happy: 'if any thing mortal is sweet, my Eton years, excepting anxieties at home, have been so!'[37] His experience there had been enlarging, had taught him self-reliance socially and intellectually, and had, as John Gladstone had intended, associated him with the mainstream of English public life. His time there had also been fun: sculling on the river with Hallam, playing cricket, drinking with the Salt Hill Club which 'went up to Salt Hill to bully the fat waiter, eat toasted cheese, and drink egg-wine'; within the club Gladstone went by the name of 'Mr. Tipple'.[38] In the habit of English boarding-school former pupils, Gladstone became nostalgic about Eton, despite its pedagogic inadequacies.

A House Man

John Gladstone next sent his son to Christ Church—Aedes Christi, the 'House'—the dominant college, politically, intellectually, and socially, of the University of Oxford.* Under Cyril Jackson, the great reforming Dean who retired in 1809 but whose nominees still ran the college, Christ Church had since the late eighteenth century become the college most linked to the world of affairs. Jackson had deliberately and successfully made Christ Church a forerunner of the French *écoles*, a college intimately linked with

---

* This step had been planned at least as early as 1824, when the expectation was that William Gladstone would take his degree, then study law in London prior to entering political life.[39]

politics and administration, with the explicit purpose of creating a governing élite of the highest quality. It was under the influence of Jackson and Christ Church that the highly competitive system of examination by classes had been introduced in a series of Statutes beginning in 1800. The college still had a rowdy element for, as is often the case with educational reform, the peer group's standards were slow to adapt to change, and there were still those who were not 'reading' men (i.e. did not intend to take an honours degree). It was, no doubt, some of these undergraduates who entered Gladstone's room on 23 March 1830 and beat him up. None the less, in so far as a large Oxford college could at that time be a centre of intellectual endeavour, Christ Church was. When Gladstone took the 'Schools' in December 1831 (the examination for honours), of the ten First Classes awarded, five went to Christ Church men. Jackson's move from Whiggery into Toryism mirrored the tendency of many of the propertied class in the French Revolutionary years and though the college still had its Whigs the dominant ethos was that of Lord Liverpool's Toryism, exemplified by the most noted of the college's *alumni*, Liverpool himself, George Canning, and Robert Peel. These men reflected an emphasis on 'practicability', administrative reform and the linking of the aristocracy with commerce and manufacturing.

The college had a certain grand reserve which characterized the inmates as well as the buildings:

The etiquette of introduction is here as strict as in general society, or even more so, I think; which seems to have something absurd in it: though when it is considered how great an advantage it is to be kept *free*, it seems on the whole, to me at least, right. It is, I think, one of the greatest advantages attending a large college like Christ Church, that you are not under obligation to any acquaintance with a person merely because he belongs to the same establishment. In a small one, each individual is much more thrown into contact with every one of the rest: and of course it must be very unpleasant & injurious in many cases to be thus obliged either to put up with indifferent associates at least those who are not to one's mind or to give offence by avoiding their company. There are people in Oxford, in small colleges, who are much abused, because they *cannot* enter into the society of & the same course of life with, those around them. Here, each individual is, more or less, insignificant in regard to the mass. . . .[40]

It was, in fact, the sort of college which required undergraduates to act as if they were already in the metropolitan polite society for which so many of them were destined.

The education provided in Christ Church was not significantly different from that of Eton, but it was better done. Jackson had reformed the examination system of the University, introducing a strongly competitive classified hierarchy of classes (from 'First' to 'Fifth', i.e. the Pass School), into which each undergraduate was placed if he was to take a degree (a considerable number in the University as a whole did not, but most Christ Church men did). On the other hand, Jackson had not strenuously sought to reform the syllabus. Changes introduced, particularly under the influence of R. D. Hampden and 'the Noetics', at Easter, 1831, opened the syllabus a little more to recent writing, but these were made too late to affect Gladstone's undergraduate studies. Moreover, though Oxford was open to talent, it was not open to non-Anglicans: unlike Cambridge, all undergraduates had to subscribe to the Thirty Nine Articles at the time of matriculation, as Gladstone did on 23 January 1828: 'matriculated, taking the oaths, & subscribing to the Articles & Statutes'. Although the English governing class avoided becoming a caste in the French mode, the restriction of the Articles was pushing Oxford towards becoming one in education. The University faced the question, could it be both national and Anglican? It never itself succeeded in providing an answer. Eventually, Gladstone himself reluctantly cut the knot, repealing the 'Tests' in 1871.

A classical education with some compulsory theology, and with mathematics as an afterthought (for under the recent reforms the mathematics and physics examination could only be taken as a postscript to Literae Humaniores), was thus thought to be the best training for the Anglican clerisy. To the many criticisms which came from utilitarians on the one hand and some theologians on the other, arguing either that a classical education was of little value to an increasingly commercially-oriented society or that the Anglican priesthood (easily the largest professional destination of Oxford graduates) required a much more specifically theological training, Gladstone responded vigorously shortly after leaving the University:

It will be attempted to prove that one and all of these objections are futile: that there is no fair presumptive argument for change in our educational systems, as regards their fundamental principles, from the changes which have taken place in military tactics, in popular science, in manufacture . . . the errors of a pagan are not only not more, but are far less likely to entrap and mislead us, than those of that mass of modern writers, who bear the badge, and profess the principles of Christianity, while their real principles rise no higher than the level of the common opinions of society . . . not only do the classics quicken our views of Christianity by the force of contrast, and enlarge our knowledge of human nature by augmenting the stock of experimental facts whence our inductions are to be drawn: but further, that they are the best school for a study of human nature.

As Newman wrote in his Anglican days: 'put faith first and knowledge second, and Aristotle changes into Butler'.[41]

Gladstone was thus a product and a defender of liberal education in its purest form. But in contrast to the usual argument for a liberal education, that it encourages individual development and safeguards a pluralistic system of values, Gladstone believed that it would reinforce orthodox Anglican Christianity.

The deficiencies of his Eton education, especially in Mathematics, had been to some extent compensated by a rather unsatisfactory interim spell with a crammer, the Revd J. M. Turner of Wilmslow, another moderate Evangelical.[42] For most of his time at Christ Church, Gladstone worked hard, but not very hard:* he did not have to, until a spurt in his last year. Then he worked very hard indeed. His obvious ability was marked by his elevation by Dean Smith to a Studentship of the College in 1829. The only set-backs of his academic career were his failure to win the Dean Ireland Scholarship for which he entered in 1830 and 1831 (coached by Charles Wordsworth), the Craven in 1830 (being defeated on each occasion by a member of the Shrewsbury School coterie of textual analysts), and his entry 'Tyre' for the latin verse prize was unsuccessful; however, his memory in old age that he had entered for the Newdigate Poetry Prize was erroneous.

Milnes Gaskell noted 'He is among the very few who are thought sure of his class',[43] and the expected Double First (in Literae Humaniores and Mathematics and Physics) was obtained in December 1831,† despite alarms about the Mathematics, which a year earlier his father had agreed he need not offer, and despite a substantial amount of time in the summer term before the examinations being spent in organizing the Oxford petition against the Reform Bill and writing a long pamphlet (never published) opposing it. Naturally, such an achievement was accompanied by nervous strain: one Oxford School in a month is enough for most undergraduates! But arduous though Gladstone found the ordeal, he kept control, helped by his friends and some sedatives. It was a performance to be repeated many times in his life: for the work of assembling the budget and presenting it to the Commons, the concentrated effort of his oral examination before R. D. Hampden in the

---

* His formal timetable, undated but probably in 1829, may be of interest:[44]

Sunday	Church
	Divinity Lect I (6pm)
Monday	Mathematics 11
	Evening Lecture 7
Tuesday	Thucydides 11
	Romans in Second Century 12
Wednesday	Mathematics 11
	Evening Lecture 7
Thursday	Thucydides 11
	Romans in Second Century 12
Friday	Mathematics 11
	Juvenal 12
Saturday	Romans in Second Century 12
	Hall 2

† At that time, an undergraduate could offer himself for examination, with very little notice, when he felt ready, the examinations being provided several times a year.

Schools was—with many friends and others present—a good training. Gladstone found the preparation valuable:

Term is now approaching, and the critical time too. Taking into consideration *together* the amount of mental labour and of physical trial, and the anxiety arising from uncertainty of results, it is a sort of thing which ought not I think to come more than once in one's life, though for once it is very well, and the benefits certainly, as I think, exceedingly great: I doubt whether the intellect of the nineteenth century will ever set up a system of education more fundamentally sound.[45]

Years later, he disputed the value of such examinations with John Ruskin, who a decade after Gladstone had broken down during his preparation at Christ Church and could not take the honours examination: 'Gladstone gave, as a strong argument, *pro* the value of the sudden strain and effort, the vast concentration of mind, the hasty calling into play of all the intellectual powers, as a training for political life'.[46]

The set books a student reads, if taught properly as texts and not via commentaries,* stay with him or her throughout life: they have a peculiar grounding quality which is unequalled by later reading. This was certainly the case with Gladstone's undergraduate studies. The set books at Oxford were prescribed under the general rubric of 'a sufficient acquaintance with the Greek and Latin language and ancient history ... and Moral and Political Science, as derived from the ancient Greek and Roman authors, and illustrated, if need be, from modern authors.' They introduced him, amongst others, to Homer, Plato's *Phaedo*, Aristotle's *Ethics* and *Rhetoric*, Joseph Butler's *Analogy* and Thucydides' *History* (partly studied via Thomas Hobbes's 'Summary'): this last may be a clue, because of these, only Thucydides did not become a lifelong influence.† These and other books were exhaustively studied.

Gladstone's method of learning was, as at Eton, the detailed Epitome, and the way he made these Epitomes shows that he learned his set books while making a direct relationship between them and his own times. For example, his Epitome of Aristotle's *Rhetoric* is written on the right-hand side of the page; on the left are given examples from contemporary Parliamentary speeches by such as Canning, Peel, and Palmerston to illustrate the Aristotelian categories.[47] Of course, the full significance of these works was not apparent to him at the age of 21, when he took the Schools, but their categories were his instinctive points of reference for the rest of his life.

* It is interesting that on this ground Gladstone disapproved even of the introduction—after his time—of the aid of Liddell and Scott's *Greek Lexicon*: 'I had to make my own Homeric Lexicon, and the labour did me good.'[48]

† In the course of the Literae Humaniores examination—oral and written—Gladstone recorded being examined in Rhetoric, Ethics, Butler's *Analogy*, Plato's *Phaedo*, Homer's *Iliad* and *Odyssey*, Virgil, Persius, Aristophanes, Herodotus, Thucydides; he was prepared for, but was not examined in, Hellenics, Livy, Polybius, Select Orations, Horace, Juvenal, Aeschylus, Sophocles; he added 'I fear that unless they alter this, no one will get up his books' (17 Nov. 31).

It will be noted that Gladstone's set books offered him a number of models of how the world should work or had worked, but none of how it actually did work. Everything was by analogy and inference: parallels and analyses of the modern world were drawn by comparisons with the working of human nature and institutions in the ancient. Butler's *Analogy*, which itself of course reinforced this method of thinking by comparison, was the only set book for Literae Humaniores written after the first century.

The ways of thinking offered to the undergraduate were thus all pre-industrial, and prior to that body of writing on political economy which by the 1820s was well-established and considerable. None of the Oxford teaching dealt with political economy except through Aristotle, an author profoundly hostile to the division of labour both as a fact and as a means of social organization (except in the crude division between citizens, women, and slaves). Gladstone had thus no awareness of the Smithian revolution in political and economic thought which was already prescribed reading in the Scottish universities. There was no objection in itself to secular authors, for he was taught secular, classical authors as a contrast to Christianity, but the extensive debate as to whether Christianity and political economy were compatible passed him by. The laws of the market, the division of labour and the consequent concept of a world free trade market were to dominate the politics and intellectual life of Gladstone's century, but he finished his university studies with nothing more than a third-hand Malthusianism.

Though Gladstone's formal education at Oxford was much more rewarding than that of Eton, a good deal of the value of his time there sprang from what were really extensions of the Eton Society: the university Debating Society (which soon became the Oxford Union) and the Essay Club which he and others founded in Christ Church in October 1829. The intention of the founders of the Essay Club was to provide an Oxford equivalent of the Cambridge Apostles, of which Hallam was a member, and which gave Gladstone the idea of the Club.[49] It often met in his rooms in Canterbury, the small, 'very *fashionable*'[50] quadrangle—then a new building—built with money from Richard Robinson, late Archbishop of Armagh, and the Club became known by his initials, the WEG.* The club does not long seem to have survived his time at Oxford. Certainly the aim of an elitist, intercollegiate, private but notorious intellectual club, which would be self-perpetuating, was not achieved. In the Union, a mirror of

---

* The names of the members give an impression of Gladstone's Oxford circle; original members were: T. D. and A. H. D. Acland, J. Anstice, F. and O. B. Cole, F. H. Doyle, J. Milnes Gaskell, Gladstone, Benjamin Harrison, J. T. Leader, H. Moncrieff, Frederic Rogers later Lord Blachford, H. Seymer, E. H. Grimston; members joining later, Lord Abercorn, I. and J. Bruce, T. Egerton, H. G. Liddell, Lord Lincoln, H. Lushington, F. D. Maurice, N. Oxnam, C. Thornton, H. H. Vaughan, C. Marriott. The last recorded meeting was the 56th, in June 1832, with H. G. Liddell as secretary (Add MS 44804).

Parliament of which Gladstone became President for 1830, the same enthusiasm for political conventions as had dominated the Eton Society trained its active members for the debates in the Commons; it differed from the Eton Society in being generally open to membership and in being able to debate contemporary politics.

In these contexts Gladstone continued old friendships with Etonians, but made no burning new ones. He enlarged his circle of friends, naturally, but his contacts with his contemporaries—as varied as Lord Lincoln, F. D. Maurice, the Acland brothers, Sidney Herbert, Robert Phillimore, Walter Kerr Hamilton, Henry Manning—were amicable but not intense, though a number of them became so in later years. Intimacy was encouraged amongst those who regularly received Communion (in addition to the chapel-going which was compulsory for all undergraduates). This group was, Gladstone felt, deplorably small. He noted on 1 November 1829: 'Sacrament. Drake, Anstice, [Benjamin] Harrison, Ld Grimston & his brother, the two Aclands, [Martin] Tupper—& perhaps the servitor—I did not observe'; and again on 6 December 1829: 'Sacrament: as cold and unprepared as usual. Ld Grimston & his brother, Acland jun., Tupper, Anstice, [Penry] Williams(sen) & myself.' Several of these were members of the WEG. Gladstone felt a special bond with them, nurtured by the intensity common in an undergraduate group which feels itself besieged—as Gladstone certainly did by the general want of religious fervour which he identified as characteristic of the Oxford of his time. Tupper, later the author of the best-selling *Proverbial Philosophy*, was not a member of the WEG, but, despite finding him in later years rather tedious, Gladstone kept up with him even when he had fallen on hard times, sometimes giving him small 'loans' without expectation of repayment and eventually, in 1873, securing him a Civil List pension.

Of this group, Joseph Anstice and the Acland brothers were the closest to him. Anstice and Gladstone, together with Walter Kerr Hamilton, spent some time in the summer of 1830 at Cuddesdon, near Oxford, on a reading party supervised by A. P. Saunders. All three of these undergraduates were brought up under an Evangelical influence and moved in the 1830s towards a Tractarian or High Church position. It was in conversation with Anstice on 3 August 1830, as they walked back to Cuddesdon from a visit to Oxford, that thoughts 'first spring up in my soul (obvious as they may appear to many) which may powerfully influence my destiny'. Gladstone shared with Anstice 'that awful subject which has lately engrossed my mind'—the possibility of becoming a clergyman, whose full context and consequence will be discussed shortly. Thomas and Arthur Acland joined with Gladstone in the 1840s to found 'the Engagement', a laymen's substitute for clericalism, as no doubt Anstice, who also settled in London, would have done had he not died in 1836. At that time Gladstone noted: 'Heard to my deep sorrow of Anstice's death on Monday. His friends—his young widow—the world can spare him ill: so at least says the flesh'; next day he wrote some verses in his memory.

Though Christ Church reflected the self-confidence of a ruling class which had successfully beaten the French and avoided revolution at home (Gladstone's first Union speech defended Pitt's repressive legislation of 1795, an 'exceedingly easy' subject[51]), the Oxford of Gladstone's day had an undertone of unease. The dynamic entrepreneurial spirit of the north of England was not reflected in the south. Certain sections of the University maintained the old Tory non-juring tradition and a number of the younger dons, though not part of that tradition, were, like J. H. Newman, vicar of the University Church of St Mary, tinged with cultural pessimism.

As the Church of England in the 1820s began to appreciate the sheer scale of the reforming problem that it faced if it hoped in any real way to retain its position as the national Church, Oxford, the chief nursery of its incumbents, was neither buoyant nor energetic. The University saw itself threatened at almost every level—intellectually, politically, ecclesiastically, and constitutionally—a threat supposedly confirmed by the disintegration of the Tory party, the passing of Catholic Emancipation, and the victory of the Whigs in the General Election of 1830. Those who tried to sponsor internally generated constitutional reform to broaden the basis of the University by abandoning the requirement to subscribe to the Articles got short shrift from their colleagues, and in a panic of spurious orthodoxy R. D. Hampden, Principal of St Mary's Hall, was censured for rationalism in 1836–7 when Melbourne appointed him Regius Professor of Divinity. But for Parliamentary business, Gladstone would have gone to Oxford to vote against Hampden, an intention he later regretted.[52]

For any thinking member of the Church of England, the 1830s was to be a decade of ferment as groups within the Church of England and the University sought to regain the initiative for Anglicanism. Gladstone was to find himself a leading protagonist of this movement. While contemplating his future in 1831, he told his father: 'One of the most formidable features in the present frightful circumstances of the country is, that we have so long been blessed, contrary to our deserts, with ease and peace & settled habits, that the upper classes in this country cannot bring themselves to believe they are about to be wrested from them, and in consequence sit with hands folded and look on while the Revolution is in progress, instead of making strenuous exertions.'[53] Gladstone never sat with hands folded. His strenuous exertions were to form an unusual episode in the history of British Conservatism.

CHAPTER II

Gladstonian Conservatism: from Oxford to Westminster

A Young Conservative—A Serious Call?—The Tories' Rising Hope—
Towards a 'Science of Government': Plato and Aristotle—Church Principles—
Political Action—Wooed and Married and All—Money and Morality—
A Confident Conservative?

The time and circumstances are difficult in which I have to steer my little boat: but the pole-star is clear. Reflection shows me that a political position is mainly valuable as instrumental for the good of the Church: & under this rule every question becomes one of detail only.[1]

A Young Conservative

Gladstone left Oxford University after dramatically carrying in the Union an amendment stiffening a motion opposing the Reform Bill. In the manner of his time, he then made an extended visit to the Continent, travelling widely in France and Italy. While he was abroad, the Duke of Newcastle, father of his Christ Church acquaintance Lord Lincoln—and at the latter's instigation, for he was much struck by Gladstone's anti-Reform speech—approached John Gladstone with the proposal that William should sit for Newark, a town in which the Duke had influence, though not an exclusive influence. It was a good example of that 'representation of mind, for the political training of youth upwards, of the most capable material of the country' through the pocket borough system, a system which for that reason Gladstone always defended.[2] Rather to his surprise, Gladstone found himself in the new post-Reform Commons.*

This political destination in retrospect seems natural, and it seemed natural at the time to Gladstone's friends and to his father. To see why it came to seem appropriate to him, we must look in more detail at certain aspects of his life in early manhood.

The young Gladstone was a Tory. If we look at his letters, writings, and speeches in the late 1820s and early 1830s, it is not difficult to portray him as

---

* He also guarded himself against subsequent failure by eating a few of the dinners required by Lincoln's Inn for joining the bar—the original plan he and his father had devised, and a common one for young men in his position.

a very hard-nosed Tory indeed. Like many of his generation, he shared, at certain moments and especially in 1831–2, a millenarian feeling that European society stood on the brink of revolution and moral disaster.

. . . The signs of the times are so appalling. . . . Who can look abroad and say what the morrow shall bring forth, or hope that the dove of peace may find where to rest her foot amidst the deluge that is spreading . . . society seems, by the promulgation of new, pestilent, impracticable theories, shaken to its very foundations . . . this country is the main remaining home and hope of the cause of order throughout the world and even this last bulwark is assailed from within as well as from without.

The Reform Bill was 'the monstrous Bill which Ministers have introduced. It seems to me that they come nearer to deserving impeachment than any Ministry this country has had since the Revolution.'[3]

This view was not confined to the Reform Bill. In 1835, as the fall of the brief Peel government loomed, Gladstone told his mother: 'if we are beaten tonight as we are humanly certain to be, Sir Robert Peel will resign tomorrow, and with him will depart not indeed the last hope, for God still reigns, but (in my mind) the last ordinary, available, natural resource against the onset of Revolution'. Like others at the time, and especially those seeking a development from Evangelicalism, Gladstone was interested in Edward Irving's apocalyptic Catholic Apostolic Church, but when he visited it he found 'a scene pregnant with melancholy instruction', and Irving 'little short of madness'.[4] Gladstone's concern about what he saw as revolution was genuine but it was not cranky, that is, it was a concern conceived within the established categories of English political analysis. It is interesting that several of Gladstone's most urgent analyses—including that quoted above—were made in the context of a defence of rational exposition as against a flight to Pentecostalism by such as Bulteel and Irving as the means of responding to the crisis of the epoch. The change Gladstone feared was a constitutional, parliamentary revolution carried through by a Whig government; he showed no sign of alarm at the possibility of popular revolution. It was this constitutional revolution, a betrayal of its role by the aristocracy, that Gladstone worked to prevent.

As an undergraduate and as a young MP his votes, with the important exception of Catholic emancipation, were hostile to Whiggish and radical causes: political and church reform, abolition of Jewish civil disabilities, and abolition of hanging and flogging. His organization of the very strongly worded Oxford petition against reform and his newspaper articles written in 1833 in his early days as an MP suggest a simplistic stridency and a lack of qualification uncharacteristic of his later career. Gladstone later regarded this phase of his political life as one of 'folly', the problem being that he had not yet learned 'the great fact that liberty is a great and precious gift of God, and that human excellence cannot grow up in a nation without it'.[5] This recollection of 1892 is a little misleading. In certain small respects Gladstone was antilibertarian—for example, he several times tried to get the utilitarian *Westminster Review* struck off the Oxford Union's list of purchases—but he was never antilibertarian in a thoroughgoing way and, in the Protestant tradition, he always allowed for scruples of conscience. Rather, he held a view similar to that put forward as a main theme of David Hume's *History of England*, to which as we have seen he paid close attention as a schoolboy, the view that there was no necessary correlation between liberty and parliamentary institutions, and that liberty was more a judicial than a political concept. The exercise of such liberties was the fulfilment of an obligation rather than the exercise of a right. In the sense that Gladstone did not think in terms of rights, he was certainly fundamentally separated from the secular liberal tradition exemplified in his day by the *Westminster Review* and the Mills. Gladstone's view of society, rather, was of a social order whose gradations were related to each other by duties, and whose legitimacy derived from Providence. 'Man . . . comes into the world under a debt to society [and] to his parents', Gladstone told the WEG Club in answer to Moncrieff's support for the view that liberty was the end of government.[6]

The function of the British constitution was thus to permit the living of a Christian life: it had no other legitimacy, and certainly no natural rights inherent in it. Property, in Gladstone's view, had duties but no absolute rights. Its tenure was a convenient and on the whole beneficial social arrangement which could be changed. Society should be a community of believers, not of property-owners, and above all society existed for discipline. As he put it a little later:

The whole experience of life, all that befalls and belongs to him [mankind] in it, his domestic position, his social position, whatever is his, whatever lies around him, is one comprehensive system of discipline, devised by Divine Wisdom for the purpose of contributing to the accomplishment of that great design, the renovation of the nature of God in a race that had fallen away.

So Gladstone was a Tory. But we must take care not to make him too Tory.* He recognized that the political and ecclesiastical aspects of the constitution as it existed in the 1820s contained major 'anomalies' which neither could nor should be absolutely defended. Though influenced by Burke's organic analysis of the social and political order, he did not at that time take a Burkean view of 'prescriptive rights' and he did not, as many in Oxford increasingly did, argue that the Church had inviolate rights of a temporal kind unassailable by the State. He was, therefore, never an 'ultra', as the last ditchers in 1828–32 were called. Having consistently supported

---

* The terms Conservative and Tory were both used in the 1830s; Gladstone usually, but not always, used the former.

Catholic emancipation while a schoolboy, in Oxford he came out boldly against Wellington's administration when the duke declared against all Parliamentary reform at the end of 1830. The evening he was elected president of the Oxford Union, 11 November 1830, he moved and carried by one vote a motion of no confidence in the duke's government. He accepted the need in the regrettable circumstances—as the Huskisson group saw them—for modest political reform. As he put it in an unpublished pamphlet written in July 1831, a measure might have been introduced 'to restore as completely as possible the balance of the principles' of the constitution, achievable by a variety of means: modest redistribution, franchise reform, corrupt practices reform. If this had been done, 'though all might not have adopted the whole of these opinions, rational men would in general have admitted that the object was fair and attainable and that the means proposed did not necessarily imply the action of any destructive principle'. As it was, the thoroughgoing, wholesale reconstruction of the electoral system, even, as Gladstone saw it, of the constitution itself—'a revolution bill and *not* a Reform Bill' he called it—which the Whigs proposed in 1831 and eventually carried, threw him off balance, and kept him off balance for the rest of the decade.[7]*

Gladstone's very strong political reaction to the Whigs' reform proposals in 1831 mirrored his alarm at what he saw as the appalling state of religion at Oxford. He was shocked that 'a seminary for furnishing with ministers a reformed and Apostolical Church' should, given all its advantages of wealth, learning, and reputation, be so sterile: 'Here irreligion is the rule, religion is the exception.'[8] Neither the moral virtues of a classical education nor the proper qualities of the national priesthood could be achieved if the Church in Oxford, and generally, did not revive itself. Given the central importance in the nation's morale which Gladstone accorded to Oxford, the situation he believed he had found there amounted to a national disaster, calling for thoroughgoing remedies. Gladstone tried to respond to the situation at two levels, the personal, by considering whether he should himself become a clergyman, and the national, by trying to develop an active conservatism in public affairs.

A Serious Call?

A linear move from strict Evangelicalism to a High Church position has commonly been seen as characterizing Gladstone's religious 'development' in the 1820s and 1830s. This is an oversimple view. As has already been shown, it would be misleading to describe him simply as an Evangelical in his schooldays, even though he retained some Evangelical qualities

---

* In 1865 he recalled: 'The Reform bill frightened me in 1831, and drove me off my natural and previous bias. Burke and Canning misled many on that subject, and they misled me'; Morley, i. 70.

throughout his life. At Oxford, in a context he clearly felt religiously unsympathetic whatever its other strengths, he sought to stabilize his religious opinions. He found strict Evangelicalism inadequate though he often used Evangelical terminology. But he also seems to have felt that he ought to be able to respond better than he did to the Evangelical challenge. Confronted by 'national apostacy', he felt it his duty in 1830 to offer himself as a potential clergyman; his tutor, Biscoe, had earlier asked him if he was considering the clerical profession.[9] But the way he made this offer was most curious.

During the reading party at Cuddesdon in July–August 1830, Gladstone worked not only on the classics but on the Old Testament with Anstice. In a conversation, Anstice stressed 'the love of God, *not* selfishness' as the motive for actions. Gladstone was filled with remorse for his own inadequacy: 'I should have been in ecstasy to hear such an avowal of grand and high truths: but as it was the working[s] of my Satanic heart were far otherwise, as the day of judgment will show.' Fearful for the salvation of mankind, 'I ask myself the question why I am slumbering and trifling over matters which have at best but an indirect connection with religion, while souls throughout the world are sinking daily into death?' He felt a powerful duty to offer himself as a clergyman, but also a duty to ask his father's permission to do so. He wrote asking this permission already knowing that his father was hostile to the suggestion. He told John Gladstone: 'I do not now see my own view can or ought to stand for a moment in the way of your desires. In the hands of my parents therefore I am left.' Since John Gladstone had educated him to go into the law with a view to a career in politics, only one answer was likely.

Gladstone's attempt to become a clergyman had none of the committed determination of his brother John's wish to become a sailor. William Gladstone felt he *ought* to be a clergyman—it was his duty to God to offer himself—but he had had no clear call. 'O that, whithersoever he calls, I may follow!' Gladstone wrote in his diary when writing to his father and while 'much distracted with doubts as to my future line of conduct'. But God did not call. If Gladstone had had a clear call, if he had seen his way instead of being 'utterly blind', God's authority would have trumped his father's. There was relief rather than disappointment when John Gladstone's temperate reply urged public life as a broader profession, and counselled delay in making a decision: 'Had a most kind letter from my father for which I ought to be very thankful.'[10]

If Gladstone had not had a call, so also had he not experienced a conversion in the strict Evangelical sense, and this separated him from the Calvinist predestinarianism which he found in the Oxford Evangelicals, represented by the St Edmund Hall set and the Revd H. B. Bulteel, whose church and sermons Gladstone quite often attended. He wrote a long memorandum, 'The Doctrine of Conversion', to show that conversion was wrongly understood when measured by 'signs commonly arbitrary and frequently erroneous and improper' described, in a caricature of the Evangelical experience, as 'ideas of inspiration sudden and sensible, of bodily convulsions, of wild and idle speculations and imaginations'. Conversion was a '"turning" . . . so far from being the work of a moment that it cannot even be considered as the work of a life'. It was thus a lifelong process, involving a 'turning-point' when the balance tipped between one 'general ascendancy' and another, but it was a 'turning-point' invisible to man.[11]

This was at most a very moderately Evangelical view of conversion. Gladstone found himself turning to a less inward-looking religious stance and more to the Church as a body of believers, 'the Church militant here on earth', the institutional representation of Christ on earth. When he came again to declare his intended profession, it was again in the form of a letter to his father, written in January 1832 in the light of the reform crisis of the second half of 1831:

I cannot help believing, from circumstances around me, that the human race, or at least the civilized world, is rapidly approaching its crisis: that no great number of years will in their revolutions bring the time when the whole fabric of human society shall be rocked to its very foundations. . . .

The consequence was a duty to enter 'what is called public life' with a view to resisting social disintegration, since 'intercourse *with subordination* forms the essence of what we understand by "society" in its largest sense'. The first symptom of the destructive 'new philosophy' which was spreading, 'a kind of calculation of interests', was the attack (as Gladstone saw it) on the Church, an attack which, he believed, could ultimately lead 'through the degradation of the British nation to wide and irremediable ruin through the world'.[12]

The Tories' Rising Hope*

Religion led Gladstone to 'public life' and his attitude to it thus focussed on two related points: the stability of society and the well-being of the Church. The attempt to define, to relate, and to justify the importance of these two foci was to be his chief preoccupation of the 1830s, and, in various complex restatements, of the rest of his life. This preoccupation reflected his movement away from a rather inward-looking, self-directed, faith to a much more ecclesiological and institutional position.

'Society', 'State', and 'Church' were all in the 1830s 'essentially contested

* Macaulay's famous comment, often misquoted, that Gladstone was 'the rising hope of those stern and unbending Tories', was added in the margin of the draft for his *Edinburgh Review* article on Gladstone's book; his first deleted formulation appears to read 'the darling hope of those stern and uncompromising Tories'. I am obliged to Mr William Thomas for drawing my attention to this.

concepts': that is, they were those terms which lay at the centre of ideological and political dispute, used by different groups to mean different things, but commonly agreed to be the focal points of argument. The intellectual debate of the age therefore centred on their definition. The Whig cabinets in office between 1830 and 1841 (with the brief caesura of the Wellington–Peel minority government of 1834–5 in which Gladstone gained office for the first time) marked a sharp change of direction from the financial and administrative reforms of the Tories in the 1820s. The Whigs were primarily institutional reformers, unafraid of facing head-on the difficulties of definition which major institutional reforms raised in a stark, confrontational form. The Whigs thus reformed the representative system of the constitution both nationally and locally, and attempted a reconstruction of the national church and its allied educational system. Sometimes dismissed as foppish cynics, the dominant Whigs of the 1830s in fact represented Broad-Churchmanship in action, with a clearly-defined ideology, owing much to Richard Whately and Thomas Arnold, which was integrative and anti-dogmatic.[13]

Young Tories such as Gladstone thus found themselves faced with 'a gigantic scheme of speculative amelioration',[14] an ideological as well as a legislative challenge. Beyond the Whigs was seen an even more dangerous menace, a thoroughgoing secular utilitarianism represented in the Commons by the Radicals on whom, with O'Connell's Roman Catholics, the Whig government was dependent for votes after 1835. Tories such as Gladstone saw the Whigs as sometimes their abettors, sometimes their dupes. In discussing Gladstone's reaction to this situation, it is important to remember the wider context. The government's legislation in the 1830s, together with a general awareness (expressed inside and outside Parliament) of the fundamental shift in British society which industrialization and urbanization were producing, encouraged widespread questioning and justifying of values and assumptions hitherto taken to be so self-evidently right as not to need contemporary systematic justification. As Gladstone observed, 'Do we not live in an age when everything is made a subject of question and doubt. . . . It is the critical period in the history of nations, when men begin to question themselves respecting everything around them. . . .'[15]

Often such investigations, originally conceived in a defensive spirit, came to have radical consequences, as many of the leading authors of the *Tracts for the Times*, begun by J. H. Newman in Oxford in 1833, discovered. Works such as William Palmer's High-Church *Treatise on the Church of Christ* and F. D. Maurice's Platonic Broad-Church *The Kingdom of Christ*, both published in 1838 at almost the same time as Gladstone's *The State in its Relations with the Church*, reflected this general concern. The problem was one confronting any nation state with a liberal constitution, as was shown in the French case by Lamennais' rather earlier *De la religion con-*

sidérée dans ses rapports avec l'ordre politique et civil (1825–6):[16] what was author-ity and legitimacy in the modern state, and how justified was the Church of England (in the English case) in claiming that authority?

It is proper to discuss Gladstone's position in this intellectual context. As a young MP he was of course involved in routine parliamentary duties, for example sitting on Select Committees on bribery petitions, but it is clear from his diary and from the voluminous memoranda written through-out the 1830s that the chief direction of his energies lay in intellectual pursuits.[17]

None the less, his obvious political abilities were quickly recognized. After his first speech in Newark following the hustings in 1832, the *Nottingham Journal* concluded, 'he is a young gentleman of amicable manners and the most extraordinary talent; and we venture to predict, without the slightest exaggeration, that he will one day be classed among the most able statesmen in the British Senate'.[18] Gladstone made his inaugural speech, on slavery in the West Indies—he had hoped to make it on the Irish Church Bill—in June 1833: 'House 5–1. Spoke. my first time—for 50 min. My leading desire was, to benefit the cause of those, who are now so sorely beset. The House heard me very kindly, and my *friends* were satisfied. Tea afterwards at the Carlton.' Two days later 'Sir R. Peel came up to me most kindly & praised the affair of Monday night.'[19] Gladstone's attacks on the terms of emancipation of the slaves—but not on the principle—and his defence of the church establishment in Oxford, Eng-land, and Ireland, gained him a place in the minority Tory government of 1834–5 as a Commissioner of the Treasury (usually known as a Junior Lord of the Treasury) with routine responsibilities, and on 26 January 1835, Peel 'offered me the Colonial Under Secretaryship. I accepted this great responsibility.' Less than a month later the government was defeated on the election of the Speaker, and its end was certain: 'Of the state, of wh. this div. is a symptom, I can form but one opinion.' On 18 April 1835, he 'bade farewell to the Colonial Office', ending his time there with a partial dis-agreement with his superior, Lord Aberdeen, over West Indian education, Gladstone wishing that any educational scheme for the ex-slaves there should be explicitly Anglican.

This sort of difficulty with a much respected fellow Tory, which, had it been brought to a head 'would have been extremely painful', encouraged Gladstone in the view that his intellectual position required deepening and systematizing. In the long recess in the winter following the return of the Whig government in 1835, he went to Fasque and undertook what repre-sented, in scope and intensity, almost a second education. His mother's death and his own unrequited love for a society beauty, Caroline Farquhar, sister of one of his college and political friends, seem to have intensified rather than deflected him from his studies. He read, amongst others,

Hume's *History* (again), beginning at the Commonwealth, Locke's *Essay Concerning Human Understanding*, Augustine's *Civitas Dei*, Tocqueville's *Democracy in America*, Thomas Chalmer's *Bridgewater Treatise*, Bolingbroke, Blackstone, Dante, and especially Aristotle's *Politics* which rather curiously had not formed a chief part of his Aristotelian studies at Oxford; he found it 'a book of immense value for all governors and public men'. This programme of reading was buttressed before and after the recess by Gladstone's usual wide-ranging studies. The reading of Augustine and Dante, and especially the thorough study of the latter, gave a catholic balance to the list, and Gladstone maintained his reading, finishing 'the dear Paradiso' for the first of many times in March 1836.[20]

The striking feature of much of this reading is its theoretical nature. As a young MP, Gladstone sought right rather than results. Unlike many in his position, he did not try to make himself an authority on some particular topic, though because of his father's business interests he found himself speaking frequently in defence of the West Indian plantation owners in the period of 'apprenticeship' which intervened between abolition of slavery in principle and abolition in practice, and his experience as Colonial Under-Secretary added some authority to his interventions on imperial affairs, especially with respect to Canada, in the later years of the Melbourne government. The many private papers which he wrote in the 1830s are almost wholly theoretical (in the sense of abstract) in tone; they deal with the nature of obligation in State and Church, and usually with little or no reference to the circumstances of the day, except by implication by way of comment on periods of earlier constitutional crisis.

While revising for his Oxford examinations in 1831, Gladstone had 'an idea . . . of gathering during the progress of my life, notes & materials for a work embracing three divisions—Morals—Politics—Education'. He kept some such notion of a book in his mind, recording it in 1835 during his period of reflection at Fasque as 'Idea of the Church. What the Church is: idea as it should be.' After a good deal of preparatory writing in 1837 it had by March 1838 taken a rather different form: 'I spoke to Mr. G. after dinner on the point I opened to Mahon at B[ridgewater] H[ouse]—viz. a definite principle on religious matters in the event of any C[onservative] Govt being formed.' Thus a work originally conceived in rather secular, classical categories (though obviously their treatment if it had any contemporary content would have involved religion), had become more explicitly religious in direction and more directly linked to the principles on which conservatism should act. If 'the science of Government', he told the Commons in 1835, was to exclude 'the consideration of religion—the most vital of all subjects to our permanent happiness and advancement', the result would be that 'so far from the science of politics being, as the greatest philosophers of antiquity fondly proclaimed it, the queen and mistress of all other arts, and discharging the noble functions of the mind, it will be an occupation degrading in its practice, and fitted rather for the very helots of society'. The Aristotelian good life of the property-owning gentleman must be conditioned and legitimized by the Anglican Church. Gladstone thought 'this matter of speaking is really my strongest religious exercise'.[21]

He published his views on this question in two books, *The State in its Relations with the Church*, published in December 1838, and *Church Principles Considered in their Results*, published in November 1840, which together represent the political and theological position reached by Gladstone in his twenties.

Three areas of influence bore upon Gladstone as he faced the controversies of the 1830s and attempted to forge conservatism for his generation: first, intellectual, the classical legacy of his education; second, ecclesiastical and theological, his increasing interest in the question of authority within the church; third, political, the participation in the political debates of the 1830s.

Towards a 'Science of Government': Plato and Aristotle

Gladstone was, as we have seen, steeped in the classics. But the classical school, though it suggested the basis for an analysis of society by analogy, in itself suggested no single view. Gladstone found himself attracted to both its two chief combatants, Plato and Aristotle. Unlike many of his contemporaries he was not simply a Platonist or an Aristotelian. The comment 'Optime' in the Christ Church Collection [Report] book on his work on both Plato and Aristotle reflected his balanced approach. From Aristotle Gladstone gained categories of analysis—the family, the local community, the state—which encouraged him to analyse society as a natural organism. From Plato he gained the concept of a vision of human society not yet realized. He found himself unable to decide decisively in the long battle between these two philosophers and their supporters. Aristotle's *Ethics* took no account of the fallen nature of man or of the possible reward of a future life; they were therefore deficient and feeble in lacking the concepts of retribution and reward. Looked at as to character Plato seemed superior: 'The *motives* are the main spring of every ethical system. Aristotle's are common: Plato's exalted: an approach far more in character to those proposed to us in the Word of God.'* Thus Gladstone concluded an essay comparing the two offered to the WEG Club. None the less, Aristotle's supposed 'practicality' appealed: 'It seems to me therefore that no one would deny the ἰδεα [nature, form] of Plato's scheme to be

---

* Plato's *Phaedo*, the main Platonic text for undergraduates, was, with its stress on an afterlife and on the fallen nature of man, the most convenient of Plato's works for instruction in a university whose tutors and students all subscribed to the Thirty Nine Articles; Gladstone and his generation were thus given a very unbalanced view of Plato.

finer, *except* possibly from the supposition that Aristotle's is more practical.'[22] It is clear that Gladstone's chief interest in making this comparison was in its political consequences; he was not interested in the more philosophical aspects of the debate. In refusing to side with one rather than the other, he was, for his time, rather unusual, and this refusal reflects a very general eclecticism in his intellectual position. Quotations can always be found with which to pin Gladstone to a particular school, political, ecclesiastic, or philosophical, but they always misrepresent the gallimaufrous nature of his mind, taken as a whole.

Gladstone took from Aristotle an analysis of society which was stable, almost static, each individual in his or her natural place, fulfilling social and political obligations rather than exercising rights. Thus his starting point for writing 'On the Principle of Government', written shortly after his essay comparing Aristotle and Plato, was strongly Aristotelian in its stress on natural status:

A state of graduated subordination is the natural law of humanity. . . . Civil government then is not a matter of option but of nature. . . . It is the prevailing error of all times, and particularly of the present ones, that men are looking at the power of self-government as intrinsically and essentially a good: whereas I think any reasoning lover of freedom would admit that it was not necessarily a good *when alone*, although he might contend for it as not only *a condition* but a *part* of the chief good. People talk and act as if the faculty of choice was the one thing needful—instead of the disposition to choose rightly.

This 'disposition' would be paternally encouraged and consequently

the right principle seems to me to be, not to give as much political liberty to the subjects as can be conceded compatibly with the maintenance of public order, but as little. A minimum of representation and not a maximum is I think the first object to be desired.[23]

Gladstone's detailed study of Aristotle's *Politics* in 1834–5 deepened his view that the social order was both natural and, when Christian revelation was added to Aristotle, divinely orchestrated; for of course Gladstone believed that classical authors could only offer a partial truth, to be modified and illuminated by revelation. At Fasque he wrote a long paper 'Of the Law of Social Obligation':

Society possesses, both from the *nature of the objects* it contemplates, and from the *debt which by benefits conferred* it has imposed upon every one of us, has a natural and binding right to our allegiance, anterior to, and wholly independent of, any individual conviction on our parts . . . this right, not having its *formation* and origin in the will of society, or of any member of it, is not determinable in its specific requisition by individual members of the community . . . though distinct from absolute right, and capable of deviation from absolute wisdom, it has a Divine sanction as well as a human reasonableness. . . . We are therefore placed in our nation, as in our family: and must discharge our social, as our domestic duties, in deference and subordination to naturally that is Divinely constituted ordinance.[24]

This Aristotelian viewpoint offered the basis for an attack on the idea of 'original contract, as advocated by Hooker, Locke, the Whigs of 1688, and Mr. Burke' and on 'original contract as held by Rousseau'. This long paper entitled 'Prevalent theories of government', written in December 1835, disposed of all these, and of absolute and indefeasible hereditary monarchies, and of the will and numbers (i.e. *vox populi*) as a basis for a constitution, and it concluded in a passage headed 'The true position of Will in Government':

> We have striven to overthrow the persuasion, which in various shapes of prejudice, habit, opinion, affection, and even conviction, is so popular, that human will is a rightful and original arbiter in the main and essential matters of government. . . . The doctrine is in itself so totally unable to bear the light of investigation, that in no form of government can it be acceptable to the inquiring mind: it hides from view and takes refuge in some artifice, as that the king's will is wiser than the people's, or the people's than the king's, but from thence to the occasion of action, and in the excitement of selflove, it is ever ready to come forth again and animate the crowd of tumultuous passions which a single moment can evoke, and become, even though unconsciously, the governing motive of men or bodies of men. Such is the subtlety of evil. It is therefore our duty in the security of study and contemplation, firmly to grasp by the understanding, the truth that human will, as will, though it has power has not authority, in the fundamental matters of government: nor can we more forcibly concentrate the sentiments which belong to this proposition, than in the nervous declaration of Aristotle 'οὐκ ἐῶμεν ἄρχειν ἀνθρωπον',[*] For it is against man, against king, nobles, people, all alike, when considered as creatures of mere will, that our objections and accusations lie.

In his reflections about society, Aristotle was the predominant influence in the early 1830s, though Gladstone's many notes on him often express qualification or objection. Aristotle explained why society was what it was; he did not say what it could become. Here Plato's *Republic*, begun in August 1832 (i.e. after leaving Oxford), offered an image of perfection: 'Aristotle built upon the practical unity of φιλία [family affection] (on which a larger unity may however be raised)—Plato wrought synthetically & removed existing instincts and affections to substitute one visionary in great measure.'[25]

Gladstone offered a self-confident hierarchical conservatism abstractly defended. When linked with a visionary view of what Christianity could become, it was to be a heady mixture. The difficulty with it was that while it offered an analysis of the present and a prescription for the future, it did

---

* 'This is why we do not allow a *man* to rule, but rational principle, because a man behaves thus in his own interests and becomes a tyrant', *Nichomachean Ethics* (1134 a. 35); Add MS 44725; paper of 11 December 1835.

not offer either a means or a method. It might be a science of society, but it was not a science of government.

Church Principles

Parallel to this analysis of society, related to it but never wholly fused with it, Gladstone in the early 1830s developed his views of the Church. He completed his formal education in the usual way, a tour of the Continent, made in 1832 with his brother John. This tour awakened his internationalism but also strengthened his nationalism—a duality which he retained throughout his life. Raised, as was his generation, to instinctive but largely uninformed hostility to Continental liberalism and the French Revolution,* he experienced on visiting the field of Waterloo a curious mixture of emotions, of patriotic separation, anti-popery, and prudent reformism:

The sight of this field, especially under the present aspect of circumstances, suggests many recollections of an overwhelming interest. How dearly the honours and the benefits of that field were brought: and how does the very grandeur of the victory itself bear a melancholy witness to the intensity of the struggle. If indeed that battle were fought in a wrong cause, how painful has been our guilt: if in a right one, and if in accordance with the commands of God, yet with how much alloy of baser motives has the great enterprise been prosecuted! Yet after all, if the cause were good, this is indeed a spot where an Englishman's heart should beat high with exultation.

But what if the tide of our national destiny is turned, and if we are now about to go hand in hand with those alien principles, against which we once waged an implacable war? God forbid, and direct all for good. And indeed in the grand division of continental parties, it is very much easier to predicate evil of one side, than good of the other. It may be painful to see Church Establishments overthrown—but who would wish for the renewal of the Empire of Popery in all its pride? It may shock our feelings to see the kingly office first misunderstood and misdefined, and then degraded, yet who can say that the ancient despotism was a wholesome government for France?[26]

This duality was strengthened in another dimension by Gladstone's experiences of religion in Italy. While at Oxford he had developed his earlier interest in Roman Catholicism by making an extended analysis of 'Roman Catholic Doctrines and Ceremonies'. In March 1832 he experienced Roman Catholicism at first hand—for he knew no English Roman Catholics—when he made the first of many crossings of the Alps into Italy, then a patchwork of states, most of them ruled by the Hapsburgs, the Bourbons, or the Pope. He immediately made a pilgrimage to the valley of the Vaudois, Milton's 'slaughtered saints' in whom he had been interested

---

* Gladstone's tour made him aware of his ignorance; on his return he noted: 'I find so much the want of knowledge in detail of the French Revolution, that I begin Scott's account of it [in his *Life of Napoleon*]', so as to be able to evaluate the French authors such as Sarrans and de Bourrienne whose works he recently begun.

since Eton, and was dismayed to find those legendary Protestants to be rather ordinary and undistinguished.[27] Travelling south towards the Papal States, he was soon fascinated by the Roman Catholic church services, in his view a curious mixture of beauty and inaudibility. He formed contempt for the temporal power of the Pope—'there seems to be every absurdity involved in the idea of an ecclesiastical sovereign—whether legislative or executive'—and his instinctive reaction to seeing St Peter's for the first time was to note 'my humble homage is reserved for that Gothic style, which prevails in our own English cathedrals'. None the less, he soon 'experienced the truth of the universal opinion, that St. Peter's grows upon one's continuing contemplations'. And not only architecturally:

In entering such a Church as this, most deeply does one feel the pain and shame of the schism which separates us from Rome—whose guilt (for guilt I at least am well persuaded there always is where there is schism,) surely rests not upon the Venerable Fathers of the English Reformed Church, but upon Rome itself—yet whose melancholy effects the mind is doomed to feel, when you enter this magnificent temple, and behold on its walls the images of Christian saints and the words of Everlasting Truth. . . . May God bind up the wounds of his bleeding Church.

This visit to St Peter's made an abiding impression. When he visited Rome again in 1838, he noted of his visit to St Peter's: 'Here I remember almost to have experienced the first conception of unity in the Church—acquired alas! by the existing contrasts—and first to have longed for its visible attainment: an object in every human sense hopeless· but not therefore the less to be desired. . . . That idea has been upon the whole, I believe the ruling one of my life during the period which has since elapsed.'[28]

Gladstone's first direct experience of Roman Catholicism in its majesty thus both attracted and repelled him. It opened a vision of what Christendom might be and it exposed the worm in the bud. As he attended the Palm Sunday Service in the Sistine Chapel, in the presence of the Pope, he felt: 'its principle of life, has left it. Even so stood before us the great members of the papal system, as the cold and pale spectres of the highest and most powerful domination the world has ever beheld.'[29]

The dualism of Gladstone's reaction to Rome not surprisingly encouraged inquiry into the Church of England's place—or potential place— in the religious world order, an inquiry reinforced by the ignorance of the Church of England which he discovered in Italy. He began to look at 'some of the details of the system of the English Church, as set forth in the Prayer-book, with which I was before less acquainted'. His experience in Roman Catholic countries gave him 'an idea' of the nature of a Church 'very much higher & more important than I had previously any conception of'.[30]

This concept of 'an idea', a vision, an image, was of growing importance. In opposing Whig reforms of the Church of England and Ireland in 1835, Gladstone showed himself a more than competent combatant at the statistical level, using the old device of quoting the opposite side's figures to refute its arguments. At one level this was satisfactory and effective. But it was not in itself adequate. Like many of his generation of Oxford men, Gladstone found a decade of Whig reforms driving him increasingly to look for a more systematic defence of the establishment and claims of the Church of England. He sought a more thoroughgoing explanation of the State's relationship to it than 'commonsense' conservatism of the sort offered by, for example, Sir Robert Inglis, the successor to Peel in one of the Oxford University seats, and by Peel himself in the buffer device of the Ecclesiastical Commissioners set up during the 1834–5 minority Conservative government and continued subsequently by the Whigs. Gladstone did not oppose this sort of reform, though he strongly opposed some of its subsequent recommendations, but his writings, his reading, and his demeanour in the 1830s reflect a yearning for a more theoretical base.[31] He always despised 'the miserable policy of mere resistance to change, and of tenacious adherence to civil privilege'.

Unlike some of his Oxford contemporaries, Gladstone was not led by this process to question or to test the legitimacy of the Church of England, but rather to inquire into what should be the relationship of the State towards it. On the contrary, the 1830s brought to him an increasing awareness of, and devotion to, the Church of England. His continental experiences in 1832, and his subsequent reading, coming at a time when he was beginning to be interested in 'system' in the Church, convinced him of two things. First, that there is 'a real and not merely supposititious personality of nations, which entails likewise its own religious responsibilities' and, second, that the Church of England represented truth and thus, in its geographical context (i.e. England, Wales, Ireland, and the Colonies, but not Scotland), represented the 'religious responsibility' incumbent on the state, and was also the criterion of deciding, in Aristotelian terms, what the disposition of a good citizen should be.

From these two beliefs sprang that concept of 'religious nationality' which was fundamental to Gladstone's view of the state, whether English, British, or elsewhere.[32] In certain respects, this placed Gladstone close to the Noetics of Oxford.* His elevated view of nationalism (at this stage, it should be noted, owing little to Liberal views of self-determination) related him to the nationalism of Thomas Arnold's *Principles of Church Reform* (1833), the classic advocacy of antidogmatism in the Church in order to achieve the confessional state.[33] The idealism which permeated Gladstone's views on the State in the late 1830s was mainly derived from

---

* It is interesting that his specific complaint against Richard Whately, the doyen of the Noetics, several of whose sermons he attended as an undergraduate, was about 'his antisabbatical doctrine ... as mischievous as it is unsound' (18 Sept. 1831). Gladstone might have been expected to have been much more quickly and more generally hostile.

Coleridge's *On the Constitution of the Church and State According to the Idea of Each*, the classic defence of the confessional state. Both Arnold and Coleridge held out an Ideal, derived through the inspiration of Plato, against which present-day institutions might be measured, Coleridge arguing, in a famous phrase, that the congruity of the English state and the Church of England was a 'blessed accident', enabling the Ideal to be observed in actuality. In notes made in 1837 on Coleridge's *Church and State*, Gladstone commented: '*We* do not claim to be the Universal Church of the whole earth—but we claim to be the Church of this realm corresponding in all material laws with that model which was established and intended to be universal.' Coleridge's book was published in 1830. Gladstone did not read it until 1837—he had earlier read other of his works—but when he did read it he read it very carefully, as the annotations in his copy show.[34] Similarly, though he had read Plato's dialogues as an undergraduate, he did not read the *Republic* until late in 1832. He turned energetically to Idealist authors, and especially Coleridge, from 1836 onwards. 'Finished Coleridge's Idea' is, significantly, the way Gladstone refers to the end of his study of Coleridge's book—not the short title by which it was or is usually known. Not surprisingly, therefore, Arnold saw Gladstone as a quasi-ally.*

This rather unsystematic contact with the Idealist tradition was important. We have seen Gladstone, both deeply trained at university and by his own subsequent studies in the 'practical' Aristotle, dissatisfied with the inadequacy of 'low' defences of the Church. Seeing the established Church as useful rather than transcendental played into the hands of its opponents. Plato and Coleridge gave Gladstone an intellectually perhaps rather dangerous means of expressing and developing his already half-thought-out views about the relationship of the State to the Church.

Gladstone was also concerned about what he saw as the increasing materialism of the age: 'There is danger when we are led to fix our thoughts on possession, rather than use. Here one [?our] peril arising from money's becoming the basis of all relations: because it has no intrinsic value.'[35] Such materialism, an obvious, even a defining feature of industrial Britain, could only be met by a national antithesis. Those like Thomas Chalmers who met political economy on its own ground and stressed the central role of the moral autonomy of the individual consequently, in Gladstone's view, neglected the high place of a national Church based on an apostolic ministry. Gladstone was completing a draft of a work on 'Ch & St.'

---

* Thomas Arnold, *Introductory Lectures on Modern History* (1842), 51: 'I would unite one half of the Archbishop of Dublin's [Whately] theory with one half of Mr. Gladstone's; agreeing cordially with Mr. Gladstone in the moral theory of the state, and agreeing cordially with the Archbishop in what I will venture to call the Christian theory of the Church, and deducing from the conclusion, that the perfect state and the perfect church are identical.'

previously worked on in 1837 and perhaps earlier,* when he attended
lectures on establishment given in London by Chalmers in the spring of
1838. Stung by Chalmers's low view of apostolicity and the corporate
Church, he refurbished his draft to stress the importance of these factors.

Gladstone's acquaintance with the 'high' Idealist image of perfection
seemed to give him the analytical tool he needed. Coleridge offered an
argument 'alike beautiful and profound', and Gladstone was especially
drawn to Coleridge's argument that the '*cultivation* of the inward man,
which is the root, the corrective, and the safeguard of *civilization*' should
be nourished as 'a paramount ingredient of national life' by a 'natural
"clerisy" of a state'. Of the various writers whose views on the relationship of State and Church Gladstone surveyed—Hooker, Warburton,
Paley, Chalmers, Hobbes, Bellarmine, Coleridge—it was the last whose
definition was the most acceptable, its deficiency being that 'he does not
carry his conceptions into detail'.[36] Gladstone concluded his public statement of his views, his book *The State in its Relations with the Church* (1838),
with quotations from two of the high priests of the Idealist movement,
Herder and Plato.

Gladstone was concerned to develop a view of a confessional State on a
'high' ground. He was equally concerned to assert not merely the Anglican
Church's function within such a State, but what was regarded as a High-
Church view of the nature of that Church. 'Church principles' involved a
strong stress on 'the divine constitution of the visible Church' as exemplified by bishoprics and the apostolic succession. Thus, while the confessional, national aspect of Gladstone's view of the State seemed to point
towards Arnold's antidogmatic, integrative reforms, his view of the Church
led him towards a rather narrow apostolicity which linked him clearly both
with the older High-Churchmen such as William Palmer, whose *Treatise*
came out too late to have much impact on the first edition of Gladstone's
book, and with the Puseyite element of the Oxford Movement, or Tractarians as its members were known. Faced with a choice, Gladstone always
put Anglican apostolical purity first. For the Greek tradition of civic
humanism, important though it was, was not enough and Aristotle and
Plato were merely 'pagans': 'great as is the importance of our civil and
social life, it is not an essential but an instrumental importance: it is
important for what it yields and generates, not for that which it is. . . . It is in
the history of the Church that we have the final consummation of all human
destinies.'[37] *Church Principles* attracted much less attention than *The State in
its Relations with the Church*. But it was, from the author's point of view, a
more comfortable book. It did not have the awkwardness of Glad-

---

* The absence of the MSS of the early drafts of *The State in its Relations with the Church* makes it
difficult to be sure how the bouts of writing on this subject, mentioned in the diary from 1836 onwards, relate to the final version.

stone's attempt in *The State* to meld the Aristotelian with the Platonic–Coleridgean way of thought.

Gladstone's stress in both his books on the legitimacy of the Church of England meant that he was strongly hostile to concurrent endowment (i.e. the notion that the State should take religions as it found them and organize education through whatever denominations, Roman Catholic or Protestant, might be found to exist side-by-side with Anglicanism). After formulating this view in the 1830s he subsequently always preferred no State patronage to mixed, pluralist State patronage in religion and education, a situation he described as prevalent in Prussia and in France, where, despite the predomination of Roman Catholicism in the latter, 'the principle of national religion has been essentially surrendered, and the state joins hands with all creeds alike—a marked and memorable result of her first Revolution'.[38] Gladstone did not argue that the Church of England was in an absolute sense the representative of true religion in the areas where it was established, but, following Bishop Butler's view of probability, he argued that the government maintained it as 'that form of belief which it conceives to contain the largest portion of the elements of truth with the smallest admixture of error'.[39] Thus Gladstone disagreed sharply with some of William Palmer's less qualified statements, such as his view that Nonconformists were outside the Church and therefore beyond salvation.[40]

In the British case, Gladstone thought, 'we still seem to have ground which is defensible, and which is worth defending' 'Our country', he believed, 'seems to promise at least a more organised, tenacious, and determined resistance to the efforts against national religion as well as to the general principles of democracy, than any in the civilized world.'[41] In thinking this, in the light of the difficulties of Romanism, Socinianism, paganism, and dissent of which he showed himself well aware, Gladstone revealed himself as an optimist. In this sense, his Idealist phase placed him in a different position than the High-Churchmen of the Palmer sort, who defined and guarded the Anglican tradition and deplored the Roman drift of the Newmanites, but offered little that was positive or forward looking.

The State in its Relations with the Church and *Church Principles*, as we have seen, were amongst other things deliberately intended as a guide to Conservatives as they prepared for office. This was, probably, the last point at which a general defence of Anglican hegemonic nationalism could be attempted. If conservatism was to be more than a Fabian defence against, and consequently a pragmatic accommodation of the liberal, pluralist, and industrial state—if it was to be an ideology rather than a reaction—Gladstone's position, or something like it, had to be held. Gladstone contributed to the very high expectations which Conservatives placed upon the coming Peel government, an almost apocalyptic expectation which by its very existence added to the difficulties of that government and to its failure and the subsequent disintegration of the Conservative Party. Ultra Tories looked to him, as they were to do in 1845, but they looked ultimately in vain. Gladstone's Canningism seemed suspended in the 1830s, but it was not dead.

The difficulties into which Gladstone's first book led him in the 1840s will be considered in the next chapter. In the context of Conservatism of the 1830s, it is worth noting two points. First, his view of Anglicanism denied the 'subjective immobility' of any religious system and accepted that each age produces 'particular modifications', with doctrine therefore being essentially secondary. Though cautious and conservative, his position therefore accepted renovation and growth: an analogy with Aristotle's view of the organic growth of society from family to State is supported by Gladstone's use in the Church context of the famous Aristotelian simile used in the *Politics*, 'as an oak unfolds the life which it has carried seminally within it from the acorn'.[42] The function of the conservative was to locate, by historical awareness, where on this path of growth the present stood. However cautiously applied, and however different the intended conclusion, Gladstone's use of development associated him with the dominant progressivism of the age. Second, Gladstone was, even with respect to fundamentals, sometimes less confident about his party position than his public persona suggested. In 1836 he privately surveyed the positions of the two main parties (without naming them); the one, he thought, was based on the 'major principle that control and restraint are in themselves good for human nature and are not to be accepted merely as disadvantages necessarily entailed by a social status', that power was 'in itself intoxicating' and must be curtailed by 'that passionless agency of Law and fixed institution which most restricts individual caprice and lowers pride'. The other party assumes 'that the right of government finally resides in the mass: that man is the best judge of his own interests in political as much as in private matters: that the principle of birth and wealth are rather the tolerable accidents, than the valuable auxiliary, of social excellence . . .'. It would appear obvious which side Gladstone was on—and it is interesting to note that he assumed party was based on fundamentally differing principles—but his conclusion was more tentative than might be expected:

Who may be right and who wrong in this fundamental principle lying at the root of party distinctions, is a deep and difficult question, and one in which we must perhaps rely mainly upon perceptions and persuasions incapable of analysis and ranking among the ultimate facts of our nature. The details of Revealed truth seem to me to bear out the choice which my mind has made: to indicate that we are as children and pupils, seeing in a glass darkly, appointed to self-government for the purpose of growth and strength, but not intended to regard it as an end valuable in itself: and as on the other hand necessary, but *less* necessary, than the counterpoising principle of obedience, while the two together as the active and the passive principle form the harmony of our nature.[43]

As Gladstone's life progressed, he was to find harmony difficult to achieve, for in his nature the active clearly dominated the passive.

Political Action

Following Bishop Butler, Gladstone saw man as an agent, with the need to act. Man was not an observer, but a participant: a participant participates, as best he can, in situations given by history. Taking decisions involves the risk, even the expectation, of being wrong, and much effort must be taken to minimize error. It was to try to establish the best criteria for right action that Gladstone's works and speeches in the 1830s were devoted.

In 1835, he described how a politician should approach the business of politics. The passage sums up very well his own approach to his Parliamentary activities—it being always remembered that he only saw these as a partial fulfilment of his calling to 'public life'—and is worth quoting at length:

In that gradation of instruments through means of which this lofty standard is applied to the varieties of practice in the government of human societies, next to the standard itself are those contemplative and philosophical faculties by which we handle the grounds and principles of the highest sciences. Partly analytical and discriminative: partly such as generalise and compare. The union of these two great branches of intellectual power is perhaps nowhere more necessary than in the politician, who has for his object not to delineate an ideal picture, but to frame a practical system, which embodying many principles of Divine wisdom from which human depravity is averse, shall nevertheless be adapted to operate upon the masses of human beings without violence, to change their opinions and habits for the better, without arraying those opinions and habits against itself. He is to give every consideration, like the ethical teacher, to the needs and frailties of human nature, to combine the indulgence of sympathy with allegiance to everlasting truth. He ought therefore to be familiar with each of those two mental moods so rarely found in union, analytical disquisitiveness, and creative contemplation. In his observation which has amassed, in his judgment which classifies his experimental facts, and in his reason which contemplates the fixed principles of human nature and Divine Will . . . we find a copy as it were of that Divine Will as regarding human societies: faint and dim and mutilated, but still the best which our capacities can attain, and therefore the most authentic evidence of political right, which is to be found on earth.[44]

Being an MP obviously suggested activity, even if it was only participation in the process of politics by voting in the lobbies. For Gladstone, the presupposition was always that it would mean speaking as well. He had written on 'Rhetoric' for the *Eton Miscellany*, and he wrote a further article (unpublished) on 'Public Speaking' in 1836. His education had been in large measure a training in and through rhetoric. Involvement in rational debate—winning the argument—was always for him a central function of political activity, for from the winning of the argument, if it was a right argument, would come political success. Thus the argument that the Church of England represented truth rather than numbers was always his point of departure. In England, there was—or was thought to be—a congruence between truth and numbers; in Ireland there was not. The point of defence thus became the establishment of the Church in Ireland. The Church in Ireland deserved to be established there because it represented true religion. The failure of the Roman Catholics there to recognize this implied, not disestablishment or concurrent endowment, but inadequacy in the presentation of this truth to the Irish peasantry. Thus Gladstone consistently defended the Irish establishment, and church rates generally, and worked towards a refurbished system of Anglican education in Ireland.

'The Protestant faith', he told his constituents in Newark in 1835, 'is held good for us, and what is good for us is also good for the population of Ireland.' But this depended on a peculiarly English view of British nationality, already, by the establishment of Presbyterianism in Scotland, in fact and in law pluralist in character. Gladstone accepted this with respect to Scotland. There, despite his strong reservation about the Presbyterians' supposed want of apostolicity, he found a form of national religion perhaps purer than in England: 'I have myself found in the nationality of Scottish religion . . . a cause of its comparative purity.' It might not seem a large step to recognize that the Episcopalian Church in Ireland was no more 'national' than it was in Scotland. Yet in the context of the parliamentary politics of the 1830s it was a huge step, and with huge consequences. Defending the Irish Church, Gladstone found himself unable to explain how that Church could become more broadly based, even if great abuses in it were conceded to exist. He was forced back on consequential arguments—more consequential than at the time he can have realized: 'we have abundant reasons, even of a political complexion, for maintaining that Church: after its destruction we should not long be able to resist the repeal of the Union, partly by loss of strength, and more from abandonment of our principles'.[45] This was not simply a question of numbers—the Anglicans' lack of support. Gladstone could be appealed to on more positive grounds, and in 1839, as he sat waiting 'to obey my superiors' by answering the Whigs in an Irish debate, and as the Tories began to anticipate a return to office, a remark of Lord John Russell's struck Gladstone 'ineffaceably', as he recalled thirty-one years later: 'You [Russell] said, "The true key to our Irish debates was this: that it was not properly borne in mind that as England is inhabited by Englishmen, and Scotland by Scotchmen, so Ireland is inhabited by Irishmen."'[46] Parliamentary action to defend the Anglican establishment in Ireland was becoming problematical.

The active side of Gladstone's nature also led him in the later 1830s to a number of practical initiatives, mostly in the religious sphere. He was closely associated with Bishop Blomfield's Metropolis Churches Fund, founded in 1836 to supply by subscription what the State declined to pay for by taxation, and in 1838 on Blomfield's invitation he joined the council of the National Society for the Education of the Poor in the Principles of the Established Church, and from this position he energetically opposed the Whigs' programme for a permanent committee of the Privy Council to promote education on the principle of concurrent endowment. He was prominent in the founding in 1837 of the Additional Curates Society, a High Church breakaway group from the evangelical Church Pastoral-Aid Society.[47] Developing the High Church or Tractarian side of his interests, he co-operated with E. B. Pusey in promoting reform along the lines of Pusey's pamphlet, 'Remarks on the prospective and past benefits of Cathedral institutions' (1833): 'Breakfast with Acland [in May 1838] to meet Dr. Pusey: conversation on Ch. Govt of Cathl question—wh is now fermenting in my mind.' The association between Gladstone and Pusey was a natural one, for they shared an Anglo-Catholicism which was thoroughly non-Roman, however much their willingness to go beyond High Church passivity might be misunderstood by many of their contemporaries.[48]

Initiatives such as these placed Gladstone at the front of the young Conservative MPs, a number of whom were, like him, associated with the Tractarian movement while not really part of it. His Puseyism dismayed some of the older MPs, always extremely cautious of any implication of a concession to Roman Catholicism, but it was not necessarily a disadvantage with his own Tory generation. In 1839 J. S. Mill, not a sympathetic observer, made a sharp analysis of 'the Oxford School . . . a new Catholic school without the Pope . . . one of the forms, & the best forms hitherto, of the *reaction* of Anglicanism against Methodism, incredulity & rationalism'. Mill concluded, echoing Macaulay's famous phrase: 'Among others of their proselytes it is said that Gladstone, the only rising man among the Tories, is one; the man who will probably succeed Peel as the Tory leader, unless this prevents him.'[49]

Gladstone's conservatism in the 1830s was highly romantic, even Utopian, much more so than that of the Young England movement of the 1840s which it anticipated. It was also much more systematically worked out than that exotic initiative; Gladstone's timing was poor—he was at least a generation too late—but it was not as poor as Disraeli's.

His highminded view of the functions of Conservatism contrasted markedly with the realities of electioneering in the two-member constituency of Newark, where he was returned in the general elections of 1832, 1835, and 1837 (in the last two of which he was unopposed), and 1841. It was not that Gladstone was ignorant. In Newark, bribery and 'treating' (i.e. free drink) were, as in most constituencies at the time, the accepted means of political persuasion and elections were extremely rumbustious. On his first appearance on the hustings, in 1832, his elaborate speech was totally inaudible: 'Mr. Gladstone then endeavoured to address the electors, but an outrageous noise, in groaning, hissing, and shouting, prevented him proceeding'; Gladstone struggled on for fifteen minutes undaunted—but he could not be heard. At the 1835 election, his attempts at a complex statement of belief were cut down to a brief broadsheet manifesto (though this was partly because of the absence of an opponent). Working for a Tory in a by-election in Westminster in 1835 he noted: 'A stormy scene. Got cut over the nose with a piece of wood.' The negotiations he had to carry on between the Duke of Newcastle, his father, and the Tory political agent about overspending in the elections reinforced the knowledge he gained from sitting on Commons committees inquiring into bribery in other constituencies. Not surprisingly, Gladstone concluded that the 'most singular argument' he found in his Aristotelian studies in the 1830s was the view that 'the clubbed intellects of the multitude may render them fitter to govern than the few'.

So it was not that Gladstone was ignorant of the realities of constituency politics. It was rather that, as yet, he did not think the rank-and-file elector capable of sophisticated political judgement. As he told the House of Commons soon after joining it, 'in what did the heinousness of bribery consist? Was it not in the bartering of a man's conscience? . . . those in the humbler walks of life could not be supposed to have very correct abstract opinions upon the nature of bribery. The utmost, perhaps, that could be reasonably expected from them would be, that they should consistently adhere to one political creed.'[50] But it was largely Church questions which were at issue at the hustings and which were being decided by a bribery which Gladstone accepted was understandable enough and perhaps rational from the individual voter's point of view. This suggested a curious process of electing the body which was in effect the synod of the Church of England and Ireland. Of course, this had been one of the Tories' objections to reform in 1830. But since the Church must be a community of self-aware believers, where then did this leave 'Church Principles' a decade later? For a national Church could not be national unless it had men as well as officers.

His view of Conservatism also left Gladstone curiously dissociated from his own mercantile origins. In an article written in 1834, but never published, he observed: 'A new population has sprung up in the manufacturing districts, with new habits, wants and wishes, and has greatly diverged from the ancient and indigenous national character.'[51] This was an uneasy position for John Gladstone's son to hold. None the less, it was a common view in the Tory circle—often Oxonians living in London—in which Gladstone moved. His two close friendships of the 1830s, with Henry Edward Manning (a man of rather similar origins) and James Hope, were formed in 1836 in the context of his idealistic High Church Conservatism. Like Gladstone, Manning (Balliol) and Hope (Christ Church) had been privately tutored by Charles Wordsworth; both had become Fellows of Merton College. Again, like Gladstone, Hope, a Scottish Episcopalian, had thought of taking Orders, but became a lawyer; Manning, of Evangelical upbringing, served briefly in the Colonial Office, but took Orders in 1832: both specialized in a rather arid legalism. Gladstone knew them as undergraduates, but not intimately. On reading Arthur Hallam's *Remains* in 1834, Gladstone had noted, 'if I were *now* to meet one such, still the old affection might be initiated but could not be renewed'.[52] He was to be surprised. In his rather lonely bachelor life in London he found with Hope, especially, a congruence of personal and intellectual attraction which was irresistible, as great perhaps, and certainly longer lasting, than that of Hallam. From today's perspective it is hard to understand the fascination exercised by Hope, who was high-minded but rather limited. But fascination there undoubtedly was with both Hope and Manning, and their apostacy to Roman Catholicism in 1851 contributed greatly to Gladstone's nervous sexual crisis of the early 1850s.

The friendship with Hope and Manning brought joy for the time being. They helped with advice about the writing of *The State in its Relations with the Church*, a time of enthusiasm and friendship as well as energetic intellectual work. In 1838 Manning was with Gladstone in Rome where they compared the Church of England to the Church of Rome and, fatefully, Gladstone 'took Manning to Wiseman's'. Wiseman, the leader of the English Roman Catholics, arranged for them to go to the English College to attend Mass 'with the parts of which I am beginning to acquire a little acquaintance'. Gladstone, at least, was 'confirmed in the idea that the mass implies & carries less of active mental participation than the English Liturgy'. Also in 1838 Gladstone drew up plans for a 'Third Order' in which clergy and laymen would share their religious thoughts and charitable activities, and the sort of spiritual, religious affinity which Gladstone felt for his friends would be given an institutional setting.[53] In the 1840s, as we shall see, something of the sort was achieved by the 'Engagement'. Religion in the male context—and the religious revival of the 1830s was very male-orientated—was thus for Gladstone personally uplifting.

It was also disturbing. The only two dreams recorded by Gladstone in the course of a lifetime of self-analysis date from just before this time. They were both dreams about Christ, the second apocalyptic and similar to the visions of the then fashionable artist, John Martin. Gladstone, in character, drew a moral lesson from each. Their interpretation must be hazardous, but the reader may like to have Gladstone's own account of them. First, on 19 July 1834, while in London during the Session:

Had last night a very curious dream of an appearance of our Saviour. Oh that he were ever present to the eye of my mind, as other visions often are.

Second, on 25 August 1834 while at Fasque and after writing the previous day (a Sunday) on 'God is love':

This morning I had a painful and appalling dream. I stood with ——, looking out towards the S. and E.—Over the sea there arose a light strange in colour, between blue and green, indescribably clear—it extended its arch upon the heaven: 'look, look, look!' and as we looked, it brightened into a clear flame, a white consuming flame, masses appeared to [be] crackling and dissolving in it: its advance was steady and rapid over the intervening space, it gathered up and devoured all the rival elements on its way: the truth flashed upon me, it is the coming of the Son of Man! I turned and saw one drawn by a resistless power, in convulsive struggles down, down to the ground, and under the ground: my tongue said mechanically, Glory to thee, O God! but I felt within me the mass of sin, of flesh, of self, a death from which I could not escape and along with which I too must surely and how deservedly be destroyed—but here my vision ended, I awoke. It should be useful: may it be.

Wooed and Married and All

Relationships with women were much more problematical than with men such as Hope, which followed a code well-established at school and university. For men with an Evangelical upbringing, the psychological pressures to marry were very strong. Some, like Newman, countered this by developing an ethos of celibacy, but Gladstone always seems to have seen marriage as his natural destiny. His education had left him with hardly any day-to-day experience of women of his own age, save for his sisters during the holidays. In the wholly male society of Eton and Christ Church—his Eton Dame was the only woman who played any part in his formal education—he developed a tendency to masturbate. This was in the circumstances natural enough, but like almost every male in his century who underwent a similar education, Gladstone saw it as a sin requiring forgiveness, a desire to be suppressed, even while recognizing it as a 'natural (& vigorous)' tendency. He was tantalized by this temptation through the 1830s and perhaps beyond. From an early age he began to counter it by (in the 1830s) occasional approaches to women in the street who were either destitutes or prostitutes, and with these he would hold religious conversations and sometimes give a charitable donation.

Living as a bachelor in London, he was left to make his own way, and this amounted to meetings with society women during the elaborate rituals of Conservative political society: 'dined at Sir E. Kerrison's—& sung! at Lady Salisbury's'. For a vulnerable youth with a tendency to introspection such opportunities cannot have been easy to take. Always anxious as a young man about the rightness of amusement and relaxation, Gladstone cannot have been at ease on such occasions. As always, he saw retribution hovering, and he agonized over the propriety of his attending balls and parties.

All three of the women to whom Gladstone proposed marriage were daughters of the aristocracy. Each was therefore socially superior to his father (though less so to his deceased mother) and each fell within the class whose value to the constitution Gladstone particularly revered. In his approach to marriage, Gladstone—no doubt subconsciously—sought to consolidate the social position to which his education had accustomed him.

His first two attempts at proposals were disastrous. Caroline Farquhar was well-known in society for her beauty. She was the daughter of Sir Thomas Farquhar, the sister of Walter Farquhar, an Eton and Christ Church friend, and a cousin of W. K. Hamilton, also of the House. She was clearly bewildered by the Gladstonian barrage, episodically maintained in 1835 and 1836 and probably exacerbated by his brother Robertson's marriage—albeit in an Anglican church—to a Unitarian in January 1836. Religious difficulties and differences were compounded by an absence of attraction on Miss Farquhar's part, Walter Farquhar telling Gladstone bluntly after some eight months of courtship, mostly by letter: 'The barrier you have to overcome is the obtaining of my sister's affections.'[54] Aged twenty-seven at this time, Gladstone began to brood about marriage, and in a melancholy mood:

> I know not whether any other boon
> Except the holy treasure of a wife
> Could make me love this anxious load of life
> Or think if now I died, I died too soon.[55]

This despondent frame of mind probably explains his sudden proposal to Lady Frances Douglas, daughter of the Earl of Morton. Having met her two years earlier, he courted her during a brief visit in November 1837 to her father's house, Dalmahoy, near Edinburgh. E. B. Ramsay, the famous Episcopalian dean of Edinburgh, acted as an intermediary, but achieved nothing, having to send Gladstone 'a crushing letter'.[56] Ramsay continued to intercede on Gladstone's behalf, but on 31 January 1838 he 'heard conclusively from Mr. Ramsay'—the Mortons had ordered an end to the correspondence.

These two attempts at marriage left Gladstone uncertain and disorientated. For the only time in his adult life he experienced something like despair. To gain a change of scene he asked his father to let him make a voyage to the West Indies so as personally to investigate the controversial plantations. The request was refused. The diary in 1838 has a number of mournful entries: 'The world outside me seems somehow dismantled now, because of the icy coldness of my heart. . . . This results from a few very bitter things which have gone the wrong way for me'[57] '. . . the daily sadness that is upon me in the midst of this painted life of inward trouble' '. . .I live almost perpetually restless & depressed.'[58] The tone is Byronic; *Childe Harold* had offered a model of romantic restlessness to Gladstone's genera-tion, and he read it as the fruitlessness of his suit of Caroline Farquhar began to be apparent.[59] His depression partly reflected distress at the state of public affairs, for Gladstone was finishing the manuscript of his book in a mood less optimistic than its pages suggest: 'Conversation with Pusey. I told him for himself only—I thought my own Church & State principles within one stage of becoming hopeless as regards success in this genera-tion.' But no public developments could entirely account for this inward malaise. With relief, Gladstone left for the Continent as soon as the Session ended. He went in the company of Arthur Kinnaird, a Liberal MP 'at once frank and gentle, and set singly upon the truth'.[60]

A few days before leaving, he met Catherine and Mary Glynne, sisters of his Eton and Christ Church acquaintance, Sir Stephen Glynne. The Glynnes were also bound for Italy. Gladstone had stayed a weekend at their family seat, Hawarden Castle in Flintshire (now Clwyd) in January 1836,[61]—immediately after his brother Robertson's controversial wedding and while he was courting Caroline Farquhar by letter. At that time he made no note of either of the Glynne sisters in his diary, though he found time to commend the sermon of Henry Glynne, their brother and Rector of Hawarden.

The Glynnes were an old Flintshire family—Sir Stephen was the ninth baronet—modestly well-off and attempting to sustain its position by asso-ciating itself with industrial development in the area—a move whose disas-trous consequences were already becoming apparent with respect to the over-extended Oak Farm brick company in Staffordshire. Sir Stephen was Whig MP for Flintshire. He was a remnant of those Pittite Whigs who had not begun to call themselves Tories; Pitt the Younger was Catherine Glynne's first cousin twice removed and the family was linked to the Gren-villes and the Braybrookes. Glynne's obvious conservatism both impressed Gladstone and, as was the case with his travelling companion Kinnaird, flew in the face of his adversarial view of party relationships in the 1830s. Glynne was also a pillar of the Church of England in Wales and his huge collection of notes on all the old churches in Wales is a major achievement of nineteenth century antiquarianism, as well as showing the enthusiasm for Wales (and its ancient apostolic Christianity) characteristic of many of the Welsh gentry, so often dismissed as an alien presence by the Non-conformists. On the Italian journey he was a charming and knowledgeable companion, quite apart from the attraction Gladstone felt for his sister

Catherine. Gladstone took his own sister, Helen, to Ems on a cure for her health, but moved on quickly to Italy with Kinnaird to fall in with the Glynne party. While on this journey, he had a long conversation at Milan with Manzoni, the author of *I Promessi Sposi* which he had read earlier; Gladstone found him 'a man of rather strong Transalpine principles, but of fervent piety and charity'. The party visited Rome and Naples, Gladstone correcting the proofs of his book on the wing. Gladstone and Kinnaird went on for a month's tour of Sicily.

On returning to Rome, Gladstone renewed his courting of Catherine Glynne, almost bringing himself to a proposal in the moonlight in the Colosseum. For the first time his attentions were received with under-standing. On 17 January 1839 he proposed by letter,[62] even though he was frequently in the Glynnes' company. The statement of important feelings by letter rather than word was common at this time both generally and in the Gladstone household. An extra reason on this occasion was Glad-stone's wish to avoid the 'precipitancy' which he believed had spoilt his chances on earlier occasions.

Love for Catherine partially dispelled the malaise characteristic of the first part of the year. The change from the private diary to a travel diary written to be read at home and even more widely—the Sicilian sections were later rewritten to form the relevant part of Murray's *Handbook for Sicily*—means that the course of Gladstone's wooing and depression both go unrecorded. On resuming the private diary in February 1839, he noted:

In my accustomed review at the end of the past year [1838] I found that I had passed through more real depression in the earlier part of it, than ever before. . . . The truth is I believe my affections are more worthless than ever. Poured forth more than once & more than once repudiated they have become stale and unprofit-able; and I am strangely divided between the pain of solitude in the heart and the shame of soliciting a love which I sometimes fear it is impossible for me to repay. I am so deadened and exhausted by what has taken place. . . . And yet I suffered more & more from being *inwardly* alone . . . in my circumstances a nature truly noble would probably come to the conclusion that it had nothing left to give which would be worthy of any woman herself such as to be worthy of its attachment.—I offer myself therefore with many conflicting feelings: but this time must I suppose be the last, were it only for shame's sake.

In her C.G. I saw what I desired, as I think distinctly developed: the admiration of sacrifice made for great objects—and a gentle not unwomanly contempt for the luxurious pleasures of the world.[63]

Faced with the prospect of permanent union with a man whose character was transparently extraordinary, Catherine Glynne asked for time. A week later Gladstone and Sir Stephen Glynne returned from Rome to London for the opening of the Session. Courtship continued with the return of Catherine and Mary Glynne to London in May, Gladstone eventually telling his father of his suit, 'concealment became too heavy for me'. At last, on 8 June 1839, during a walk by the river at Lady Shelley's house near Fulham, Catherine Glynne accepted him. Both saw the marriage in intensely religious terms:

We walked apart, and with an effort she said that all doubt on my part might end. I intreated her to try & know me well: I told her what was my original destination & desire in life, in what sense & manner I remained in connection with politics—all this produced no revulsion in her pure and lofty spirit. She asked for the earliest Communion, that we might go together to the altar of Christ.

Purity of behaviour was further established by an exchange of information about each other's earlier suits, Gladstone wanting 'to show her the letter of September 1835, and explain to her, at the least, that subject', i.e. the Caroline Farquhar affair. In his diary he noted, using Greek letters, the names—a considerable list—of her suitors, commenting, 'I could not fail to become more and more attracted by such goodness':

σημερνευαρκίλλϝαυάνὲγερτονὰνϛονάρκουρτλευιϛμορδαυντ⁶⁴*

The couple were very quickly married on 25 July 1839 in Hawarden parish church with Francis Doyle as best man in a double wedding with Mary Glynne and George, Lord Lyttelton, whose engagement was even shorter. 'It has been more of heaven than of earth today' wrote Gladstone on his wedding day. But, characteristically, he qualified the joy: 'it has had its warning voice'; the brooding figure of Lady Glynne, too depressed to attend the ceremony, was a reminder of 'the contrasts of this mortal life'.

Gladstone was almost certainly a virgin when he married. Always highly susceptible to beauty, he had often been tempted and his diary contains many scattered references to sins of temptation of an unspecified sort. In his usual way of being precise without being explicit, Gladstone noted on the day Mary Glynne became engaged to George Lyttelton: 'I now know enough to be convinced that not without the faithful Providence of God have I been reserved for access to a creature so truly rare and consummate as my Catherine.'⁶⁵

Catherine Glynne was a strong-minded, healthy, independent, and beautiful woman with, as her husband noticed after their wedding night, 'a pure, enduring brightness'. She had Gladstone's mother's sense of repose but combined it with a life of energy and action directed at the family and at charities for the service of children, estate workers, and, later, East-Enders. She thus stood somewhat outside Gladstone's conception of womanhood as exemplified by his mother and his sister Anne. For all his adoration of them, he did not marry their image. 'What am I', wondered Gladstone, 'to charge myself with the care of such a being, and to mix her destiny in mine.'⁶⁶ Catherine Glynne must have been aware at the time of her

* i.e. Seymer, Newark, Hill, Vaughan, Egerton, Anson, Harcourt, Lewis, Mordaunt.

marriage of the extraordinary potential of her husband's public life. She can hardly have anticipated its astonishing private developments.

Money and Morality

The Gladstones were a comfortably-off couple, in every sense. Well connected, their honeymoon was a tour of great houses in England and Scotland. Marriage to Catherine brought a wide range of contacts with every level of the aristocracy save the very top, and their life-style in London reflected this. Marriage also placed her husband in a curious relationship to the great social classes of the country. Never actively in business, commerce, or the professions, Gladstone was none the less 'middle class' and always regarded himself as such, though his use of the preposition 'still' in the following quotation suggests his recognition of ambiguity: 'I . . . with the family of which I am a member, still claim to belong to that middle class',[67] he told the citizens of Liverpool in 1843. On the other hand, though not landed himself, he soon found himself, through marriage and through Sir Stephen Glynne's financial incompetence, the effective head of the Hawarden estates, with a country as well as a town base. Gladstone was, in fact, ideally placed in social terms later to develop the position which gave him such power in British politics, the arbitrator and mediator between the aristocracy and the middle class.

Catherine Glynne brought with her, by her husband's calculation, £10,716. 13s. 4d.[68] This roughly balanced what William Gladstone already had. His father had launched him on his career as an MP with a gift of £10,000, with further gifts of East India stock in 1837, valued at £2,150, and of £2,000 in 1840. To this was added an annual allowance of £2,500 and various generous gifts towards furnishing and day-to-day expenses such as 'Linen, Books, Carriages, Plate &c.'. To have a carriage was important in London society: it was the demarcating line between the wealthy and the pretenders.

As a bachelor MP, Gladstone lived in L2 in the Albany, off Piccadilly. When he married he bought the lease of 13 Carlton House Terrace on a mortgage of £6,500 paid at 6 per cent. Both these addresses were impeccable. Always a stickler for form—far more so than his wife—Gladstone's choice of houses reflected not merely convenience, but a desire for the best that orthodox London society could offer.

Apart from his salary during his brief period of office in 1834–5, Gladstone had earned not a penny of his wealth, which he valued in 1840 (including the mortgaged house and his wife's money) at £34,270. Given his view that society was based on obligations and duties rather than on rights, Gladstone naturally took his money seriously, though he was never embarrassed by it:

We ought to care about money: as a means, to be utterly regardless of it, as an end. We ought to be careful 1. to spend it—always to have either a) a present or

b) a prospective purpose for it. 2. *so* to spend it, that we may be the better able to open our books of pecuniary account, along with the rest of our proceedings, before God at the day of judgement.[69]

Consequently, Gladstone was exact about his charitable donations, the usual way of demonstrating proper stewardship. While an undergraduate, he reckoned that he had about £35. 10s. 6d. for 'Charity and Religion', and that this was 'under 1/11th' of his income (not of overall wealth); this had risen by 1835 to £211. 8s. 0d. ('about 1/9th'): for the years 1831–40, the average was, he calculated, 1/8th, or a total of £1,887. 1s. 0d. It is a little surprising that Gladstone seems to have seen these sums as residues after expenditure had been subtracted from income, rather than as sums set by forward planning. None the less, he had, in fact, done rather better than the Biblical tithe or tenth often used as the guide for personal charitable donations. In 1840 he planned in future to give 1/6th of his income. Later in the 1840s he partly separated charitable donations from his own expenditure pattern by setting up a separate charity fund, especially invested and generating its own income. In 1885 he calculated that, since 1831, he had given £52,113 to 'Charity & Religion'.

The Gladstone household was run religiously. The married couple read the Bible together, and household prayers—that Evangelical habit which in the early 1840s was becoming widespread—were regularly held. William Gladstone wrote a remarkable series of sermons which he read to the servants on Sundays, a habit he had developed while a bachelor—the series runs from 1834 to 1866.[70] On Sundays Gladstone always also privately read some printed sermons. As the 1830s progressed these tended to become High Church or Tractarian in tone: sixteenth-century divines such as John Jewell (Hooker's patron), Arminian and Caroline divines such as William Laud and Jeremy Taylor, or Tractarians such as Keble, Newman, and Pusey. As an undergraduate, Gladstone often read Thomas Arnold's moralistic sermons, but as the 'church party' tension of the 1830s developed and Arnold denounced the Tractarians as 'Oxford Malignants', he figures less in Gladstone's reading. Even so, this reading never became exclusively devoted to writers in the apostolic tradition.

In worship, Gladstone became increasingly Tractarian. For the time, he communicated very regularly, regarding 'the Eucharist, as representing food rather than remembrance'.[71] He made private notes for regular use in preparation for communion, one of his Eucharistic verses later finding its way into *The English Hymnal* as hymn 322. He usually attended his local parish church—St James's, Piccadilly, when living in the Albany, St Martin-in-the-Fields after his marriage—but he felt strongly drawn to the new ecclesiological and Tractarian developments in worship. In a paper written in 1839 on the need for beauty and veneration in worship, he wrote:

There is a true wisdom—varying in its application through a thousand degrees according to temperaments and circumstances—in the tinted lights, the rich and solemn architecture, in the plaintive chanted prayer, in the many voiced celestial organ: because they do for certain portions of our complex nature (instrumentally under God) what mental effort does for certain other portions.[72]

This view places Gladstone, as do his private devotional habits as developed in the 1840s, very much in the Puseyite tradition, however cautious publicly he was about some of its tendencies.

A Confident Conservative?

In concluding this review of Gladstone's years of high-Conservatism, it would be wrong to argue that his position was either clear or easy. Even in his chosen area of State–Church relationships, there was a wide range of influences pulling in differing directions. Two of these—the Broad Church nationalism of Coleridge and Arnold, and the apostolic semi-separatism of the Tractarians—both led in the context of the century to Liberalism, though for very different reasons. It was a great irony that almost all those Oxonians of Gladstone's generation who in the 1830s wrote books and pamphlets to counteract the dangerous tendencies of Liberal intellectualism and Liberal politics—Gladstone, Pusey, Manning, Newman—later found themselves its political beneficiaries.

None the less, Gladstone's Conservatism was characterized by boldness. That guarded qualification typical of the later Gladstone was already present, but it was not dominant. In the 1840s Gladstone came to prefer the 'lean and stunted affirmations' of Bishop Butler as he used probability as his guide to conduct. In the 1830s 'probability' lurked in the small print; Gladstonian Conservatism appeared certain and unyielding.

In certain important aspects of Conservatism Gladstone showed no interest. In particular, on the great question of fiscal policy he had as yet no well worked-out views of the sort that he had on Church questions. Brought up a Huskissonian moderate tariff reformer, he remained so during the 1830s, but without much scrutiny of his position. There are a few clues. Gladstone's method was already clear. In the second order world of fiscal arrangements he judged by facts rather than by abstract, a priori premises and deductions. In 1826, aged 16, he defended his Huskissonian position on the Corn Laws in anonymous letters to the *Liverpool Courier*, arguing he was 'as much opposed to the Levellers and visionaries of the one side, as to the Bigots and Monopolists of the other'. 'I admit facts, and abstract principles only in subservience to facts, as the true standard of Agricultural, Commercial and Financial Legislation' he told the electors in his election address in 1832, without mentioning the

Corn Laws. In the 1830s, these facts were thought to support the modified Corn Laws:

surely we are aware that if they were repealed, the landlords would be impoverished: no rents would remain . . . the landlords would become farmers themselves . . . the farmers would become labourers; and the labourers . . . must be contented with such wages as foreign countries give.

This comment, written in a draft pamphlet on the dismissal of the Whigs in 1834, Gladstone chose not to publish, and it is, among his many statements about the politics of the 1830s, almost a lone comment on the contemporary situation.[73] Early in 1841 he had an interesting confrontation with Richard Cobden on the Anti-Corn Law League. Cobden, not yet himself an MP, campaigned for the League at a by-election at Walsall, where J. N. Gladstone was the Tory candidate. Gladstone campaigned for his brother, and made a speech. Cobden wrote to complain at Gladstone's claim in his speech that 'this Anti-Corn Law League was no better than a big borough-mongering association', and challenged him to a public debate. 'I propose to show', Cobden wrote,

that the corn and provision laws are partial and unjust, that they are calculated for the temporary enrichment of a small part of the community, at the expense of the millions who subsist by honest industry, that they are an interference with the dispensation of divine Providence as proved by the revealed word of God and the obvious laws of nature, and that therefore they ought to be totally & immediately repealed.

This assault by the Anglican Cobden used a terminology which would have appealed to Gladstone, though he would not himself at any stage have made such a mechanical link between Providential dispensation and the need for repeal. It caught Gladstone slightly off-balance, and, declining the debate, he replied by separating the League from the Laws and attacking the former:

You desire me to meet you in discussion not upon the League but upon the Corn Law. I cannot imagine two subjects more distinct. I admit the question of the repeal of the Corn Law to be a subject fairly open to discussion although I have a strong opinion against it. But as to the Anti-Corn Law League I do not admit that any equitable doubt can be entertained as to the character of the proceedings: &, excepting a casual familiarity of phrase, I adhere rigidly to the substance which I have expressed.

Not surprisingly, he concluded in 1841 that 'Cobden will be a worrying man on corn'.[74]

A tariff structure implies, to a degree, a managed economy. In that sense, it was not incompatible with the confessional State which Gladstone spent much of the 1830s contemplating. Indeed, in the twentieth century, advocates of a confessional State have often been explicitly corporatist in their view of the economy. But Gladstone drew no such conclusion. He made no attempt to link a national economy with a national religion. When in 1843 he commented on a pamphlet by Friedrich List, the chief apologist of a national economy in the nineteenth century, he attacked 'those anti-commercial ideas which have lately been propagated in Germany by Dr. Liszt [*sic*]'. In keeping with the traditions of his education, he did not connect political thought with political economy: indeed, as we have seen, he was largely ignorant of the latter. Like most of his generation, nurtured on the supposed evils of the national debt incurred during the wars against France, he was an instinctive retrencher. From his first manifesto in Newark in 1832, Gladstone declared himself an economic reformer, i.e. in favour of the curtailment of government spending. This meant that he did not support the plans put forward by Sir Robert Inglis and some other Tories for extensive grants to the Church of England for its expansion into the areas of new population. The means of achieving 'national religion' were, therefore, in Gladstone's view to be voluntary means: the modern state should have a national church, but without it being paid for from government revenue.

There was in all this the embryo of a method, but no developed view. Partly this may be explained by the fact that for most of the decade fiscal policy was, compared with constitutional reform and Church questions, relatively unimportant: 'from 1833 to 1841, was a period the most inactive we believe in the improvement of our commercial legislation, since the peace of 1815', wrote Gladstone in 1843 when he had turned to consider such matters.[75] It was possible for a young MP living in the Albany not to have to be confronted by the practical consequences of industrialization in any very direct way. Yet it remains curious that Gladstone gave little attention to the social and economic organization that would have to underpin 'national religion', particularly as the role of the landed aristocracy in his system was bound to be prominent.

As with many of his contemporaries who looked to the Tory Party as their best hope, Gladstone lacked the intellectual categories with which to discuss such issues. The language of Toryism did not embrace concepts such as industrialization and modernization. The vague notion of 'improvement' to which Gladstone subscribed was an insufficient guide. At certain moments in the decade, Gladstone yearned for a fusion of intellect and religious zeal. He tried to see them as complementary rather as Coleridge in the social and political area saw the concepts of 'progress' and 'permanence', and in general attempted a fusion of knowledge and belief. Gladstone hoped to 'direct the mental eye of man in a course intermediate between speculation and idolatry', and he used the image of the steam engine to describe his vision:

It is true that we have hitherto seen but too often the principle of intellectual excellence & the spirit of religious zeal in collision rather than in harmony, but let us hope that it may be otherwise, even as the elements of fire and water . . . now are blended to accelerate the passage of man over the wide ocean.[76]

It was, of course, just such a fusion that the Oxford Noetics were attempting with respect to philosophy, theology, political economy, and social organization. The experience of the Peel government of 1841–6 was to provide the shock which completed the first phase of Gladstone's education, and then in the very un-Noetical direction of a disaggregation of functions: Church and State, government and economy, was each to ride its different way.

The 1830s as a decade turned out to be something of a red herring for Gladstone. He later believed that the 1832 Reform Act delayed the repeal of the Corn Laws by a decade. A similar delay may be suggested in his own development with respect to Church–State relations. But the reasons for both were the same. It was not generally apparent in the 1830s that intellectual, administrative, economic, demographic, and political pressures were all pointing towards a free-trading solution. Nor was it apparent, though it was perhaps easier to see, that similar pressures were rendering redundant both the Tory and the Whig versions of 'national religion'.

Learning this was to be a hard lesson, with permanent consequences.

CHAPTER III

Church, State, and Free Trade: the Public Crisis of the 1840s

*Gladstone in the 1840s—'A book upon a portion of political science'—
National Religion—Peel's Government—Idealism versus Practicability: the
Maynooth Grant and Resignation—Maynooth and the Oxford Movement—
Church Affairs—Free Trade and Experience—International Morality—
Liberalism and Politics in the Early 1850s—A 'Mixed Government':
the Aberdeen Coalition*

The last years have woven strong cords upon me that I had not before:
but my vocation does not seem as yet to struggle against them. I am older
than was the Redeemer in the flesh. Is He in any sense my pattern, in any
sense that is not a mockery? Have I made any true progress in the work of
salvation? Habitually my hope preponderates over fear: but it is not free
itself from the fear that it may be a sin-wrought delusion.

Gladstone in the 1840s

Thus Gladstone wrote in his diary (or journal, as he always called it) on
his birthday, 29 December 1844, as he prepared to resign from Peel's
cabinet on the Maynooth question. And indeed strong cords were being
both woven around him and released, cords which, partly by his own
tying and partly by the developments of the day, came to bind him to
political and intellectual positions which in the 1830s he would have
regarded as inconceivable, even satanic. The predominant features of
Gladstone's life in the 1840s are those of sharp change and sometimes
painful consolidation: change in domestic, political, and intellectual
affairs; consolidation in the gradual establishment of life-long attitudes
and commitments.

Domestically, Gladstone's marriage in 1839 marked the start of wide-
ranging responsibilities and changes. The 1840s and early 1850s saw the
birth of all his children and the death of one of them, the death of his
father, the apostasy of his sister and of some of his closest friends, and the
start of his regular attempts at the redemption of prostitutes. His marriage involved him in the bankruptcy of the Oak Farm company, the
consequent mortgaging of his wife's family estates at Hawarden, and his
life-long commitment to their rescue. These domestic developments,

together with the stress of public life, forced upon him a severe psychological crisis whose expression took a sexual form. He risked ruin 'all'anima ed al corpo' (to the soul and body).

They made for Gladstone a personal and sometimes intrusive background for the dramatic public developments of the 1840s. The resurgence of the Tory party ended in 1846 in one of the three major schisms of modern British politics, causing party instability and long-standing personal bitterness. The Oxford (Tractarian) movement had a development *pari passu*, of influence, defeat, and disintegration. The government and the governing class came to terms with the social, economic, and political problems of the most industrialized nation in the world, and tried to deal with those of its regional antithesis, rural Ireland.

The years between 1840 and 1855 were one of those periods which force men from their courses, and of no figure is this more true than of Gladstone; they have, at least between 1840 and 1848, a sustained and heightened feel of political crisis not again met until the 1880s. In those years Gladstone reached the Cabinet (and resigned from it) and held three offices in it, two of them of central and even decisive importance: President of the Board of Trade (1843–5), Secretary of State for War and the Colonies (1845–6), and Chancellor of the Exchequer (1852–5). The 'swan, very white and tender, and stuffed with truffles' which Disraeli observed at a dinner party in 1835, spread its wings and dirtied its feathers: the Tory Tractarian became the nation's leading financial statesman, and the colleague in Cabinet of the radical Utilitarian Sir William Molesworth. Intellectually and ecclesiastically the author of *The State in its Relations with the Church* witnessed the collapse of his political and ecclesiastical system and built anew on the basis of free trade, a colonial empire and, however reluctantly, an increasingly secularized State.

These years were, therefore, of central and pivotal significance for Gladstone's political, intellectual, and ecclesiastical development. His diary chronicles them and their consequences relentlessly, sometimes in the form of passages of reflection, always in the form of detailed records of reading and correspondence which show the changing pattern of his social and political involvements and intellectual interests.

Though by 1840 well established as a political figure, Gladstone never saw himself as merely a politician; he saw, or tried to see, political life as merely a function of a more general calling. As he put it: 'it is especially true that he who holds office of public trust runs a thousand hazards of sinking into a party man, instead of a man employing party instrumentally for its ulterior purposes; into a politician, instead of a man in politics; into an administrator, instead of a man in administration'. When in 1840 he drew up a list of 'plans at present in view', all were extra-parliamentary and only two were concerned with politics, and those very obliquely.* In principle and in theory, therefore, withdrawal from political life would be a natural enough move, and he considered it on several occasions during these years. The reader may judge for himself whether, having experienced real power, Gladstone found a satisfactory alternative in his out-of-office pursuits.

'A book upon a portion of political science'

Like George Eliot's Dorothea in *Middlemarch*, Gladstone's mind was 'theoretic, and yearned by its nature after some lofty conception of the world'. Throughout his life and to an extent far beyond that of any other British politician who was regularly in office, he spent much time yearning after such a conception, and attempting to define it in such a way as would be true and at the same time applicable to the realities of British public life. Gladstone approached problems in two ways. First by massive and detailed analysis resulting in a practical solution advanced and defended by overwhelming empirical argument, laborious correspondence, and dextrous use of institutional manipulation; second, if the problem moved him sufficiently, by a reflective article or book review, or, in a major instance, by a book. Thus his response to the Reform Bill of 1832 and its Whiggish aftermath was *The State in its Relations with the Church*; to university reform and the justification of classical studies as the basis of a Christian education, *Studies on Homer and the Homeric age*, to the general problem of right conduct in public life, his edition of Joseph Butler and his *Studies subsidiary to Butler's works*, begun in 1845.

We shall not, therefore, get far in understanding Gladstone's behaviour without considering the background: *The State in its Relations with the Church*, first published in 1838, twice reprinted, with a second edition in two volumes in 1841, and its companion volume *Church Principles considered in their Results* (1840). For these, and especially the first, intended as 'a book upon a portion of political science', sum up what he thought, *circa* 1840, the essentials of public life and social order ought to be. The consequences of the discovery of the impracticability of this approach, the crisis which this forced upon him, and his attempts to resolve that crisis, constitute the framework for the reading, correspondence, and self-analysis which provide the bulk of the entries in his diaries. An examination in some detail of the arguments and implications of these volumes is therefore necessary.

---

* '1. Publication of my book on Church principles.
    2. Enlargement of my book on Church & State.
    3. Scotch College [i.e. Glenalmond].
    4. Church at the Oak Farm.
    5. Certain rules to be established at my Father's new Church in Liverpool.
    6. A new School & a Board of Education at Newark.
    7. To concentrate & reorganise those operations now carried on through 'Societies'.
    8. Church at Fasque.'

Gladstone's first two books, certainly the most remarkable of British Prime Ministers' publications, cannot be dismissed as *jeux d'esprit*, youthful aberrations whose theories were either painlessly or quickly abandoned.* We have seen in the previous chapter the extensive reading and emotional energy through which Gladstone in the 1830s developed his intellectual and religious position. Of the books, *The State in its Relations with the Church* is the more important of the two, for *Church Principles* largely derives from its premisses. Though described famously and wrongly by Macaulay, followed by Morley and many others, as *Church and State*, the emphasis falls on the State, and this constitutes its chief interest. Though intended as a contribution to the revival of Anglicanism in the form of the Oxford movement, the work is not a characteristic Tractarian production. It relies strongly on Hooker for its approach to the Church, but on Burke and Coleridge for the State. Based on the Coleridgian concept of the Ideal, Gladstone defined the State as an 'organic body' in which persons were to be considered 'not as individuals, but only as constituents of the active power of that life . . . the state is the self-governing energy of the nation made objective'. Thus the State was not merely an aggregation of individuals, but an organic whole with 'a national conscience . . . formed upon a pure and comprehensive idea of right and wrong'. Definition of right and wrong was the function of the Church: 'religion is directly necessary to the right employment of the energies of the state as a state'. From this derived the role of the Established Church and the necessity for its preservation.

These arguments from within the Idealistic tradition implied strong hostility to the Utilitarian position, and Gladstone denounces 'the philosophy which holds that the latter [the individual man] will do best to choose his actions by a consideration of their general consequences, and which maintains that presumed advantage is to the human mind the best and most available criterion of right'. 'The injurious legacy of Locke' had spawned 'the twin sister of that degraded system of ethics or individual morality' which reached its full development in Bentham and James Mill.

Gladstone had made very bold claims for the theoretical authority of the State—bolder perhaps than he knew. For, as Macaulay observed in his famous attack in the *Edinburgh Review*, he had developed a major premiss to support a minor. Gladstone had no time for the old High Tory Establishment arguments of convenience and social stability, a

---

* Gladstone's reaction to criticism was to expand to two volumes, not disavow, his book. Historians have tended to isolate the comment in 'A chapter of autobiography', 'scarcely had my work issued from the press when . . . I found myself the last man on the sinking ship', without heed to the subsequent time-span. Morley does not meet head-on the role which *The State in its Relations with the Church* and its aftermath played in the development of the intellectual aspects of Gladstone's views on politics. The condition of the Liberal party, the debate about the nature of Liberalism 1899–1902, and Morley's own difficulties about making a systematic analysis of political Liberalism may well have discouraged him from this confrontation.

kind of Protestantism, with which I have no sympathy whatever ... which grew into fashion during the last century and has not quite grown out of it: that hated everything in religion which lived and moved: which lowered and almost paganised doctrine: loosened and destroyed discipline, and much defaced, in contempt of law, the decent and beautiful order of the Church: which neglected learning, coolly tolerated vice ... heaped up abuses mountain-high in the shape of plurality, non-residence, simony, and others more than I can tell ... made the Church of England, I say it with deliberate sorrow, instead of being the glory, in many respects the shame of Christendom.

The object of the book was to erect a framework of justification for establishment in theoretical terms strong enough to outweigh the objections—legitimate as Gladstone thought—to High Tory practice and expediency. Hence the very strong major premiss. The implications of the major premiss of the organic State are not worked out. Indeed, when he came to consider the rights of individuals and the historic position of the right of dissenters to exist without persecution, Gladstone was forced back upon that utilitarian tradition which he had earlier in the book so vehemently condemned. Notwithstanding his claims for the State, Gladstone asserted that 'the individual man, in virtue of his rational understanding and free agency, is entitled and bound in the sight of God to be in the last resort the arbiter of his religious creed, subject to his own full responsibility for employing the means most calculated to put him in possession of the truth';[*] and he mentions Locke's *Letters on toleration* as merely a step towards the goal. Thus at the heart of the book lay a profound contradiction, the result of the attempt to use two quite separate philosophical traditions to justify first an Ideal of society, then practical anomalies to that Ideal which already existed. There was, therefore, a lifeline to utilitarianism and consequently pluralism when the ship sank.

National Religion

Before considering the practical implications of these ideas, two other characteristics of the volume may be noted. Most striking is the high role given to nationality and its definition. The organic definition of the State and its close marriage to the Church would reflect the national character: 'national religion is the vivifying and ennobling principle of all national life'. 'National organization is evidently of divine appointment ... nations are the families into which the human race has what may be termed its primary distribution.' Keble, in his review in the *British Critic*, regarded the passage on the nationality of Anglicanism as the most original section of the book. The State, 'the natural organ of the nation', must choose the religion, guided by its ruling élite, which in Gladstone's view should resemble Coleridge's clerisy. Thus embodying their various national

---

[*] An aim of religion is 'the greatest holiness of the greatest number'.

characteristics, the English élite chose Anglicanism, the Mohammedans Mohammedanism, the United States a diversity of beliefs. Though the two last fell short of the ideal, they were acting not wrongly but naturally: the national Church reflected the innate characteristics of the nation it served. This belief was to be crucial when Gladstone came in later years to confront the problem of nationality in the Empire and in America. An expression of this view and of the practical application of what Gladstone called 'religious nationality' can be seen in his denunciation in 1851 of the Whigs' anti-Buddhist policy in Ceylon. In the Anglican context, therefore, the consequence was that the laws of Church and State, though of great importance, were merely the legal expression of English 'religious nationality': 'the union of the Church and the State is not a law of a primary kind, but a consummatory result of the development of Christianity in a people'. Believing this, Gladstone naturally had difficulty in justifying the Anglican establishment in Ireland, and the passages defending it in his book are much more mechanistic and less organic in tone than those on England. This emphasis on national religion, on locality, and separate traditions, distanced Gladstone somewhat from the Newmanite group within the Tractarians, and associated him rather with the High-Churchmen such as William Palmer, a group increasingly concerned about the 'Romanizing' tendencies of Newman's circle.

Because of this deeply-rooted belief that the form of religion was conditioned by nationality, Gladstone was never inclined to Roman Catholicism, whatever the Protestant press maintained. Of all those regarded as Tractarians he was perhaps most personally appalled at the progressive apostasy which overtook that movement, and no layman can have done more by correspondence and admonition to try to prevent it. For Gladstone already regarded Roman Catholicism as, at least in the nineteenth century, necessarily ultramontanist. He regarded what he saw as the Liberal Catholic Montalembert's failure to put truthful statement of fact and argument as a necessary and 'crucial instance of that fundamental antipathy between ultramontanism and freedom which at this moment constitutes one of the darkest omens for the future of Christendom', and he regarded Montalembert's Liberal Catholicism an 'imposture . . . he little knows what freedom means'. Gladstone naturally found 'startling' the 'general view of the ulterior section of the Oxford writers and their friends', for the ultimately ultramontanist position of the supporters of Newman's Tract XC seemed to him unnecessary, unhistorical, and deplorable, as he pointed out in drafting an anonymous letter to *The Times* in 1842 (though he thought better of sending it).

Another pronounced feature of *The State in its Relations with the Church* is its preoccupation with moral progress in this world. Coleridge's *On the Constitution of the Church and State* (1830), which, as we have seen, influenced

Gladstone from the mid-1830s, was ethical in tone and Gladstone was very much concerned with the ethics of the clerisy, an intellectual élite 'inherent in every well-constituted body politic', and with the morality of the nation as a whole. (His interest in the clerisy—a 'class . . . sufficiently supported . . . freed from corroding want and care'—led naturally to his later enthusiasm for the administrative grade of the civil service.) Though he spent much time himself on personal analysis, he was less concerned than other Tractarians with individual spirituality; the world of affairs not John Keble's Hursley vicarage was his natural home. Indeed Keble, in a review whose nuances are today of more interest than Macaulay's sledge-hammer blows, found Gladstone's book deficient in a number of Tractarian virtues. It had an 'unconscious tinge, we will not say of Erastianism, but of state as distinct from Church policy'; Gladstone had failed 'to keep his language clear of a certain utilitarian tone'; he should have given 'less encouragement to the enemies of Christian discipline'.

Peel's Government: Idealism versus Practicality

These then were the high aims of the young Tory of the early 1840s: the dream of a moral State married to a cleansed Church together countering 'the moral movement . . . of the day, away from religion and towards infidelity' and so achieving a peculiarly English and nationalistic form of ethical and religious progress. Other countries were seen in terms of Britain's salvation. Thus when in 1840 he spoke strongly against the infliction of the opium trade upon China, Gladstone was motivated partly by sympathy for the Chinese but also he was 'in dread of the judgment of God upon England for our national iniquity towards China'. Similarly, Ireland in 1845 was 'that cloud in the West, that coming storm, the minister of God's retribution upon cruel and inveterate and but half-atoned injustice!'* But national virtue depended on individual conviction. Individual and institutional leadership was therefore vital to establish a context of moral progress: 'the people must recover their moral health as individuals (in a polity where they exercise a main controul) before they can enjoy its consequences as a combination'. Gladstone continually stressed, in a characteristically Anglican way, the superior advantages of the Church of England as an effective compromise, in which all reasonable persons might find a mansion.

Individual leadership was provided by individual Tractarians; institutional leadership would come from the Tory party and the Anglican establishment secured by that party. Tactical success thus depended, as Gladstone and Keble both observed, on the Tory party as the guardians of

* Letter of 12 October 1845, in A. Tilney Bassett, *Gladstone to his wife* (1936), 64; the context of this famous quotation appears to refer to the Church question, not to the famine, but the nature of the 'injustice' is not made clear.

the Establishment and on the 'chosen band' of Tractarians within it 'to assert those principles'. The role of the Tory party was therefore crucial to the Gladstonian conception of State–Church politics, for the Whigs and Radicals were certain to act against it. But the idea of the chosen Tractarian band persuading the Tory country worthies to lead the nation along Tractarian paths of spiritual, ethical, and ecclesiastical progress seems odd enough, as some Tractarians, such as Newman, had already recognized by the late 1830s. As the prospect of office in 1841 became a certainty, Gladstone began to question the practicability of his concept, a matter of fundamental importance to his political life, for if the Tories failed to live up to their role, he would have to reconsider his own function and position in politics. 'Supposing the party abandon altogether the recognition of the Church, I mean of the Church as *the* Church', Gladstone wrote in May 1841, then he would have to 'accept the conditions of the age', 'leave a way which is hopelessly barred' and perhaps abandon parliamentary action altogether.

The recognition that the way to the realization of his dream was indeed barred by 'the conditions of the age' was to be slow, painful, and critical. During the collapse of the Whig ministry in the summer of 1841, Gladstone was included in Peel's meetings to discuss Tory tactics. His hope of the Cabinet and of a post in Ireland—for 'since the Address meetings the idea of Ireland had nestled imperceptibly in my mind'—were unrealized. (The Anglican establishment was most obviously vulnerable in Ireland.) Reluctantly, and with qualifications about the morality of British policy towards China, he accepted the vice-presidency of the Board of Trade. At first he regarded this as a limited and technical activity which left him 'morally free' (because he was outside the Cabinet) with respect to the administration's general policy. He immersed himself in minutes, tariff and corn law revision, and reading on economic questions. Peel had chosen wisely. In the Board of Trade Gladstone, from the start virtually its president as the records of the minute books show, discovered an absorbing fascination with the details of administration. Despite his self-confessed earlier ignorance, Gladstone was soon sufficiently informed and self-confident to challenge Peel—the accepted financial expert of the age—on the details of corn law revision, even to the point of threatening resignation. In a few months Gladstone had advanced from having 'no general knowledge of trade whatever' to being one of the few who had mastered the labyrinthine detail of British tariffs, even allowing himself to draw some comfort from his new-found abilities, the more so as he realized that Ripon's lethargy as president hampered the Board of Trade's effectiveness at Cabinet level.

Peel remedied this in 1843 when Ripon retired by offering Gladstone, then aged thirty-three, the presidency with a seat in the Cabinet. Peel was careful in discussing the matter to mention 'the compromises and adjustments of opinion necessary to ensure the cooperation of a Cabinet composed of any fourteen men'. Gladstone raised difficulties about the opium trade, Graham's proposed Education Clauses for the Factory Bill, and the amalgamation of bishoprics in North Wales to provide a new see for Manchester. He wavered between entering the Cabinet and retiring altogether ('at least such is probably the second alternative'). Guided by the 73rd Psalm—the set Psalm for the relevant Sunday—and a conversation with Hope and Manning who urged acceptance despite the narrow issue of the bishoprics, he accepted the presidency and joined the Cabinet. 'My first Cabinet', on 15 May 1843, was on O'Connell's movement for the repeal of the Act of Union.

As president, Gladstone quickly developed his remarkable facility for combining in a bill both immediate and anticipatory elements. Thus his Railway Bill of 1844 tidied up the procedure for handling the mass of private bills necessary for developing a railway network sponsored by private capital, and reserved the State's rights to intervene in the concerns of the railway companies. It provided for the needs of the working-class family through the 'parliamentary train'—one train to run each day at the minimum charge of 1*d.* per mile. Gladstone also anticipated that private enterprise might not produce an adequate railway system, and so provision was made for the preservation of the national interest by allowing for the ultimate acquisition of the railways by the public under certain stated terms of compensation, a provision which reflected Gladstone's general attitude to the limitations on the privateness of property, his natural *étatisme* and, it may be said, his common sense.

The implications of this realization of the beauty, joy, and technical satisfaction of departmental work were profound for Gladstone's general approach to politics. For it launched him on that life-long passionate effort of 'working the institutions of the country', and of explaining and defending the details of administration in the Commons. The growth of this technical fascination can be seen throughout the years 1841–5. By 1845 time spent on 'business' was counted with study and devotion as time spent in a Godly way (measured daily by the hour and recorded in the diary). Though Gladstone sometimes regretted his absence from church through the pressures of administration, he never regarded the latter as unworthy, however routine the activity. His diary testifies continually to the energy with which he absorbed speeches, correspondence, reports, books, and pamphlets which allowed him to speak, write, and act on such a variety of topics.

This absorption in the realities of administration forced Gladstone to recognize that as 'a man in politics' he might have a wider function than the ethical role he had accorded himself in the 1830s and the governing élite in his book. It also brought into sharp focus the excessively theoretical nature of his earlier views. The success of political Tractarianism had depended on infiltration and control of the Tory party. But it was soon clear that the Tory party in office, and perhaps especially its Cabinet, would fall far short of the high role accorded it by Gladstone. By 1842 he noted that he had ceased to believe that in 'the adjustment of certain relations of the Church to the State ... the action of the latter can be harmonised to the laws of the former. We have passed the point at which that was possible. ... The materials waste away daily.' But he hoped a Tory Cabinet would at least avoid worsening the Church's position and that under the Tories 'the State would honestly aim at enabling the Church to develop her own intrinsic means'. At the end of 1843 he noted: 'of public life I certainly must say every year shows me more & more that the idea of Christian politics can not be realised in the State according to its present conditions of existence'. None the less some cause for optimism remained, and the impracticability of Gladstone's State and Church theory had not yet been fully demonstrated. Moreover he was directly involved in its defence by his promotion to the Cabinet: he could no longer claim the moral freedom of mere departmental responsibility.

The tortuous and technical questions which lay behind the 1844 Dissenters Chapels Bill did not prevent Gladstone from supporting it enthusiastically on 'general principles of equity and justice'. This view dismayed Tory Establishmentarians of the old school and prompted R. L. Sheil, the Irish MP, to a perceptive if slowly realized prophecy: Gladstone, 'the champion of free trade, will ere long become the advocate of the most unrestricted liberty of thought'. But Gladstone's support for this bill sprang from the awkward historicism of his general support in his book for Dissenters' rights. It did not strike at the roots of his theory, or at any rate at that section of his book which justified the apparent anomaly of Dissenters' rights by arguments of utilitarianism and historicism.

The Maynooth Grant and Resignation

The crisis, however, soon came, and on what was for Gladstone the central point of principle, perhaps because it was more significant symbolically than practically, he found the cabinet wanting in steadfast principle. Hostility to the endowment and increase of the educational grant to the Roman Catholic college of Maynooth, near Dublin, seriously proposed in January 1844, became for Gladstone the touchstone of orthodoxy, for what was this but Whiggish concurrent endowment by the back door, which his book committed him to oppose?* On the question of English education he was ready to take, once in the cabinet, a position of administrative convenience. But Maynooth he saw as the battleground for 'National Religion', and it was in that 'Serbonian bog' that Gladstone's model for State and Church sank to its axles.

* In 1842 he supported the grant before its increase, 'reluctant but convinced'.

The battle between Gladstone and the cabinet was prolonged—from February 1844 to his resignation in January 1845—but the result was never in doubt. The impracticality of Maynooth as a battle-cry was merely a measure of the impracticality of the theory it symbolized. With his recent training in Peelite techniques of administration Gladstone soon saw this. Principle rejected the Maynooth grant: good government demanded it. Thus Gladstone both resigned from the cabinet and voted for the grant: the man of theory and the man of government.

Gladstone's resignation was popular amongst many Tories, churchmen, and even Nonconformists, who looked to Gladstone as the natural leader of the opposition to Peel—and as a much more substantial and reputable focus of opposition than Disraeli. Strong pressure was put upon him to lead the opposition to the grant. Ministerial fears that the government might fall on the issue reflected strong anti-Catholicism in the constituencies, and the petitions and deputations against the bill presaged the better known demonstrations against the establishment of Roman Catholic sees in 1850–1. It was not Gladstone's resignation, but his subsequent support for the grant which seemed perplexing and casuistic.

Idiosyncratic and perverse though Gladstone's action seemed to contemporaries, it was for him a pivotal and purgative experience. Never again (except perhaps in his last officially significant act in 1894) did he resign purely on principle, never again did he invest government or party with the high ethical status of *The State in its Relations with the Church*. The crisis foreseen in 1841 had occurred; the basic assumptions of his political life had been shown impracticable. He had, he told Newman, 'clung to the notion of a conscience, in the State, until that idea has become in the general mind so feeble as to be absolutely inappreciable in the movement of public affairs'. The experience was a 'nightmare' for him for several months, but it had one immediate dividend. He met the split of the Tory party in 1846 with relative equanimity; for Gladstone and for many lesser Tractarians at Westminster, in country vicarages, and in Oxford colleges, it had already abandoned its elevated function.

Maynooth and the Oxford Movement: 'the Parting of Friends'

The personal problem facing Gladstone in the years after Maynooth was: should he remain in politics and could anything be salvaged from the wreck of his theories? Gladstone told Stanley during the Maynooth crisis that 'the lower ends of a State ought to be fulfilled even when the higher ones should have become impractical', and he had only momentary doubts about continuing as an MP. His own problem of ideological reconstruction was much more complex. It was to some extent simplified by the collapse of the Oxford movement during the 1840s. One by one the friends parted, each with his own Maynooth, but all going further than Gladstone ever contemplated by joining the Church of Rome. Newman, Hope, Manning, all the Wilberforces save Samuel, and many of lesser fame took the step against which Gladstone so anxiously watched, argued, and prayed. The apostasy of Hope and Manning in 1851 was, on both sides, a bar to further intimacy; it left Gladstone 'unmanned and unnerved' though with 'total freedom from doubts' and brought on a period of severe spiritual loneliness expressed in part in a sexual crisis when he found 'my trusts are Carnal'.*

Thus was gradually broken up the circle of friends who from the mid-thirties had been Gladstone's closest confidants, to whom he had naturally turned even on political matters. If this left Gladstone without many friends with whom he could discuss his intellectual problems—James Hope is the only man outside the family given an albeit self-conscious nickname—it meant that those who were his friends were more political in outlook and commitment and less clerical in occupation than previously. Lord Lincoln and Sidney Herbert (both Tractarians) in political, Samuel Wilberforce increasingly in ecclesiastical matters, became reliable friends, but these were not intellectual friendships of the burning intensity shared with Manning and James Hope. In old age Gladstone recalled of Manning, 'I can only look at him as a man looks at the stars', and of Hope, 'he possessed that most rare gift, the power of fascination, and he fascinated me'.

There could be no expectation of an imminent resurgence of the Oxford movement, or of that great burst of progress in English religion to which Gladstone had looked to make his theory possible: after Maynooth he concluded 'that any man, in any country, can in this age of the world, give full effect to Christian principles in the work of Government, is alas! very far beyond my belief'. The direct consequence of this realization was an alteration of position on issues affecting the legal relationship of Church and State. Gladstone never again directly defended Irish Establishment, though it was many years before he publicly supported its abolition. But already by 1847 he was privately unable to give an assurance to Phillimore while 'I can in my own mind entertain so much as a suspicion that I may some years hence be forced to abandon it. . . . We are no longer in a condition to occupy high and secure ground in arguing for the integrity of the Irish Church Temporalities.'†

Gladstone returned to the Commons in December 1847 as one of the two burgesses (MPs) for Oxford University. His success in the election against C. G. Round showed the extent to which he and his group of Oxonian Tories had moved since the 1830s. For his vote (from the constituency of all Oxford MAs whether resident or not) was made up of an

---

* See below, p. 93, for further discussion of this. Gladstone's grief at his friends' apostasy became intermingled with his work for, and temptation by, prostitutes. When James ('Jim')Hope joined the Roman Catholic Church, Gladstone immediately struck off Hope's name as an executor of his will.

† Letters to Phillimore in this and subsequent paragraphs are in the Phillimore MSS in Christ Church.

alliance between Anglo-Catholics of one sort or another—Tractarians and High-Churchmen—and Liberals. At the university level, his supporters agreed that the history of the University between the Hampden affair in 1836—when the Tractarians were ascendant—and the degradation of W. G. Ward in 1845—when they lost, Newman almost being stripped of his MA at the same time as Ward—showed that reform was essential. Gladstone's membership for Oxford thus represented and accepted a desire for change, and in a Liberal direction.

Gladstone was at this time commonly regarded as a Tractarian, and we have seen that in several respects it is quite fair to call him that. Keble described him in 1847 as 'Pusey in a blue coat: and what can be said more for any layman? . . . I am so sure of him that I don't at all mind here and there a speech or vote which I can't explain.'*

The University contests produced much vituperative literature; indeed, their campaigns, in which the candidates took no direct part, were carried on at a lower level of argument than many of the other constituencies. This Evangelical squib represents the better side of Oxford election wit, and it captures something of Gladstone's Puseyite image:

> Swell'd with his honours from the classic school,
> See Gladstone! as a legislator rule!
> A second Canning! yes, with like conceit,
> But tithing not his eloquence and wit:
> A second Wilberforce! he wrote a book,
> But, for the Gospel, Puseyism mistook!
> 'The Protestant' (our pure Reformed Faith)
> 'Is but a *negative*' wise Gladstone saith,
> 'The Roman Catholic, the *positive*,
> 'Which only, can the Christian blessings give.'
> Gladstone! what honest sect, does this betoken?
> Words, only fit, for Roman to have spoken!
> Did'st thou, from science of the loadstone speak,
> Or some recondite Hebrew, Latin, Greek!
> Was it St. Stephen's dome inspired the rant,
> Or did'st thou not know what was Protestant?
> Wou'dst thou call *virtue, negative* of vice,
> Or *courage, negative* of cowardice?
> Thou'rt not too old to learn, if not too wise;
> Oh, do not then, our humble muse despise,
> Go back to school, and learn thy Catechism;
> Add not this folly, to thy other schism!
> Can we not grave authority advance,
> How Cato Greek learnt,—Socrates to dance—

* Quoted in the useful analysis of the Oxford constituency which I have relied on for the previous paragraph: W. R. Ward, 'Oxford and the origins of Liberal Catholicism in the Church of England' in *Studies in Church History*, i (1964).

Recant! recant! ere thou presumest to be
A Candidate for the University!
Your Popish tricks shall prove impotent spell,
If Oxford-sons perform their duty well.*

Gladstone regarded himself as, and was, primarily a Church of England man; he personally disliked church-party labels, and went out of his way to avoid direct association. He told Phillimore in 1847: 'With respect to Tractarianism, it is true, but I suppose of no use to say, that I have not read the Tracts ... I do not find people denounce me as a Tractarian from my books. It is chiefly on the ground of the vote with Ward.' (Gladstone strongly attacked, in an article in the *Quarterly*, W. G. Ward's views as expressed in the *Idea of a Christian Church*, but he went to Oxford to vote against his losing his MA.) In a second letter to Phillimore he developed his point about parties: 'I must firmly say I have committed myself to no party in the Church and no party has a right to reckon me among its members. ... It is then certainly not *e confessio* that I belong to a party.' It was true that Gladstone had not read the ninety *Tracts for the Times*, but he had read some of them, and a fair collection were to be found in the library at Hawarden. It was true that Gladstone's published works on religion reflect a wide range of influences, but it was also true that his private religious observances were markedly Tractarian in character. If Keble, the originator of 'the engagement', could find Gladstone 'Pusey in a blue coat' it would seem fair to describe him as a Tractarian, while bearing in mind his own reservations, and that the label 'Tractarian', especially by the 1840s, covers quite a wide spectrum of opinion. In terms of his constituency, Gladstone gained and lost from the label. It associated him with an important and well-organized but waning group within the University, it estranged him from the Evangelicals, and it raised problems about his relationship with the Liberals, who were finding common cause with him on non-religious matters.

On his return to the Commons, his first act found him reflecting his new political position and the changing opinions of those who had supported him: he voted for the Whigs' bill to permit Jews to take a different oath and thus become MPs. This was 'a painful decision to come to. But the only substantive doubt it raises is about remaining in Parliament.' His speech and vote were given shortly after Sir Robert Inglis, the other Oxford University Member who was returned unopposed, had presented a petition of Convocation against the bill. Gladstone's relationship with some of his university constituents was thus from the first acerbic, and opposition to him at the next election was assured. His vote on Jewish disabilities marked his new awareness of the necessity of pragmatic adjustment and the relativity of theory: 'the application of the immutable principles of justice to the

---

* From *The Newmania; or, Puseyism Unmasked* (1847).

shifting relations of society must be determined by successive generations for themselves, according to their several diversities'. He admitted that his book had 'strained the facts of the case' and that members of the University and politicians must recognize 'the political temper of the age'.

This feeling for the practical, and his unwillingness again to expose himself to a practically untenable position, can also be seen in his handling of the Gorham crisis of 1850, when the State reversed a patronage decision of an ecclesiastical court. Dismayed though he was privately by the judgement,* which for some Tractarians such as Manning was the occasion for apostasy, and though at first 'resolved to try some immediate effort' he declined to take a public stance, argued that it was for the bishops to lead the Church, and refused to sign a Declaration (for which refusal he was described as Judas, so central was the issue to Tractarians) and later tried to delay further action. He argued in his pamphlet, 'Remarks on the Royal Supremacy' (1850), that the Church of England as established at the Reformation was historically justified (Manning at this time concluded that it was not), but that the constitutional basis of the Gorham judgement was not so. Maynooth had taught Gladstone not only pragmatism but political tact.

But Gladstone had not admitted, and never admitted, that his theoretical conception as expressed in *The State in its Relations with the Church* was wrong. His subsequent writing and behaviour recognized its impracticality on specifically allied topics, but a larger question remained—could something more positive be achieved, could aspects of it be made practical by other means? The decade after 1845 shows his attempt to reach an alternative if less elevated synthesis. In addition to his movement towards acceptance of an increasingly secularized Parliament, Gladstone tried to construct this in three ways: colonial affairs, the morality of free trade and finance, and the morality of international affairs.

Colonial Affairs

Despite his resignation over Maynooth and his lowered view of politics, Gladstone remained eager for office in 1845 and became colonial secretary after the political crisis of December 1845, when Peel attempted to resign when his cabinet would not follow him over suspension of the Corn Laws and Russell declined to accept the 'poisoned chalice'. His tenure of office could not but be brief, and he began no large-scale plans. He dealt firmly with West Indian questions, on which he was already well-informed. More important, however, was his involvement in constitution-making in the white settlement colonies. For here was a new interest, much developed in the years after 1846, though in the 1830s he had spoken on Canadian and New Zealand affairs.

* When the case started he told Phillimore, 3 December 1847: 'O Newman! without thee we never should have had a Gorham case showing its face among us.'

Gladstone's understanding of nationality as organic, something much more than an aggregation of individuals, led him to interest in the British nation transplanted (and transported) abroad. He was much influenced by Gibbon Wakefield and by Cornewall Lewis's *Essay on the government of dependencies* (1841). Although a Whig, Lewis was, like Gladstone, a product of Christ Church and the Oxford classical tradition and his *Essay* gave an historical dimension to Gladstone's thinking. Gladstone's speeches on overseas colonies were in substance and sentiment adapted from Lewis's *Essay*. Lewis wrote that 'On reviewing the history of the Greek colonies . . . it will be seen that the advancement of mankind is to be expected rather from the diffusion of civilized nations than from the improvement of barbarous or half-civilized tribes.' Colonies were thus one of the 'best means of advancing and diffusing civilization'; the object of colonization, Gladstone thought, was 'the creation of so many happy Englands'. Greek colonies had set the right example by being founded not in dependency but in 'the union of heart and character'. It was no coincidence that Gladstone's increased interest in colonial affairs in the late 1840s coincided with his first burst of constructive work on Homer, for was not Homer essentially the story of the early development of 'the greatness of our race'?*

'Happy Englands' were for Gladstone Tractarian Englands: if the Anglican Church could not play its full role in England, perhaps it could in the colonies. Thus Gladstone saw systematic colonization as a means to systematic Tractarianism. His personal effort in the years 1846–52 was in the establishment first of colonial bishoprics, then of the emancipation of colonial sees from metropolitan control. To this end he introduced a series of private bills, none of which was passed in the form he intended. Though unsuccessful, Gladstone was led by these legislative attempts and by his analogies from Greek history to an important conclusion: local independence and responsible government were of vital importance to a colony. Locally churches should be supported by synods involving clergy and laity—a development he also advocated for Scotland in 'The functions of laymen in the Church' (1852). Colonies likewise must have responsible assemblies.

In his attempt to reconstruct the means towards moral progress, Gladstone certainly moved more quickly in colonial than in domestic affairs. As colonial secretary he moved much more rapidly than Stanley, his predecessor, towards self-government for New Zealand, and his good relations with Gibbon Wakefield helped bring the New Zealand company and the Colonial Office together. He was, if necessary, ready to partition the colony to achieve immediate self-government, which he thought should include local control of native affairs. His diary, when at the Colonial Office in 1846, shows his frequent contacts with Wakefield and he subsequently

---

* *Studies on Homer and the Homeric age* (1858), iii. 615 (conclusion).

became a chief, if not wholly orthodox, supporter of systematic colonization. Though he did not join the Colonial Reform Association, for he wished to assert the primary importance of his own Colonial Church Bills, he was deeply involved in its manœuvres, and he worked with his wife's brother-in-law, Lyttelton (whom he had made under-secretary when he was at the Colonial Office), J. R. Godley and Gibbon Wakefield to establish the Tractarian colony at Canterbury in New Zealand.

This developing interest in colonization ('planting a society of Englishmen') by 'the Anglo-Saxon race' had two important consequences. It was the political means by which, together with free trade, Gladstone found himself allied with Liberals and Radicals such as Molesworth and Roebuck. His views on colonial subjects gave a wider, more institutional, and more directly political dimension to the implied Liberalism of his free-trade ideas, discussed below. In the years after 1846 he found himself more radical than and in frequent conflict with Grey, the Whigs' colonial secretary, and it was on Gladstone's encouragement that Adderley put forward for the Colonial Reform Association the motion which effectively caused the resignation of the Russell administration in February 1852, 'of course to escape the Cape motion'. Thus on the formation of the coalition ministry in December 1852, Gladstone was an obvious candidate for colonial secretary, and was pressed as such at court by Aberdeen, but it is hard to see how he could have sat as such in a cabinet with Grey had Aberdeen persevered.

Free Trade and Experience

As a colonial reformer Gladstone was separated from the Cobdenite Radicals who had no interest in exported nationalism. He was also at first separated from them in his free trade views, though the gap narrowed as Gladstone more and more came to see free trade as an alternative, or at least a supplement, to the Church as the means by which the conscience of the State could be expressed and the relationships of an industrial society fairly adjusted.

Gladstone approached the problem of protection through the work of the Board of Trade, that is, through the administration of the vast corpus of tariffs for which the department was responsible. His primary concern was therefore with the supply of raw materials for manufacturing, with the export of manufactured goods and with the whole framework of trade treaties with other nations. In this context the question of the Corn Law was secondary, though clearly important. Gladstone's progressive conviction that the windows of 'the hothouses of protection' should be further and further opened was thus formed partly for administrative and partly for general commercial reasons. Reductions of tariffs could be achieved progressively but gradually by good administration from within the existing system. A general movement towards free trade across the board, rather than a localized interest in the Corn Law was therefore his chief interest. This was not to say that he did not admit a strong case against the Corn Law; in 1842 he felt the old law to have been 'a very stringent and severe one' and proposed resignation when he felt it had been insufficiently alleviated. But he did not support repeal at a stroke. As he told his father, 'I viewed the Corn Law as defensible only on the ground that the agriculturist had a claim to very gradual and cautious transition out of the artificial state in which law had placed him.' He therefore showed no enthusiasm for the social and political aims implicit in the programme of 'the notorious League' which, in 1843, he thought basically ingenuous:

An enormous credulity, as it appears to us, is essentially required before a man can raise himself to the level of that dogmatic faith, wherewith some of the opponents of the corn laws appear really to believe, that the removal of the restrictions upon the trade in grain is to remove all suffering, to obviate all risks, and to introduce in short a commercial millennium.*

Gladstone at the end of 1845, rejoining the Cabinet during a political crisis, saw the Corn Law question in terms firstly of political pledges given in 1841 at the election, secondly in terms of the immediate Irish crisis. At the time he showed little interest in the law as a symbol, and he deplored the symbolic tone of Peel's famous tribute to Cobden in 1846. Experience, and the balance of the evidence, rather than a conversion to Ricardian comparative advantage theories, in the first instance made Gladstone a free trader.

With an interest in general tariff reduction Gladstone was coming to see free trade not, as the Leaguers saw it, as the field for a battle fought between two classes on the issue of the Corn Laws, but rather as the class-integrating factor in the organic state. As his system of State and Church collapsed in 1845, Gladstone, searching for a substitute, came to invest the general concept of free trade with the moral role in the nation's ethical progress earlier attributed to the Established Church. In this sense the 1853 budget was the answer to the Maynooth grant. Gladstone's search for a role was over: fiscal probity became the new morality.

Practical experiences at the Board of Trade made Gladstone consider the relationship of religion to commerce; he squarely faced the question 'whether the system of modern industry is ... fundamentally and essentially at variance with the principles of the gospel'. He concluded 'that this question must be deliberately answered in the negative'. This was of fundamental importance, since 'religion and Christian virtue, like the faculty of taste and the perception of beauty, have their place, aye and that the first place, in political economy, as the means of creating and preserving wealth' and he quoted John Wesley to prove it.†

* 'Course of Commercial Policy at Home and Abroad', *Foreign and Colonial Quarterly Review*, i. 252 (January 1843).
    † Ibid., 253.

Gladstone thus saw economic progress linked to religion in achieving moral and social development. A central function of government was to facilitate this. Gladstone believed the Board of Trade and the Exchequer had in 1841–5 achieved progress of this sort: existing departments were efficient, and could be made more so by and within the existing political structure. He therefore did not see any urgent need for further political reform and though not opposed to it in principle was certainly not its protagonist in the Aberdeen administration of 1852. In this merging of religion, ethics, and economic progress, Gladstone owed much to Thomas Chalmers, whose lectures in the 1830s had in part occasioned *The State in its Relations with the Church*. Chalmers' works on commerce are often referred to in the diary, though not always with unqualified praise.

In his changing political situation in the mid-forties, free trade became more and more the touchstone of Gladstone's political action. The Aristotelian notion of a balanced society based on obligation and duty gave way (though it did not wholly disappear) to a society in which the assertion of economic individualism gained predominance, conditioned though Gladstone hoped it would be by probity, self-control, and Christian morality. Though Gladstone sometimes continued to use the language of a pre-industrial social hierarchy (especially when discussing the duties of land-owners), his political actions increasingly in fiscal matters coincided (though he did not see them fusing) with the atomistic individualism of political economy. He read the political economists fully and repeatedly. His hostility to the Mills in the late thirties changed to an increasing reliance on them for technical competence in fiscal matters. His notes and jottings show him teaching himself Millite political economy at first at a very simplistic level. It would go too far to say that Gladstone became at any stage in his career in any full sense a utilitarian, but those utilitarian aspects of his approach to society, noted above and criticized by Keble, certainly became more pronounced.

State and Church being out of the way as the pivot of his political relationship, he found fiscal rectitude the chief bar to a return to the Tory party. Disraeli's supposed flippancy and slackness in fiscal matters and his irreverence towards fiscal canons appalled Gladstone in the same way as the approach of the Whigs and Radicals to the Irish Church had in the 1830s.

Because at first Gladstone saw tariff reduction as primarily an administrative problem, his movement towards free trade was not in the early 1840s politically dramatic, and as late as 1848–9 he spoke against complete abolition of the Navigation Acts, favouring safeguards during a transitional period for the merchant navy, and some control over colonial trade relations with foreign powers. But rather than endanger the overall success of repeal of the Acts, he did not press his scheme, much to the disappointment of Disraeli. His proposal had become futile when 'the ship owners and their friends ... would not adopt a plan upon the basis I propose'. Thus, despite occasional questionings of timing, the change in his position was, at bottom, firm and irrevocable. As such, it involved a quarrel with his father, who had supported Huskisson but would move no further in the 1840s, and opposed repeal of the Corn Laws and of the Navigation Acts in long letters from Fasque. The quarrel was especially distressing to both, for it occurred during the attempts to rescue Helen Gladstone from the drug addiction following her conversion to Roman Catholicism.

When his father in 1849 accused him of having made Peel a free trader Gladstone wrote this account of his position:

As respects my 'having made Peel a free trader', I had never seen that idea expressed anywhere and I think it is one which does great injustice to the character and power of his mind. In every case, however, the head of a Government may be influenced more or less in the affairs of each department of State by the person in charge of that department. If, then, there were any influence at all upon Peel's mind proceeding from me between 1841 and 1845, I have no doubt it may have tended on the whole towards Free Trade: I can recollect many cases in which my endeavour was to lead the Government onwards in the path of progressive & gradual relaxation, than to keep it back. In 1842 for instance it was my wish individually to have made a somewhat greater reduction of the corn duties. . . . But all this ceased with the measures of 1845 when I left office. It was during the alarm of a potato famine in the autumn of that year [that] the movement in the Government about the Corn Laws began. I was then on the continent, looking after Helen. . . .

. . . I myself had invariably, during his [Peel's] Government, spoken of Protection not as a thing good in principle but to be dealt with as tenderly and cautiously as might be according to circumstances, always running in the direction of Free Trade. It *then* appeared to me that the case was materially altered by events: it was no longer open to me to pursue that cautious course: a great struggle was imminent in which it was plain that two parties only could really find place, on the one side for repeal, on the other side for the *permanent* maintenance of a corn law and a protective system generally & on principle. It would have been more inconsistent in me, even if consistency had been the rule, to join the latter party than the former. But independently of that, I thought, & still think that the circumstances of the case justified and required the change: I should have preferred rather a different form, that is to say a low fixed duty of 4/- or 5/- per quarter to last for a greater number of years; but that was decided otherwise. . . .

So far then as relates to the final change in the Corn Law you will see that no influence proceeded from me, but rather that events, over which I had no controul, and steps taken by Sir R. Peel while I was out of the Government, had an influence upon me, in inducing me to take office.

Gladstone's separation from the Tory party was initially on the tariff issue, but it slowly broadened into a difference on fiscal policy generally, culminating in his violent and devastatingly successful attack on Disraeli's budget on 17 December 1852. This was due in part to a personal dislike of Disraeli and regret at not having been able to defend Peel in Parliament in 1846 (Disraeli would not have been able to dismiss Gladstone, as he had Sidney Herbert, with jokes about valets). Gladstone's diary and correspondence show mounting irritation and dislike of Disraeli, without the usual charitable qualifications which accompany Gladstone's remarkably rare personal censures. By 1849 Gladstone felt 'it is a very unsatisfactory state of things to have to deal with a man whose objects appear to be those of personal ambition and who is not thought to have any strong convictions of any kind upon public matters'. By 1852 he was glad not to have to speak in direct answer to him, and even to do so indirectly gave him an unwonted sleepless night. After his great personal triumph over Disraeli in December 1852, his only regret, which kept him up most of the night, was that he had 'mismanaged a material point (by omission)'—this in an overwhelmingly successful speech, which immediately preceded the defeat of the government.

But it would be unwise to attribute to as politically complex a character as Gladstone a position based purely on personal antipathy, important though that was in this instance, at least as an immediate spur. Since the Peel government's fall in 1846 little had been done, save the repeal of the Navigation Acts, to further that great plan of gradual but progressive reduction of tariffs across the board. Nor had the question of the theoretically temporary but continually renewed income tax of 1842 been tackled. Nor did either a Whig or a Tory ministry show itself likely to tackle these problems thoroughly. To the tariff question therefore was added the income tax question; the two come together in the 1853 budget, essentially an expanded version of that of 1842, but going far beyond it in general social significance and future planning. The 1853 budget was, as well as the saving of the coalition, the summit of Gladstone's early political and administrative career; it was the moment at which he became a national as well as a parliamentary figure, and one clearly marked out for leadership. Had those who heard it been aware of the highly effective tactical battle which Gladstone had fought in cabinet to maintain it intact, they would have been the more impressed. This developing view of the importance of fiscal responsibility was therefore the background to Gladstone's decision to join the coalition in December 1852, despite his lingering affection for the Tories as a party, and his antipathy to the Whigs as promoters of the Ecclesiastical Titles Bill.

International Morality

Right relations with the colonies and fiscal responsibility thus formed the two chief interests of Gladstone during his attempt to find a political role following the collapse of his State and Church structure. To these must be added spasmodic interest in international morality. China in the late thirties and early forties, Don Pacifico in 1850, Italy in 1851–2 were questions taken up with great, even violent passion and then dropped almost as suddenly, at least for a time, though Italy was a slow-burning fuse. Little attempt seems to have been made to integrate them into a coherent view of international affairs and Gladstone did nothing when Chancellor of the Exchequer after 1852 to resolve Neapolitan problems, apart from acts of personal charity towards the political prisoners. None the less his interventions in these questions made him a figure of European note even before he became, as chancellor, a first-rank politician in his own country.

Gladstone's two visits to Italy in these years were both fortuitous. The first, in 1849, was in pursuit of Lady Lincoln who had fled thither with her lover. Gladstone finally found the villa near Lake Como and entered the grounds disguised as a guitarist to get the evidence needed for Lincoln to divorce her by private bill. He later gave evidence in the House of Lords on this, an action which he had some difficulty in explaining when he vehemently opposed the bill which made divorce generally available in 1857. The general importance of this visit was that during it Gladstone began to read Leopardi, whose works he reviewed in the *Quarterly* on his return.

The second visit was in 1850–1, made for the benefit of his daughter Mary's eyesight. It was, as we shall shortly see, to have important political consequences. Neither visit, therefore, was the result of direct curiosity about Italian developments. However, their timing was important. In Italy, and especially in the Bourbon kingdom of the Two Sicilies, the thoughts about right social relations in British domestic and imperial affairs which had preoccupied Gladstone in the 1840s were brought into sharp focus. For in Naples he found a society where right relationships had manifestly not been established, and by a government indisputably conservative. The arbitrary arrests and managed trials of respectable lawyers, the realization that 'a portion' of the Roman Catholic priesthood could be informers and perjurers, the appreciation that normal British standards of justice and governmental conduct—let alone representative institutions—were regarded as liberal and thus damned, gradually forced Gladstone to the conclusion that action must be taken, privately at first, publicly if necessary: 'one grows wild at being able to do nothing' against 'the Government of Naples which I believe to be one of the most purely Satanic agencies upon earth'.

Visits a few days before leaving Naples to the prisons of the Vicaria and the Nisida, and in particular a talk with Carlo Poerio outside the latter, ensured that Gladstone reached London ardent for action. Somewhat to the embarrassment of their recipient, Gladstone published two *Letters to the Earl of Aberdeen*, the first of which described Bourbon rule in Italy as 'the negation of God erected into a system of government', the first of Glad-stone's famous phrases which punctuate the century. The reaction to the *Letters* reflected at a European level the position which Gladstone had already reached in British politics. Whatever his motives, he found himself unavoidably associated with the Liberals: European Conservatives in Britain and throughout Europe, with hardly an exception, deplored his initiative. In the third of his pamphlets on Naples, Gladstone ended by extolling the mid-century Liberal solution: 'free and unrestricted exchange ... with all the nations of the world', with Britain 'the standard bearer of the nations upon the fruitful paths of peace, industry and commerce'. Thus the 1853 budget was also the answer to King Bomba. Conservative he might still feel himself, Liberal his language was certainly becoming.

Liberalism and Politics in the early 1850s

By the early 1850s, therefore, Gladstone had shed many of his Tractarian Tory political, though not necessarily social, predilections of the 1830s. In this sense the decade 1841–51 is the crucial period of his political develop-ment. In place of his earlier views he had developed a number of interests, which were not yet necessarily coherently interlocked but which, taken as a whole, made it increasingly difficult for him to co-operate with the Tory rump.

His aim had been not to reconstruct an abstract theory of the sort given in *The State in its Relations with the Church*, but to arrive at a series of practical positions which would further national moral progress. He had developed a 'thorough Sir Robert Peelian horror of *abstract* resolutions' and he never again attempted, as he had in his book, first to state an abstract principle, then to work it out in politics. Subsequently he invested practical measures with abstract principle; here lay one of the secrets of his great public success.

To say whether this constituted Liberalism is to measure him against an undefined standard. But it can be said that it placed him with the political economists on fiscal policy (Liberals to a man)—with the Whigs on civil liberties—with the Radicals Molesworth and Roebuck on colonial affairs, and—whether he liked it or not—with the moderates of European Liberal-ism on the Italian question. On the topics which had become central to his political interests, therefore, he found himself in each case allied with groups which, whatever they were, were not predominantly Tory.* For a politician of Gladstone's type, the change in personal relationships follows the change of opinion. Of all the leading Peelites he had become the most

* The Ecclesiastical Titles Bill of 1851 and the Don Pacifico debate of 1850 were partial excep-tions to this; but on the first, Gladstone defended a pluralist position which was essentially Liberal rather than Whiggish or Conservative, and in the second his speech against Palmerston on inter-national morality was far more characteristic of Bright than of Disraeli, though Gladstone found himself in the lobby with the Conservatives.

Liberal, on many topics, in the sense of policy, but remained the most enthusiastic for a rejuvenated Conservative party permeated and controlled by the Peelite group. 'Junction with the liberals' in 1852 would be 'our least natural position'; the function of the Peelites was 'working out a liberal policy through the medium of the Conservative party'. But in saying this, Gladstone already believed that in terms of issue and policy he would find great difficulty in supporting Derby's Conservative government at least until its protectionist proposals had been defeated. Then the Peelites would be 'free & ready to pursue whatever course in point of party connection the interests of the country might seem to require'.

A 'Mixed Government': the Aberdeen Coalition

Gladstone played his part in the defeat of the minority Conservative government. Quite handsomely returned for Oxford University in the General Election of July 1852, he attended the opening of the Session in November in a state of high nervous excitement marked by a bout of self-flagellation. He contributed to the defeat of protection on 26 November: 'Divided in 336:256 and in 458:53. So ends the great controversy of Free Trade. Nervous excitement kept me very wakeful: the first time (after speaking) for many years.' But that was not all, for, on the night of 16–17 December 1852, as he noted laconically: 'Rose at one & spoke till past 3 in answer to Disraeli.' As the thunder shook the windows of the newly finished Palace of Westminster, the Peelites made clear what had been implicit in their behaviour since 1846 and virtually explicit since their refusal to join Derby in February 1852: their support for the Tory party was on conditions it could not meet, even by giving up protection. The subject was the budget; the issue, Disraeli's intention to overstep the traces of orthodox Peelite views about taxation. Gladstone's attack was, most unusually, made after Disraeli had wound up the debate in a brilliant, mesmeric speech. But certain comments about personalities had left Disraeli open to a reply. Gladstone's response, first a ticking off of the chancellor for want 'of discretion, of moderation, and forbearance', then an assault on the deficiencies of the budget, gained the hearing of an initially rowdy House. The attack appeared to be an impassioned, impromptu effort. Gladstone's diary shows most of it to have been, like most spontaneous successes, well-researched and thoroughly prepared.

Gladstone did not bring down the ministry single-handed. The General Election and the regrouping of the supporters of the previous Whig government had Disraeli already wriggling in the Commons. But his intervention, at a moment when it looked as if Disraeli's 'unorthodox' views on taxation were attracting some support, appeared decisive; it certainly showed Gladstone holding the dagger which slew the government, and it marked him out as the chief antagonist of Disraeli.* The consequence of the ministry's subsequent resignation, Gladstone concluded, was that 'the only remaining alternative would therefore seem to be a mixed Government'. Two days later he avoided a 'lion's den' in the Carlton Club only by physically removing himself from that Tory stronghold.

Aberdeen went to Windsor to kiss hands and mentioned Gladstone for either the Exchequer or his old post at the Colonial Office. According to Prince Albert, the Crown tipped the balance in favour of the Exchequer. Thus was Gladstone launched on what were to be a series of 'mixed governments' (he preferred this term to 'coalition') on the progressive side of British politics, eventually and in no very certain or deliberate way developing into the Liberal party.

In the Aberdeen coalition, as the ministry of 1852 is usually called, Gladstone found himself playing a central political role. The most effective of the Peelites in the Commons, he was also the most successful departmentally, and in two very different directions. As Chancellor of the Exchequer, he held the office whose former incumbents' proposals (Wood for the Whigs, Disraeli for the Tories) had led to disaster. What was needed, first, therefore, was a safe pair of hands. Gladstone perhaps rather surprised his contemporaries, accustomed as they were to his Tractarianism, by being in peacetime first, foremost, and *almost* always, a safe chancellor. He did not make mistakes, and he did not have to take things back. He thus provided, at the least, stability and control, qualities which were important in the very uncertain circumstances of British politics in the early 1850s. Of course, he also provided a great deal more, and it will be convenient to examine his work as a mid-Victorian chancellor in a later chapter (Chapter V).

University reform was an inevitable duty of the government. The Royal Commission on Oxford University set up by the Whigs (and opposed by Gladstone) in 1850 had in 1852 produced a powerful statement of the Liberal case. The arguments of the Tories in the 1830s, including Gladstone, that the University could and would, given time, reform itself institutionally, had been seen to be fruitless. The issue was not whether but how Parliament would reshape Oxford. As MP for the University, with a vote awkwardly, as we have seen, composed of Liberals, Tractarians, and many of the leading scholars resident in Oxford, but opposed by Tories, Evangelicals, and many of the country clergy, it naturally largely fell to Gladstone to produce the government's response to the Royal Commission,

* The intensity of the personal antagonism between the two men—rare on each side—was reflected in a tetchy exchange of letters, much of it in the third person, after Gladstone had succeeded Disraeli as chancellor, the issue being the value of the furniture in No. 11 Downing Street (the chancellor's house) and the handing over of what was thought to be Pitt's chancellor's robe, traditionally sold by one chancellor to the next; despite his support for tradition and precedent, Disraeli held on to it. Gladstone noted about one of his letters, written on a Sunday: 'Wrote (draft) to Mr. Disraeli: (I did it purposely *today*).'

for if he surrendered control of the bill, he would have effectively surrendered control of his constituency as well. The details of the bill concern Oxford more than Gladstone, but its general form is revealing about his approach to institutions and his relationship with the various political groups. The Liberals wanted a rationalized university, the traditional autonomy of the colleges broken by a powerful professoriate: a movement towards a departmental rather than a collegiate system. They expected Gladstone would back them. He did not. His bill, he told Bonamy Price, was framed on 'the principle of working with the materials which we possess, endeavouring to improve our institutions through the agency they themselves supply, and giving to reform in cases where there is a choice the character of return and restoration'.*

This method, the use of Parliament to permit regeneration rather than to impose novelty, to work from within a set of historic institutions rather than from an a priori plan, characterized the mid-century Gladstone. When the Liberals complained, he reacted sharply: 'these gentlemen, whatever they may be as irrigators are as respects Parliament merely dreamers. An English legislature would not, even if we were to ask it, force their "spick and span" Professoriate upon Oxford any more than they would adopt a constitution out of the pigeon holes of Abbé Sieyès.'† The bill was one of radical conservatism. As usual, Gladstone's conservative intentions—pruning off the rotten branch, as he later said of compulsory church rates—were misunderstood by the Conservatives; Dean Gaisford of Christ Church, for example, found the bill 'unjust and tyrannical'.

The bill secured a viable solution by borrowing something from the Liberals, and by reflecting the aims of the moderately reforming Tutors' Association; it gained support for a fundamentally conservative solution by readily giving up obvious but superficial conservative totems. Having decided on his line of action, Gladstone was determined and thoroughgoing in achieving it, and saw to its completion by insisting on the provision of commissioners to supervise its execution. The Liberals were disappointed, but the Tories were shocked. In this sense, Gladstone's making of the Oxford University Bill epitomized his relationship to British politics.

Gladstone's work on the bill involved him in a huge correspondence—again, a characteristic of his methods of preparing legislation. Springing from this, on the urging of the Broad-Churchmen Temple and Jowett, he requested Northcote (formerly his secretary) and Sir Charles Trevelyan of the Treasury to report on recruitment to the civil service. Skilful use of their brief report supporting competitive examinations through a central board made it one of the most famous British documents of the century.

---

* Quoted in E. G. W. Bill, *University reform in nineteenth-century Oxford* (1973), 151.

† Quoted in ibid., 160. The bill was introduced in the Commons by Russell who acknowledged Gladstone's predominance in its construction; Gladstone then worked it through the Commons.

Gladstone saw competitive examination as the means of achieving the ascendancy of a Coleridgean clerisy in the secular world. The almost absolute distinction between the administrative grade and the rest of the service, with admission to the administrative grade via examinations which were effectively a repeat of the Oxford and Cambridge degree examinations, would tend 'to strengthen and multiply the ties between the higher classes and the possession of administrative power'.* A civil service hitherto appointed by patronage and influence would give way to a nonpolitical administrative class educated in the moral values of a liberal education further developed by a reformed Oxford and Cambridge. It was a means of extending, confirming, cleansing, and legitimizing an existing élite. Whereas, Gladstone thought, the seventeenth century had been an age of rule by prerogative, and the eighteenth by patronage, the nineteenth would become a rule by virtue. For a liberal education attempted, above all, to produce citizens who were morally good, and such it was that would succeed in the examinations. In this objective, the Peelites were at one with the Liberals, though not with the Whigs. What the Liberals failed to gain in Oxford, the gradual implementation of competitive examinations (fully effected in 1870) gave them in the British Establishment as a whole.

'I fear', Russell wrote to Gladstone in March 1854, 'my mind is exclusively occupied with the war and the Reform Bill, and yours with university reform.'† Certainly Gladstone, though he had to raise the money to pay for it, was only marginally involved in the Cabinet's move towards war with Russia. But his position was clear and resolute: he accepted the need for British intervention in the general cause of peace, and he stiffened Aberdeen's will as the moment arrived in February 1854:

He [Aberdeen] said how could he bring himself to fight for the Turks? I replied we were not fighting for the Turks, but we were warning Russia off the forbidden ground. . . . We stand I said upon the ground that the Emperor has invaded countries not his own, inflicted wrong on Turkey & what I feel much more most cruel wrong on the wretched inhabitants of the Principalities [of Moldavia and Wallachia]: that war had ensued and was raging with all its horrors: that we had procured for the Emperor an offer of honourable terms of peace which he had refused: that we were not going to extend the conflagration (but I had to correct myself as to the Baltic) but to apply more power for its extinction: and this I hoped in conjunction with all the Great Powers of Europe: that I for one could not shoulder the musket against the Christian subjects of the Sultan: and must there take my stand.

Gladstone came to oppose aspects of the conduct of the war and of the negotiations to end it, but his view of its initial necessity as an act of public

* See J. B. Conacher, *The Aberdeen Coalition* (1968), chapter 13 for this, and for the wrangles with the Whigs which, with the onset of war and the break-up of the government, led to the loss of the proposed legislation.

† Morley, i. 500.

control remained an important point of departure for his interventionism in the Eastern Question later in the century.

The Aberdeen coalition rescued Gladstone. The private torments, which will be discussed in the next chapter, largely fell away. The public promise, sketched in his Tory career but cast in shadow by the confusion of the Maynooth resignation and vote and the disintegration of his party, was now confirmed on a wider canvass. The coalition gave Gladstone his chance at the top level of British politics, and he took it.

CHAPTER IV

Religion, Family, and Sex: the Private Crisis of the 1840s

Religion and Family Finances —Sex, Prostitutes, and the Oxford Movement—
Gleanings from the Journal in the 1840s and Early 1850s—Taking Leave of the
Early Gladstone

When I compare my convictions in religion, and the mercies that have
been poured upon me, with the extraordinary tenacity of the evil in me,
the fruit without doubt of indulgence, I cannot but deeply believe that my
debt to the justice of God is the very heaviest that can be conceived: for
have I not after all suffered that sin which I have described to have its
habitation & to find its food in me, and could it have been covered by
such flimsy pretexts but for an extreme corruption?

The pursuit of knowledge, the desire of estimating different periods &
states of the moral and religious life of man, the hope of doing good to the
persons living in sin: of all these I had utterly failed to discern the proper
bounds, and had sometimes perhaps often lost even these from view
when once upon the train of thought on imagery of which they might
have first effected the introduction. Further if at any time I had discerned
those bounds, the vision of them became dim & ineffectual at the time of
need, even if resolutions of a solemn kind had been formed, & formed at
the most solemn hour—before the Altar.

Looking back then over more than twenty years since this plague
began, I can discern two periods at which the evil was so to speak
materially limited but it may also have been formally, essentially,
enhanced. First the period of marriage: and secondly that period of
general recollection and prevision, which was vouchsafed me in my
retired life at Baden [in 1845] . . . though I might persuade myself that in
my inner heart I carried along with me a perfect hatred and disgust
towards the fruit & work of lust, yet this was not genuine, or, if genuine
was too weak to defend mind and body from the infection, especially in a
case like mine, when the habits of my life, such as being out at all hours,
place me peculiarly in the way of contact with exciting causes.*

Religion and Family Finances

The great crisis of Conservatism and of the Conservative party in the 1840s
was in part the consequence of the very high expectations of the Church–

* 19 July 1848.

State Conservatives, of whom Gladstone was a prominent member. They brought to politics expectations which the normal political process could not satisfy. The Whig–Liberal coalition expected less and was consequently better able to overcome disappointment. Like the Conservatives in 1846, Whig governments tended to disintegration, but, unlike the Conservatives, they knew how to regroup.

For the Conservative party, hitherto so bold, so assured, so knowing about the deficiencies of its opponents, the twenty years after 1846 were to be years of exclusion, ideological sterility, and a gradual acceptance of Peel–Gladstone fiscal policy. For Gladstone, as we have seen in the previous chapters, the 1840s were an education in the practicalities of politics and policies.

This reformation of political role and belief was not achieved without a price. The diary for the years after 1846 is a strange mixture of solid plodding and masked, sometimes open, anxiety. Gladstone the administrator is seen supervising a series of estate developments, railway wrangles, and reforms in voluntary institutions. In the most dramatic situations Gladstone could reinforce himself by routine actions—witness his reading Mayhew 'on the Street folk' outside the room where his father lay dying. Gladstone the thinker involves himself in petty projects such as his dictionary of 'homoionyms', as well as his classical studies, his reviews, and correspondence. All this without apparent care at his loss of office and the uncertainty of his political position, though he was much relieved to be back in the Commons in 1847 and in 1848 noted about his attendance on his father, 'this & what I have towards my wife's family must for the present stand instead of much else'. Yet there is an underlying restlessness expressed most obviously in his bizarre solo journeys to the Continent in pursuit of his sister Helen in 1845, and of the eloping Lady Lincoln in 1849, and in the start of his rescue work with prostitutes.

Before the prostitutes are considered, some account must be made of the overwhelming family disaster of these years—the failure in 1847 of the Oak Farm works, for which Gladstone was examined in the Birmingham court of bankruptcy in 1848. Gladstone became involved in the works by marriage into the Glynne family, but he soon became an important influence in its management, advising his wife's brother-in-law, George Lyttelton, not to sell his share in it in 1840. Characteristically his chief interest was to build a church for the employees in the iron works.

John Gladstone had made a fortune as a merchant; he had never been a manufacturer. He had taught his son William much about the principles of financial success, but little of the specific and technical skills on which his success was based. William had never served even a brief turn in the family offices; it was his brother Robertson who was given the role of business successor to John Gladstone. The Oak Farm was a brick and iron works near Stourbridge, in which the Glynne family was heavily involved. Its business was closely interlocked with the many other small and medium-sized works in that area. On no basis of experience and despite his father's cautions, Gladstone supported Boydell, the manager, in his over-expansion of the iron works, until the general financial crisis of 1846–7 made it too late to withdraw. The subsequent bankruptcy and mortgages, for which Boydell was blamed, but for which Gladstone must bear a share of the responsibility, forced the Glynne family for a time out of Hawarden Castle, and occupied Gladstone until the 1880s. The affair is of general interest to his career mainly because of the anxiety it caused him, which, on occasion, took a sexual form of expression.

Acute anxiety was also caused by his sister Helen with whom his relationship was close though ill-natured. He had political as well as personal reasons for regretting her conversion to Roman Catholicism (she was one of the first casualties of the Oxford movement) but his concern about her drug addiction was more important. Gladstone saw in his sister what could happen when the powerful emotions to which he was also heir broke loose from the tight middle-class conventions to which his family subscribed, despite their aristocratic marriages and purchases of landed estates. He had played some part in the development of her condition. When she joined the Roman Catholic Church he advised his father to expel her from his house and was dismayed when the old man's 'paternal affection' prevented this. For a time he forbad her to see his children. Gladstone visited Baden in October 1845 to try to persuade Helen to give up her laudanum if not her Roman Catholicism, and witnessed appalling scenes as she became paralysed by the drug and was 'held down by force to have leeches put on'; 'she stipulated I was not to touch her'. It was in this context that, already ravaged that year by the 'nightmare' of Maynooth and the demise of the State and Church system, Gladstone drew up the extraordinary list of remedies and categories of temptation which is discussed later in this chapter.

Sex, Prostitutes, and the Oxford Movement

Helen Gladstone's self-control had snapped; her brother William's came very close to doing the same. Gladstone was a man of intense, and, in the 1840s, apparently increasing, sexuality. At first it was contained by his marriage, but this also, he believed, may have 'formally, essentially, enhanced' it. His wife was nine times pregnant and recovering from childbirth or miscarriage in fourteen years. There is no indication in the diary or elsewhere of any sexual incompatibility between the two, but it is clear that there were considerable periods of enforced sexual abstinence, caused by the Victorian middle-class convention of abstaining from sexual relations during most of pregnancy, nursing, and menstruation. Moreover, it may well have been that the Gladstones, in common with many Victorian religious families, took literally the implication for the marriage bed of the Prayer Book's statement that marriage was 'first . . . for the procreation of children'. The comment on 'the ideal above the ordinary married state' in the diary at 22 April 1849 perhaps refers to this. Certainly, Gladstone told his daughter Mary in the 1880s that he hated birth control as much as he hated anything. What is definite is that Catherine Gladstone was often absent from her husband, with children or relatives at Hagley or Hawarden. It was usually during these periods that Gladstone's rate of rescue work increased, and it was certainly during her absence that nervous crises occurred in October 1845, July 1848, April 1849, and especially in the critical period of July 1851.

Anxiety about his political work, his friends' religion, the Oak Farm finances, and his personal problems, aggravated Gladstone's feelings. At first, during the 1840s, he relieved them by reading what he regarded as pornography—mostly Restoration poems, classical authors such as Petronius, and *fabliaux* (French verse fables, some of them extremely bawdy). These were all readily available in bookshops and in the libraries of friends such as Thomas Grenville.* To pornography he later added conversations with prostitutes, some of whom he found beautiful and physically attractive.

At first the 'rescue work' (as he called it) was an act of conventional charity done within the context of the 'engagement'. The 'engagement' was a lay Tractarian brotherhood organized by the Acland brothers on advice from Keble. It had a thoroughly Tractarian ethos. Gladstone was associated with its planning in 1844 and began to attend it early in 1845. It had obvious associations with the 'Third Order' which he had sketched in 1838, and several of its members had first come together in the WEG Club at Oxford. Its membership of fifteen, which met in the Margaret Chapel and included Frederic Rogers, J. T. Coleridge, Roundell Palmer, and the architect William Butterfield, was subject to twelve rules, of which the first was to perform 'some regular work of charity'.† Gladstone fulfilled this rule in the early days of 'the engagement' by work with destitutes, male and female, who were in or dependent on the House of St Barnabas (the 'engagement's' patron saint) in Rose Street, Soho. But by 1848 he found

---

* His friend Monckton Milnes had a well-known and outstanding library of pornography, though Gladstone does not mention it.

† Its rules were: '1 Some regular work of charity, 2 Attendance on the daily service, 3 Observance of the fasts of the church, 4 Observance of the hours of prayer (9, 12, 3), 5 Special prayers for the unity of the church and conversion of unbelievers at some hour: also for the other persons engaged, 6 Rule of number of hours to be spent in sleep and recreation, 7 Meditation with morning prayers—self-examination with evening, 8 To fix a portion of income for works of mercy and piety, 9 To consider with a practical view the direction of the church concerning confession and absolution, 10 Failing any spiritual director, to follow the judgement of one or more of those co-engaged in the case of breach of rule, 11 If unable to perform (1) contribute funds instead, 12 To meet, compare results, and consider amendments.'

this work 'less suitable than it was' and told Acland it was too time-consuming.

In May 1849, under stress from Oak Farm affairs and the Clergy Relief Bill, he began meeting prostitutes on the streets late at night.* In the Session, he was often in the Commons till midnight. In July 1850, following the Pacifico debate and the death of Peel, when his wife was away at Hagley, and perhaps prompted by an article in the *Westminster Review*,† he began regular meetings with prostitutes in the vicinity of the notorious Argyll Rooms, and the names of individual prostitutes start to be regularly noted in the diary.

The rescue work was at one level exactly that—the attempt to rescue prostitutes from the streets and rehabilitate them in suitable employment, or by marriage, or by emigration, after a time of training. This was done at the House of Mercy at Clewer, by Windsor, where the keeper in the early 1850s was Mariquita Tennant whom Gladstone had known since 1843. Much time was spent in persuasion and in arranging transport and subsequent employment. Catherine Gladstone was well informed about these activities and prostitutes were, almost from the start, invited to the Gladstones' house. But it is also clear that for Gladstone rescue work became not merely a duty but a craving; it was an exposure to sexual stimulation which Gladstone felt he must both undergo and overcome. As he admitted to himself, he deliberately 'courted evil'.

The redemption of prostitutes was an activity which, in principle, had an obvious Christian justification. But for Gladstone it also involved temptation. Was the danger to his spiritual well-being balanced by the good he was doing? In his talks with prostitutes he 'trod the path of danger' as regards himself, while at the same time having little success in proselytizing. By January 1854 he had spoken, 'indoors or out', to between eighty and ninety prostitutes, but 'among these there is but one of whom I know that the miserable life has been abandoned *and* that I can fairly join that fact with influence of mine'. The lack of success was not surprising, for the discipline during rehabilitation at the Houses of Mercy at Clewer and Rose Street, Soho, was stronger than that of any Victorian boarding school. Jane Bywater, a partially rescued prostitute, wrote to Gladstone in 1854 after a short spell in the House of Mercy: 'I have no doubt that you wished to do me some service, but I did not fancy being shut up in such a place as that for perhaps twelve months. I should have committed suicide.'

Gladstone completely ignored the political danger attending his rescue work. When a Scot named Wilson attempted blackmail by threatening to expose him to the *Morning Herald* for speaking to a prostitute shortly after

---

* There had been some rescue work done earlier, but not systematically.

† He was familiar with Parent Duchâtelet's work on prostitution in Paris, *De la prostitution dans la ville de Paris*, 2 vols. (1836).

the 1853 budget, Gladstone met the threat with resolute indifference, exposing it to the police and the courts without hesitation. He was well aware that 'these talkings of mine are certainly not within the rules of worldly prudence' but this was not, for him, of importance. The crucial question was whether 'Christian prudence sanctions them for such an one as me'. Despite his awareness both of spiritual danger and lack of success, the work continued.

His predilection for pornography has been noted above. In 1849 Gladstone began to scourge himself to counter stimulation from it. By 1851 he was also scourging himself after conversations with prostitutes during which he felt he had allowed himself to be excessively excited. Sometimes he went to their homes or lodging houses for talks long into the night, sometimes for tea. On occasion he was moved to almost lyrical praise of their beauty, noted in Italian.* So far as we know, and there is no evidence to the contrary, he managed to remain, in the end, self-controlled and self-critical.

Beginning in October 1845 during his visit to his sister Helen in Germany, Gladstone analysed his feelings about both pornography and prostitutes in a series of remarkable passages, some in the diary, some on separate sheets of paper which were folded and enclosed with the diary. He kept records of his temptations and of his measures to overcome them. These were listed as 'Channels', 'Incentives', 'Chief actual dangers', and 'Remedies', each broken down into several sub-headings and categories. The presence of the Aristotelian philosophical tag πρός τι (in respect of things of a certain kind) and the abstract form of the other categories shows the pervading influence of the Oxford Schools even on Gladstone's most private thoughts. It is a curious footnote to G. M. Young's observation of the basic importance of their Oxford training to both Gladstone and Newman.†

Notes of his self-scourgings were kept first on the separate sheet, later in lists in the diary, and then day by day by signs in the diary entries. The last started the day he read Froude's *Nemesis of Faith*. This series of lists, explanations, and entries must be regarded as a classic of mid-Victorian self-analysis of guilt. It is also very characteristically Gladstonian; a strange mixture of detail, thoroughness, generality, and principle, carried through with cool efficiency, passion, self-confidence, and religious repentance. A small part of one of the passages is quoted at the head of this chapter.

Gladstone's self-analysis of an explicitly sexual topic was made in

---

* As W. Acton noted, prostitutes in central London were 'generally pretty and elegant—oftener painted by Nature than by art' (*Prostitution* (1857), 53). In 1841 the Metropolitan Police estimated that in the St James's—Regent Street—Soho area there were 152 brothels and 318 prostitutes; in the Westminster—Chelsea area, 153 brothels and 514 prostitutes; ibid. 16.

† G. M. Young, 'The Schoolman in Downing Street', *Victorian essays* (1962), 86–7.

language which treated it implicitly. In this, despite the privacy of his diary and the various codes and foreign languages available to him, he remained within Victorian public conventions. Thus it is impossible to know the exact nature of Gladstone's relationship with the prostitutes he visited. The language is guarded, but occasionally suggestive. In 1896, seventeen months before he died, he assured his son and pastor, Stephen, that he had never 'been guilty of the act which is known as that of infidelity to the marriage bed'; he specifically limited himself 'to this negation', a precise and obviously qualified declaration.*

What is clear is that on occasion these confrontations were followed by self-scourging. Gladstone's use of the scourge or discipline is marked in the diary or on his lists by the sign ♭, presumably because of its resemblance to a whip. An entry characteristic of its use, and of the oblique references to what may seem to be some form of limited physical encounter, is that of 13 July 1851, in the crisis of Hope and Manning's apostasy, which literally 'demoralized' him. In the urgency of the crisis—a crisis as Gladstone saw it of national as well as of personal identity—he lost for a time his moral sense. Numbed, disorientated, overwhelmed by a development he had failed to anticipate, he

Went with a note to E[lizabeth] C[ollins]'s—received (unexpectedly) & remained 2 hours: a strange & humbling scene—returned & ♭.

This and all other entries when a prostitute was involved suggest that the flagellation was self-administered in private, following, not during, the meeting.

It is true that flagellation was known as 'the English vice' and doubtless figured in the pornography which Gladstone read.† None the less, the idea of its use for what was intended as a punishment for sin probably came to him in a Tractarian context. Newman certainly used a scourge and described it in his novel, *Loss and gain*, as 'an iron discipline or scourge, studded with nails'. E. B. Pusey asked Gladstone's closest friend, James Hope, to bring him a discipline from the Continent, and hoped that Keble, his confessor, would advise him to use it. Gladstone may well have found the discipline being used by brother members of the 'engagement', rule ten of which would have allowed for mutual instruction in this, though there is no evidence found that this was so.

From the diary it seems that Gladstone used the scourge without consultation. In 1840 he contemplated 'voluntary periodical confession', recognizing that 'for many consciences I should not think it necessary in any

---

* During the Wright case in 1927 (a libel case between Captain Wright and Herbert Gladstone which turned on the truth or falsity of Wright's allegations about the Prime Minister's private life) the Gladstone brothers felt on counsels' advice that, because of this specific limitation, the declaration could not be used as evidence on their side.

† I. Bloch, *Sexual life in England* (1901), *passim*, and S. Marcus, *The Other Victorians* (1960), 103.

degree; but for mine it is a question to be pondered'. When considering a paper by Keble planning the 'engagement' in 1844 which provided for group confession, he wrote: 'it often occurs to me what a blessing it will be to our children if they can be brought up in the habit of constantly disclosing the interior of their minds'. It is perhaps remarkable in view of this, and of his apparent Anglo-Catholicism, that he neither practised sacramental confession, as a number of his friends did, nor sought the advice of a spiritual director, lay or clerical, in these times of temptations. It is also interesting, although perhaps not surprising, that his wife is never mentioned in this context of self-examination: there is no hint in the diary or in their correspondence that she knew anything specific of these temptations, although she was involved even with those rescue cases which tempted him most. Indeed Gladstone deliberately kept his difficulties from her, as is shown by this melancholy passage from a letter which he wrote to her in July 1851—she was at Hagley—just after the high pitch of temptation with Elizabeth Collins had been reached and overcome by scourging:

When you say I do not know half the evil of your life, you say that which I believe in almost every case is true between one human being and another; but it sets me thinking how little you know the evil of mine of which at the last day I shall have a strange tale to tell.

Throughout his life Gladstone was essentially secretive (though he had in principle no political secrets from his wife) while at the same time living for the record—but the record was to be read by posterity; his diary and his many memoranda were used to clarify his thoughts and as a means of 'self-rebuke' and self-confession. In this crisis of his early middle-age (he was forty-one at the height of this bout of sexual temptation), he worked out his own salvation less like a Tractarian than an Evangelical or Nonconformist.

The use of the discipline and the other 'mechanical' means developed by Gladstone seem to have been helpful with the pornography, less so with the prostitutes. No doubt many today will find it risible that the Chancellor of the Exchequer should so have relieved his tensions rather than by taking a mistress. But Gladstone knew his own character. He was aware of his 'deadly foe' which was 'the subtle and blinding influences of corrupt sophism' and he must have realized that these passions, once fully liberated, must have destroyed his family and himself. Priggish and hypocritical he may have seemed to enemies, foolhardy to friends, but his struggles with his body and his conscience, when seen in the diary in the context of his religious, political, and family life, cannot but seem noble.

Gladstone's involvement with prostitutes was therefore in no way casual, nor was it merely charitable work which might equally have taken another form. The space taken to discuss it here reflects the time and concern Gladstone devoted to it, 'the chief burden of my soul'. The time spent on it,

the obvious intensity of many of the encounters, the courting of evil, show
how at the centre of a Victorian family and religious life was a sexual situation of great tension. It is tempting to see Gladstone, because of his religious and political prominence, as exceptional in these matters, but
perhaps if more middle-class Victorians had recorded their secret lives so
assiduously and honestly he would not seem so; indeed he might seem,
rather than a curiosity, predominantly an abstainant.

Gleanings from the Journal in the 1840s and Early 1850s

We should not see Gladstone merely as a politician wrestling with an intellectual crisis or a Tractarian flagellating his sinful body. For perhaps his
most remarkable ability was that of living life with equal intensity at many
levels, and, in these years, without being fully committed to any. It was this
ability to change levels, to design railways for the Hawarden estate, to
denounce at length Montalembert's *Des Intérêts Catholiques au XIVe Siècle* in
the *Quarterly Review*, to translate Farini's *Lo Stato Romano* and to produce
the most famous budget of the century, all within the space of a year, 1853,
which gave Gladstone his great public weapon—surprise, and his great
private resource—variety.

Despite the intensity of his feelings about his sexuality, his life with his
family never seems to have been less than happy. The diary incidentally
records the life of a fairly normal wealthy Victorian family, with problems
about the governesses, difficulties with the servants, the self inflicted
anguish of sending off the boys to boarding schools. The seven children
who lived were raised to adulthood without the sort of casualty which
Helen, Gladstone's sister, had been for her generation. Doubtless much of
this was the result of Catherine Gladstone's balance and resilience, which
seems to have been taken so much for granted that references to her in the
diary are very rarely expansive.*

Gladstone's health in the 1840s was, on the whole, good. His eyesight
gave trouble, and an exhaustive series of rules was drawn up to improve it,
with some success. Illness was occasional: a bad attack of erysipelas in September and October 1847, which he caught from his daughter Agnes, who
nearly died from it, recurred in September 1853. On the first occasion his
arms were 'more or less disabled'; on the second, 'an apparent return of my
erysipelatous inflammations' at Dunrobin, the Duchess of Sutherland
passed the time by reading to him, 'full of the utmost kindness and simplicity', thus beginning a relationship of increasing importance to both.
The male side of the family was little troubled by illness—none of the four
boys was seriously ill in these years. The girls were less fortunate. Agnes, as
we have seen, had severe erysipelas, Mary's sight was so bad that in 1850

* When apart, Gladstone wrote to his wife very frequently, and at great length, almost always
signing himself 'Ever your afft. W.E.G.'

her parents had to take her to Naples for a change of climate, a journey with results far beyond the improvement of her eyes, and Jessy suffered an appalling death from meningitis, aged 5, on 9 April 1850. Her parents could but sit and watch her die. Gladstone's response to distress and crisis was activity; the long biography of Jessy begun that day and the twenty-five letters written testify to the depth of his reaction. By himself, he took her coffin by train and coach to Fasque and saw her buried in the family vault.

Life for Gladstone was not especially hard, but it was earnest, and earnestness is the dominant characteristic of the diary. There is much material about holidays, but even on these Gladstone worked hard at relaxing. Miles walked, feet climbed, churches seen, sermons (never enough) heard, conversations held with unreliable foreigners when abroad, charitable visits to tenants (marked +), are all carefully noted, with Victorian obsession for detail and record as valuable in themselves. Even the casualties of relaxation, such as the top of his left forefinger blown off while shooting in 1842, taught a moral as well as a technical lesson: 'a foolish conceit secretly' had intruded into his shooting, 'in being or seeming able to do what others do. This silly & carnal temper has I hope received a rebuke from the Divine mercy. . . . I really wanted some lesson however little in bodily pain lest I should forget or hold only a dead remembrance of that part of the lot of mortality.'

Gladstone carefully recorded his religious observances. He almost always attended church twice, sometimes three times, on Sundays, and tried to go once each weekday, usually to an early evensong. To maintain the regularity of his attendance in Scotland, he would go if necessary to a Presbyterian church. His churchgoing in London was to some extent conditioned by easy access from Westminster, but it is clear that he gained most from Frederick Oakeley's Anglo-Catholic Margaret Chapel, where he found an 'atmosphere of devotion . . . which I know not where else to look for'. The chapel was rebuilt after Oakeley's apostasy in 1845 as All Saints, Margaret Street, by Butterfield, a member of the 'engagement', many of whose members worshipped there.

Gladstone took communion usually each Sunday, drawing great sustenance from it. His lack of worthiness for receiving it was the immediate cause of the great passage of self-analysis of July 1848 quoted earlier. His communicating was accompanied by elaborate, self-devised preparation and subsequent contemplation, which he noted as 'Secreta Eucharistica', revised at intervals throughout his life. But while his churchgoing was in many respects that of an Anglo-Catholic, in choice of church and in sacramental regularity, it continued to have a strong Evangelical underpinning. We have already noticed Gladstone's reluctance to turn to confession in times of temptation. In a more positively Protestant way he relied strongly on the old custom of waiting on the Bible to 'speak' to him, almost after the fashion of Balfour of Burley, the Covenanter in Scott's *Old Mortality*, one of his favourite novels. The Psalms, he felt, were regularly a present help in time of trouble and decision, both personal and political. Thus in 1843, when deciding whether to enter the Cabinet, he noted: 'in the occurrence of the 73rd Psalm among the services of this day I see another of those minute but striking Providential adjustments which I have often had to remark'. On 9 May 1854 he made a survey in his diary of some of the occasions on which the Psalms had providentially confirmed—never it seems altered—his inclinations.

Personal devotions were for Gladstone no haphazard matter. His morning and evening prayers were carefully planned, with long lists of persons, projects, and categories to be remembered, from the Queen, through his family, the members of the 'engagement', widows, and apostates, to the tenants of Fasque. The children were from the earliest possible age regularly instructed in the Bible, which he tried to read regularly aloud with his wife. Sunday reading was largely spiritual or ecclesiastical. There were clear rules for religious observance in the household, and for household prayers Gladstone made an abstract of the Prayer Book, which he published in 1845. He continued each week to read one of his own sermons to the servants. Though often generalized homilies on a scriptural theme, these sometimes discussed in a straightforward, fairly simple way, some contemporary event; there are some of great interest explaining the Irish famine as a consequence of Providential judgement.

Though his main personal charitable efforts were given to dealings with prostitutes, Gladstone spent much time in the mid-1840s on a project to build a church in Leicester Square, which was eventually unsuccessful. Instead, he and Sir Walter James used the funds to establish a chapel of ease in Bedfordbury in a small upstairs room, behind what is now the London Coliseum Theatre. Gladstone and James paid for a part-time curate, in breaks from the Commons they taught at the ragged school held in it, and they sometimes took the services as well. Saint Andrew's Chapel, in the grounds of Fasque but available to the villagers, and Trinity College, Glenalmond, the school through which the Gladstones hoped to Anglicize, or at any rate Episcopalianize the Scots, were larger examples of institutional proselytization.

Beyond these, Gladstone was involved in many examples of voluntary work; he was one of the chief founders of the Metropolitan Visiting Association (the chief mid-century charity caring for London destitutes), of Saint Barnabas, the House of Mercy still active in Rose Street, Soho, and of the Clewer House of Mercy (also still active), and he played an important role on other religious and secular committees. He was an active member of whatever body he joined, and he joined many. In addition to his parliamentary duties, he was one of those journeymen who work the institutions of the Establishment from the inside, and make them run. Among many such posts, he was an active trustee of the British Museum, a founder of the London Library, chairman for almost thirty years of the Radcliffe Trust which at that time ran the Radcliffe Camera and other property in Oxford, a governor of the Charterhouse and of King's College, London, a trustee of the National Portrait Gallery and of the Colonial Bishoprics Trust, and an often rather parsimonious Commissioner of the 1851 Exhibition, as well as being, when in office, *ex officio* on the governing body of a variety of institutions. Oxford and the Church of England are the important links between many of these, and certainly Gladstone was one of the chief effective Anglican laymen of his time: he earned his right to tell his Church how it should develop.

Despite his many activities, Gladstone found time, spasmodically, for his growing family. Always a cheerful, even a boisterous *pater familias*, he managed in the family circle to forget, or ignore, the public and private pressures and temptations which beset him. Away from his family, Gladstone was often forgetful of birthdays and other events; with them he was part father, part tutor. It is in the latter role that he usually presents himself in the diary. Willy, the eldest of the four boys, bore the brunt of this. Aged three and a third, he was given a course of lessons 'respecting our Saviour'. Perhaps naturally for his age, 'his interest fixes itself upon His being placed upon the cross'. Willy's Latin verses improve over the years, but only after much instruction and, on one occasion, a whipping by his father after a row with his tutor, the local priest. His preparation for confirmation gave his father much pleasure, but Willy may have looked back with more affection to the bonfire on 5 November 1849 when his family was gathered together at Fasque. His father noted: 'Poor Willy's Guy Faux in the evening had an unfortunate effect. I confessed to Aunt J[oanna] the excess into which I was betrayed.'

In the 1840s and 1850s, Gladstone's reading, which he listed with occasional commentary, continues to impress by its range. A new feature in these years is that much of it was done in preparation for a public statement of view in the form of a pamphlet or book review. His book reviews, issued in a steady stream from 1843, were at first for ecclesiastical periodicals such as the *Foreign and Colonial Quarterly Review* or for the Tory *Quarterly Review*. An important development, symptomatic of his developing Liberalism and inconceivable in the 1830s, was a review in 1852 for the Whiggish *Edinburgh Review*, a review, amongst other works, of his own translation in four volumes of L. C. Farini's attack on the Pope's temporal power, *Lo Stato Romano*.

The records of his reading indicate when and through what sources he became interested in specific topics, and what sources were used to resolve the questions raised. In 1852, for example, his reading (apart from sermons) was mostly on colonies, the United States, and Oxford reform until November when he read an article by Cardwell on finance and J. G. Hubbard's pamphlet on the income tax. From then until his budget in 1853 he read all the current pamphlets and reports on the tax, including material from other countries and from the eighteenth century.

On the Crimean war, which did much to frustrate the success of the income-tax measures of the 1853 budget, Gladstone read more patchily. In the summer of 1853, after the budget and before his involvement with the Oxford Bill, he informed himself of the historical and legal background of the eastern question from Marmont's *State of the Turkish empire* (1839) and Phillimore's study of international law, *Russia and Turkey* (1853). But despite further reading in Greek and French, it is clear that there is never that depth and urgency which characterized his reading on a problem in which he felt fully involved. The war appears in the diary mainly in the form of the mass of financial detail it required. Gladstone had firm views on how the war should be financed and fought—on the Foreigners Enlistment Bill he 'never before heard the announcement of a majority in which I had myself voted with such doubtful (if indeed doubtful) feelings'—but he does not seem to have doubted that there was any option but to fight it. He greeted the news of the Alma patriotically and got much more heated over his row with Lord John Russell about the dismissal of a Whig civil servant, Kennedy, than about the departmental reorganization occasioned by the war. The 'brute passions' aroused by the Kennedy affair created 'overflowing disgust at the conduct of Ld J[ohn] & the degradation of the Cabinet' and endangered Gladstone's relationship with the Whigs, though in the end it was probably Aberdeen who suffered most from the 'feud'.

In addition to reading on particular topics of the moment, Gladstone read steadily the literature of the day. *Uncle Tom's Cabin* 'scarcely denies exaggeration', though he thought it of sufficient value to distribute to prostitutes; *Jane Eyre* he found 'a very remarkable but jarring book', as well he might if it is compared to the minor Tractarian novels which provided, especially in the 1840s, a steady supply of undemanding sanctimony.

These brief gleanings from the diary may perhaps encourage the reader to seek out its printed volumes. Its range, political, literary, religious, social, and personal, is extraordinary. No-one will find it light work, and those seeking an easy read will be disappointed. The eclectic complexity and interrelated nature of Victorian culture pervades every entry. The reader approaching the diary will find it looming like some vast rock face seen from far off, some of it sunny and appealing, much of it bleak and uninviting. But closer inspection reveals a different aspect; it is, after all, a climbable face. The ascent is arduous, but reveals on the way a vast mosaic of events, views, descriptions, analyses, reports, changing social and intellectual relationships. As the end is gained, the pattern as a whole becomes clear.

Taking Leave of the Early Gladstone

Two figures emerge as dominating in these early political years: Sir John Gladstone and Sir Robert Peel. John Gladstone, given his baronetcy by Peel in 1846 despite his hostility to Corn Law repeal, had a business as much as a personal relationship with his son. None the less it was he who was largely responsible for creating the framework by which Gladstone reached the Cabinet. He had provided the education of his choice, he had steered 'son William' (as he docketed all his letters) away from the Church as a career; he provided the house and the income which made his son's glittering social and political success possible. The success of many of the projects close to William Gladstone's heart depended on his father's support: he made possible the building of the Scottish Episcopalian boarding school, Trinity College, Glenalmond, and of St Andrew's Episcopalian chapel at Fasque, and provided the bulk of the funds for saving the Hawarden estate, the three material successes which in these years probably pleased Gladstone most. In return Sir John expected attention and attendance. Hence the long journeys to Fasque, Sir John's estate in the Mearns, south of Stonehaven, so dramatically eased by the coming of the railway, and the long sojourns there, out of touch with religious and political developments. Games of whist and piquet, constant arguments about the evils of Anglo-Catholicism and of free trade ('stood two batteries on Free Trade' is characteristic), were the price Gladstone paid for his father's assistance. Not a high price to pay, but one which until his father's death in 1851 was being paid frequently. When with his father, he acted as secretary, a duty which irked him, forcing him to display 'inward & even outward impatience'. Gladstone enjoyed the countryside around Fasque but his service to his father and the need for constant self-containment in the face, especially in the late forties, of persistent harangues, bore heavily upon him, though he tried to turn it to didactic advantage, 'in teaching patience & a humble mind'. Catherine Gladstone must have found life at Fasque very trying, dealing both with the kind but cantankerous Sir John, and with the unpredictable Helen, often drugged and quarrelling with her brother or the servants.

His family around him, the tough old man died aged eighty-seven, in December 1851, refusing the doctor and the holy communion—the latter to William's distress—and calling for porridge. There is some indication of a craving for affection, or at least for recognition, by William at the deathbed, but he met his father's death with equanimity, carefully noting the details of the final stages, concluding with an argument with his brothers about the sacrament, the property, and free trade, and a poignant reminder of a relationship in which, though both had prospered, neither had found much more than a business intimacy: 'I kissed thrice my Father's cheek & forehead before & after his death: the only kisses that I can remember.'

With the death of Sir John, Fasque passed to the eldest brother Tom, and Gladstone took his 'final adieu to Fasque as a home'; despite all the quarrelling, Fasque had become his instinctive home, to which he had taken the body of his dead child Jessy to lie in the family vault. His suggestion that he rather than Tom should take over Fasque came to nothing. Hawarden, reopened after the financial difficulties of 1847 largely as a result of Sir John's generosity, replaced Fasque: Gladstone's 5,000 books were moved to Hawarden and the metamorphosis of the Gladstones of Biggar, so carefully designed by Sir John, was complete: 'son William' was in all but name the owner of an aristocratic estate, walking with pride from Chester to Hawarden castle 'thro' my land'.*

Sir Robert Peel, the nation's 'greatest statesman', had died eighteen months before Sir John, thrown from his horse two days after Gladstone's great speech in the Don Pacifico debate. Gladstone remembered 'with joy with how pure true and vigilant a conscience he always seemed to act'. The diary is a continual witness to the influence of Peel. Peel's very different view of Anglicanism led to disagreements, but Gladstone realized that in the 1841 ministry he was receiving the sort of governmental education which few had the luck to get. If Aberdeen taught Gladstone gentleness, generosity, and justice in politics, Peel taught him method. It was on this method that Gladstone's political success depended, for it provided an indestructible base to which he could return from the ideological forays which many of his political colleagues found extraordinary. Thus on a speech in 1848, 'Peel was gratified & that was enough for me'.

A final word may be said about Gladstone's political development in his Peelite years. It took place within a clearly defined social and parliamentary environment, which, if anything, narrowed as the years passed. As MP for Newark until 1845 Gladstone had some contact, at elections, in correspondence, and through occasional visits to his constituency, with ordinary citizens otherwise unconnected with him. As burgess for Oxford University after 1847 he was, by custom, prevented from direct electioneering, and his constituents were all, by definition, graduates, many of them priests. His fellow-Peelite, Sir James Graham, already felt that Oxford excessively muzzled him, telling Aberdeen in 1853: 'the defeat of Gladstone at Oxford at this precise juncture would be a misfortune; but for his own sake hereafter, Emancipation from the Thraldom of that Constituency would be a blessing'. This may have been true on some issues, but it does

---

* Gladstone technically only owned Hawarden for a few months in 1875 but he and his wife regarded their eldest son from birth as the probable heir. Gladstone bought in his own name considerable property around the Hawarden estate.

not seem to have restricted Gladstone at this time. For Oxford controversies were either of the symbolic sort, such as the feeling about the Jewish
Disabilities Bill, or progressively inward-looking. In developing his ideas
on the major imperial and national issues of the day Gladstone was largely
free, in the 1840s and 1850s, from the normal constituency pressures which
affected even other Peelites, themselves an unusually cushioned group in
their choice of seats. Rarely can a politician undergoing an intellectual
crisis have had more like-mindedly perplexed constituents than Gladstone
and the Oxford MAs in the decade between the degradation of W. G. Ward
in 1845 and the Oxford Reform Bill of 1854.

At the Board of Trade Gladstone had met many deputations of manufacturers, but he seems to have been influenced less by them than by his
reading and by the views of permanent members of the department. Thus
his contacts, apart from those with prostitutes and tenants, and his correspondence were overwhelmingly with MPs, civil servants, clergymen
(mostly Anglican), lawyers, and gentry.* Nonconformists, Chartists, even
ordinary electors, made little impact on his diary and impinged on Gladstone only indirectly, in the pages of reports and pamphlets on their condition.† An exception was Gladstone's visit to Manchester in October
1853, when he made his first important extra-parliamentary speech as a
Cabinet minister, and his first speech to a large audience since the 1841
election. It was the first of those great public orations before an 'enormous
auditory' of which he later became the master, and perhaps also the slave.
In Manchester he unveiled a statue of Peel and made an important declaration on government policy towards the Crimea. It was made 'before a great
assemblage—of *men* almost exclusively, & working men. There I spoke, to
the cracking of my voice.' He clearly enjoyed the occasion; it was a portent
for the future.

---

* His correspondence with West Midlands creditors of the Oak Farm—mostly small manufacturers—was an exception to this.

† He was a special constable against the Chartists in 1848 and wrote an anti-Chartist declaration of loyalty to the Crown; however, he helped the Spitalfields ballast heavers in 1843 and at the
Board of Trade he introduced an employment register for London coalwhippers, and he addressed
a meeting of Shadwell coalwhippers. His work with prostitutes gave him a thorough knowledge of
a specialized aspect of working-class life, though it did not lead him to attempt its systematic
prevention or alleviation, save by voluntary effort.

CHAPTER V

Chancellor of the Exchequer: Free Trade, Budgets, and Franchise Reform

*A Peelite and mid-Victorian Politics—Gladstone as Chancellor—
The Politicization of the Chancellorship—The Social Contract of the
mid-Victorian State—Income Tax, Virtual Representation, and Franchise
Reform—The Emergence of a National Politician: Regionalism, Speech-making,
Class, Trade Unions—The 'People's William' and the Press—A Broadening
Political Base—A 'smash . . . without example': Franchise Reform 1866—7—
Regaining the Initiative: Ireland and the Premiership*

But I feel like a man under a burden under which he must fall and be crushed if he looks to the right or left, or fails from any cause to concentrate mind and muscle upon his progress step by step. This absorption, this excess, this constant ἄγαν is the fault of political life with its insatiable demands which do not leave the smallest stock of moral energy unexhausted and available for other purposes.

They certainly however have this merit: they drive home the sense that I am poor, and naked, and blind and miserable: and they make forgetfulness of God not a whit less unintelligible than it is excusable, though it is one thing to remember and another to obey.

Swimming for his life, a man does not see much of the country through which the river winds, and I probably know little of these years through which I busily work and live, beyond this, how sin and frailty deface them, and how mercy crowns them.*

A Peelite and mid-Victorian Politics

Thus Gladstone, twenty-six days after kissing hands in 1868 as first lord of the Treasury for the first time, celebrated his arrival at 'the top of the greasy pole'. It had not for him been a difficult climb, though there had been the odd slip and loss of grip. Nor had the conditions been especially arduous in the decade since the Crimean War. The crises of 'the hungry forties' gave way to the spectacular prosperity of the 1850s and 1860s. Britain moved towards democracy by the rule book, recalcitrant theorists proving a worse problem for the government than the demonstrations of loyal artisans, eager to ally themselves with political democracy. Problems of public

* 31 December 1868.

order, the chief feature of the earlier years of Gladstone's career, gave way to the limited adjustment of relationships between unalienated groups: whereas the Chartists had wished to overturn the political order, the Reform League merely wished to associate itself with it.

The 1850s and early 1860s showed the Victorian constitution working in its most characteristic form, in a context of economic progress at which contemporaries wondered, though without complacency. By the late 1860s the propertied classes were becoming disconcerted by the re-emergence of those 'great social forces' which suggested that the mid-Victorian settlement might not, after all, hold. But the early 1860s—the 'Age of Equipoise' in W. L. Burn's phrase—were years in which the achievement of progress—material, moral, intellectual—seemed to be Britain's contribution to an envious and admiring world. 'Greater World' was Gladstone's slip of the pen when Dilke's 'Greater Britain' was intended: it characterized a generation.

For Gladstone personally most of these years offered a similar tranquillity. The great crises of his public and private life which characterized the 1840s and early 1850s had been largely resolved. The tensions in what he saw as political and sexual temptations became the tensions of tactical not of strategic decision: the path of his life seemed finally charted, the set of his thought consolidated.

This is not to say that the problems of political tactics were not extremely complex, as we shall see; but the great questions for Gladstone of the 1830s and 1840s, of whether politics was for him a legitimate career, of the nature of the Christian State, and of the relationship between ambition and duty, no longer form the central themes of his diary.

Politically, the diary of these years records a series of decisions and manœuvres whose context is quite different from that in which Gladstone could seriously offer to Peel the amalgamation of two Welsh sees as a reason for not joining the Cabinet. For Gladstone, the relationships of Church and State had ceased to be a chief point of theoretical controversy: his decisions in 1868 about the abolition of compulsory church rates and Irish disestablishment were decisions about timing and tactics, no longer about great moral issues; the latter, he believed, had already been settled by the failure of the Oxford movement in the 1840s to convert the nation.

However, in purely tactical political terms, the years 1855–9 were the most personally complex in Gladstone's career. The success of the Peelite–Liberal coalition of 1852 was, from Gladstone's point of view, broken by the events of January and February 1855, which he records in very great detail. But no great ideological difference separated Gladstone from the Palmerston government (in which some Peelites, notably Argyll, continued to serve) except the character of its leader. On the other hand, no great question of policy seemed to bar his return to the Tory party. As he put it, anonymously, in the *Quarterly Review* in 1856:

The interval between the two parties has, by the practical solution of so many congested questions, been very greatly narrowed. He who turns from Pall Mall towards the Park between the Reform and Carlton Clubs will perceive that each of those stately fabrics is mirrored in the windows of the other, and it may occur to him, with horror and amusement, according to his temper, that those mutual reflections of images set up in rank antagonism to one another, constitute a kind of parable, that offers to us its meaning as we read with conscience and intelligence the history of the time.*

The Peelites found themselves standing in the street, exiles from one club, fearful to join the other, though willing to visit it.

Thus while there was a tendency to co-operation with the Liberal party, as in 1852, when, as Gladstone told Aberdeen in 1857, 'the act was done, which would probably have led to a real & final amalgamation with the Liberal party', there was also a tendency to reunion with the mass of the Conservatives who appeared to have abandoned the fiscal views which after 1846 had made continued co-operation with them impossible.

In his attempt to reassess his notion of a moral organic society, Gladstone had in the late 1840s travelled a very considerable distance in certain aspects of his thought towards a liberal position. His difficulty was that politics had not continued to divide on the question of free trade on which this liberalism was founded, and the national dedication to free trade seemed belied by the later stages of the Crimean war and the disasters of the general election in 1857 in which many of the free trade Radicals lost their seats. Foreign policy during Palmerston's government of 1855 to 1858 had certainly not followed what Gladstone regarded as moral policies, and that government had in his view also been misguided in its financial and immoral in its divorce policy. Gladstone thus found it easier to work on some questions with the Radicals, on others with the Conservatives, but rarely with the Whigs.

However, the position of a politician assessing motion by motion on its merits was not congenial to Gladstone's executive turn of mind: 'He must be a very bad minister indeed, who does not do ten times the good to the country when he is in office, that he would do when he is out of it.' The Radicals he found irresponsible, in the sense that they were critics with no desire to become actors. He could work with them on specific issues, but they could offer no solution to the question of the execution of policy. Similarly the Conservatives, much though he might appreciate Derby's

---

* [W. E. Gladstone], 'The declining efficiency of parliament', *Quarterly Review*, xcix. 562 (September 1856); this important and neglected article, an expansion of a letter to Aberdeen, written in the light of his 'memorandum on finance' of 15 February 1856, gives a clear and revealing account of Gladstone's views about the proper development of British politics.

probity, offered no prospect of a satisfactory executive position, for Gladstone believed, very probably rightly, that the Peelites did not constitute a political grouping substantial enough to assist the Conservatives to a working majority in the Commons. Moreover, Gladstone found that co-operation with the Conservatives on financial matters broke down on the important question of the social implications of different types of taxation, an issue which in 1856 raised the question whether the apparent agreement between the Peelites, the Radicals, and the Conservatives on the defects of Cornewall Lewis's financial policy, could in the long term be maintained.*

Gladstone had become essentially an executive politician. As he told Samuel Wilberforce in 1857, 'I greatly felt being turned out of office, I saw great things to do. I longed to do them. I am losing the best years of my life out of my natural service. . . .' This was by no means a characteristic attitude for a mid-Victorian politician. Even more uncharacteristic was Gladstone's action in drawing up in opposition (in February 1856) a great programme of measures to be passed through when next in office.

This programme of twenty-one financial measures included, amongst others, what became the Exchequer and Audit Act of 1866, the assertion of treasury control over all other departments, a reappraisal of the role and profits of the Bank of England, the abolition of the paper duties, the reduction of the wine, malt, sugar, coffee, insurance, and stamp duties, the reform of the taxation system by 'the extension and increase of the House Duty upon the determination of the Income Tax', and a series of technical measures. Where Peel had moved hesitantly and experimentally, Gladstone codified a large but miscellaneous body of fiscal and departmental reforms into a coherent plan for an all-powerful 'ministry of finance', and one which only his formidable political will was likely to be able to translate into legislative and administrative reality.

Not surprisingly, therefore, Gladstone regarded his period of opposition after 1855 as an anomaly to be ended by entry to the Cabinet of either a Whig–Liberal or a Conservative administration. Although he does not say so, he must have realized that his choice of party must now be final: he could hardly expect forgiveness from either side a second time. This may well account for his caution. His personal inclination in the period 1855 to 1859 lay on the whole with the Conservatives, whom he saw as less capricious than Palmerston; but, apart from Derby and Spencer Walpole, he had little intimacy with Conservatives of Cabinet rank. The Conservatives, for their part, while keen to capture Gladstone, made it clear to him that the extent of demand for office within their own party would leave no room for a general occupancy of senior Cabinet posts by the Peelite group.

* Gladstone's argument that finance benefited from having the Conservatives in office because the Liberals were more effective retrenchers when in opposition hardly offered a long-term solution.

Gladstone, however, consistently argued that the problem of party after the break-up of the coalition in 1855 could not be solved by men, but by measures. By measures, he meant the fulfilment of the programme of financial reform which he worked out in February 1856. Other Peelites, however, without exception worked to push him away from Derby and appear on several occasions to have exercised at least a decisive negative influence upon him. His failure to join Derby in 1858 was crucial, for, if he was again to hold office, there was no alternative left for him but to join the government of 1859, consequent upon the overthrow of the Derby Cabinet.

The Ionian Islands commissionership extraordinary, held by Gladstone in 1858–9 at the request of the Conservative government, was not from his point of view a move towards the Tories, though it was so intended by them. Gladstone had never, by his votes or speeches in the 1850s, hidden his view that the Conservatives deserved respect and, when possible, support. Though accepting the position from a Conservative ministry might seem to suggest a movement towards holding domestic office in that ministry, this was not the consequence seen by Gladstone's subtle mind. In Gladstone's analysis of the political situation it added nothing and subtracted nothing: it did not involve the Peelites as a group, and it did not involve 'measures'. If he had found insufficient reason to join the Derby ministry at its outset, there was no further reason to contemplate joining later, for the life of the ministry was agreed by all to be certain to be short. The Ionian interlude is certainly of interest, but not in the party political context; it will be discussed later.

There was also 'the difficulty of Disraeli', by the late 1850s firmly established as the leading Conservative in the Commons and the probable Leader of the House in any Conservative ministry. As Sir James Graham said to Gladstone, the Peelites could not expect Derby to throw Disraeli away 'like a sucked orange'. Gladstone personally felt 'unable to enter into any squabble or competition with him for the possession of a post of prominence'. To join with Disraeli was, in the Peelites' view, to place political morality at the service of chicanery, though in Gladstone's opinion Palmerston was not much better, despite being like himself a Canningite in origin, having 'dishonour as the great characteristic of [his] Government'.

By biding his time and accepting Peelite cautions against Conservatism, Gladstone solved the problem by elimination. Always reluctant to admit the role of ambition in politics, Gladstone was none the less aware of his abilities and their lack of application since 1855; his entry to Palmerston's Cabinet in 1859 thus involved no great moral choice and produced no great passage of self-analysis in the diary.* It was the hard-headed response of an able politician with a programme for action, invited to join a Cabinet at the

---

* The aftermath of the general election of April–May 1859 did, however, occasion one night of self-flagellation and a half-sleepless night.

outset of its formation.* In discussing political contingencies in 1856 with the other MP for Oxford University, Sir William Heathcote, Gladstone remarked:

That as to union, it was quite impossible to treat it as a matter of mere choice or will: whether it were a question of rejoining our late colleagues, or any other persons, our proceeding to be warrantable, must be founded on convictions of the public interest & on community of views evinced to the world by co-operation on great questions of the day which as they arose would speak for themselves & would open the path of duty.

Robertson Gladstone, by now Mayor of Liverpool and a leader of Lancastrian Radicalism , put the political point more directly:

No one, who knows you, if he ever thinks, can suppose, that you would coalesce with D'Israeli: when *you* join with another, that move, we know, will have some sort of principle, at least, to boast of.

Italy was, or could be made to seem, such a question in 1859. But in the general context of Gladstone's position in the years after 1855, of his failure to find a similar basis for co-operation with the Conservatives despite his violent and publicly voiced hostility to Whig foreign policy, of his persistently expressed criticisms of the financial policies of successive governments, of his own solution to financial ills, and of his demand in 1859 for the Exchequer alone, it is hard to see Italy as more than a convenient issue on which to combine with the Whigs on their own ground of foreign policy. This is not to say that Gladstone was using the Italian question deceitfully: he undoubtedly believed in the policy to which in the latter part of 1859 he contributed, but he can hardly have seen Italy as the basis for a government, and it did not figure in the list of public questions which he believed in 1857 to be of primary parliamentary significance.

Gladstone's visit to Venetia and Piedmont in the spring of 1859 on his way back from the Ionian islands undoubtedly quickened his interest in the subject, though his view of what should happen there was largely negative and even anti-Piedmontian: Austria should be removed, but not to Piedmont's advantage, and the temporal power of the Pope diminished. Despite his opportunities, Gladstone did not much encourage the Italianate sympathies of the English radicals, with their republican over-

---

* Palmerston had been confident Gladstone would join, and hopeful that he could be kept out of the Exchequer. On 30 March 1859 he had listed Gladstone for the Colonial Office, as he also did on an undated list, and for the India Office on another (undated) list. On these lists he had put Lewis down for the Exchequer. But Gladstone apparently saw Palmerston, knowing that Lewis would cede the Exchequer to him; see A. Hayward (to his sisters, 16 June 1859) *Correspondence* (1886) ii. 34: 'It was through me that Sir George Lewis communicated to Gladstone his readiness to give up the Chancellorship of the Exchequer to him if he wished and it was I who first told Lord Palmerston that Gladstone would join.' This is probably the meeting recorded by Gladstone on 2 June 1859, i.e. before the vote of 10 June which felled Derby's government, in which Gladstone voted against the motion of want of confidence. Gladstone told Herbert he would only have accepted the Exchequer.

tones, and his behaviour during Garibaldi's visit to England in 1864 can only be described as shuffling. Despite his later claims, Gladstone played an important part in persuading Garibaldi to abandon his planned provincial tour.

Appalling though Gladstone believed Palmerston's policies to have been between 1855 and 1858, their direction had advantages from his point of view. Gladstone argued that Palmerston's

stock in trade as a Peace Minister was wholly inadequate, or rather nearly null. It followed that he could only be a Peace Minister by keeping alive the passions, maintaining the sentences, and thus ever walking on the giddy brink of war.

But, to last, a peace-time government must offer more than this; it must offer a substantial programme of domestic legislation. This Gladstone could provide. There was 'a policy going a'begging', already prepared in some detail, which could provide the basis for the domestic programme of the government. A prime minister whose chief interest was bound to be in the area of foreign policy could have advantages for a Chancellor of the Exchequer with his own programme of legislation, and a programme it was. Gladstone as chancellor between 1859 and 1866 introduced, step by step, the items of the programme he had drawn up in 1856, the last item, the Exchequer and Audit Act, being passed shortly before the government resigned in 1866. This was a remarkable, perhaps unique, achievement in Victorian politics, and one which showed that, at least for Gladstone, the construction of policy could be something more than the accidental product of the politics of personality.

Gladstone as Chancellor

Gladstone was Chancellor of the Exchequer from December 1852 to February 1855, and from June 1859 until July 1866, the latter the longest continuous tenure between Vansittart and Lloyd George.* It may be useful, therefore, to set out the context of what was probably the most satisfying period of his political career, and certainly his most sustained period of departmental success.

A Victorian chancellor was not much troubled by the sort of crises characteristic of British history since 1914; the only peace-time occasion on which Gladstone had to act unexpectedly was the 1866 financial crisis caused by the failure of Overend and Gurney's bank, and even this was, from the chancellor's point of view, intrusive only for a weekend: 'Although the case was perplexing at the onset, & will be so in the *hereafter*, yet when we obtained the facts of the operations of the day our course became at once perfectly clear.' For the most part the chancellor

* Gladstone beat Hicks Beach (1895–1902) by five days, and was beaten by Lloyd George (1908–15) by a month.

was concerned with strategy, with the construction of an efficient 'Ministry of Finance', as Gladstone usually called it, and with the measured preparation of the annual budget. This pattern was disturbed only by the spasmodic need for extra revenue for imperial exploits, and by sudden calls for extra domestic defence expenditure through last minute changes in the departmental estimates. As chancellor, Gladstone was rarely involved in the day-to-day activities of the Treasury. The sort of detailed work which at the Board of Trade he had done himself, such as the day-to-day correspondence with other departments, was the responsibility of the financial secretary to the Treasury. It would seem that Gladstone involved himself more in departmental matters than most chancellors, but even this involvement was chiefly in the area of contract negotiations, especially as they affected overseas communications, for example the Red Sea telegraph and the Galway packet contract for postal communication with North America.

Gladstone usually drew up the heads of his spring budget the previous Christmas, at Hawarden, and without any reference to the Treasury. On one occasion he began earlier, in August: 'I dreamt of the next Estimates: with a dour sense of the work I have to do.' He would then request information from the various departments, such as the Board of Inland Revenue and the national debt commissioners, about the likely effect on revenue of changes in taxation which he contemplated introducing. He did not consult the Treasury or the departments on questions of policy, but merely on administration, nor did the Treasury or the departments propose policy changes to him. Least of all did he involve his Cabinet colleagues. As he told Cornewall Lewis when Lewis succeeded him as chancellor in 1855: 'I advised him to keep his own Counsel & let the Cabinet as a whole not know his plans till his mind was made up in the main, & the time close at hand.'

As chancellor, therefore, Gladstone acted independently. He also acted aggressively. His years at the Treasury coincided with reform of that institution from within which Gladstone both shared and encouraged.* The Treasury was asserting its right to control the activities and personnel of the civil service as a whole; Gladstone asserted the political position of the chancellor in Cabinet, in Parliament, and hence in the country generally. Hitherto the Exchequer had either been held by a man of importance, but not of the first importance, or by the First Lord of the Treasury himself. Peel had, between 1841 and 1846, used Goulburn more as a financial secretary than a chancellor, and had prepared and introduced budgets almost without reference to his chancellor. Whig chancellors had been second rank men without aspirations to real power. Disraeli had been the first chancellor also to be the obvious second man in the government.

---

* See M. Wright, *Treasury control of the civil service, 1854–1874* (1969).

By deliberately asserting the overall suzerainty of the Treasury, Gladstone not surprisingly clashed with the spending departments, particularly the Admiralty and the War Office, for army and navy estimates constituted 43% of all government spending in 1861. Defence and the charges on the national debt together accounted for about three-quarters of central government expenditure, and were therefore the chief areas of concern for the chancellor on the expenditure side.* He battled with the Admiralty and the War Office about what he considered unnecessary expenditure, though always, to the distress of some of the Radicals on the back-benches, accepting the need for both an efficient army of considerable size and a large fleet. The debt, he attempted to deal with by conversion in 1853 and 1866–7 (a happy co-operation with Disraeli) and, to a lesser extent, by redemption.

In the Cabinet struggles of the early 1860s, Gladstone tried to force the defence departments to work within the Treasury's framework of taxation reform; that is, he appeared to give priority over imperial considerations to a financial programme of mainly domestic political importance. But this was to a considerable extent only appearance. Because Gladstone could not decide whether spending on imperialism was chronic or merely spasmodic, he failed to develop a policy to deal with it, save the negative one of making colonies of predominantly European settlement pay for their own defence. Thus he found himself treating each imperial crisis in non-white areas separately and in its own terms only, and, as each imperial action could be made to seem plausible, Gladstone, as Cobden so often complained, found himself raising funds for imperialism as effectively as any Whig or Tory.

The other contentious item was the plan to fortify the southern coast against French invasion. Here Gladstone had an alternative policy: the

* As % of total gross central government expenditure

	Debt charges	Defence	Civil government
1836–40	57.7	24.6	10.0
1841–5	54.5	25.8	10.4
1846–50	50.2	28.9	12.0
1851–5	48.8	27.9	12.2
1856–60	38.6	39.9	12.4
1861–5	37.7	39.4	15.4
1866–70	38.2	36.1	15.8
1871–5	38.1	33.1	17.2
1876–80	34.8	32.5	20.0
1881–5	34.4	31.3	21.7
1886–90	28.5	34.4	21.2
1891–5	24.3	34.7	19.8
1896–9	21.0	36.6	19.9
1900–3	12.3	56.5	19.9
1904–8	22.9	43.1	20.2
1909–13	11.7	38.0	31.2

Compiled from B. R. Mitchell and P. Deane, *Abstract of British Historical Statistics* (1971), tables 4 and 4a. The total to 100 is made up by administrative costs, Post Office, etc.

French commercial treaty of 1860, and on this question time proved him right. The fact that the war secretary was his close and already ailing friend, Sidney Herbert, made no difference to Gladstone, who relentlessly exposed Herbert to a full-scale battle by correspondence. But Herbert had behind him the Duke of Somerset, First Lord of the Admiralty, and, more important, Palmerston, one of the very few men who could equal Gladstone in political stamina.

In 1860 Gladstone pressed his hostility to the brink of resignation, but not over it. 'My resignation *all but* settled': the significance lay in the italics. Gladstone, unlike Randolph Churchill in 1886, never offered resignation formally. Moreover Palmerston, unlike Salisbury with Churchill, did not wish him to go, and despite their differences went to considerable lengths to keep him in the Cabinet, the Duke of Argyll acting as mediator. In these protracted struggles, each side convinced itself that it had won at least the odd battle. In the sense that imperialism was paid for and some of the fortifications built, the Admiralty and War Office gained most of their objectives. Gladstone pressed through the French treaty and, eventually, the repeal of the paper duties. He gained politically what he lost fiscally, and, by not resigning, remained to realize the programme of treasury control which, if apparently unsuccessful in the short term of the 1860s, in the long term seemed to triumph.

The Politicization of the Chancellorship *

Some of what the chancellor had to do was technical: the details of the small print of the handling of various taxes and of the national debt, though even these were never uncontroversial. Gladstone was very good at this sort of behind-the-scenes management, but it was not this that gained him his fame as chancellor. In 1857, when reacting to Cornewall Lewis's budget, he drew up a list of priorities:

To maintain a steady surplus of income over expenditure—to lower indirect taxes when excessive in amount for the relief of the people and bearing in mind the reproductive power inherent in such operations—to simplify our fiscal system by concentrating its pressure on a few well chosen articles of extended consumption—and to conciliate support to the Income Tax by marking its temporary character & by associating it with beneficial changes in the laws: these aims have been for fifteen years the labour of our life.

The Peelites liked finance to be neat, regular, and seen to be so. The balanced budget, its income raised by a simple, pared-down structure of direct and indirect taxes, its expenditure given to a few absolutely necessary departments of government, exemplified a nation with its bowels in

---

* In this and the next section I have introduced some material originally quoted in my article 'Disraeli, Gladstone and the politics of mid-Victorian budgets', *Historical Journal* (1979), which has more detail on various aspects of Gladstone's chancellorship.

good working order. 'Finance is, as it were, the stomach of the country, from which all the other organs take their tone', Gladstone wrote in 1858. For this to be so, a high political profile for the chancellor and the Treasury was essential.

Gladstone aggressively and consistently politicized the chancellorship, through the preparation and prosecution of budgets. In 1853 he immediately established almost complete independence from his old department, the Board of Trade, remembering perhaps the way it had, under his direction, influenced budgetary preparation in the 1840s. The 1853 and 1860 budgets (especially the latter) were of course in large measure tariff budgets, but in their preparation the Board of Trade was consulted merely on technicalities.

The 1860 French treaty, a central feature of that year's budget, was negotiated almost independently of the Foreign Office, and largely independently of the Cabinet. The 1860 treaty was a quite deliberate interference in Whig foreign policy. It was presented politically as a further step towards free trade, though technically it was a reciprocity treaty and criticized as such by some theoretical free traders. Its financial importance was chiefly confined to its effect on the English silk and glove trades, and to Gladstone's plan to solve the drink problem by creating a nation of wine drinkers consuming their cheap 'Gladstone claret', as it came to be called, in decorous cafés which paid their licence fees to the government, instead of in public houses under the licence of local and often independently minded magistrates. The French treaty was the first of several such treaties in the 1860s, but it was the only one to which Gladstone attached much political importance. To counter Whig suspicions of France and the consequent construction of massive fortifications along the English south coast, Gladstone was determined to get a commercial treaty with France, at almost any cost. He told Cobden, who negotiated the treaty in Paris, of

... the great aim—the moral and political significance of the act, and its probable and desired fruit in binding the two countries together by interest and affection.

Neither you nor I attach for the moment any superlative value to this Treaty for the sake of the extension of British trade. . . . What I look to is the social good, the benefit to the relations of the two countries, and the effect on the peace of Europe.

Similarly the repeal of the paper duties in 1860 and 1861, involving the first major institutional row between the two Houses of Parliament since 1832, deliberately allied the chancellor with political radicalism in a way that Gladstone had been careful to avoid with respect to the 'taxes on knowledge' during his previous chancellorship in 1852–5. Both Gladstone's most famous budgets, of 1853 and 1860, were pressed through an unwilling Cabinet. We have already seen his finesse in getting eventual Cabinet acceptance for his 1853 budget. In 1860, on the paper duties question, he was only supported by Gibson and Argyll in the Cabinet, and in 1861 only by Gibson, yet he was eventually able to prevail. Moreover, since it became quite clear from the press, and from the behaviour of Palmerston in parliamentary debates, that paper duty repeal was at Cabinet level very much Gladstone's own policy, the political advantages to Gladstone of the eventual success of the repeal and of the outflanking of the House of Lords were all the greater.

Much of Gladstone's work as chancellor was self-consciously in the tradition of Peel, but it was executed in a political style more dramatic, more rhetorical, and less discreet than the Peelite reforms of the 1840s. This was not accidental or merely the result of personal differences. Gladstone believed that big bills and budgets were a necessary feature not merely of executive government but of post-1832 politics. He attacked Macaulay for articulating the eighteenth-century view that it was not the function of the Executive persistently to initiate legislation, and he denounced Palmerston between 1855 and 1858 for acting like the eighteenth-century Duke of Newcastle—a domestic programme of quiescence designed to placate placemen.

This was therefore not merely the Pitt–Peel argument that there were reforms to be done and abuses to be remedied, but a much more political argument that it was politically essential that reforms should persistently be seen to be done, for 'it is rapid growth in the body politic that renders stereotyped law intolerable'. 'Public opinion', Gladstone argued, 'is disposed to view with great favour all active and efficient government.' In this sense Gladstone's chancellorships represented the politicization of Peelism. For Gladstone, therefore, big bills and big budgets* represented a means of regular renewal of the legitimacy of Parliament and the political system; for Palmerston and the Whigs they represented a continuous threat to stability and moderation.

At first glance there was something of a paradox here: the less budgets and the fiscal system were intended to superintend or direct the national economy, the more they became the centre-pieces of the political year. But this was not really paradoxical because an important, indeed a central, feature of the mid-Victorian finance of which Gladstone was the dominant exponent was what may be called positive retrenchment. The direct relationship between government and the economy should be minimal, but the indirect relationship, through the setting up of a self-sustaining economy, would be considerable. The reduction of government superintendence of the economy by the abolition of the tariff structure and the maintenance of a low level of government spending was intended to have positive results. First, the economy would be self-regulating. This would

---

* Ironically, the Queen, later to be so alarmed by the Gladstonian habit of big bills, encouraged him in this direction, telling him in 1859 that a big budget was required.

have the economic benefit, it was thought, of allowing the maximum of capital accumulation in a free market; 'in giving legal freedom to the energy of capital and skill of Englishmen, we were adopting a true and powerful means of extending our commercial prosperity'.* It would also have the political benefit of dissociating government and Parliament from the need to bargain with economic pressure groups. 'Government' and 'the economy' would thus be quite separate entities—good citizenship would not be compromised by economic interest.† Indeed, a society in which the political process was mainly concerned to deal with such groups would be a corrupt society.

By 1880 Gladstone had come to see protection as a 'poison', sheltering nothing 'but the most selfish instincts of class against the just demands of the public welfare'; it armed producers with 'power and influence largely gotten at the expense of the community, to do battle, with a perverted prowess, against nature, liberty and justice'.‡

This stress on a concept of citizenship which discounted the economy would allow Parliament to be seen as 'fair' and dispassionate by all classes in the State.§ Consequently, although 'classes' would undoubtedly exist and indeed Gladstone's view of the distribution of taxation took direct account of them, politics would not appear essentially to be about class. By

---

* The success of this strategy was remarkable. At a time when, as Gladstone pointed out, the proportion of government spending to national wealth was rising rapidly in Continental nations, in Britain it remained both low (relative to a world power's responsibilities) and fairly constant (though falling markedly in the years of Gladstonian suzerainty, 1860–75), as the following table shows:

Proportion of Central Government Gross
Expenditure to Gross National Product

	Expenditure £m	G.N.P. £m	%
1853	55.3	642 (1855)	8.6
1860	70.0	702	10.0
1865	67.1	846	7.9
1870	67.1	953	7.0
1875	73.0	1136	6.4
1880	81.5	1101	7.4
1885	88.5	1120	7.9
1895	100.9	1459	6.9
1905	149.5	1814	8.2
1913	202.2	2322	8.7

Source: B. R. Mitchell and P. Deane, *Abstract of British Historical Statistics* (1971), Public Finance 4 and 4a, and C. H. Feinstein, *National Income, Expenditure and Output of the United Kingdom 1855–1965* (1972), Table 1.

† See G. Stedman Jones, *Languages of Class* (1983), 177–8, for the success of this strategy in countering Chartism.

‡ W. E. Gladstone, 'Free Trade, Railways, and the growth of Commerce', *Nineteenth Century* (February 1880), 377; in this article, he was careful to reserve his position on infant industries.

§ See Ross McKibbin, 'Why was there no Marxism in Great Britain?', *English Historical Review* (1984).

its wider ranging fiscal reforms, and especially its abolition of protective tariffs, the House of Commons had acted, Gladstone told it in his 1860 speech on the budget and the Cobden treaty,

on behalf of the masses of the people, and not on behalf of them alone, but on behalf of every class, on behalf of the Throne, and of the institutions of the country.... By pursuing such a course as this it will be in your power to scatter blessings among the people, and blessings which are among the soundest and most wholesome of all the blessings at your disposal; because in legislation of this kind, you are not forging mechanical supports and helps for men, nor endeavouring to do that for them which they ought to do for themselves; but you are enlarging their means without narrowing their freedom, you are giving value to their labour, you are appealing to their sense of responsibility, you are not impairing their temper of honourable self-dependence ... [these sorts of laws] win more and more for the Throne and for the institutions of the country the gratitude, the confidence, and the love of an united people.

But the advantages were not merely domestic. Defending in 1853 the use of 'the mighty engine' of income tax, so essential to the financing of the war effort against the French Revolution and Napoleon, and now so valuable as the agent of free trade through commercial and fiscal reform, Gladstone claimed a world mission for the British model: 'in reforming your own fiscal and commercial system, you have laid the foundations of similar reforms—slow, perhaps, but certain in their progress—through every country of the civilized world'.

This view of the relationship of central government to the economy presupposed two premisses, both of which turned out, in the long run, to be false. First, it presupposed that equilibrium in the economy would naturally be achieved at the full utilization of available resources, both capital and labour—that, as J. S. Mill put it, an excess of supply was, except in moments of temporary dislocation, an impossibility. Second, it presupposed the capacity of a vast network of voluntary organizations to superintend, through the participation of active citizens and in cooperation with local government, most of the range of moral, charitable, educational, and welfare services. The absence of initiative by central government in such areas was thus premissed on the vigorous involvement of the citizen in local affairs, in charitable giving and administration, in savings societies, and in the many religious organizations which aspired to offer a very wide range of services, many of which would today be regarded as outside the area of 'religion'. Gladstone himself, as we have seen, was active in a private capacity in exactly these sorts of endeavours. There was no divide between his public advice and his private thought and action. As an Anglican, however, he had a rather different perspective on such matters from a Nonconformist or a strict Liberal. Anglican welfarism necessarily had national objectives which implied, ultimately, national standards,

1. Gladstone in 1833. *Oil sketch by George Hayter for the group portrait of the 1833 Parliament*

2. Sir John Gladstone in old age. *Calotype by D. Hill and R. Adamson*

3. Catherine Gladstone. *Watercolour, 1843, by George Richmond*

4. 'The Flight of Daedalus and Icarus! illustrated under a new aspect', by H. B. (John Doyle), July 1844, with Gladstone seeking the free trade sun even more energetically than Peel

5. Gladstone in 1858, wearing 'Broughams', the checked trousers named after Henry Brougham with whom he became friendly in the 1850s; from Maull and Polyblank's *Photographic Portraits of Living Celebrities*, one of the first such series

6. Tenniel's cartoon 'Critics', captioned: 'MR. G–D–S–T–N–E.
"Hm!––Flippant!" MR. D–S–R–LI. "Ha!—Prosy!"'. *Punch*,
14 May 1870. Unlike Disraeli, Gladstone's features posed problems
for cartoonists; this is one of Tenniel's best

7. (a) Agnes
Drawing by G. Richmond

7. (b) Catherine Jessy, died
April 1850
Portrait by G. Hayter

7. (c) Mary

7. (d) Herbert John

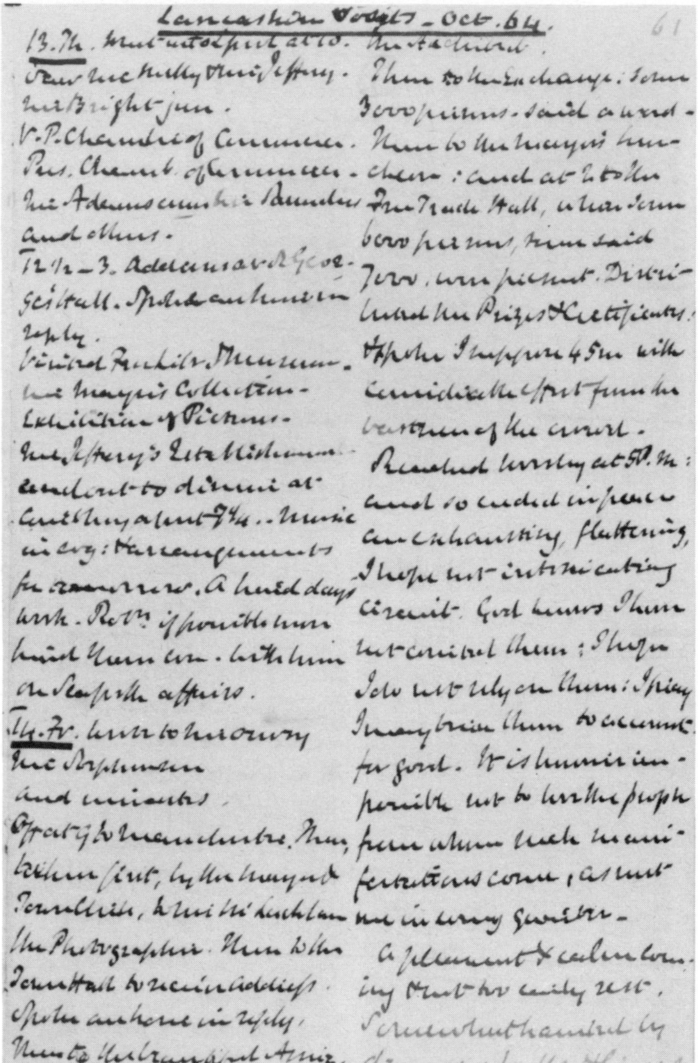

Lancashire Visits – Oct. 64. 61

13. Th. Went off at 10. [illegible]

Saw [illegible]

Mr Bright jun.

V.P. Chamber of Commerce.

Pres. Chamb. of Commerce.

Mr Adamson [illegible]

and others.

12½–3. Addresses at St Geo[rge]'s Hall. Spoke an hour in reply.

Visited Peel Park Museum – the Mayor's Collection – Exhibition of Pictures.

[illegible] Establishment [illegible] to dinner at [illegible] about 7¾. – Music in evg: & arrangements for tomorrow. A hard day's work. [illegible] if possible [illegible] on Scapular[?] affairs.

14. Fr. Wrote to [illegible] Mr Stephenson and minutes.

Off at 10 to Manchester. Was taken first, by the Mayor [illegible] to the Photographer. Then to the Town Hall to receive Address. Spoke an hour in reply. Then to the [illegible] Assize Courts. [illegible] the Architect.

Then to the Exchange: some 3000 persons – said a word. Then to the Mayor's luncheon: and at 2 to the Free Trade Hall, where were 6000 persons, some said 7000, very patient. Distributed the Prizes & Certificates. Spoke I suppose 45m with considerable effort from the vastness of the crowd.

Reached Worsley at 5 P.M.: and so ended in peace an exhausting, flattering, I hope not intoxicating circuit. God knows I have not courted them: I hope I do not rely on them: I pray I may turn them to account for good. It is however impossible not to love the people from whom such manifestations come, as meet me in every quarter.

A pleasant & calm evening. Went too early to rest. Somewhat haunted by dreams of bells & lines of

8. Gladstone's diary of his tour of Lancashire, 13 and 14 October 1864

coverage, and measurement. In this pattern of voluntary action, the Church of England must be included, for it was expected to raise its revenues by voluntary means. But it was not to be expected that its members could accept without reserve the aberrations which a voluntary system of welfare and education were bound to produce.

Consequently Gladstone's retrenchment ethos and his preference for a voluntarist society were tempered by an absence of dogma, a willingness to see problems in a national context, and a maintenance of executive authority. His programme of legislation was, as has been mentioned above, set out privately in 1856 and carried through between 1859 and 1866. Its aim was the construction of an independent and controlling Treasury, represented at Cabinet level by a powerful 'minister of finance', supported in the legislature by annual inquiry through the Public Accounts Committee, set up in 1861, and by a House of Commons dedicated to vigilance and retrenchment. The Public Accounts Committee checked abuses in expenditure retrospectively. Enthusiastic though he was for retrenchment, Gladstone was also very careful not to yield executive control of the planning of expenditure. At an early stage of its existence, in 1862, the Committee showed interest in prospective expenditure and its control. Gladstone explained in evidence to the Committee that if a spending department and the Treasury could not agree, 'they would go to the Cabinet, and the Cabinet would decide questions for that period'. He then considered another possibility: 'the other choice would be that of presenting the transaction to Parliament before it had become final, and while it was subject to modification. I think if it were to be presented in that way it must go to some Committee or to some separate body; it could not go to the House of Commons at large.' This opened the possibility in the working of such a Committee of an alliance between Parliament and the Treasury for the pursuit of retrenchment. But Gladstone, despite his wide-ranging plans for the extension of Treasury control, his frequent appeals for public demand for retrenchment, and his lament for the 'declining efficiency of Parliament', never advocated the setting up of such a Committee; control of prospective expenditure remained effectively and firmly in the hands of the executive, and in this he acted wholly in character.

Gladstone is well known for his phrase that money should 'fructify in the pockets of the people', but what he actually meant was that it should fructify in the deposit vaults of the National Debt Commissioners. Much though he extolled the virtues of self-help, his actions as chancellor were consistently *étatist*. While Gladstone often used pluralist free trade arguments to justify the use of exchange as an impartial arbiter of social morality, in practice as chancellor he often returned to the organic, almost corporatist view of the State which he had set out in his first book. The aim of his Post Office Savings Banks plan was to give the Treasury more independence from the Bank of England. His Working Class Annuities Act, passed against strong hostility from the Friendly Societies, was in direct competition with them, and denounced by them as quite contrary to the self-help ethos, but was welcomed by trade unionists anxious to associate themselves with the State.*

The aim of his Country Bank Notes Issue Bill, which had to be withdrawn, was to speed up the working of the issue centralizing clauses of the Bank Charter Act of 1844. But the strengthened Bank of England was to make less money from its role as the government's bank, and was to be less firmly entrenched as the pivot of fiscal crisis, for Gladstone contemplated a radical alteration to the 1844 Bank Act, by which an issue of bonds, controlled by the Treasury, would expand the money supply in times of crisis, controlled by an ever-increasing rate of interest. The failure of the Country Notes Bill showed the strength of the lobby for the existing banking system, and the plan for the revision of the 1844 Act, also strongly opposed within the Treasury, never became more than a privately canvassed proposal.

Gladstone's mistrust of the existing banking system stemmed from his experiences after his wife's family business had been bankrupted in the fiscal crisis of 1847. Partly as a result of this, partly in keeping with a general change of view characteristic of mid-Victorian Britain, Gladstone came to believe, at least in the 1860s, that market forces could not produce a just society. Moreover, he had never been an out-and-out Ricardian. His youthful Idealist approach to the organic nation had been in direct contrast to Ricardianism and though in the late 1840s he had abandoned as unworkable the view of State–Church relations set out in his first book, he had specifically not forsworn his view of the organic nature of the State.

As chancellor, Gladstone compared himself to an architect altering a fine but decaying eighteenth-century mansion to a form fitted for the industrial age, designing the new building, controlling its construction, modifying its form as the years passed. Technically put, the function of the chancellor was to create a model of international free trade and then to interfere at the margin of the domestic economy on grounds of social justice:

Once security has been taken that an entire society shall not be forced to pay an artificial price to some of its members for their production, we may safely commit the question [of cheapness of goods] to the action of competition among manufacturers, and of what we term the laws of supply and demand. As to the condition of the workpeople, experience has shown, especially in the case of the Factory Acts, that we should do wrong in laying down any abstract maxim as an invariable rule.

But this absence of 'abstract maxim' led in practice to considerable flexibility, for

---

* In practice, the response was disappointing; about 13,000 annuities *per annum* were taken up.

There is no one, I should imagine—at least I know of none—who thinks that savings banks, or the grant of annuities or assurances for the people, are matters with which it is desirable abstractedly for Government to deal. If it could be said that the operation of the great law of supply and demand is generally satisfactory and sufficient, and that the failures which occur are incidental to the principles on which commerce must be conducted, that would merely be a conclusive condemnation, not merely of the law you passed two years ago for Post Office Savings Banks . . . and also of the laws as to the grant of annuities and the old savings banks.

Government interference could be of three kinds:

The highest form in which it has been carried out is that of positive regulations requiring this thing and that thing to be done in the course of private commercial arrangements, for the sake of obviating social, moral or political evils . . . the second kind of Government interference . . . has been interference by sheer naked prohibition . . . the third and . . . mildest description of Government interference . . . [is] that by the interference of the Government you enjoin nothing and you prohibit nothing, but you offer to such members of the community as may be disposed to avail themselves of your proposal certain facilities for what I may call self-help.

The most notable exercise of Gladstone's *étatism* would have been the putting into effect of the 'nationalization' clauses of his 1844 Railways Act, which provided for the option of purchase by the State after twenty-one years (i.e. in 1865) of railways constructed in or since 1844.* Such State action would not have been in character with the age, but it was not wholly fanciful, as the Tory nationalization of the telegraph system in 1868 showed. If it was to be done, Gladstone noted, it would have to have 'the support of a general and impartial public opinion'.† Gladstone certainly toyed with the possibility of nationalization. As the moment for review of the 1844 Act came, he raised the matter (without mentioning the Act) with Palmerston, who showed himself by no means in principle opposed. Encouraged, Gladstone reminded him of the 1844 clauses and, in reply to further queries, wrote:

We suppose the Railways 1. To have been purchased and taken into possession by the State. 2. To be worked by commercial firms or companies as lessees from the State, in conveniently divided groups. And probably 3. To be superintended, as far as the State is concerned, by a Board or Department having a qualified independence from the Executive Government.

Palmerston, alarmed about cost, found this 'on the first Blush a wild and more than doubtful Project'. Gladstone backed off, pointing out that his scheme had been hypothetical, 'Upon the assumption of a certain state of things, not . . . showing that the state of things ought to exist.'‡ The matter

* See above, p. 67.

† 19 Dec. 64. For telegraph nationalization—a Tory Act following up a Liberal initiative—see J. L. Kieve, *The Electric Telegraph* (1973), chs. 7 and 8.

‡ See the correspondence between Gladstone and Palmerston in October–December 1864 in P. Guedalla, *Gladstone and Palmerston* (1928), 291–319.

was referred to a Royal Commission which Gladstone intended would make merely a factual inquiry which would not 'compromise or commit either ourselves or Parliament with any reference to any legislation upon a matter of this vast importance'.* The Commission, however, pronounced strongly against putting the 1844 option, or a developed version of it, into operation, and there the matter of State purchase effectively rested until the Labour party made nationalization one of its leading objectives.

It is not clear how committed Gladstone was to nationalization. In his correspondence with Palmerston and in his statements in the Commons he was careful not to be tied to executing his 1844 option; but he was equally careful not to forswear it. This was quite in line with his policy of not being publicly committed to general propositions which had no immediate prospect of becoming statutes. Cabinet considerations of the railway question coincided with a major row over defence expenditure. Although Gladstone's plan 'was one which would have created no debt in lieu of stock, and which only looked to a distant reversion', it may be that he was alarmed about the costs, or worried at Palmerston being given an opportunity to present himself as the retrencher and Gladstone the spender. He may have felt that public opinion would not be sufficiently favourable. Whatever the reason, or reasons, he did not raise the question again, and his own government after 1868 made no progress even on the relatively minor and probably less controversial issue of the nationalization of Irish railways. Had Gladstone pressed through the scheme he adumbrated which was very similar to the Liberals' solution in the 1920s for the coal industry—public ownership leased to private management—the administrative history of the nineteenth century and perhaps the political history of the early twentieth would have been very different.

The Social Contract of the Mid-Victorian State: Income Tax, Virtual Representation, and Franchise Reform

To permit movement towards freer trade for Britain, Peel's government had in 1842 imposed income tax: a spectacular departure, since the previous income tax had been a war measure, removed with indecent haste and with little concern for a fair balance of taxation, in 1816. At the Board of

* Gladstone's reply to Roebuck's question about the Royal Commission in *Hansard*, clxxvii. 232 (14 February 1865); for the Royal Commission's report, see *Parl. Papers* 1867, xxxviii. The Commission found it 'inexpedient at present to subvert the policy which has hitherto been adopted, of leaving the construction and management of railways to the free enterprise of the people, under such conditions as Parliament may think fit to impose for the general welfare of the public'. The Commission thought 'the Act of 1844 warns us of the extreme difficulty of making prospective arrangements to take effect after many years. Instead of facilitating the acquisition of the railways by the State, it has rendered the operation more difficult, and indeed almost impracticable with a due regard to the guarantees it has accorded to the railway companies.' This was a little hard, since if the 1844 Act had not existed, it is unlikely that the question would have had a serious airing in the 1860s.

Trade in 1842, Gladstone had regretted the imposition of income tax, favouring instead an increase in a different form of direct tax, the house tax. He had not, however, disagreed with Peel's view, that the balance of contributions to government revenue was too far weighted to the disadvantage of the indirect tax payers.

In the arguments about the income tax in the 1850s and 1860s, this concern for the balance between the direct and indirect tax payers had continued to be of central importance, and Gladstone's attempts to remove the income tax must always be seen in the context of that concern. In 1853 his chief aim had been to prevent the existing tax being discredited, as he saw it, by differentiation (that is, the taxation of different forms of income at different rates).

This he had triumphantly done. The Aberdeen coalition, defeated in the Commons three times in the week before the budget in 1853, was not again seriously threatened until the worst days of the Crimean war. Gladstone's budget in 1853 retained the income tax but did not reform it; his 1860 budget confirmed this position. In maintaining the income tax unreformed Gladstone strove to achieve a balance. On the one side, the Radicals through the Liverpool Financial Reform Association called for abolition of all indirect taxes and the raising of government revenue only through the income tax, but an income tax differentiated to accommodate the claims of 'precarious' professional income tax payers such as lawyers and doctors. On the other side the landed interest favoured indirect taxation and, if there was to be an income tax, one not altered to favour the professions. Gladstone's budgets struck a balance between the two.

Gladstone's first budget, a speech of four-and-three-quarter hours delivered on 18 April 1853, struck a keynote of energetic resolution which was repeated in his subsequent performances. He made finance and figures exciting, and succeeded in constructing budget speeches epic in form and performance, often with lyrical interludes to vary the tension in the Commons as the careful exposition of figures and argument was brought to a climax. The 1853 budget and its background thus deserve some attention.

The role of Peel's income and property tax of 1842 was ambiguous in character. It was introduced to balance the Whigs' deficit and to permit the remission of indirect taxes and protective tariffs. The understanding was that once the remission was made, the tax would be removed, but Peel never explicitly committed himself to this position. The tax limped on and a substantial demand for its reconstruction developed among articulate members of the propertied classes, who wanted differentiation for the benefit of the 'precarious incomes'. Wood, the Whig chancellor of the late 1840s, lost his budget of 1851 because of this, and Disraeli's ambitious attempt—too imaginative for its day—at the reconstruction of the tax was partly the cause and certainly the occasion of the minority Conservative government's defeat. The existence of the tax and the question of its differentiation had become the focal point of fiscal and political controversy. Gladstone realized, as had Disraeli in 1852, that whoever settled the income tax question would earn his party and himself a great political dividend.

This settlement was thus in 1853 'the corner stone of our whole financial plan'. Gladstone continued the income and property tax for seven years (the previous maximum had been three) and, following Disraeli, extended it to Ireland, but with a step-by-step reduction intended to lead to its abolition in 1860. He thus offered hope both to those who wished to see the tax abolished and, by the length of its renewal, to those direct taxers such as the members of the Financial Reform Association and the Cobdenites who wished to see it permanent. He dramatically increased the number of those paying income tax by reducing the starting point from £150 to £100, thus increasing its yield and broadening its social base. He strongly opposed formal differentiation because of the anomalies it would produce, but, with spectacular political finesse, he introduced an effective differentiation by an exemption from tax of savings which took the form of premiums for life insurance policies or deferred annuities. He thus aimed to meet the 'public feeling' that 'relief should be given to intelligence and skill [i.e. the precarious incomes] as compared with property'. This exemption formed the point of departure for one of the chief forms of saving in middle-class families until it was abolished by the Conservatives in 1984.* Such families were also conciliated by the development of the legacy duty. 'This', Gladstone told the Commons, 'is a tax which will leave wholly untouched the intelligence and skill of the country. It is a tax that gives the relief, and more than the relief that you aim at by the reconstruction of the income-tax, but it does it without the danger which would necessarily attend that reconstruction.' It also offered for the future a permanent form of direct taxation and a tax on capital held by Liberal economists such as Mill to be a fair exception to the general rule of avoiding the taxation of capital.

The propertied classes were thus offered a more palatable income tax, a tax more widely based in terms of numbers paying it, and a tax with a planned redundancy. The working classes, and consumers generally, were offered a substantial remission of indirect taxation by reduction and abolition of duties which it was hoped would, as in previous Peelite remissions, ultimately pay for itself because the reduced duties would stimulate demand and consequently a lower duty could raise as much as a higher.

In the budget, the propertied classes and the working classes confronted each other in the distribution of taxation, and Gladstone as chancellor

---

* By the end of the century about a fifth of income-tax payers claimed the relief, commonly spending 5% or more of their incomes on insurance; see L. Hannah, *Inventing Retirement* (1986), 5 and 154.

acted as broker between them. The result was the social contract of the Victorian State: the budget brought the direct and the indirect taxpayers face to face,* and, as we shall see shortly, it related them not only as payers of taxes, direct and indirect, but as voter and non-voter by fixing as £100 the level at which payment of income tax began. 'Declining [as Gladstone said] to draw any invidious distinction between class and class', the budget offered much to each. As the great economist Joseph Schumpeter observed in 1954, 'Gladstonian finance ... translated a social, political, and economic vision which was comprehensive as well as historically correct, into clauses of a set of co-ordinated fiscal measures.'†

In political terms the 1853 budget consolidated the Aberdeen coalition and provided a point of reference for Liberal politics for much of the rest of the century. For Gladstone, his technical triumph—for the budget had many neat but complex details of the sort the Victorian press admired—married with his understanding of the central, reconciling importance of taxation to 'right relations' between the great classes of the State to give him not only a prime position in the history of British finance, but a strong reserve of political capital.

Gladstone mistrusted and feared the peacetime income tax, but in all his years as chancellor he never abolished it. It played too central a role in the great taxation compromise which legitimized the Liberal State in Britain.

The effect of Gladstone's handling of the income tax was to entrench the ambiguity which, as we have seen, was inherent in Peel's reintroduction of it. This was reflected in the way that Gladstone's proposal of 1853 appealed both to those who wanted the tax continued and to those who wanted it abolished. The tax could not be reconstructed and differentiated because that would imply permanence to what was soon to be abolished (and the Peelites declined for this reason to sit on the 1851 Select Committee on the tax); on the other hand, the propertied classes must accept the unreconstructed tax so as to permit social and economic progress. Gladstone unconsciously caught the ambiguity in his summary of Peelite finance made in 1857; there, as already quoted, he aimed both 'to conciliate support to the Income Tax by marking its temporary character & by associating it with beneficial changes in the laws'. Was it possible for the same tax both to be marked by a 'temporary character' and to be associated with 'beneficial changes', for was not the character of those changes likely to be of an on-going, shifting nature? Gladstone's position implied that a permanent peacetime equilibrium of the state and its finances could be achieved. The

* Even if the abolition of income tax had been achieved in 1860, Gladstone planned to replace it with the direct tax he had originally favoured in 1842, the house duty, thus preserving the direct/indirect tax balance. He had a similar plan in 1874, on that occasion wishing to use the death duties.

† J. A. Schumpeter, *History of Economic Analysis* (1954), 403.

rest of the century was to be the battleground on which he fought the forces which prevented it.

It was not Gladstone's intention, but it was his achievement, that at the end of the century Britain had the income tax which the governments and progressive politicians of Germany, France, and the United States craved but could not gain. In the competition between the need for a fair ratio between the 'twin sisters' of direct and indirect taxation on the one hand and dislike of income tax on the other, Gladstone kept the tax to maintain the ratio.

In 1853 the phased reduction of the income tax to permit its abolition in 1860 was hedged about by many conditions. First, it assumed that the *pari passu* reduction and abolition of customs and excise duties would be offset by an increase in consumption by which those duties remaining—especially tea, drink, and sugar—would produce more revenue; in other words it assumed at the least no economic recession. Second, it assumed no intervening disaster requiring a large increase in government expenditure. Third, it assumed that the new succession duty, an alternative direct tax, would yield a substantial amount. Finally, it assumed a diminution of ordinary government expenditure.

It was unlikely that all of these conditions could be met, and they were not all met, even if the Crimean war is discounted. Faced in 1860 with continuing the income tax or substantially increasing the burden of indirect taxation as a necessary consequence of repealing the income tax, Gladstone unhesitatingly chose to continue the income and property tax, which at that time contributed about 13% of central government revenue. The switch to indirect taxation which its unilateral abolition would have involved would have been politically quite unacceptable to the Liberals.*

At the same time, maintaining and extending his Board of Trade work of the 1840s and the budget of 1853, Gladstone abolished, together with the changes resulting from the French treaty, the Customs and Excise duties and tariffs on nearly 400 articles. He thus left only about fifteen articles subject to duty and contributing a significant income. Virtually none of these remaining duties constituted a protective or differential tariff. Protection was all but eliminated from the British fiscal system (Gladstone's first government completed the process by abolishing the 1s. od. duty on corn left from 1846). Among the duties abolished was the excise duty on paper, thus providing for cheap newspapers and preferred in the budget to a reduction to a minimum of the duties on tea and sugar. The House of Lords rejected this proposal. In 1861 Gladstone consolidated all his financial measures in a single finance bill, the first time that this had been done. The Lords, faced with a single package of legislation, passed it, including the paper duty abolition.

* A position energetically taken by Palmerston in 1865; see Guedalla, op. cit., 321.

1860 was thus the last of what Gladstone later called 'the cardinal or organic years' of the introduction of 'the Free Trade factor'. The legislation of that year gave almost universal effect to two principles:

1. That neither on raw produce, nor on food, nor on manufactured goods, should any duty of a protective character be charged.
2. That the sums necessary to be levied for the purposes of revenue in the shape of Customs' duty should be raised upon the smallest possible number of articles.*

The British fiscal system was thus as open as it could be. The indirect taxes, reduced to a tiny number, were imposed on goods proportionately important for the working classes. The consumption of the goods on which these remaining duties fell—for example, tea, coffee, beer, spirits, sugar, tobacco—was held by some to be 'voluntary', so that those wage-earners who chose not to consume such articles would not have to pay any central government taxes at all.

This notion, widely held by mid-nineteenth-century political economists—more so than by Gladstone and the Peelites, who emphasized particularly the cheapness of administration and the high yield of these few taxes—was really a justificatory device, for if the labouring classes had acted 'voluntarily' so as not to pay taxes, the revenue would have been thrown into confusion. In fact, these items were so remunerative because they fell on goods culturally central to working-class budgets; in 1866 Gladstone remarked that 'undoubtedly not less than one-third, probably a good deal more than one-third, of the sixty-eight millions at which our revenue now stands, is contributed by the working population of this country. My belief is that the working man pays taxes in as high a proportion to his income as is borne by the wealthier classes.'†

The consequence of this limiting of the number of indirect taxes was that it made the raising of extra revenue much more controversial than if a wider tax base had been maintained, for extra central government revenue (beyond that created by increasing consumption and income) could be obtained only by raising the existing duties on food, drink, and tobacco,‡ or by controversially introducing new indirect taxes, or by raising direct taxes, i.e. the income and succession duty taxes. This limitation was quite deliberate; it was intended to shackle British peacetime governments to the minimum expenditure required by the minimum state. *Étatist* Gladstone certainly was, evolutionary in his view of politics and political policies he had learnt to become; but in his financial policy a different tone

---

* W. E. Gladstone, 'Free Trade, Railways, and the Growth of Commerce', *Nineteenth Century* (February 1880), 374.

† Speech in Liverpool, 6 April 1866, in *Speeches on Parliamentary Reform in 1866* (1866), 71.

‡ This was because the technique of reducing taxes to stimulate consumption of particular articles had obvious limits of elasticity; the technique had probably reached its limits by the end of the 1860s.

predominated: he aspired to a timeless equilibrium undisturbed by other than temporary dislocations.

The equilibrium never became timeless, but it was remarkably enduring, as the table on p. 115 shows. There was a difficulty as far as Gladstone's position was concerned. Once he had become a Liberal leader and especially once the franchise had been extended in 1867, any extra revenue-raising was, because of the narrow indirect tax base and the general Liberal predilection for improving the contribution of direct taxation, likely to be forced largely on to the income tax, making its abolition the less probable. His emphasis on retrenchment was thus reinforced.

The 1853 and 1860 budgets reflected, amongst other things, a close attention to the social balance of taxation. The years of Peel–Gladstone finance saw a slow but on the whole steady movement towards the equalization of the contribution from indirect and direct taxes.* Gladstone's attitude to income tax was always qualified by the need, if it were to be abolished, to replace it with some other form of direct tax and by its relationship to indirect taxation. In the years after the Crimean war, he consistently supported reduction of customs and excise duties. In 1857, during what was potentially the most successful of his various negotiations with the Conservative party in these years, he broke off the negotiation rather than give way on this point. In the Commons the difference between them was made clear: Disraeli moved the reduction of the income tax, Gladstone proposed to move the reduction of the tea and sugar duties. Derby told Gladstone that his Resolutions

not only point distinctly to an infraction of the *implied* engagement that the Income Tax should terminate in 1860 but also to an alteration of its positive enactment during the term of its continuance; and this, not to meet any sudden and unfore-

* Percentage of United Kingdom exchequer revenue contributed by indirect and direct taxation

	Indirect	Direct
1836–40	78.7	21.3
1841–5	75.2	24.8
1846–50	69.8	30.2
1851–5	69.2	30.8
1856–60	64.8	35.2
1860–5	64.9	35.1
1866–70	66.6	33.4
1871–5	65.4	34.6
1876–80	65.3	34.7
1881–5	59.3	40.7
1886–90	56.1	43.9
1891–5	56.0	44.0
1896–1900	52.4	47.6
1901–5	48.8	51.2
1906–9	48.3	51.7

1844 was the first full year of property and income tax returns; for details of the compilation of this table and of the indirect/direct tax question, see Matthew, art. cit., 638 ff.

seen emergency, but to enable the Government to reduce other Taxes, by again raising the Income Tax to its original amount.

As Chancellor of the Exchequer the need for a balanced reduction of direct and indirect taxation was one of Gladstone's chief concerns. But since the maintenance of the balance greatly increased the difficulty of abolishing income tax, and since its abolition depended on the substantial reduction of government expenditure, Gladstone determined to increase equally substantially the number of income-tax payers. For he believed that the more persons made to pay the tax, the greater would be the demand for the reduction in expenditure which would permit its eventual abolition. Hence the important reduction in 1853 from £150 to £100 as the amount at which incomes became liable to pay the tax, a drop which roughly doubled the number of income-tax payers on Schedule D. The £100 line was, Gladstone argued, 'the dividing line . . . between the educated and the labouring part of the community'. It was, as the statistician Dudley Baxter observed, 'the equatorial line of British incomes'.*

There was therefore intended to be a rough correlation between the income-tax payers and the electorate, which should consequently vote to hold down public expenditure. As Gladstone wrote in a public letter in 1859 to J. L. Tabberner, a propagandist for direct taxation: 'it is desirable in a high degree, when it can be effected, to connect the possession of the franchise with the payment in taxes'. This then was the social contract: the indirect taxes (now chiefly on items of working-class consumption) fell mainly on the non-electors or the 'labouring' section of the poulation, and the direct taxes (chiefly the income tax) on the 'educated' classes, those likely to be enfranchised. The £100 exemption thus represented the line at which the doctrine of trusteeship by the electorate on behalf of the unenfranchised wage-earners began. The wage-earners were, uniquely in Europe, virtually represented in Parliament by a self-taxing class of income-tax paying electors. Income tax thus reminded the propertied class not merely of its fiscal but of its political responsibilities; it united the two factors which Victorians regarded as cardinal to stability in the State: fiscal and political probity. It was for the electorate to support the chancellor in achieving probity by retrenchment.

The experiences of the 1857 general election, when Gladstone campaigned unsuccessfully on an anti-expenditure basis in Flintshire for his brother-in-law, Sir Stephen Glynne, and when most of the anti-expenditure Radicals lost their seats, and of the long battle with Palmerston and the service ministries over military and naval estimates between 1860 and 1863,

---

* The figures worked neatly; Gladstone calculated that to attain a £10 household qualification, an income of £96 p.a. was required, with the consequence that 'I do not think that a £10 franchise can in the fair meaning of the word be said to be within the reach of the working man' (*Speeches on Parliamentary Reform in 1866* (1866), 53).

showed that the House of Commons as then constituted was an unreliable check against government expenditure, however many of its electors also paid income tax. Moreover, Gladstone came to see income tax not as the restrainer of expenditure through its unpopularity, but as the creator of expenditure through the ease with which it could be levied, and the predictability of its return.

This left two possibilities: abolish the income tax, or reform the House of Commons. In the winter of 1863, Gladstone toyed with both. The arguments against income tax abolition had been resolved, and the contacts Gladstone had with trade unionist artisans during the preparation of the Government Annuities Bill in the spring of 1864 encouraged him in the view that a moderate increase in the electorate through the addition of articulate artisans would strengthen the economical wing of the Liberal party in the House of Commons. He also developed the view that the franchise should be related to taxation by arguing that, as working men contributed almost half of national income and, through payment of indirect taxes, a third or rather more of the government's revenue, it was fair that about a third of the borough seats should have a predominance of 'working class' voters.* Gladstone's 'pale of the constitution' speech of 1864, and his subsequent strict adherence to the £7 annual rental level of qualification in the Reform Bill crisis of 1866 and 1867, have therefore to be seen in the context of his views on the role of taxation in politics.

The effect of Disraeli's Reform Acts of 1867–8, which introduced a much wider (if still quite limited) urban franchise than the abortive Liberal Reform Bill of 1866 would have allowed, was to remove the basis of the 1860s settlement which Gladstone had helped to create. For the extended franchise of 1867 introduced problems of political communication, organization and policy of a quite new order. Gladstone's franchise proposals of 1866 were designed to consolidate an existing order; Disraeli's destroyed it.

The Emergence of a National Politician: Regionalism, Speech-making, Class, Trade Unions

Gladstone's budgets represented a compromise and a balance—a settlement in accord with the House of Commons as it was between the first and second Reform Acts. As such, they gave Gladstone a central place in the success of the Whig–Liberal ministries between 1859 and 1866. They also allowed him to construct a new kind of constituency in the country. Gladstone had no personal political base of the sort normal in post-1832 politics. He could not even get his brother-in-law elected in 1857 in the small county constituency in which they were together important land- and coal-owners. His position in his own university seat—which had no constituency in the normal sense of the word—was increasingly uncertain.

* Speech in Liverpool, 6 April 1866, in *Speeches on Parliamentary Reform in 1866* (1866).

After he joined Palmerston's ministry it was evident that his candidacy at Oxford would always be contested as it had been in 1853 (a contest in a university seat was in itself a grave mark of disfavour)* and few doubted it would soon be defeated. In 1860 Gladstone drafted an address stating his intention not to contest the Oxford seat again, though he did not send it. In the early 1860s he rejected a number of offers of alternative seats, though he did not wholly disavow his selection by the Liberals for the new, third, seat in South Lancashire, and his candidacy for Oxford in 1865 was, especially after his statement in 1865 on Irish disestablishment, virtually a challenge to the university to throw him out. Gladstone's rejection in 1865, and his famous arrival 'unmuzzled' in Lancashire, dramatized the role of popular politician which he had cultivated during the 1860s with considerable skill. Defeat in a wholly Anglican and largely clerical constituency also made Gladstone's position in the Liberal party much simpler. As he told Sir Walter James in July 1865:

These good people, my opponents, have been resolved, in their blind antagonism, to *force* me into the confidence of the Liberal party, and it really seems they are succeeding.

It has rightly been emphasized that changes in the nature of national and local politics in the 1850s and 1860s made possible the emergence of a new kind of popular politician.† We may notice here, however, Gladstone's own contribution to his success, since his emergence as the chief beneficiary of the changing political order was not accidental.

Gladstone had made himself a national politician in a literal sense. He travelled frequently, widely, and conspicuously, and he kept his friendships warm. There were few parts of the mainland of the United Kingdom with which he did not have intimate links and where he did not have powerful friends.

In Scotland the Gladstone family was, of course, well known. In this period, as first Rector of Edinburgh University from 1859 (elected by the undergraduates)‡ Gladstone made annual visits. Appointments to Chairs were made jointly by the university and the city corporation under the rector's chairmanship and he took his duties seriously. Gladstone in this capacity made several political friendships, and laid the base to which he returned for the Midlothian Campaign in 1879. He could, and did, remind his audiences of his family's roots in the Borders and Lothians and in the port of Leith. In Glasgow his stockbroker, Sir James Watson, was a powerful member of the corporation, and soon to be Lord Provost. In Wales,

* After Gladstone's defeat in 1865 there was no contest for either Oxford University seat at a general election until 1918, and only one at a by-election (1878).

† John Vincent, *The formation of the Liberal party* (1966), especially ch. 2.

‡ He was defeated when standing as Chancellor of Edinburgh University in 1868, the electors for the chancellorship being the graduates. His proposal (included in a permissive clause of the 1858 Universities (Scotland) Act) that the Scottish universities would use their resources more efficiently if they became colleges of one Scottish National University, was not popular.

Gladstone could and did show himself as an important landowner in a rich farming area, an encourager of industrial development in the Dee estuary, a well-known holiday-maker, and local personality.

In England, Gladstone's areas of contact were numerous. He could tell his Lancastrian audiences of his youth on the sandhills of the Mersey, and almost all his speeches in his Lancastrian campaigns showed local knowledge. In the Midlands his contacts with the Duke and Duchess of Sutherland, with the Earl of Dudley (his creditor in the Oak Farm disaster, also a Tractarian friend), his relationship to the Lytteltons of Hagley, and his links with sundry influential local solicitors (many started by Oak Farm correspondence but now maintained on a political basis), his experience with Midland capitalists during his arbitrations of railway disputes, all these made him familiar and prominent in the heartland of industrial expansion. In the capital Gladstone was a noted pedestrian by day and night, active in many of its institutions as well as being one of the best known lay Christians in the city, whose appearance in church could of itself abate an anti-ritualist riot, as at St George's in the East in October 1860, when Gladstone sat prominently in the churchwardens' pew with police in attendance.

Such a geographical range of interests might be forced upon a great Whig landlord by the accident of heredity. In Gladstone it was present largely by the assiduous nourishment of interests which, not being landed, would otherwise soon have withered. Railways allowed politicians to treat the British mainland as a single political constituency in a way physically impossible in the pre-railway age. But if Gladstone was the beneficiary of this new national political community, it was in large measure because he imposed himself upon public attention not merely in the metropolis, but also at many points on the periphery.

The nurturing of these regional acquaintances could encourage an impression of national reputation, but it could not bring that reputation to influence the practicalities of power. This could be done more directly first by the impact of things done at the periphery upon Westminster politics, second by astute use of the press, third by the control and demonstration of executive power. These three prerequisites of Gladstone's political success will now be discussed.

Gladstone's use of extra-parliamentary speech-making, dormant in the late 1850s save for addresses to societies such as the Society for the Propagation of the Gospel, was recommenced in 1862 with tours of Lancashire and Tyneside. Public orations increased his reputation in the regions in which he spoke, in the newspaper reading nation as a whole through verbatim reports of his speeches, and at Westminster, for one result of his platform speeches was to emphasize his separation from the conventional Whiggery of the rest of the ministry's leadership. The extent of Gladstone's platform activities of the 1860s should not be exaggerated—he turned down many more invitations to speak than he accepted—but they were large in comparison with his previous platform appearances, with his ministerial colleagues, and with his own behaviour as Prime Minister in his first ministry. By these speeches Gladstone, hitherto known mainly at Westminster, at Court, and amongst the intelligentsia, became a national figure, a household name among the middle-class families which attended the meetings or, a far larger number, read the six columns of closely-set type, reporting the speech in the morning newspapers.

Gladstone's relationship with the middle classes in the provinces, and also with the working classes, is to be seen, from his point of view, primarily in terms of his fiscal strategy. He visited factories and he marvelled at the achievement of the middle class: it was at this time that he hoped Samuel Smiles would write his father's biography. Similarly he assessed groups of working people according to the extent to which they complemented and buttressed that strategy, which to a considerable degree they did.

Viewed *en masse*, Gladstone found the working classes amorphous, obscure in their tendencies and potentially dangerous. He noted on Harrison Ainsworth's historical novel: 'Finished that singular and for the masses dangerous book Jack Sheppard',* and just after the débâcle of the Reform Bill in 1866 George Eliot's reconstruction of the riots in 1832 disconcerted him: 'Finished Felix Holt: a most inharmonious book. It jars and discomposes me.' But when 'the masses' were presented to him in an organized and particularized form, his reaction was almost always enthusiastic.

As chancellor, Gladstone received deputations from working people. As is well known, these deputations had a considerable effect upon his views on working-class 'responsibility'. What is rarely emphasized is that these were trade union deputations. In particular, the trade unions requested the privilege of using the new Post Office Savings Banks, a concession expressly conceded,† and in 1864 the well-known deputation in favour of the Annuities Bill, which spurred Gladstone to his 'pale of the constitution' speech, was a deputation from the 'Junta' offering the support of the new unionism for the government's proposals.

The consequence of this was that, when in 1867 and 1868 trade unionism became a question of primarily political discussion, Gladstone defended the 'Junta' (the Liberal trade unionists led by Robert Applegarth who turned their backs on Chartism) as being a useful adjunct to

* Another important source of contact with London artisans were the exhibitions organized by Newman Hall, the Congregationalist minister, and patronized by Gladstone.

† See S. and B. Webb, *The history of trade unionism* (1902 edn.), 245. An echo of this request is to be found in the only 'fancy franchise' of the Liberal Reform Bill of 1866—a right of registration for holders of a savings bank account of £50 for two years, in lieu of qualification through the property qualification; this would chiefly assist those in the counties whose houses were under the £14 qualification.

the consolidation of the 1860s economic settlement. In an important speech opening a Mechanics Institute in Oldham in 1867 he declared himself not hostile to the right to strike and while arguing an orthodox view of the wages fund, he did not 'deny, in principle, that it is perfectly fair, as an economical question, for the labouring man to get as good a share of it as he can'.* In saying this, Gladstone placed himself in an advanced position in the intense debate about the labour question in the late 1860s. But he did so believing that the 'Junta' and its moderate policy represented the likely development of the trade union movement; he rejected the more extreme demands of George Potter when Potter led a deputation hostile to what he saw as the moderation of the Oldham speech, and in his contacts with working-class support for the 1866 Reform Bill, he declined contact with the Potter faction.†

Gladstone confirmed his advanced position and his optimistic view of union moderation when he was chairman of a remarkable meeting of the National Association for the Promotion of Social Science in July 1868. At this meeting he stated his conclusion reached through his contacts with those of the 'Junta' who favoured co-operation rather than confrontation with capitalism: 'Experience convinces me that with respect to those from whom perhaps we might anticipate the greatest difficulties, viz. the artisans and skilled labourers of this country, we have only to approach these in the right way, in order to find them thoroughly amenable to reason.'‡

Gladstone's call, therefore, was for working people's allegiance to the economic order of a marginally modified free trade society. He sought exactly the allegiance reflected in these lines written in 1865 by Janet Hamilton, the blind working-class temperance poet of the Scottish lowlands, lines characteristic of the enthusiasm of at least the politically aware Liberal working class for the fiscal system:

> That gleg birkie, Gladstone, has weel dune his part;
> Exchequer's big pouches o' siller are fu',
> An' mony's the taxes that's dune awa' noo,
> An' labour's weel paid, an' the flour an' the meal
> At a wanworth—an' sae we micht fen unco weel.§

* On the other hand, Gladstone also argued that the capitalist should improve his machinery and 'make himself independent of those who resort to strikes', thus anticipating the 1871 Criminal Law Amendment Act. He also opposed 'restraint in industry' and restrictions on piece-work.

† Gladstone told Potter that the employer's right of dismissal was 'a natural mode ... of self defence in that friendly strife which must always go on between the capitalist and the labourer'.

‡ The remarkable assembly, in addition to 'advanced' employers such as A. J. Mundella and T. Brassey, included John Ruskin, W. Allen, R. Applegarth, Frederic Harrison, J. G. Holyoake, Lloyd Jones, and J. M. Ludlow; the meeting was to set up a committee, of which Gladstone was elected chairman, 'to diffuse information as to the natural laws regulating the rate of wages and the demand for and supply of labour, and to promote industrial partnership and the formation of courts of conciliation'.

§ Janet Hamilton, 'Rhymes for the Times, 1865' in her *Poems and Ballads* (1868).

Working-class movements that buttressed that economic order Gladstone encouraged, those that challenged it he disparaged. Thus he approved of co-operative ownership, because 'in the cooperative mill the operative becomes a capitalist', but the co-operative store could be commended only in so far as it encouraged a more competitive retail system, for the existence of the co-operative store could only be 'indicative of some defect, removal of which would restore things to their natural course' of capitalist entrepreneurship.

The great tours of Tyneside and Lancashire in 1862 and 1864 were celebrations of achievements, not campaigns for a better future: free trade, the French Treaty, the repeal of the paper duties, these were the themes of speeches which were already by 1868 retrospective. Criticism was confined to government expenditure, and the need for the new electorate to reduce it. As we have seen, Gladstone's call for reform in 1866 was for a carefully limited addition of frugally minded artisans to the franchise. Frustrated in this, he attempted to enrol the household suffrage of 1867 under the same colours: 'There are those who tell us that a Parliament more highly popularised would become more extravagant than parliaments resting upon a more limited suffrage. It depends upon you to falsify that adverse prediction (Cheers).'

The 'Cheers' may have caused a moment of optimism in the ex-chancellor's mind, but it was not to last. Gladstone believed that the extension of the franchise to thinking and articulate artisans would force the Commons to reduce expenditure; Cobden had likewise believed that it would reduce militarism. But the experiment was never tried, and Gladstone soon began to find after 1867 that appeals to frugality were incompatible with the *étatist* measures which as chancellor in the 1860s he had begun to introduce. His appointment of the rigidly orthodox Robert Lowe as his Chancellor of the Exchequer in 1868 suggests that he had already made his choice in favour of frugality.

'God knows I have not courted them: I hope I do not rely on them' recorded Gladstone after a Lancastrian tour in 1864. But the courting lay in the very existence of the tours. Many contemporaries supposed that the novelty of Gladstone's electioneering must also involve a novelty of message to the electorate. In fact Gladstone consistently used such occasions as an appeal for support for an already existing order;* only three times did he appeal for popular support for a novelty: in 1862, 1866, and 1867.

In 1862, on his visit to Newcastle, he made his famous claim that the Confederate leaders had 'made a nation'. Much repented and explained away later, this claim was both premeditated and popular. Gladstone had

---

* The 1868 election campaign was retrospective, in the sense that it requested popular support for an Irish Church policy already approved by the House of Commons.

used the same phrase three weeks before in a letter to Arthur Gordon,* and the same sentiments, less dramatically expressed, in a speech in Manchester in April. The speech was well received in Newcastle; Gladstone's view was not as heretical in Liberal and northern circles as was subsequently made out. If Gladstone's aim in making this speech was to use extra-parliamentary oratory to force the Cabinet into recognition of the confederacy, it was unsuccessful.

In 1866 Gladstone appealed at the Liverpool Amphitheatre for popular support for reform, but for reform as expressed in the very limited Bill with the £7 limit. He told his audience (shocking many of his fellow MPs): 'it is, to a great extent, in these great assemblies of our fellow countrymen, that the opinions and sentiments are formed, which become ultimately the guides of the public mind and public policy'. Even so, extra-parliamentary oratory had little effect on the Adullamites. Gladstone, though offered many opportunities, declined the next logical step, public collaboration with the Reform League.

In 1867, in his speech at Southport, he raised the general questions of Irish land and the Irish Church, but with no specific proposals, no personal commitment save by implication, but with an appeal for popular involvement and awareness: 'Ireland is at your doors. Providence placed her there; law and Legislature have made a compact between you; you must face these obligations: you must deal with them and discharge them.' The Southport speech and its exhortation suggested a departure from a mere appeal for consolidation but its consequences were not to be immediately apparent. Radical activity in the 1860s consisted chiefly of groups appealing for inclusion in the working of the political community. It was such groups that Gladstone addressed; it is not therefore surprising that his consolidatory appeals met so enthusiastic a response. It was his aim to encourage the disaffected Irish to behave similarly: 'What we want is that those sympathies in Ireland which now hang and float bewildered between law and lawlessness shall be brought into active alliance with it.'

Consolidatory though Gladstone's public appeal might be, his enunciation of it on platforms in industrial towns in vast speeches, nationally reported, created an unprecedented focus of popular interest in an executive politician, which in turn gave him in a parliamentary context a patina of strangeness, even of menace. As yet Gladstone had not tried to use his popular following against the Commons; but the threat existed, exemplified in the London crowds which followed him daily in the streets during the 1866 debates, that he might do so.

A further result of these speeches may be noted. They were the chief means by which free trade, for long associated with Radicalism and in

* '. . . it has long been (I think) clear that Secession is virtually an established fact & that Jeff. Davis & his comrades have made a nation.' Gladstone to Gordon, 22 September 1862.

a vaguer way with Whiggery, became an absolute article of faith for the Liberal party as a whole. It has been argued that the Liberal party was made up of groups whose chief point of identification was religious or parochial, that Liberalism was not an exact creed and that most Liberal MPs were not much more than men of good will.* None the less, the 1860s was the decade in which the Liberal party moved from being the party amongst which free traders were most likely to be found, to being the chief free trade party in European politics, with an absolute commitment to the doctrine which survived as the article of party faith virtually unchallenged until 1929.

Through Gladstone's chancellorships free trade became an administrative reality, but also something much more remarkable, for through his oratory the creed of the Cobdenites became the orthodoxy of the electorate. Further, the years of Gladstone's chancellorships came to be generally regarded as 'normal' years, the point of reference by which subsequent decades in the period before 1914 were measured. The early 1860s represented for the nineteenth century, as the 1950s did for the twentieth, the period in which the British economy behaved 'naturally', the years in which capitalism seemed to have created a balanced society.

The 'People's William' and the Press

Public appreciation of Gladstone as a new kind of executive politician had depended greatly on the rapidly expanding provincial and metropolitan daily press. Gladstone's awareness and use of the newspaper press was much more acute than has hitherto been allowed. He was, of course, the benefactor of the popular quality provincial and London dailies by his repeal of the paper duties in 1861, which made possible the development of the penny press. He exploited this advantage deliberately. When J. A. Froude wrote in 1861 to criticize Gladstone's handling of the press, he replied:

The whole subject of working through the press for the support of the measures of the financial departments is very new to me: I have commonly been too much absorbed in the business of the offices I have held to consider as much as I ought of the modes in which my proceedings or those of others could be commended favourably to the public notice. I will with your permission bear the subject in mind.

Gladstone found a remedy with little difficulty. The chief London paper to benefit from the repeal of the 'taxes on knowledge' was the *Daily Telegraph*, owned by the Levy-Lawson family. Virtually restarted as a penny daily in 1855, it had reached a circulation of nearly 200,000 by 1871, far outdistancing *The Times*. Gladstone had come in contact in 1860 with one of its

* See John Vincent, *The formation of the liberal party* (1966), *passim*.

reporters, Thornton Leigh Hunt, son of the essayist, J. H. Leigh Hunt. In 1861 they corresponded on the paper duty repeal. By 1862 Gladstone was helping Hunt gain access to details about the Ecclesiastical Commissioners, and a spasmodic but substantial flow of information passed from Gladstone to Hunt during the later years of Palmerston's government. In 1865, for example, Gladstone sent papers on the annuities legislation with encouragement to write on it, but with instructions about not disclosing the name of Scudamore, the source of the information. Hunt organized at Gladstone's request an Irish visit in 1866 by the eldest Gladstone boy, Willy, as a result of which some of Willy's articles on Ireland were published in the *Telegraph*.

During the Reform Bill crisis, Hunt's name is very frequently mentioned in the diary, as it is during the Irish Church resolutions and Church rate debates in 1868. The *Telegraph* was a strong supporter of Gladstone through the crises of the 1860s, and this appears to have been largely encouraged by his links with Hunt; certainly there is little evidence of contact with its proprietors.

The *Telegraph*'s view that Gladstone was the coming man was persistently pressed from at least 1862 onwards:

We have enshrined Free Trade at last in a permanent act. . . . The time must come, though patriotism wishes it far away, when the failing hand of the Premier will relinquish the helm of state. It would be ill for England, in prospect of such a day, if she had not one pilot at least to whom she could look with proud and happy confidence. She can, she does, so look to Mr. GLADSTONE, because in all a long career of public life he has never swerved from the path of manly and straightforward policy. His words and deeds alike have confuted the fools who hold that statesmanship is intrigue, and diplomacy chicanery. His words and deeds have alike confuted the cynics who think religion and morality are well in every place but a Cabinet. In his person it is not only a grand commercial theorem that has been triumphantly vindicated, but the sterling worth of veracity and the irresistible strength of honour.

Since much of the provincial press followed the *Telegraph*'s lead respecting Westminster politics, these contacts between Gladstone and the *Telegraph* are of great importance. As W. T. Stead pointed out, it was the *Telegraph* which created the 'People's William'.

Gladstone's attention to publicity in the 1860s was always exact, from instructions to his secretary about the release of budget figures, to his insistence on his photograph being sold for 6*d*. or under. That this was combined with an appearance of unworldliness was particularly irritating to opponents. Even during his commissionership in Ionia in 1858–9 the flow of copy for the press was undiminished, provoking Disraeli's exasperated complaint to Lytton, the colonial secretary: 'The daily advertisements respecting Gladstone, his intentions & movements, are becoming ridiculous. Pray give direction, that it should be stopped.' But this was a futile plea: Gladstone had reached that point when his own efforts as a publicist were no longer fundamental to his persistent appearance in the press: an action or a speech was news because he did or said it, regardless of its intrinsic interest. This enabled Gladstone sometimes to appear un-interested in publicity, but this unworldliness should not be allowed wholly to mask an acute and purposeful flair.

A Broadening Political Base

Gladstone's relationships with regional politics and the press were characteristic of a Radical; as such, they caused dismay and distrust among the leaders of the Whig–Liberal party; they were certainly not sufficient in themselves to carry him to the party leadership. The informal but tight group of Whig elders—if Palmerston may by the 1850s be so included—still played a role of great importance. But the ability of the Whigs to control the Liberal party fully was uncertain. In 1855, in the last great political crisis of the closet in the eighteenth-century style, the true Whigs had, between them, failed to form a ministry, thus letting in Palmerston. In 1859, a Liberal ministry only became a certainty after a party meeting. But if the Whigs' patronage was in decline and their hereditary right to rule in question, party had not yet risen in a formal sense. The prediction of divi-sions was risky, and a ministry could expect to be defeated quite frequently on minor questions and even, on occasion, on major ones, without being expected to resign or dissolve. Nor was the size of the electorate yet such as to require the strict party allegiance of individual MPs, many of whom still expected to be returned almost regardless of how they voted in the House.

Gladstone stood to benefit from this Parliamentary situation. By the 1860s, while not rivalling the Whigs in executive service, he was, of the non-Whig Cabinet members, much the most experienced. Italy had been the question which sustained the unity of the ministry at its formation, but Italy could not have more than a passing effect on party politics. Gladstonian finance pro-vided the staple legislation around which the Whig–Radical–Peelite coali-tion of 1859 could coalesce. The technical aspects of Gladstone's work as chancellor have already been discussed. Politically, his 1853 budget stabil-ized the Aberdeen coalition. The defection of the senior Peelites in 1855 was caused by the personal loyalty of Gladstone, Herbert, and Graham to Aber-deen and Newcastle, not by differences on general policy. The budgets of the 1860s and the gradual fulfilment of Gladstone's programme of treasury legis-lation constituted the main domestic achievement of Palmerston's govern-ment. Cobden told Gladstone in 1863, 'I consider that you alone have kept the party together so long by your great budgets.'

By his combination of administrative achievement and political moralis-ing, Gladstone appealed, not merely to the established Radicals such as

John Bright, but to the leaders of the coming generation of Liberal MPs, men of moderate but none the less firmly held Radicalism, such as H. A. Bruce, H. C. E. Childers, W. E. Forster, James Stansfeld, W. P. Adam, G. J. Shaw-Lefevre, Lyon Playfair: representatives of the moderate but committed readership of the *Telegraph*, men who were to epitomize the non-Whig element and to be the work-horses of the Liberal party in the 1870s. For his part, Gladstone gave these men their chance in his first administration. They were mostly men more interested in policy than in party, and this accorded with Gladstone's own view.

Gladstone's successes as chancellor balanced the mistrust which his Tractarianism caused amongst many of the Whigs. His Church policy was always liable to lead to conflict. In July 1857 he had prolonged the Session to prevent the Divorce Bill then being passed from forcing Anglican priests against their consciences to remarry divorced persons. But in Palmerston's 1859 ministry Gladstone avoided religious wrangles. His interference in episcopal appointments was cautious and he refrained from playing a public role in the Colenso case and in the outcry about the controversial Broad Church volume, *Essays and Reviews* (1860). Although Gladstone's personal beliefs remained resolutely 'catholic', in the sense that he used the word in his book on *Church Principles* (1840), he enlarged his experience by a series of meetings with Methodists and Congregationalists, organized by Christopher Newman Hall. Though Newman Hall carefully balanced the denominational membership of these meetings, Gladstone regarded them all as 'Dissenters': 'A conclave of Dissenters chiefly Ministers: the teeth and claws not very terrible.' These meetings did not encourage intimacy, but they developed respect on both sides. A potentially important barrier to Gladstone's party leadership was being removed. At a personal level, the many meetings at Penmaenmawr with Unitarian guests of Samuel Darbishire were of importance.

Developments within the coalition hierarchy fell favourably for Gladstone. Cornewall Lewis, the ablest of the younger Whigs of Cabinet rank, regarded by some as a likely successor to the Palmerston–Russell duumvirate, died in 1863. Of the Peelites, Lord Aberdeen died in 1860, Sidney Herbert and Sir James Graham (already retired) died in 1861, the Duke of Newcastle, the Lord Lincoln of Christ Church days, once regarded by Gladstone as a future Prime Minister, died in 1864, his mind, his family, and his estates in chaos.

With the death of Palmerston in 1865, this left only Russell and Gladstone in obvious contention for the premiership; Granville and Clarendon, the other possible candidates, would have to challenge in order to be considered. Some of Gladstone's friends had encouraged him to bid for the post-Palmerstonian leadership. But the circumstances of Palmerston's sudden death found Gladstone quite unprepared and 'giddy'; the Queen told Russell to be ready even before Palmerston died, and Gladstone, isolated at Clumber sorting out Newcastle's chaotic estate, sent an unsolicited letter of allegiance to Russell, who insisted on his taking the leadership of the Commons in addition to the chancellorship. Gladstone's position of heir-apparent to Russell was thus reached without any explicit struggle for power. His formidable political skills were known; they did not have to be directly employed.

A 'smash . . . without example': Franchise Reform 1866—7

The serious commitment of the Liberal Cabinet to a reform bill in the autumn of 1865 to some extent altered this. Gladstone's great measures of the 1850s and 1860s had all been carefully balanced compromises: the Oxford University Bill of 1854 which achieved a middle way between the Liberal reformers and the college traditionalists, the budgets of 1853 and 1860 which satisfied both Radicals and Whigs. Once Gladstone had achieved what he regarded as a balance, he stuck to it with obduracy. This was particularly noticeable in the case of the Taxation of Charities Bill of 1863. Gladstone believed that many charities were inefficient, corrupt, and misnamed, and that bequests by the dead which went untaxed encouraged posthumous vanity, while donations by the living, made regularly and unspectacularly, came out of income which was taxed. To round off his reform of the income tax, already extended in 1853 to Ireland, he wished to extend it to charities. Gladstone saw this as a reasonable and fair bill, a logical part of his great series of reforms; its failure was an unusual rebuff.

Gladstone saw the Reform Bill planned by Russell and himself early in 1866 in the same light. He had voted for Baines's Borough Franchise Bill in 1861, and had made a famous speech in 1864 in which he argued that every male 'who is not presumably incapacitated by some consideration of personal unfitness or of political danger, is morally entitled to come within the pale of the constitution', a declaration which caught the spirit of the Liberal press, infuriated the Prime Minister, Palmerston, and became one of the famous political quotations of the century. It was generally interpreted to herald a wide-ranging extension of the franchise. However, Gladstone explained that by 'capacity' he meant 'self-command, self-control, respect for order, patience under suffering, confidence in the law, regard for superiors'. The vote was a privilege granted to those with such qualities; it was not a right. Gladstone thought that a lowering of the borough franchise from £10 to an annual rental of £7 would bring within the constitution's pale a rather clearly defined group of men (and exclusively men) with rather clear qualities.

This was quite definitely not a call for what contemporaries called 'household suffrage' (a vote for all male heads of households). The £7 line was, despite the difficulties of the data, carefully calculated. Introducing the 1866 Bill, Gladstone told the Commons that a £6 rental qualification was too low: it 'would place the working class in a clear majority upon the constituency. Well . . . I do not think . . . we are called upon by any . . . sufficient consideration . . . to give over the majority of town constituencies into the hands of the working class. We propose, therefore, to take the figure next above . . . namely a clear annual rental of £7', which would represent 'an income very generally attainable by the artisans and skilled labourers of our towns'.* Like many mid-Victorians, Gladstone developed an acute sense of the labour aristocracy, and his bill was intended to complete its integration into the political community. In the context of the various schemes for parliamentary reform being discussed in the 1860s, it was, short of doing nothing, the minimum that could be proposed.

Gladstone's views reflected general contemporary ambivalence about 'class'. On the one hand, it was clearly recognized to exist, and the 1866 proposals made a carefully calculated distinction between the labour aristocracy and the rest. On the other hand, Gladstone believed—and it was a belief necessary and central to the Liberal case for parliamentary reform— 'that there is no proof whatever that the working classes, if enfranchised, would act together as a class'.† The thrust of the argument for incorporation through religion, education, fiscal fairness, and political reform, rested on this being so in the future. Certainly, in the 1860s Gladstone believed that such an incorporation was being achieved and that modest parliamentary reform would consolidate it. England's peculiar historical and geographical position, if wisely nurtured, cherished, and developed, would 'improve' her position 'for the sake of preserving it'. For England stood uniquely between the old world and the new, with aspects of both: 'she stands between those feudal institutions on the one side under which European states were formed, and which have given to England her hierarchy of classes, and on the other side, those principles of equality which form the base of society in the United States'. This blending of hierarchy and egalitarianism gave the English both their peculiar class structure and their chance for 'a forward and onward movement . . . an increase of attachment of the people to its laws, its institutions and its rulers'.‡

Gladstone's proposal for a limited extension of the franchise was based on arguments about the declining efficiency of Parliament and the virtues of the labour aristocracy which seemed to him self-evident: there were self-evident reasons why reform was needed, and self-evident reasons why reform should be limited to the £7 ratepayer. Moreover, this was just the sort of balanced measure which had stood the coalition well in the past.

---

* See F. B. Smith, *The Making of the Second Reform Bill* (1866), 67.
† Speech moving the Second Reading of the Reform Bill, 12 April 1866, in *Speeches on Parliamentary Reform in 1866* (1866), 109.
‡ Speech in Liverpool, 6 April 1866, ibid., 85.

This is not the place to trace the complex débâcle of the 1866 Reform Bill. Certain aspects of it as it affected Gladstone and his political position may however be noted. Unlike previous major legislative measures for which he had been responsible in the Commons, Gladstone had only partial control of the drawing up of the Bill. His usual exhaustive mustering of figures and facts gave way to confused discussions in a committee of Cabinet working with rushed and inaccurate data. It became clear to Gladstone at an early stage that the bill was in difficulties; he told his Tractarian friend and legal adviser Sir Robert Phillimore even before the bill was introduced: 'I cannot see how I am to succeed or how I am to be beaten.' He began to bring into play alternative political forces.

First, in early February 1866 he raised in Cabinet the question of a compromise on the long-standing Dissenter grievance on compulsory Church rates. By the time the Reform Bill was in serious difficulties, agreement had been reached with the Dissenters and a bill was introduced. Gladstone ran Church rates side by side with the reform question from the drafting of the Reform Bill early in 1866 until his Church Rates Bill emerged in its final form to confirm his links with Radicalism in 1868.*

Second, once the bill was seen to be in danger, he made two speeches in Liverpool attacking the Adullamite minority, an unprecedented extra-parliamentary appeal by a Cabinet minister on behalf of legislation before the Commons, ensuring that, whatever the fate of the Bill, he would have been popularly seen heading the 'fight for the future'. His support for dissolution and a 'purge' of the party, rather than resignation, in June 1866 followed from this activity. The Cabinet's overruling of Gladstone's and Russell's calls for dissolution saved Gladstone from what was potentially the biggest set-back of his career: a poor general election result, fought on an issue at that time intensely divisive for the Liberal party, might have created the circumstances for an organized opposition to his succession to Russell. Resignation, removal from British politics by a winter in Rome, and the extraordinary passage of the Derby–Disraeli bill in 1867, did not. Indeed, in the crisis of April 1867, it was Gladstone who considered writing a letter threatening resignation from the leadership in the Commons, while Granville and Brand, the Liberal chief whip, begged him not to send it.

The 'smash perhaps without example' of April 1867, when forty-five Liberals paired or voted against Gladstone's amendment to the Conservatives' bill, certainly was a 'smash' in the short term in the Commons. But what was smashed was not Gladstone's position of Liberal leader in the Commons, but rather his attempt to avoid household suffrage and keep

* For the details, see O. Anderson, 'Gladstone's abolition of compulsory church rates', *Journal of Ecclesiastical History*, xxv. 187 (1974); the Act was a characteristic compromise, seeming more radical than it was.

reform to the moderate £5 limit. Gladstone's political ferocity had been a ferocity of consistent moderation. The effect of Disraeli's intricate manœuvres was, as Gladstone told a 'Monster Deputation' of the Reform Union after the 'smash', to cut Gladstone loose from moderation: 'my proposal of the £5 is gone (cheers). I do not see the circumstances under which I am likely to revive it. I must reserve to myself perfect liberty. . . .' It was not difficult for Gladstone then to move quickly to support, before Disraeli's unexpected acceptance of it, Hodgkinson's amendment which seemed to lead the way to thoroughgoing household suffrage. Nor, given the extraordinary complexity of the implications of the various amendments, incomprehensible to many MPs, let alone electors, was it difficult for Gladstone to be presented in the country as the champion of the bill, the man who forced reform upon the Commons. On the other hand at Westminster he could be known as the proponent of that bill which the Adullamite Whigs would have preferred if they could have seen the end at the beginning. Disraeli's desire for any bill at any price so long as it was his bill, for any amendment so long as it was not Gladstone's amendment, could discompose the latter but not displace him.

Regaining the Initiative: Ireland and the Premiership

In December 1867 Russell announced his intention that he would not again take office. By telling Gladstone a week before he told Granville, his successor in the Lords, he effectively made Gladstone his heir. Gladstone heard the news in bed at Hawarden, almost blinded by a stray splinter of wood, a hazard of his hobby. Russell's parting gift to British radicalism was a pamphlet series on the Irish Church, calling for not merely disestablishment but almost complete disendowment as well.

Gladstone's Irish Church Resolutions of 1868 had therefore an immediate and impeccable Whig as well as Radical pedigree: indeed in the context of such proposals as Russell's and of those of the Liberation Society, Gladstone could even present his Resolutions as being a compromise to save the Irish Church, rather than to break it. The Resolutions, added to the Church Rates Bill already in the Commons, allowed Gladstone to continue to behave as he had behaved since the ministry's resignation in June 1866, as if he were a government minister rather than an opposition leader. Gladstone's first ministry had in a legislative sense started with the beginning of the autumn session of 1867, though he did not return to office until December 1868. He brought forward and successfully pressed through the Commons legislation and resolutions in 1868 as if he were in office and sitting on the government rather than the opposition front bench. He introduced his Suspensory Bill for the Irish Church exactly as if he were leader of the House, and indeed it was soon assumed, and has often been assumed since, that the Church Rates Bill was passed by his government and that therefore his first ministry must have begun early in 1868, rather than in December.*

This appearance of competence and control consolidated Gladstone's position within his party. Disraeli was caught in his own web: he could not put Gladstone's confused position of 1867 quickly to an electoral test because the tail-ends of the reform legislation in 1868—Scottish and Irish Reform Bills, redistribution, corrupt practices—took as long to pass as the England and Wales Representation of the People Act on which most interest had been centred.

As soon as Derby resigned through ill-health in February 1868 and was succeeded by Disraeli, Gladstone began to consider 'the personnel of our party with a view to contingencies'. In July he reached what appear to have been amicable agreements with the Whig leaders—first Granville, then Clarendon—about the distribution of offices, Clarendon being promised the Foreign Office. These conversations insured, so far as possible, against any move by the Crown to form a Whig-led ministry.†

Such a move was unlikely. Gladstone's standing at Court was still good. During Albert's life he had been a Court favourite.‡ Certainly his reverential manner had been in marked contrast to that of Palmerston and Russell. After Albert's death he had had an important and intimate audience with the Queen. His account of it shows the start of that unbendingness which Disraeli so adroitly exploited. The reserve this caused on the part of Victoria was apparent to Gladstone at Osborne in 1865; but so great was his reverence for the institution of monarchy that he seems to have been unable to adapt himself to the needs of its holder. Gladstone had had considerable opportunities as minister in residence at Balmoral in 1863 and 1864. He seems to have got on well, but not very well. Lady Augusta Stanley recorded the effect: 'Mr. Gladstone left us today, to our sorrow. He is most pleasant, but perhaps a thought too systematic.' But these were as yet minor, largely personal difficulties. Gladstone had handled the batch of royal marriage financial settlements in the early 1860s with skill. He had been the leader of the 'peace' party in the Schleswig-Holstein affair, his Reform Bill had had strong royal support. The Queen disapproved of the Liberal party's Irish Church policy, but, since the whole party was committed to it, this was not a question on which the choice of leader could have an effect. The summons from the

* The fact that the Tory budget of 1867 was largely and admittedly based on Gladstone's debt proposals of the previous year reminded MPs of his executive importance even during his worst humiliations in the spring of 1867.

† The court was ignorant of these mid-summer talks and decisions, General Grey, the Queen's secretary, thinking in November 1868 in terms of preventing an offer of the Foreign Office to Clarendon.

‡ As a member of the 1851 Commission which met often throughout the 1850s, Gladstone maintained his contacts with Albert even when not in office.

Queen in December 1868* after the Liberal victory in the General Election was therefore surprising only in the sense that Disraeli's resignation without meeting the Commons was unprecedented. From the point of view of the Liberal party it merely recognized a supremacy unchallenged, if not universally welcomed.

Certainly Ireland had played a large part in consolidating that supremacy, and these observations on some of the aspects of Gladstone's political life in the 1860s may fittingly close with a comment on his Irish policy.

On 23 November 1868, when the general election was virtually over, Gladstone published 'A Chapter of Autobiography'. The 'Chapter' explained Gladstone's changing views about establishment, but it did so first, almost entirely in terms of the effect on Gladstone's political development in the late 1830s, Peel's ministry of 1841–6, and the Maynooth Grant of 1845, and second, almost entirely in terms of changes in the 1840s in Gladstone's own position on State and Church. We have seen earlier that by the late 1840s Gladstone had indeed significantly changed the orientation of his political views. It can easily be understood why the 'Chapter' was originally intended as an election tract: its effect was to concentrate discussion of the Irish establishment on Gladstone, on the Gladstone of the 1840s, and on the Oxford movement.

By its compelling prose—it is the best written of Gladstone's pamphlets, with several passages reminiscent of Newman's artful simplicity—'A Chapter of Autobiography' deflected attention from Ireland to England, and from the policies of the Liberal party in the 1860s to the problems of the Conservative party and the Oxford movement in the 1840s. Though it alluded to 'silent changes, which are advancing in the very bed and basis of modern society', it placed these changes in the England of the 1840s. But if, from the late 1840s 'that principle—the application of a true religious equality to Ireland—was biding its time', why was 1868 the moment when that time had come? 'A Chapter of Autobiography' gave no analysis of Gladstone's assessment of the 1860s, save for documentation of his statements in 1863 and 1865. It gave no clue to the part that the parliamentary situation, Fenianism, and agitation for tenant right, played in Gladstone's conclusion that Irish disestablishment had ceased to be 'a remote question'. 'A Chapter of Autobiography' answered the immediate political questions of the day as obliquely as Newman's *Apologia* answered Charles Kingsley.

Gladstone's spasmodic comments help to establish a chronology of his thinking about the Irish question. In 1857, rather surprisingly, he told Aberdeen that 'Ecclesiastical questions in Ireland' were one of the 'great

---

* Victoria appears to have summoned Gladstone immediately and without hesitation, being concerned more with keeping salacious Whigs—Clarendon and de Tabley—out of office than with Gladstone.

subjects of public policy, which may be said to lie within reach'. Before the election in 1865 Gladstone, apparently with the desire of not deceiving his Oxford constituents, made a statement that the Irish establishment was in principle indefensible, but he committed neither the government nor himself to any action. But as Gladstone had believed this since the late 1840s, standing in the meantime at three contested and three uncontested elections for the University constituency, his need to state it publicly must mean that he anticipated imminent circumstances in which secret belief would have to become public practice.* Three days after making this statement, Gladstone notes on the question of a select committee on Irish land tenure: 'We *persuaded* Lord Palmerston.' In 1865, therefore, Gladstone was moving towards an active policy on what he perceived were the twin remediable evils of the Irish question: the Church establishment and the land tenure system.

Gladstone was by no means unique in this; indeed he had hardly reached the position held by the Whigs since 1835, let alone that of the Radicals. The difference was that he alone held a position which could offer success on both wings of the policy; he could throw behind disestablishment—the question which would immediately involve public opinion—the widely based range of political skills discussed earlier, and behind a new land settlement—involving the dislocation of an interest group—the formidable executive capacity which his years as chancellor had demonstrated. In February 1866 a large 'Budget' of possible Irish legislation was sent to him by Chichester Fortescue, the Whig with whom at this time he had a close relationship second only to, and perhaps equal with, Granville. From this, Gladstone strongly pressed for a large-scale extension of the 1860 Irish Land Act, urging Fortescue, 'if progress can be made in such a question as Landlord and Tenant I quite think it should be done by a Bill'.

The 1866 Land Bill, caught in the breakdown of party business and discipline caused by the Reform Bill, had to be withdrawn, though Gladstone was seen publicly attached to it. Gladstone had therefore given priority to land over disestablishment, arguing that the latter was too contentious and 'unripe'. The heat of Fenianism seems to have caused a sufficient ripening of both points, bitter though they might be. Gladstone explained his views to Fortescue in December 1867:

I am going into Western Lancashire next week, & I have just had an intimation that the *Liberal* Farmers are for maintaining the Irish Church as it is! This I suppose is the tendency which Fenian manifestations make on stupid men. Of course I do not mean my constituents.

* His statement in his letter to Hannah, sent on 9 June 1865 (which Gladstone knew would be widely circulated if not immediately printed), that 'the question is remote, and apparently out of all bearing on the practical politics of the day' apparently showed little awareness of the activities of the Nonconformists and Irish, until it is noted that Gladstone wrote in 'A Chapter of Autobiography' that by 'remote' he meant 'Heaven knows, perhaps it will be five years, perhaps it will be ten'.

The Irish question which has long been grave is growing *awful*. In my opinion this Empire has but one danger. It is the danger expressed by the combination of the three names Ireland, United States and Canada. English policy should set its face two ways like a flint: to support public order, and to make the laws of Ireland such as they should be. This is what we must try: but I believe we shall have to go to martyrdom upon it, which is a graver consideration for men of your age than of mine.

. . . Maguire has given notice of his Resolution only to occupy the ground—so at least I understood him.

I hope you will use every effort to come to an understanding with him & with others perhaps through him, as to a new Land Bill. Except the quantities which may be afforded by loans of public money to the Landlords, I do not *know* in what the Bill of 1866 can be greatly improved.

It would have been with the utmost difficulty that we should have got that Bill well supported by the Cabinet & our friends and a more ultra measure would only mean more splitting.

Gladstone's views on Irish land in 1867–8 were thus only loosely formed and he was as yet engaged in the question in principle rather than in detail. Moreover, the tender condition of the Liberal party did not allow an attempt in opposition to bring forward land proposals: that could only be achieved with the full panoply of executive authority. Resolutions of principle on the Irish Church, however, both unified the party and were possible within the limitations of opposition. It was towards these that the Liberal leadership moved in the winter of 1867–8, Russell's pamphlet giving the clarion call.*

Gladstone summed up the position in February 1868 to Clarendon, who was well known for his caution on the land question:

I have not yet seen Lord Russell's pamphlet but it is in the act of being born. It recommends I understand distribution of the Irish Church Revenue among the different bodies—this may be reasonable, but it appears to me to be impossible. The Irish land question becomes more and more complicated with delay. I am afraid it is passing from the stage of compensation for improvement into the very dangerous and unsound one of fixity of tenure in some form or other. In truth the aspect of affairs is to my mind more gloomy than it has been for a quarter of a century.

Gladstone's Irish Church Resolutions of March 1868 should therefore be seen not merely as an individual initiative on a single Irish issue, but as part of a general move by the Liberal leadership to solve both their party and their policy problems, Gladstone wishing to preserve more of an equality of urgency between Church and land than the propertied Whigs.

In the General Election campaign in the autumn of 1868, Gladstone

---

* Russell also prepared, shortly before announcing his intention to retire, an initiative on education, in which Gladstone was not included. Gladstone would certainly not have been able to unify the party on the education issue.

made this clear. His last speech in Lancashire worked up to a mighty peroration linking the various proposals for Irish legislation to the fundamental evil of the Protestant ascendancy, alarming the Whigs and using the simile of the Upas tree, a fabulous Javanese tree so poisonous as to destroy all life in its vicinity:

The Church of Ireland . . . is but one of a group of questions. There is the Church of Ireland, there is the land of Ireland, there is the education of Ireland; there are many subjects, all of which depend on one greater than them all; they are all so many branches from one trunk, and that trunk is the tree of what is called the Protestant ascendancy. . . . We therefore, aim at the destruction of that system of ascendancy which, though it has been crippled and curtailed by former measures, yet still must be allowed to exist. It is still there like a tall tree of noxious growth, lifting its head to heaven and darkening and poisoning the land so far as its shadow can extend; it is still there, Gentlemen, and now at length the day has come when, as we hope, the axe has been laid at the root of that tree, and it nods and quivers from its root to its base. It wants, Gentlemen, one stroke more, the stroke of these elections.*

As anticipated, the strength of anti-popery in the area meant that the majority of the electors of south-west Lancashire kept their axes sheathed, but Gladstone had already been elected at Greenwich as a precaution. The electors, old and new, in the country as a whole reaffirmed the reunited Liberal party in power with a majority of 112.

This, then, was the background to the famous scene in Hawarden Park on 1 December 1868, witnessed by Evelyn Ashley, formerly Palmerston's secretary, and memorably described by him (though getting the date wrong) in 1898:

One afternoon of November, 1868, in the Park at Hawarden, I was standing by Mr. Gladstone holding his coat on my arm while he, in his shirt sleeves, was wielding an axe to cut down a tree. Up came a telegraph messenger. He took the telegram, opened it and read it, then handed it to me, speaking only two words, namely, 'Very significant', and at once resumed his work. The message merely stated that General Grey would arrive that evening from Windsor. This, of course, implied that a mandate was coming from the Queen charging Mr. Gladstone with the formation of his first Government. I said nothing, but waited while the well-directed blows resounded in regular cadence. After a few minutes the blows ceased and Mr. Gladstone, resting on the handle of his axe, looked up, and with deep earnestness in his voice, and great intensity in his face, exclaimed: 'My mission is to pacify Ireland.' He then resumed his task, and never said another word till the tree was down.†

The description rings true. But like most descriptions of a Gladstonian moment, it was a partial truth only. It reflected Gladstone's capacity to

* Speech in Wigan, *The Times*, 24 October 1868, 6c.
† Ashley's obituary of Gladstone in *National Review*, June 1898, mostly in Morley, ii. 252.

harness an issue and to personalize it. It obscured his political breadth and all-round strength, which allowed him so often to surprise his colleagues and opponents alike.

The same day, Gladstone wrote a memorandum, not on Irish disestablishment but on the welfare of the Irish poor, for whom some of the monies from disestablishment were used. In his journal, he wrote at the end of this notable day:

Ch. 8½ A.M. The Lessons, as usual in times of crisis, supplied all my need. 'The Lord shall give thee rest from thy sorrow, & from the hard bondage wherein thou wast made to serve. . . . The whole earth is at rest, & is quiet: they break forth into singing.['] Isa. 14. Blessed central peace! Tried a little revision of Homer: but only a little. Read Swift. The Ball in evg till 12. Much babblement: & saw divers.

Two days later he went by train to Slough on the scheduled service. Hearing that Victoria was out driving in her carriage, he visited his son Harry at Eton College and then walked unnoticed from the college to Windsor Castle, avoiding the large reception planned at Windsor railway station. He kissed the Queen's hands and formally began the work of forming a government.

9. 'The House of Commons debating the French Treaty of 1860', Mezzotint after the oil painting by J. Phillip. Lewis, Russell, and Gladstone are on the front bench, with Palmerston speaking

10. 'Gladstone's First Cabinet', by Lowes Dickenson. Seated, clockwise: Lowe, Bright, Argyll, Clarendon, Bruce, Hatherley, Ripon, Grenville, Kimberley, Goschen, Gladstone. Standing, left to right: Hartington, Fortescue, Cardwell, Childers

11. (a) Gladstone speaking at Blackheath, 28 October 1871: 'I spoke 1 h. 50 mins.; too long, yet really not long enough for a full development of my points: physically rather an excess of effort'

11. (b) Speech at Blackheath, 28 January 1874, *Illustrated London News*, 7 February 1874. Note the real audience, the press stenographers

12. (a) Two views of Laura Thistlethwayte, as a courtesan (miniature by Girard) and as an evangelical

12. (b) William and Catherine Gladstone in the 1860s

12. (c) Harriet, Dowager Duchess of Sutherland. *Bust by J. Noble*

13. (a) Gladstone in the
1860s

13. (b) Gladstone in Privy
Councillor's uniform

13. (c) Sir Stephen Glynne

14. (a) A typical Gladstonian note, ordering books from a catalogue, his handwriting just past its prime but striking by its quasi-italic modernity, with none of the loops and flourishes characteristic of most of his contemporaries

14. (b) A holiday snap at Penmaenmawr in August 1874

15. (a) W. H. and W. E. Gladstone *à la mode*, as imagined by the *Tailor and Cutter*, June 1870: 'Mr Gladstone, like many other gentlemen who have made themselves a lasting fame, is by no means a "dandy", neither is he ever seen slovenly dressed, but is always neat and gentlemanly in his appearance'

15. (b) Gladstone (nearest the camera) at Edgware Road Station on 24 May 1862, the first trial of the Metropolitan railway, in which he was a shareholder

16. Gladstone as Prime Minister. He always wore a glove or a finger-stall to hide the forefinger mutilated in a shooting accident in 1842

CHAPTER VI

Travel, Family, and Affairs in the 1860s

Weekends and Holidays—Homer and Civilization—Religion and 'rescue work':
Gladstone as Pre-Raphaelite Knight—Family Life and the Political Circle—
Abroad: Ionia and Italy—'A rebellion . . . against growing old'

I am well past half a century. My life has not been inactive. But of what kind has been its activity? Inwardly I feel it to be open to this general observation: it seems to have been & to be a series of efforts to be and to do what is beyond my natural force. This of itself is not condemnation, though it is a spectacle effectually humbling when I see that I have not, according to Schiller's figure, enlarged with the circle in which I live and move. More condemnatory by far is the moral judgment: such snares of lurking unextracted sin in so many forms: and suspicion of secret sin that is secret only because conscience has become dull to it. In other quarters some better gleams of light. In the great hand of God I stand: how well that it is so.*

Weekends and Holidays

As a politician Gladstone was well known, even notorious, for hard work. His diary shows, however, that even a life lived at full stretch by the standards of the day left a considerable time for relaxation and activities not directly political—writing, holidaying, and weekending. By the 1860s the weekend had become an established form of relaxation, combining comfort in the great houses of England with the development of political relationships. Gladstone's weekends were spent almost entirely at Whig houses, particularly with the Sutherland family and their relations the Argylls, at their great houses of Chiswick and Cliveden; during the holidays he also visited Trentham, Dunrobin, and Inveraray. He was also a fairly frequent visitor to Lady Waldegrave and Chichester Fortescue at Strawberry Hill in Twickenham. The other main Whig houses visited were Chislehurst and Chatsworth (the Cavendishes), Mentmore Towers (the Rothschilds), Woburn (the Duke of Bedford), Brougham Hall (confirming an interesting friendship with Henry Brougham which developed in the late 1850s), Eaton Hall (the Grosvenors), Pembroke Lodge (Lord John Russell), and Broadlands (but only after Palmerston's death). The

* 29 December 1863.

only Tory roofs under which Gladstone slept in the 1860s were those of Lord Penrhyn in Wales, where courtships between Penrhyn's daughters and the Gladstone boys were proceeding, the Duke of Marlborough at Blenheim, an odd and unexplained visit in 1861, and, curiously, Lord Salisbury at Hatfield, where he stayed as his administration was being completed in December 1868.

Certainly politics was a chief reason for many of these visits but, especially at Chiswick and Cliveden, politics often took second place to religion and literature. A characteristic comment in the diary is 'Off with the Argylls and others to Cliveden. Conversation with Argyll on Future Punishment. We had a delightful evening.' Tennyson was also a friend of the Dowager Duchess of Sutherland and read his poems to the company. In keeping with this intellectual atmosphere, Gladstone contributed the Latin inscription for the frieze on the entablature of Cliveden House.

The Cliveden set of the 1860s represented Whiggery at its most high-minded and progressive. For Gladstone, this was an important political connection. Indeed, in the decade after 1858, Harriet, the Dowager Duchess, to a considerable extent took him in hand.* The Sutherlands were among the most influential, and were certainly the richest, of the great Whig families. In her day a great society beauty, Harriet linked the Sutherlands with the Howards and the Cavendishes; Lord Granville was a close relation on the Sutherland side (and consequently also Acton, his step-son); the Duke of Argyll was her son-in-law. The Dowager Duchess was perhaps the last of the Whigs to be on genuinely confidential terms with the Queen (she was Mistress of the Robes in various Whig governments until she retired in 1861). She was, therefore, a powerful political patron, and Gladstone's fairly successful movement into the Whig political circle in the 1860s probably owed a good deal to her shrewd management. He saw her frequently, both at the weekends at Cliveden, and in brief visits to Chiswick during the week. The link between the families was later consolidated when, after the Dowager Duchess's death, Willy Gladstone married her granddaughter Gertrude.

Life at Hawarden and holidays in North Wales constituted Gladstone's chief relaxation. In the autumn, he usually spent several months in the country. When chancellor, for example, he was away from London in 1863 between 31 July and 10 November, in 1864 from 2 August until 7 November. Business was conducted by letter from Hawarden, but heavy though the correspondence was—one day when his secretary was away Gladstone had to open forty-four envelopes—it could almost always be dealt with in the morning.

In mid-August the family usually took a house for three or four weeks

---

* Unfortunately, Gladstone's letters to her cannot now be found; Morley, however, printed a selection; Morley, ii. 183 ff.

on the North Wales coast at Penmaenmawr, near to where Dean Liddell
of Christ Church, the father of 'Alice in Wonderland', owned a house for
holidaying. At Penmaenmawr business was confined mainly to letters
with leading politicians; administrative correspondence seems to have
been occasional. While on holiday Gladstone worked on his classical
studies, walked and swam daily—'I find it a very *powerful* agent'—noting
the number of times, and days missed, in his diary. He liked the water
astringent, complaining at Brighton that the sea on Whit Monday was
'over-warm'.

    In North Wales Gladstone led his family great distances over the
mountains of Snowdonia, though he suffered from vertigo, much to
Henry Liddell's amusement (and perhaps relief in finding a chink in the
armour). A crisis on the Great Orme ended with these two Christ Church
dignitaries clutching each other on the heights, 'the Dean leading Mr.
Gladstone along, with eyes closed, while the rest of the party formed a
sort of buttress to protect him on the seaward side'. Gladstone also took
his family frequently to church, in Penmaenmawr on occasion to a service
in Welsh, though he was not impressed by the language. At Hawarden
the boys joined in silviculture—mostly cutting, but also planting—a
regular occupation from 1858. Cataloguing the already vast collection of
books, pamphlets, and private papers, including 'a bonfire of papers on
private business to 1866 inclusive', took up much time, as did the
servicing of the porcelain collection, which was lent out to exhibitions. In
the diaries 'worked on China' almost always refers in the 1850s and 1860s
to the collection rather than the country, even at the height of the Canton
crisis.

    Gladstone did not try to make Hawarden a centre of political activity.
There were some visitors of political importance. There was an important visit in 1855 from Lord Stanley, later 15th earl of Derby; the French
Treaty was suggested by Cobden in the Hawarden garden, Bagehot made
a visit in December 1865 to discuss the country banks issue question,
Lord Clarence Paget came to arrange a compromise on the fortifications
issue, an attempt at reconciliation with Northcote included a visit by the
latter to Hawarden, Anderson of the Treasury came to discuss Treasury
matters, and there were visits from Lancashire Liberal organizers such as
George Melly. But Hawarden Castle was not on the great house circuit,
and Gladstone did not attempt to put it there. Gladstone's many visits to
the great houses of the Sutherlands and the Argylls were reciprocated
only twice, in 1855 and 1867. Indeed he bore most visitors only with
reluctance and because they pleased his brother-in-law, Sir Stephen
Glynne, still the nominal owner of the Castle. Visitors whom he enjoyed
were usually academic or ecclesiastical, or close friends such as Robert
Phillimore and Sidney Herbert. Hawarden was a family home, with

'ordinarily a family song or dance after dinner', not, as yet, a political headquarters. Among the many family amusements was the writing of comic verses; these are two of Gladstone's contributions, written in 1862:

> There was an old woman of Ewloe
> Her habits were really too low;
> She drank like a fish
> And she ate off the dish
> This ill-mannered old woman of Ewloe.
>
> There was an old woman of Broughton
> Whose deeds were too bad to be thought on;
> She poisoned her brother
> And throttled another
> This flagitious old woman of Broughton.*

Gladstone built on to the Castle the famous 'Temple of Peace'—a library and working room—into which books were moved in October 1860, and it was at Hawarden that most of his literary work in these years was done. Before joining the Aberdeen coalition in 1852, Gladstone's books and articles had been very largely theological or at least ecclesiastical. Out of office in 1855, his attention turned to the classics, and in the subsequent decade he hardly published on church questions at all, though, as the diary shows, there was little slackening in his religious reading.† The exception was his extremely influential review of Seeley's *Ecce Homo*.

Homer and Civilization

Between 1855 and 1868 Gladstone published seven long articles on classical topics, a book of *Translations* (with Lord Lyttelton) of classical and romantic poetry, a three-volume work, *Studies on Homer and the Homeric Age* (1858), and prepared a popularized version of it, *Juventus Mundi*, published in 1869. Gladstone's abstinence from theological composition is to be accounted for partly by the fact that his earlier writings had led him into an impasse, partly perhaps because open conflict with the Liberalism of *Essays and Reviews* (1860) and Bishop Colenso's publications on the Pentateuch—the two theological storms of the 1860s—would have led to political complications, partly because, as his review of *Ecce Homo* showed, Gladstone had reached a position of some ambivalence on

---

* These would today be called Limericks; Gladstone called them 'Penmaenmawrs' after the resort he was visiting at the time. It may well be that this sort of nonsense verse was commonly called by its place of composition; Ewloe and Broughton are villages near Hawarden.

† Gladstone was publicly though not spectacularly involved in the Colenso case, being sued, as one of the trustees of the Colonial Bishopric Fund, by Colenso; the Fund had cut off his salary. He was involved in the case of Archdeacon Denison, found heretical on the eucharist; he wrote, with Phillimore, Denison's statement for appeal.

theological modernism, but partly also because he believed classical writings, and especially Homer, made a real and neglected contribution to European civilization.

He believed that the neglect of Homer at Eton and Oxford during his years there was similar and parallel to the neglect of true religion. In Gladstone's mind the two were inseparably linked. The ideal of the Christian gentleman was in his view not the erastian pentameter-construing cynic of the late eighteenth century, but the churchman suffused with the civic qualities of the Homeric world. His concern touched upon a fundamental problem for Victorian middle- and upper-class education: if the aim of education was to produce godliness and good living, how could the predominance, at school and university, of the study of a pagan society be justified?

Briefly put, Gladstone's argument was that civilization was 'a thing distinct from religion, but destined to combine and coalesce with it. The power derived from this source was to stand in subordinate conjunction to the Gospel, and to contribute its own share towards the training of mankind.' Thus the Old Testament was a guide to man's relationship to God, a 'master-relation'; it was not intended to present 'a picture of human society, or of our nature drawn at large'.* The earliest statement of the values and organization of a civilized society was to be found in ancient Greece, and especially in the works of Homer. Though he still worked on Aristotle, Gladstone came to find in Homer and his gods rather than in Aristotle's sophisticated secularism the most attractive parallel to a society based on a true revelation. Indeed, Gladstone believed that Homer represented the remnants of a Divine parallel revelation made to the Greeks as well as to the Jews and not, as some Victorians thought, borrowed from the Jews. To many Victorians, this was a shocking, startling, and almost blasphemous claim. As so often, Gladstone found himself closer than he expected to Broad-Churchmen such as Milman, who had so alarmed the Church by calling Abraham a 'Sheik or Emir'. Milman had shocked by demoting the Old Testament; Gladstone alarmed by elevating Homer to a prophet. It was not accidental that it was Broad Church classicist, Connop Thirlwall, who read the proofs of *Studies on Homer*. Greece therefore had in Gladstone's view a special place in the 'providential order of the world', and it was the duty of those involved in the construction of a modern society to study and expand its lessons.

---

* W. E. Gladstone, 'On the place of Homer in classical education and in historical inquiry', *Oxford Essays* (1857), 3–5. An examination of Gladstone's competence as a classicist and of his place in classical historiography will be found in Hugh Lloyd-Jones's paper, 'Gladstone on Homer', read to my seminar and reprinted in *The Times Literary Supplement*, 3 Jan. 1975 and in *Blood for the Ghosts* (1982).

Homeric writings were therefore not an alternative but a supplement to religious works. Gladstone noted on the day he finished the MS of *Studies on Homer*: 'If it were even tolerably done, it would be a good service to religion as well as to literature: and I mistrustfully offer it up to God.' Vast effort was lavished on these works, even when in office. A translation of the Iliad (never published), a translation of and concordance to Aristotle's Politics, and a 'Trochaic Version' of Homer, worked on 'even in Crewe waiting room at midnight' were attempted while Gladstone was chancellor. He noted: 'This attempt is of the utmost interest & attraction: it threatens to be a snare. I think of beginning to inhibit myself from touching it except after dinner. This will pretty well starve it.' But in 1864 he started work on the 'Shield of Achilles' instead. Not surprisingly, Gladstone was aware of the clash between his literary and political work: 'Worked on Translation in German & English: an agreeable way for a C. of E. to pass his time.' He was also aware why, as chancellor, he did it: 'Restlessness drives me to this.' In 1868 the preparation of *Juventus Mundi* was a clear antidote to rising political excitement as the result of the election became clear.

Classical studies were therefore both a vocation and a distraction. But they were doomed to fulfil the second role more effectively than the first. For Gladstone's studies of the society of the ancient world, while contributing to the eclecticism of Victorian culture, were not much more than an *ex post facto* justification of that culture. Gladstone used classicism to buttress religion: his habits of thought were at bottom apologetic (in the sense of being a vindication): he could never have seriously considered an intellectual framework alternative to Christianity. The implications of his views of comparative myth could have led him via the Broad-Churchmen towards *The Golden Bough*, but instead they did not amount to much more than a plea for more Homer at Eton and Oxford. *Studies on Homer* showed that John Gladstone had been wise in his choice of his son's profession.

Amid this prolonged period of classical studies, Gladstone's signed review in 1868 of J. R. Seeley's *Ecce Homo* (published anonymously in 1865) stands in lonely but interesting contrast. It is surprisingly favourable. Whereas most High Church/Tractarian and Evangelical comment was bitterly hostile, Gladstone's review was essentially a defence. Yet once more he was placed in association with the Broad-Churchmen. Carefully distinguishing the book from Strauss's *Das Leben Jesu* (which he had studied at length in the 1840s) and from Renan's *Vie de Jésu* (re-read for the review), he went to great lengths to show that the author was working in a tradition of exegesis scripturally defensible, and that the book was in its freshness and directness 'eminently suited' to 'the needs of our particular day and generation'.

The review represents, in fact, a recognition that the intellectual tide had turned against Christianity. The balance of intellectual presumption, thought to be so obviously favourable in the 1830s, was now uncertain: 'the evidences purely traditional have lost their command (among others) over those large classes of minds which, in their times, before a shock was given, or the tide of fashion turned, would perhaps most steadily and even blindly have received them'. Gladstone's own religious thought and practice remained unchanged, but he recognized that it was beginning to be a personal faith practised by a limited section of the community: the rest of the community was subject as it were to 'a distemper that infects for a time the moral atmosphere'.* Thus while he saw Strauss and Renan as intending to destroy, he saw Seeley, on the whole rightly, as intending to cleanse.

Religion and 'rescue work': Gladstone as Pre-Raphaelite Knight

If classical studies in the 1850s and 1860s represent an alternative to theological writings, Gladstone's religious activities after 1855 also show considerable change. While religious activity remained very important to him, religious experience appears to have become less intense. The diary for the 1850s and 1860s dwells little on preparation for communion, failures in observing Lent (though this was partly on doctor's orders), or on the obsessive distinctions between godly and worldly activity, hitherto a persistent characteristic of Gladstone's self-analysis. The dimension of the secret male fraternity of the 'engagement' has wholly disappeared. Of the lay Tractarian generation of the 1830s, only Sir Walter James continued in intimate contact with Gladstone, and even in this case, their fund for charitable work in Leicester Square was wound up in 1855. Contact was renewed with H. E. Manning and James Hope-Scott, the two catalysts of the great sexual crisis of the summer of 1851 but in 1861 with nostalgia rather than intensity:

Saw Manning: a great event: all was smooth: but quantum mutatus: Under external smoothness and conscientious kindness, there lay a chill indescribable. I hope I on my side did not affect him so. He sat where Kossuth sat on Friday: How different!

Liberal politics encouraged Manning and Gladstone to establish a working relationship, and this was done. But Manning's inflexible ultramontanism meant intimacy was impossible.

If less intense, Gladstone's religious observances were as regular as ever. Church daily, whenever possible, remained the rule; 'ejaculatory prayer' was to be secretly practised at odd moments, such as the striking

---

* *Gleanings*, iii. 41 ff.

of the clock. W. E. Heygate's *The Good Shepherd*, a popular Anglo-Catholic work of the period, whose subtitle, 'meditations for the clergy', is a reminder of Gladstone's youthful desire to be ordained, was read daily as he dressed in the morning and for dinner. Less obviously predictable is an interest in Jansenism; the works of Nicole, the sisters Agnès and Angélique Arnauld, and of others of the seventeenth century Port-Royal group were studied in French in considerable detail. Gladstone's Evangelical origins, still discernible in some of his notes ('The hours of our mirth are not the hours in which we live ... the hours in which we live are the hours of trial sorrow care evil & struggle'), may account for this interest in Jansenism, but his interest in ecumenicalism and his growing horror of ultramontanism in the 1850s and 1860s also led him to investigate any form of Catholicism which was unsullied by Rome. This was certainly the reason for his growing interest in the 1850s and 1860s in the Orthodox religion of the Eastern Churches.

As with politics, Gladstone appears to have become tougher and less vulnerable in religion. His religious charity work with prostitutes caused, or was the occasion for, much less highly charged encounters than between 1850 and 1853. The sign for flagellation occurs only once in the diary for the late 1850s, on 25 May 1859, as the political crisis of the fall of the Tory government developed, and the comments in the diary on prostitutes are on the whole formulaic and routine rather than agonized. This is not to say that there was any diminution in rescue work. It remained persistent and regular whenever Gladstone was in London, spasmodic but prominent when elsewhere, except at Hawarden. To a certain extent 'rescue work' had become a habit. If anything his success rate seems to have declined. Nowhere in the 1860s does Gladstone analyse its usefulness or its results, nor does he seem to have made any link between his own 'rescue work' which was conducted on strictly individualist principles, and his early and determined support in Cabinet for state control of dock-town prostitution through the Contagious Diseases Act.

Most of the girls to whom he talked appear to have been common prostitutes met on the streets and appealed to there. However, there were exceptions. On 30 July 1859 Gladstone met an artist's model named Summerhayes, who also seems to have been a courtesan, a common enough situation; she was 'full in the highest degree both of interest and of beauty'. After Gladstone returned from Hawarden in September, without his wife, although he realized his thoughts 'require to be limited and purged', there were several highly-charged meetings: 'a scene of rebuke not to be easily forgotten'. Miss Summerhayes was a striking beauty in the pre-Raphaelite style. Gladstone introduced her to his friend, the painter William Dyce, and arranged for her portrait to be painted. Dyce

painted her as 'Lady with the Coronet of Jasmine'.* The picture certainly
bears out Gladstone's remark that 'Altogether she is no common speci-
men of womanhood.' Later when she had changed her name and perhaps
her station to Mrs Dale, Gladstone met her at a meeting of the Fine Arts
Club held in his house, and their meetings continued fitfully until 1867.

Lucy Sinclair, also known as Phillips, was a courtesan of some substance—she had a housekeeper. Gladstone met her in August 1866. They
appear to have got on convivially ('singing, luncheon'), but though on
occasion they had a 'smart contest', Gladstone's feelings about her do not
seem to have become intense. The same was true with H. Hastings, to
whom he 'read the whole of [Tennyson's] Guinevere aloud' and Miss
Rigby, to whom he 'gave Shakespeare' (*The Tempest*, perhaps?) 'for a
practical purpose & advised to think of emigration'. Miss Cowper, a
courtesan 'at the very top of the tree . . . she has driven her open carriage
and pair daily all this year in the Park', did constitute a success, at least
for a time. Gladstone arranged for her to go to Harriet Monsell's House
at Clewer, the responsibility for the welfare of her King Charles spaniel
falling upon the chancellor.

Laura Thistlethwayte was to prove a very different case. Gladstone
probably met her in 1864, riding in Rotten Row where he often rode, and
where she was well known. She was the daughter of Captain Bell of Bell-
brook, county Antrim, and the wife of Augustus Frederick Thistlethwayte, a gentleman of means, with a house in Grosvenor Square a few
doors from Lord Shaftesbury, a brother at Eton and Christ Church, and a
lineage in Burke's *Landed Gentry*. Gladstone always referred to her in his
diary as 'Mrs. Thistlethwayte', or 'Mrs. T.', not giving merely a surname
(perhaps with an initial) as was done with regular rescue cases. She was
not therefore a 'rescue case', but she had been well known, even notorious, in the *demi-monde*. In 1869 she wrote a lengthy autobiography to
show Gladstone that her reputation had been unfairly treated, but unfortunately this work has not survived. It is clear, however, that probably
some time after her marriage in 1852, she experienced a religious conversion to a nondenominational ethical Christianity, about which she
lectured at the London Polytechnic. Gladstone attended one of these
lectures and noted: 'I do not much wish to repeat it.' After her conversion
she became a friend of the Duke of Newcastle and Arthur Kinnaird, and
it was in this context that her early conversations with Gladstone
occurred. At first their relationship was one of interested acquaintance.
They met and corresponded on occasion, but not very regularly. It was
not until Gladstone was Prime Minister, in the autumn of 1869, that there
occurred one of those Gladstonian emotional explosions of extraordinary

* This painting is reproduced in *The Gladstone Diaries*, V, plate 3.

force and danger. We shall meet Laura Thistlethwayte again, for she did not die until 1894, and the emotional crisis of 1869 was an important part of Gladstone's life as Prime Minister.

Through Gladstone's rescue work ran a strong pre-Raphaelite streak. He read 'The Princess' and 'Guinevere' to rescue cases; he compared Mrs Thistlethwayte to the second; he was reading Tennyson and Malory when he suggested that Miss Summerhayes should be painted as 'Lady with the Coronet of Jasmine'. The blend of duty and romance of the Arthurian knights was recreated in alleys, on street corners, and in Rotten Row. 'Lofty example in comprehensive forms is, without doubt, one of the great standing needs of our race' is Gladstone's opening comment in his review of Tennyson's *Idylls*.* London accommodated this easily enough. The controlled and perceivable relationships of provincial towns with their respectable nonconformity meant nothing there.

Together with the image of womanhood, Gladstone wondered at the image of London and the relationship in it of two worlds: 'the west and the east . . . I wish that those who inhabit the western portions of this great metropolis could, each for himself, endeavour to realise their immense responsibilities towards the vast masses of population which are as completely unknown to the inhabitants of the magnificent squares and streets of London as if they were neither fellow-countrymen nor even fellow Christians. Aye, they might be better known if they inhabited the remotest quarters of the globe.' Courtesans, prostitutes, and servants lived in both these worlds, hence, in part, their fascination.

Gladstone agreed to Laura Thistlethwayte's request that she should have a veto on what he told his wife about their relationship: 'I shall say no more to my wife, except it be with your free and full concurrence, and approval.' This placed their relationship in the same category as the flagellating rather than the charitable side of the rescue work: the only topic on which Gladstone did not consult his wife. It is clear that his relationship with Catherine Gladstone, while stable and very affectionate, had a clear limit to intimacy. Gladstone spent a good deal of time away from her, and she from him. He noted that his weekends at Cliveden without her were 'selfish', but did not remedy this. He told Mrs Thistlethwayte: 'from morning to night, all my life is pressure, pressure to get on, to dispatch the thing I have in hand, that I may go to the next, urgently waiting for me. Not for years past have I written except in haste a letter to my wife. As for my children, they rarely get any.'

---

*Quarterly Review, cvi. 465 (October 1859); this review is usually recalled for its criticism of 'Maud', but most of the review is a highly favourable appraisal of Tennyson's Arthurian poetry and of the Arthurian legend and its social implications: 'The Arthurian Romance has every recommendation that should win its way to the homage of a great poet. It is national: it is Christian . . . and, though highly national, it is universal.'

Family Life and the Political Circle

Gladstone's expectations of his wife in her post-child-bearing years seem unclear. He noted in 1862 when he had been reading *Tannhäuser*: 'Dearest C's. birthday. How much might I say of her as a hero-woman.' Certainly she often offered advice, on politics as well as family affairs. She handled Arthur Gordon's proposal to Agnes and helped the boys with theirs. 'Walk with C.—now rare' exemplifies the references of Gladstone to his wife after twenty years of marriage: he took it for granted that she would be on hand when needed, valued her advice and energy, but did not go much out of his way on her behalf.

On the occasion of her great need—the lingering death of her sister Mary Lyttelton in 1857—Gladstone paid only fleeting visits to the Lytteltons' house at Hagley, remaining in London to oppose and amend the government's Divorce Bill. After Mary's death, Catherine suffered a severe breakdown in health, the doctor finding 'her whole system much deranged'. This may also have been linked to her menopause (she was forty-six in 1858), though Gladstone says nothing directly on this point. The decision to go to Ionia later in 1858 may have been influenced by a desire to improve Catherine's health, as the visit to Rome in 1850 had been to help his daughter Mary's.

By 1868 Willy Gladstone was twenty-eight, and Herbert, the youngest of the seven living children, sixteen. No serious illness afflicted the children in these years, and their upbringing was on the whole uneventful. Willy bore the brunt of his father's expectations as he worked his way through Eton and Christ Church, never short of admonition and instruction. Encouraged, even forced into a political career, he was not even allowed to write his own election address. 'Most satisfactory though taciturn', he acted as his father's secretary in 1865, as did his brother Stephen. Stephen at the age of eleven announced his intention to enter the church, and apparently never deviated from it; he was ordained deacon in 1868. Harry, aged twelve, said he would be a merchant, which he later became. Herbert already showed signs of an easy relationship with his father, whom he also puzzled: 'Herbert's [eighth] birthday: he will hardly be an ordinary man, seems to have both breadth and depth.'

The three girls, Agnes, Mary, and Helen, figure in the 1860s chiefly as objects of education—unlike the boys, they were educated entirely at home by governesses and by their father. Although Agnes, the eldest girl, was in her late twenties, there seems to have been only one (unsuccessful) proposal of marriage, that by Arthur Gordon, who had fallen in love with her when he was Gladstone's secretary in Ionia. Lucy Lyttelton, Catherine Gladstone's niece, became almost one of the family after her mother's death. She often stayed at Hawarden or Carlton House Terrace, rode with Gladstone in Rotten Row, and listened to his speeches in the Commons. Her marriage to Lord Frederick Cavendish, which was not without important political implications for the Gladstone family, was the chief moment of formal family rejoicing recorded in the 1860s.

Much more worrying than the immediate family were the affairs of the Glynnes and George Lyttelton. Lyttelton was melancholic after the death in 1857 of his wife Mary, who died almost certainly from bearing their twelfth child. Gladstone tried to draw him out of himself by joining him in authorship of a volume, *Translations*, published after several delays by Quaritch in 1861, and by encouraging him in his educational activities. Lyttelton found some consolation in a liaison with Sybella, wife of Humphrey St John Mildmay, the Liberal MP. The Gladstones did not discourage this, and Lyttelton married her after her husband's death.

Sir Stephen Glynne's business affairs improved at this time, but the prosperity hoped for from the coal-mines opened on the Hawarden estates in the late 1850s was not realized. However, the mining finances were conducted by Burnett, the agent, with none of the abandon of Boydell at the Oak Farm fifteen years earlier, and the estate finances were not over-extended. The residual problems of the Oak Farm disaster were no longer acute and by the 1860s the way to an eventual solution was clear, so much so that funds were available for the development of the estuary of the Dee.

More dramatic were the personal affairs of the widowed Henry Glynne, Catherine Gladstone's brother and rector of Hawarden, who became entangled first with a Miss Lowder, then with a Miss Rose, daughter of a local pit owner and for a time governess to his motherless daughters. Henry Glynne's remarriage was of great potential importance, for, should he have a male heir, Hawarden would not pass to the Gladstone family, and the intricate structure of mortgages and loans, constructed in the aftermath of the Oak Farm crash on the assumption that Willy Gladstone would ultimately inherit, would be overturned. The Gladstones were strongly opposed to a marriage to either lady, as becomes clear from the diary, though no reason for this hostility is given.

Unfortunately full documentation of the Lowder and the Rose affairs has not come to light. It seems, however, that a breach of promise action against Henry Glynne was only avoided by a payment by Gladstone to either Miss Lowder or Miss Rose, probably the latter. The affair was publicly referred to in the *Cork Constitution* in 1861 when the paper, trying to discredit the chancellor because of his part in cancelling the government contract with the Galway steamboat packet company for postal services to the United States, stated that he had paid £5000 to avoid summons as a co-respondent in a divorce case. Gladstone told his solicitor:

In the present case it happens that some circumstances have happened to a relative of mine which recently caused me to be the medium of transmitting to a lady through a London Bank a sum of money: it is possible that this may have grown without any intentional falsehood into the fiction we now have to deal with.

When your contradiction has been inserted into the *Cork Constitution* I should prefer not taking steps to inquire whether other papers have carried the paragraph. It seems to me that with a public denial my duty terminates, if the idea of legal punishment or redress is not to be entertained.

This was the end of the matter publicly and privately; there was no legal action, and Henry Glynne did not remarry.

Gladstone saw more of the Glynnes and the Lytteltons than he did of his own kin, who were met chiefly at deathbeds. His brother Robertson was an exception to this, though, already in decline, he played less of a part in Gladstone's electioneering in Lancashire than might have been expected from a former radical mayor of Liverpool. Two of Gladstone's brothers' wives died during these years, Elizabeth, wife of John Neilson Gladstone, and Mary Ellen, wife of Robertson Gladstone. John Neilson Gladstone did not long survive his wife. At her funeral in 1862 Gladstone noted: 'There I found my three brothers & sister. I think not assembled since my Father's death.'

Despite this family disintegration, two important relationships were restored. The visit of Sir Thomas Gladstone and his family to Hawarden in 1856 was reciprocated by a nostalgic trip to Fasque, now Thomas's house, in 1858; the brothers were not intimate, and Tom continued to vote against William at Oxford University elections, but the hostility of the early 1850s declined. Helen Gladstone, whose harrowing experiences consequent upon her apostasy were of such central importance to her brother William in the 1840s, and who had largely disappeared from the diary in the 1850s, appears in the the 1860s considerably restored: 'Helen's birthday. Well, it is brighter than once it was.' He visited her at St Helen's Convent on the Isle of Wight and she became quite a regular visitor to the family. She remained a source of political embarrassment, being the only convincing evidence for the many charges of Popery levelled at Gladstone in Lancashire, especially in the 1868 election campaign.

One figure on the fringe of the family circle deserves some attention: Frank Lawley. Lawley, a relative of Catherine Gladstone, resigned his seat and his position as Gladstone's secretary in 1854 after being caught gambling with the funds. This lapse of probity by no means discredited him with Gladstone who assisted in his financial rehabilitation and subsequently employed him as a less spectacular version of Disraeli's political factotum, Ralph Earle. Lawley sent information from Virginia about the attitude of the Confederate Cabinet during the Civil War and, on his return from America, he acted as Gladstone's intermediary with the Adullamites during the Reform Bill crises, during which Gladstone records seeing him almost daily. Gladstone clearly tried to use Lawley to counter the chief weakness in his political armoury: his relationship with the party in the Commons, and with its organization. But if he had identified a problem, he had not solved it.

Gladstone knew Cabinets and the executive machine and he had to a considerable extent outflanked the party by his development of extra-parliamentary appearances. But, though he accorded party an important, indeed crucial, constitutional role, he had given little attention to the details of its management.

It is true that he might be called the first psephologist, for in 1857 he calculated the median percentage swing for five polling stations in the Flintshire and Flint boroughs constituencies at the general election, but this was not an interest followed up in his post-Oxford elections. At Oxford, tradition compelled him not to interest himself directly in the details of political management. In Lancashire and Greenwich in 1865 and 1868, he was content to continue this practice, leaving the details of campaigning almost entirely to the local experts, in Lancashire to George Melly and the Heywood family, in Greenwich to Alderman Salomons.

Though he had thought about the nature of the new electorate, and though he had a perception and active awareness of the dynamic economic and social condition of the nation, Gladstone had not developed any view of the relationship of the Liberal party as such to it. His technique as chancellor had been to gather the party in Parliament and in the country around 'measures'. But the specific financial reform measures used for this purpose were now almost all achieved. 'Measures' could be divisive as well as integrative, as 1866 showed. Gladstone had not developed any countervailing force to this divisiveness; his solution was more but different 'measures', presented as Gladstonian initiatives. The Liberal whips of the period, Brand and G. G. Glyn, were, as members of great banking families now also landed, well placed to manage the parliamentary party of the 1860s. But they had no answer to the constituency problems implied by the Reform Act of 1867. Certainly Frank Lawley, Willy Gladstone, William Gurdon, Algernon West, and the others who formed the immediate group of personal assistants around Gladstone when he became Prime Minister were not the sort of men to answer or even to address themselves to this problem.

Abroad: Ionia and Italy

During periods of exclusion from parliamentary office in the mid-century years, Gladstone twice took his family on extended continental expeditions, the first on government business (to govern Ionia in 1858–9), the second to escape it (to Italy in the recess after the Reform Bill débâcle, 1866–7). Both are of considerable interest.

The Ionian Islands off the coast of Greece and Albania became a British Protectorate in 1815. In the confused political situation of the minority Derby government of 1858, Gladstone, as described earlier (see p. 107), went there to act as Commissioner Extraordinary alongside Sir John Young. Young was a Peelite of the second rank who had failed to deal constructively with the Risospast ('union with Greece') movement in the islands—the start of many British encounters with nationalism in the eastern Mediterranean.

The Gladstones travelled to Ionia via Dresden, Prague, and Vienna. While in Vienna, they learnt of the theft and publication in London of a dispatch written by Young the previous year proposing the transfer of all or most of the islands to Greece. Gladstone thus arrived in Corfu to find a situation of considerable political confusion. After meeting the local dignitaries—for Corfu had the full complement from an archbishop and a chief justice downwards—Gladstone quickly began a paper on the islands' future. He also recommended that Young should be replaced and Young was consequently recalled. Gladstone then acted briefly as lord high commissioner until Sir Henry Storks arrived to take his place.* His function was therefore to offer a means by which Young, regarded by Derby as incompetent well before Gladstone was sent, could be eased out without a scene, and to make recommendations about the future of a potentially important strategic Protectorate†—the islands being with Gibraltar and Malta the only British bases in the Mediterranean.

As well as their general strategic importance (limited for want of a good harbour), the islands were one of the many factors in the Eastern question; 'this small question', Gladstone correctly observed, 'is the narrow corner of a very great question, one no less, in all likelihood, than the reconstruction of all political society in South-Eastern Europe'. Gladstone's appointment thus directly confronted him with a problem involving questions of strategy, imperialism, and nationalism, and in a crisis in which he had to act. As so often, his instinct was consolidatory. Though he went to the islands with some predisposition for their partial union with Greece, familiarization with the situation decided him in favour of

---

* Holding this office meant that Gladstone vacated his seat in the Commons; some Peelites indeed saw the whole Ionian episode as a Disraelian plot to draw Gladstone into a by-election which he would probably lose; consequently they saw to it that Storks's arrival was as speedy as possible; thus, by the time the writ for the by-election was moved, Gladstone was no longer lord high commissioner; he was returned unopposed in February 1859.

† Important in the sense of being denied to the Russians, though the union with Greece was regarded as dangerous because Greek politics were so unstable as to be unable to prevent Russian penetration of the islands, should they be annexed to Greece.

a bold attempt to convert 'the abstract sentiment of nationality', which he found to be 'universal', to an acceptance of the benefits of an imperial protectorate. This was to be achieved by 'Responsible Government', which 'may now be said to form the fixed rule of the policy of the British Empire' in all areas 'not stamped with an exceptional character, either as purely military Possessions, or as being in mere infancy, or as being too critically divided between dominant and subject races'. Nationalism, Gladstone argued, subsumed all grievances, whether strictly related to national feeling or not; approached, however, 'by reason rather than by reproach', nationalism could be contained, since 'free institutions' would create an educated class receptive to imperial considerations. Even after the loss of the islands was certain in 1863, he was anxious to avoid the Ionians being seen 'as "deciding" on their destiny'.

Not too much should be made of the obvious comparisons which can be drawn from this analysis; Ionian nationalism was pro-Greek and pre-imperial, rather than primarily anti-imperial and anti-British. None the less, Gladstone made it clear in a remarkable dispatch to Lytton that he saw the Ionian question in a general imperial context, and that comparisons with problems about the compatibility of nations within the United Kingdom were also in his mind. His analysis of Ionian nationalism was acute, and overran his conclusions in the earlier part of the dispatch: he did not succeed in showing that his proposals for constitutional reform were in practice likely to woo middle-class Ionians from their Risospast (unionist) position. It is unfortunate that Gladstone never attempted to set down in similar detail his thoughts on Irish nationalism which, as he hints, were in his mind as he wrote the dispatch. Had he done so, he would have had to think more exactly about the relationship of practical reform to nationalist sentiment in the United Kingdom, and about the precise meaning of the 'justice' he claimed for Ireland.

Ruritanian though the islands' society and politics sometimes seemed, Gladstone took his mission to Ionia seriously: no sense of irony is to be found in his observation that his work in the islands had absorbed him as much as any parliamentary business. But despite his pains and intensive lobbying, his proposals were completely rejected by the Ionian Assembly, which petitioned for union with Greece instead—an instructive lesson to which he seems to have paid little attention.

HMS *Terrible* was at the lord high commissioner's disposal and the Gladstones had a splendid time in the islands, with picnics at Homeric sites, expeditions by boat, dinners, speeches in classical Greek (incomprehensible to the audience, some of whom supposed them to be in English), and in Italian (the language used by the professional classes in the islands), and two visits to the mainland. The first of these was a stay of five days in Athens where they saw the classical sites and met the

British community and the Court, which used Gladstone's visit to encourage anti-Russian feeling by excluding pro-Russian Greeks from the
proceedings. Gladstone was less excited by his visit to the Acropolis than
might have been expected. Perhaps it was too rushed ('The view—the
ruins—& the sculptures, taken together are almost too much for one
day'), perhaps his dealings with the unpopular Court (the King was
forced to abdicate in 1862) spoilt the atmosphere. The second visit was an
overnight trip to Philiates in Albania, then part of the Ottoman Empire.
His only visit to Turkish soil dismayed him:

Off at 11½ for Filates: 1½ h. steam, 3 h. hard walk. We were the guests of the Validi
Jaffier Pacha. Visited the mosque, heard the muezzin, & went through the town.
Turkish dinner, in rude abundance: after wh I smoked my first & last Chibouk.
Conversation by interpreters with our hostess respecting her Son whom she
wants me (!) to get appointed Pacha in Albania: & with the Moodir. Turkish
night accommodation too. The whole impression is most saddening: it is all all
indolence, decay, stagnation: the image of God seems as if it were nowhere.
    But there is much of wild & picturesque.

    While in the Mediterranean, Gladstone had much opportunity to
observe the Greek Orthodox Church at work, which he had hitherto
studied only theoretically. He was impressed by the fusion of the Church
with the people, and in visiting the monastery on Corfu where Capo-
distria is buried he noted 'I have not in the Latin countries seen any
monastery like this.' His view of Roman Catholicism was becoming
increasingly pessimistic, and this sympathy for Orthodoxy was to have
important consequences when the fate of the Orthodox Christian subjects
of the Ottoman Empire became a central concern at the time of the
Bulgarian atrocities in 1876.
    While returning from Ionia in 1859, Gladstone passed through north-
ern Italy, which was virtually in a state of war. In Milan he met Cavour
and other Risorgimentist leaders who took him into their confidence
about their plans, as a result of which Gladstone arrived in London
sympathetic to change in Italy, a sympathy reflected in his article in the
Quarterly and in his early activity in Palmerston's ministry. This sympathy was chiefly for moves against Austria and against the Pope's
temporal power; in 1859 Gladstone did not in principle favour major
increases in Sardinia's territory, though he shifted his view on this in
1861.
    Gladstone visited Italy again in 1866, to recover and to distance himself
from English reform politics. While in Rome he had two audiences with
the Pope, observed the making of the Vatican Council of 1870, and was
dismayed, a feeling shared by Sir John Acton, also in Rome at that time.
During this visit, Gladstone's relationship with Acton considerably deepened. Hitherto it had centred round exchanges of letters and meetings

in company at Gladstone's breakfast parties. When they had met more privately, as at Cliveden, Gladstone had been much impressed: 'the more I see the more I like. *Si sic omnes*.' Drives and dinner parties in Rome allowed Gladstone's opinion of Acton to be confirmed. One of Gladstone's aims in visiting Italy at this time was to assist his friend Father Tosti in saving the monastery of Monte Cassino, then in the process of being secularized. The exact details of Gladstone's part in the compromise reached are not clear; he raised the matter when visiting Florence (then the Italian capital) on his way home, when he also advised Scialoja on the preparation of the Italian Budget.

These two foreign journeys occasioned none of the emotional crises which characterized all Gladstone's previous expeditions abroad. They did however confront him with two of the problems which were to be in the forefront of his mind in the early years of his first ministry: nationalism and ultramontanism.

'A rebellion . . . against growing old'

Gladstone's diary in the 1860s contains no single theme to which the diarist returns, almost obsessively, as was the case in the 1840s. That there was no such theme accounts perhaps for Gladstone's feeling of suspension: 'the horizon enlarges, the sky drifts around me' and 'a man does not see much of the country through which the river winds'. In the 1850s and 1860s, Gladstone used his financial policy, interpreted in its widest sense, to stabilize and check this feeling of drift. He was remarkably successful in suggesting to himself and to his countrymen an illusion of stability and, following it in the second half of the 1860s, of change to consolidate that stability. Whether Gladstone's view of the State, a strange mixture of organic and pluralist practice and theory, could offer a permanent solution remains to be seen. What is clear is that Gladstone faced the world bleakly and increasingly alone:

There is a resistance to the passage of Time as if I could lay hands on it & stop it: as if youth were yet in me & life and youth were one.

All the world seems to lie before me, none behind.

I feel within me the rebellious unspoken word, I will not be old.

The strangest though not the worst of all in me is a rebellion (I know not what else to call it) against growing old.

Above all, the 1860s show Gladstone progressively isolated but persistently resilient. Resilient, in that the years after 1865 showed him flexible and inventive enough to move from the settled and predictable field of government trade and finance to a central point in the increasingly volatile and complex politics of British Liberal-Radicalism in such a way as both to encourage and control them. Isolated, in that he lived on, both the only survivor of the Tractarian politicians of the 1830s, and the chief relic of the Peelite Conservatives, still described in *Dod's Parliamentary Companion* (until 1870) as a Liberal-Conservative. He noted in 1864:

Newcastle's death removes the very last of those contemporaries who were also my political friends. How it speaks to me!
  'Be doing: and be done'.

To 'be doing' was never a problem for Gladstone; to 'be done' was to prove a painful process, for him and for others.

CHAPTER VII

The First Government: Ireland, Education, and External Policy

Gladstone and the Victorian State—Expectations of Office—Cabinet and Court—Foreign Policy: united Germany and re-united United States—The Colonies Old and New: free trade, retrenchment, and expansion—The Upas Tree: the Irish Church—The Upas Tree: Irish land—The Upas Tree: Irish education—Education in Scotland and England, 1869–70

'Truth, justice, order, peace, honour, duty, liberty, piety', these are the objects before me in my daily prayers with reference to my public function, which for the present commands (and I fear damages) every other: but this is the best part of me. All the rest is summed up in 'miserere'.

And so falls the curtain on another anxious and eventful year [1872]: probably the last of the present cares, and coming near the last of all.

The year [1873] ends as it were in tumult. My constant tumult of business makes other tumult more sensible. Upon me still continued blessings rain: but in return I seem to render nothing except a hope that a time may come when my spirit instead of grovelling may become erect, and look at God. For I cannot, as I now am, get sufficiently out of myself to judge myself, and unravel the knots of being and doing, of which my life seems to be full.

Gladstone and the Victorian State

That Gladstone regarded the premiership which began in December 1868 as his last as well as his first, can hardly be doubted by any reader of his journal. Anticipation of retirement is perhaps the most frequently reiterated theme in moments of recorded private reflection and in hints in private correspondence. The foreknowledge of the dramas of subsequent decades should not warp the reader's perspective on Gladstone's attitude of mind as he kissed hands as First Lord of the Treasury, thus becoming Prime Minister of the only world power.

Politically, Gladstone's view was consistent. For the previous two decades he had seen politics and policies from the perspective of the Treasury. As Chancellor of the Exchequer he had been the codifier, legislator, and guardian of the canons of Peelite finance. Under his suzerainty the Treasury had become the guarantor of the 'minimalist' State.

No industrial economy can have existed in which the State played a smaller role than that of the United Kingdom in the 1860s. Government had appeared to forswear responsibility for fiscal and economic management and it had abolished virtually all tariffs, save those non-protective duties required for revenue purposes. As yet, government responsibility for education existed only through its relationship with the Established Church and its schools and universities, and through small grants to non-established denominations. Government involvement in industrial relations and legislation was largely confined to labour relations in the royal dockyards and to the inspectorate created by the Factory Acts. The concept of social welfare in the twentieth-century sense did not exist. Government grudgingly accepted a 'last resort' responsibility in the specific areas of public health and pauperism, but this was a responsibility to prevent disease in the first case and death in the second, not a responsibility for any positive concern in the welfare of individuals.

Gladstone's part in the construction of this model had been self-conscious and deliberate. His Chancellorship had had as its first aim 'to complete the construction of a real department of Finance' and this had been achieved. There remained outstanding items, aspects of the great plan of 1856 which had not yet been executed, but their absence did not detract from the fundamental success of the plans of the 1850s and 1860s.

Even by the 1860s, the 'minimalist' State in Britain was under attack, both directly and by attrition. It was already clear that neither the Established Church nor voluntaryism could meet the demand for education. Gladstone himself had introduced, in direct and controversial competition with the friendly societies, state-guaranteed annuities which, although self-financing, voluntary, and in practice ineffective, pointed the way to National Insurance.

As a good Peelite, Gladstone had always accepted that the reserve powers of the executive must be retained. He did not accept constitutional devices which would impede executive spending should the policy for such spending be agreed upon, and his criticism of the Bank Act of 1844 was not that it was monopolistic, but that it was inefficient. One of his Cabinet's first acts was to consolidate the preceding Tory government's nationalization of the telegraph system. Gladstone's religion, his Peelism, and his innate political and executive activism prevented him from ever being a thoroughgoing *laisser-faire* Liberal. Indeed, as we have already seen, there was always a strong *étatist* element in Gladstone which lay ambivalently and uneasily side-by-side with his fiscal liberalism. For he certainly looked to free trade as providing, in the realm of secular affairs, what he regarded as a second-order political morality, his own first-order concept of a confessional, Anglican State having been set aside in the 1840s, though not wholly abandoned.

There were always, therefore, substantial qualifications both in Gladstone's mind and in the minds of most mid-Victorians to the view that minimal 'interference' was the best government. It is probably the case that, although the minimalist State was achieved in Victorian Britain in the fullest form compatible with the social requirements of an industrialized population, none the less, in these qualifications were contained the assumptions which were to lead to its gradual disintegration. But the consequences of these qualifications upon the minimalist State were as yet faint and ill-perceived. Though many of the measures of Gladstone's first administration prepared the ground for future developments, these were not intentionally pursued, at least at Cabinet level. For this was a Cabinet, not just a Prime Minister, in deadly earnest about retrenchment. In one area at least—that of the Poor Law now supervised, from 1871, by the new Local Government Board under G. J. Goschen—the administration could claim spectacular success in enforcing a dramatic reduction in supposedly sentimental and unsystematic outdoor poor relief, and in making, in co-operation with the Charity Organization Society (1869), the most sustained attempt of the century to impose upon the working classes the Victorian values of providence, self-reliance, foresight, and self-discipline.*

Looking at the architecture of the State in the late 1860s, Gladstone saw the grand design largely fulfilled. The odd cornice remained to be completed, but the foundations and superstructure were built. Gladstone saw his first government not as the new dawn of thoroughgoing liberalism emancipated by democracy, but as the setting of the sun at the end of the day of the building of the mid-century edifice. The long-term implication of the household suffrage was, no doubt, the destruction of this creation. But it must be remembered that, as we have seen, Gladstone had not sought the household suffrage of 1867, had resisted it until it was forced upon him, and had promoted limited franchise reform in 1866 as a means of consolidating the mid-century order of State, party, and politics, not of undermining it.

There is an interesting contrast between Gladstone and Disraeli. Disraeli, though relating the nineteenth century to an ideal model of a Tory constitution corrupted by Whiggery and now unattainable, saw the politics of his own day as a process, an endless series of contingencies, one leading on to the next. A part of Gladstone certainly shared this sense of contingency, also sharing the sense of a relationship to a past ideal now unattainable. When dealing with questions in which general principles related to particular legislative proposals—disestablishment, franchise reform, women's suffrage—Gladstone showed a subtle, perhaps an over-subtle,

---

* See M. E. Rose, 'The crisis of poor relief in England 1860–1880' in W. J. Mommsen, ed., *The emergence of the Welfare State in Britain and Germany* (1981) and C. L. Mowat, *The Charity Organization Society 1869–1913* (1961); Gladstone was associated with its first Report in 1870, ibid., p. 19.

understanding of the value of time. Privately held views required a sense of 'ripeness' of public opinion before their disclosure. There was a world of difference between an abstract resolution and its legislative expression in a Statute. Hence a political leader could use time as a solvent; the process of politics discouraged the expression of final positions with respect to the future.* But an important part of Gladstone did not share this sense of flux and impermanence. To an extent, bounded particularly by his financial and administrative policies, he sought a final settlement of the State, the establishment of modes of conduct which should require no fundamental review. Although placing himself on the side of historic development— 'time is on our side', the 'forward and onward movement' of social forces— Gladstone had no sense of the evolution of the fiscal or perhaps of the administrative State beyond his own time, and many of his boldest policies were intended to confirm the future in the mold of the present. Of course, we must not overemphasize this yearning for permanence; the active side of Gladstone's political nature assumed change and responded to it—few politicians could do so more formidably. None the less, Gladstone was unusual among British Prime Ministers in expecting the permanent settlement of some fundamental questions of economic policy.

Expectations of Office

Unlike 1859, Gladstone came into office in 1868 with no overall legislative programme. He entered office intent on making the existing structure of government work, improving it at the margin, and legislating on Ireland. No great lists of topics to be tackled were drawn up, and apart from the Irish Church, the programme for the first session ('Bankruptcy—Middle Schools—Scotch Education—Irish railways—Rating clauses') was modest. It was not, of course, the case that a government would play all its cards in its first session—and the Cabinet in 1868 could theoretically expect the norm of six years of office—but there seems little evidence that Gladstone in December 1868 had a clear view of the overall legislative future of his administration.

Of course, there was nothing unusual in this. Peel had been exceptional among Prime Ministers in being seen as the originator of many of the legislative measures of his administration. It would not have occurred to Melbourne, Aberdeen, or Palmerston that his duty as Prime Minister was personally to stimulate, far less personally to draw up, bills for Parliament, or that his government should be judged by legislative achievement. Russell's view in 1848 had characterized the epoch between the first two Reform Acts: 'It is not the sole or principal duty of a government to introduce legislative measures or to carry them through Parliament.'

* Gladstone's method (in this case with respect to women's suffrage) is well described in Ann Robson, 'A Bird's Eye View of Gladstone' in B. L. Kinzer, ed., *The Gladstonian Turn of Mind* (1985).

It was Gladstone's problem that his career had hitherto been unusually associated with great legislative successes, and that many of his supporters expected legislation of a dramatic sort to follow the 1867 Reform Act and the great electoral victory of 1868. Allied to this was Gladstone's view of the minimalist State, which was primarily fiscal. Fiscal policies for Gladstone always implied moral principles: he never took a narrow or mechanistic view of fiscal questions, but rather regarded them as being the political and administrative expression of a comprehensive set of moral beliefs. But the form of this expression was fiscal, a general Peelite emphasis, intensified for Gladstone by his long tenure of the Chancellorship of the Exchequer.

The curious dislocation of early Victorian politics had meant that fiscal liberalism had been achieved while political liberalism had been barely begun. Such had indeed been the Peelite objective: to show that fiscal liberalism was possible without political reform; equality of opportunity should be the gradual consequence of fiscal measures, not the result of deliberately pursued programmes of social and political reform. Gladstone by no means shared the view that free trade in tariffs should be mirrored by free trade in religion, or that the Burkean social structure of England should be disrupted save by the slow consequences of economic competition. He reminded his supporters of his move towards pluralism in the 1840s by publishing 'A Chapter of Autobiography' at the end of the election campaign in 1868, but in practice his interest in disestablishment was confined to Ireland. A politician might perceive a result to be politically probable, without having an onus personally to promote it. Indeed Gladstone seems in the late 1860s more sceptical about the value of political liberalism generally than he had been in the days of readjustment of theoretical questions of Church and State in the late 1840s.

Not so his supporters. Buoyed up by the great Nonconformist revival of the 1860s, Dissenters saw the victory of 1868 as the occasion for an assertion of the political priorities of Nonconformity: general disestablishment, abolition of university tests, a Burials Bill. The disestablishment of the Anglican Church would lead to social and political equality in the same way that Peelite finance had led to fiscal and economic equality. Allied to these proposals were those of the intellectuals, especially demanding educational reform, the abolition of university tests, the ballot, and equality of opportunity in entrance to the Civil Service. Most of these Gladstone regarded with caution, and some with hostility. He particularly disliked the complete repeal of university tests, which he succeeded in avoiding in its extreme form. He also regretted the introduction of the ballot which he came to see as unavoidable but with a 'lingering reluctance', and whose various delays he contemplated with some satisfaction, partly because the issue helped to hold the party together in 1871 and 1872. Certainly the days were over when, as in the later years of Palmerston, Gladstone had been regarded by many, not least by Palmerston himself, as almost a Radical. Given the completion of his radical fiscal programme, this was not surprising, but it came to surprise many who had seen in Gladstone's espousal of Irish disestablishment early in 1868 the implication of his general espousal of the Radical political programme.

The problems of Gladstone's personal relationship with Radicalism worked themselves out against the canvas of the electorate and constituencies created by the 1867–8 reform measures. The picture on this canvas was as yet like a preliminary charcoal sketch, of which only the vague outline was apparent. The household suffrage in the boroughs had expanded the electorate, more than Gladstone had wished, in practice less than many had expected. The 1868 election had taken place in considerable bureaucratic confusion, with registers hastily and often imperfectly drawn up, and constituency boundaries so new as to make identification with the candidate on the part of the elector difficult and confusing. It was certainly not clear that Conservative resurgence was to be a chief consequence of the Act. Acton's observation that 'by sinking a shaft through the Democratic drift they would come to a Conservative substratum' was coming to be understood in many an individual constituency, not least in Gladstone's own constituency of Greenwich; but its implications for the Liberal party at a national level were only slowly grasped. Indeed the party in a national, organizational sense, barely existed. It had no framework save the moderate discipline that the whips could exercise through the distribution of patronage and small sums of money; it had no permanent structure in many constituencies; and it had no membership.

No lead from the centre was given throughout this period of government as to how these problems could be solved. Glyn and A. W. Peel, successively the chief whips of the ministry, had nothing to contribute to the development of the Liberal party in an extended electorate. They saw their roles in strictly traditional terms. Gladstone had no John Gorst, nor did he look for one.[*] Neither was it the duty of the Cabinet to consider the party, save at moments of crisis. Though it was the only forum for joint discussion that the Liberals had, the Cabinet did not attempt to deal with the structure of the party; 'party' only intruded into its discussions when that structure had, in the Commons, disintegrated. Initiative, when it came, came from the provinces, and especially from Birmingham. Confusion in the constituencies and mismanagement and ill-discipline in the Commons were distinctive features of the administration, and the latter came to be predominant.

The dismantling of the patronage system in the previous fifty years

---

[*] The historian of Gladstone's own constituency (until 1880) observes: 'the Greenwich electoral register between 1870 and 1900 was largely a creation of the Conservative Party'; G. Crossick, *An Artisan Élite in Victorian Society* (1978), 213.

meant that the party in power had little of the 'pork-barrel' left to offer its followers save honours; as Gladstone correctly reminded Lowe in 1869, when the latter urged Cabinet discussion of the topic, the opening of the Civil Service to competition would critically change some of the functions of the whip's office: 'the change would affect more or less the basis of his [Glyn's] office, his *quid pro quo*'. Patronage in the Civil Service had been almost the last '*quid pro quo*' left of the old system of familial government; there remained after 1870 only the odd Lord-Lieutenancy, the Church, the colonies, and the Justices of the Peace. For Nonconformists, the first was as yet beyond their aspirations, the second impossible by definition, the third inimical and expensive, the fourth the preserve of a Lord Chancellor almost certain to be an Anglican. To the eighteenth-century Lord Chesterfield, patronage had been the 'pasture for the beasts we feed'; for Gladstone, the process of legislation became the sustenance of his followers, and he promised more of it in his election address in 1874.

But if legislation was the primary expectation of the backbenchers and party workers, it was by no means the only concern of the incoming premier. Indeed, the advantage of the Irish Church Bill was that it ensured at least a session of relative concord within the party. Unanimously supported at least as to its principle of disestablishment by the party before the election, confirmed by the electors, admitted as in some form legitimate by the opposition, opposed in full only by the Anglican Establishment in Ireland, but certain to provoke severe infighting in Commons and Lords on details, the Irish Church Bill offered a sure means of stabilizing the majority and preventing the dreadful disintegration which had followed victory in the 1865 general election. The future for the first Session could not but be bright in the main.

Cabinet and Court

But if the mass of the party looked to legislative achievement, the Prime Minister's immediate duties were more traditional: the making of a Cabinet and the management of the Court. The two were closely related. The Cabinet as formed in December 1868 had fifteen members; the Whigs predominated as a group with seven: Clarendon, Granville, Fortescue, Hartington, Kimberley, the Whiggish Hatherley, and Argyll (a Peelite/ Whig); three Whigs, Halifax, Russell, and Sir George Grey had declined to serve. There were two Peelites, Gladstone and Cardwell (Roundell Palmer, a Peelite, declined to serve), one Radical quasi-Peelite, de Grey (from 1871, Ripon), two contrasting Radicals, Lowe and Bright, and three Liberals, Childers, Goschen, and Bruce. All were nominally Anglicans, save Bright, a Quaker; only ten of the fifteen had been to university (four to Christ Church, Oxford, three to Trinity College, Cambridge), most were substantial landowners, and one, Bright, had some direct experience of industrial management. All, save Bright, had held at least minor office before, but, surprisingly, in view of the long predominance of Whig–Liberal governments, only just over half (eight) had sat in Cabinet before: Gladstone, Cardwell, Clarendon, Granville, Argyll, de Grey (Ripon), Goschen, and Hartington. The refusal of the three old Whigs to serve gave the Cabinet a fresh look—indeed five of its members were still in Cabinets in the mid-1890s, and one, Ripon, lived to sit in Campbell-Bannerman's Cabinet of 1905.

One general point about the assumptions of the Cabinet may be made. That the future government of Britain and the Empire was to lie with the 'Box and Cox' alternation of Liberals and Tories was by no means clear to contemporaries. 'The swing of the pendulum', as politicians at the end of the century came to call it, lay in the future: there may be a case for saying it began to swing in 1874, though 1880 or 1886 may be seen as its true start; in practice its arc was almost always irregular. 1868 may seem in retrospect to be the start of 'modern' party politics, but it was not seen as such then. The Cabinet represented a ruling political coalition whose only absence from office had been the result of internal disputes: since 1846, the Whig–Liberal–Peelite alliance had occasionally lost office, but never power. The Cabinet thus worked very much within assumptions to which it anticipated no serious challenge save that of spasmodic obstruction; it did not expect the reversal of policy or legislation, and it gave electoral considerations a low priority.

The assumption of most Liberals was that the worst that could follow the first Gladstone government would be another minority Tory administration, which would allow time for the party of progress to regroup and then again take power. That the Tories would replace the Gladstone government with a substantial majority in the Commons was beyond expectation; that the Tories would begin their administration in 1874 by reversing Liberal legislation was a precedent for the twentieth century, not a precept of the nineteenth. After losing the election of 1874, Gladstone complained about a Tory bill: 'This is the first instance on record, so far as I have been able to ascertain, of any deliberate attempt being made by a Ministry of retrogression.'[*] Adversary politics were on the doorstep, but the door was

---

[*] The Endowed Schools Amendment Act; it is worth having Gladstone's exposition (*H* ccxx. 1707): 'This is a Bill for undoing part of the work of the last Parliament. It is in that respect unusual. I do not wish to deny or to qualify or weaken the fact that the party which sits opposite possesses, after having been many years in a minority, a large majority. What I wish to point out is this, that the history of our country for the last 40 or 50 years, presents to us, as a general rule, this remarkable picture: The initiative of policy in almost every instance—I do not know of even one exception—both of administrative and legislative, was supplied by the Liberal party, and subsequently adopted in prudence and in honesty by the party which is called Conservative. Take the financial—take the colonial—take any of the Departments; and I venture to say that you will find that this is a true description of the history of which we have all been witnesses. When the Conservative Government came into power in 1834, and again in 1841, after the first Reform Act had been the

still closed. In certain respects, therefore, ministers simply did not think in those terms of party which were soon to become dominant. In other words, ministers were closer to the eighteenth than to the twentieth century in the way they saw their role.

Considering its obvious importance, and the place which Bagehot assigned it as the central and co-ordinating element of the British constitution, the Victorian Cabinet has been remarkably little studied. In part this has been the consequence of poor documentation. The documentation of Gladstone's Cabinets is far more thorough than that of any other Prime Minister until records began to be officially kept in 1916. For most Cabinets before 1916, the Prime Minister's letter reporting its transactions to the monarch is the chief regular source. But these letters have obvious and severe limitations, especially when they describe the affairs of a Cabinet to which the monarch was hostile. Gladstone's letters to the Queen were intended to instruct, Disraeli's to entertain; neither attempted to describe the details of Cabinets often lasting several hours. Gladstone's method was to tell the Queen of important decisions which the Cabinet had made, particularly in those areas of foreign and colonial policy which especially interested her. Cabinet discussions on prospective policy, on details of domestic policy, and on party matters and Commons business, are rarely alluded to. To take a random example: the letter reporting the Cabinet of 8 July 1871 only mentions the first of the five items discussed by the Cabinet, the state of play in the row about abolition of purchase.*

Gladstone is unique among Victorian Prime Ministers in keeping systematic records of his Cabinets. These records provide, at the least, a comprehensive guide to topics discussed. The Cabinet usually had a weekly meeting during the parliamentary session, several meetings in the autumn for the discussion of the Estimates and of business accumulating during the Recess, and several meetings for planning the work of the session and the preparation of the Queen's Speech; crises, political and foreign, required extra meetings as occasion demanded. The average number of Cabinet meetings for each year between 1869 and 1873 was about fifty. Gladstone's minutes provide information on almost all of these. Exceptions are those meetings at which he was absent through illness, in which case Granville presided, meetings held hurriedly in the Commons during great crises, such as the deadlock over the abolition of army purchase in 1871, and occasional meetings held in odd places, such as that of

subject of a long dispute and much contention, there was absolute security in the mind of the country and full conviction that the party coming into office would not be so unwise and so unpatriotic as to retrace the steps taken by their Predecessors.'

* 'There was no other subject treated by the Cabinet to-day which it is necessary for him [the Prime Minister] to bring before Your Majesty'; the other subjects discussed were proposals for a Law University, the cumulative vote in School Board elections, bishops' resignations, and Contagious Diseases Acts.

21 March 1871, when the Cabinet met in a GWR. railway carriage, 'to consider the Telegram on the U.S.', as its members returned from Windsor. Very occasionally, a Cabinet held in normal circumstances has no surviving minutes.* Although kept entirely on Gladstone's initiative, these minutes had some official standing, or could be used officially, for Granville wrote to General Schenck, the American minister in London during the crisis over the Alabama negotiations, of a Cabinet decision on Alabama 'as recorded in a minute by Mr. Gladstone'. Gladstone's minutes are almost always brief; they are in fact a combination of topics for discussion and consequent decisions for implementation.

This brevity is not to be explained merely by shortage of time. Gladstone had little interest in the gossip of politics. In all of his vast correspondence it would be hard to find a single letter, outside those dealing with family affairs, which could be called gossipy. The odd pleasantry from time to time occurs at the end of a letter, but it is rarely *ad hominem*, and never malicious. The spirit of futility about the usefulness or success of democratic politics which usually characterizes letters of political gossip was entirely lacking in Gladstone. His minutes and letters carry the same assumption of self-confident purpose.

This is not to say that Gladstone was naïve about the content of much of political life. Commenting on an obituary of the fourteenth Earl of Derby, Gladstone observed:

Politics are at once a game and a high art; he allowed the excitement of the game to draw him off from the sustained and exhausting efforts of the high art. But this was the occasional deviation of an honourable man, not the fixed mental habit of an unprincipled one.

Whether or not this description is true of Lord Derby, it is certainly the case that Gladstone saw politics as 'at once a game and a high art'. Much of their fascination for him sprang from the problems posed in working out the detailed consequences of great principles in the context of Cabinet and Parliament. Gladstone saw the process of politics as inseparable from its principles; nothing delighted him more than the evolving of a policy which was both internally coherent and at the same time outflanked the enemy. This combination of gamesmanship and morality gave Gladstone much of his power. He was as alert to political manœuvring as the most formidable of his opponents, as flexible and resourceful at defending or exploiting a position, and more than a match in stamina for any of his contemporaries when it came to a pitched battle. On the other hand, he appeared to act within a general context of moral objectives which allowed him to personify the moral imperatives of Victorian Liberal politics.

* Records also survive for some 'conclaves'; a 'conclave' was a meeting with non-Cabinet members present, usually for the purpose of discussing a specific problem or emergency, such as the Irish Church Bill's progress, or the state of the Alabama negotiation.

With respect to politics as a game, Gladstone's first ministry was in one sense not dramatic, for many of the players at Cabinet level were remarkably unambitious. Gladstone's position as Prime Minister was unassailable and unassailed, and his role as party co-ordinator was essential. None of the other Cabinet members made any persistent attempt to act as an alternative focus of power or influence within the Cabinet, save on certain specific issues: for example, the Whigs on Ireland and foreign policy, Bright on education.

Gladstone looked back in 1897 on this ministry as 'a Cabinet easily handled'. This was not rose-tinted nostalgia, for what Gladstone meant was that, despite the arguments, personal relationships within the Cabinet were easy: the presence of 'several members who were senior to myself' facilitated business. These older Whigs were unambitious but not embittered; they fought on policies much more than on personalities. Gladstone's happy relationship with Granville is well known, but he believed he also came to be on good terms with Clarendon (who died in June 1870), with Halifax (once the Charles Wood of the disastrous budget of 1851) and, to a lesser extent, with Kimberley, the leader of the younger Whigs. These Whigs were inclined to find 'Merrypebble', as Clarendon nicknamed Gladstone, in principle almost ridiculous, with his Tractarianism and his moralizing, but during the first ministry their personal relationships with him remained amiable, though they fought tooth-and-nail on policies. While their doubts about Gladstone's restlessness and unpredictability increased, these were, at Cabinet level, still doubts fairly easily contained within the existing structure of politics. When Kimberley believed the government was at an end after the defeat on the Irish University Bill in March 1873, he noted in his journal a judgement clearly relative to his experience of administrations since 1852: 'We have been wonderfully harmonious during our four years of office and power.'

The Whigs were a first and particular worry for Gladstone. Though a diminishing force in the country, they remained essential for government. They controlled the Foreign and Colonial Offices almost as by right, and with their great landholdings they dominated the Irish offices. They were an essential link between Court and Premier (here the appointment of Halifax as Lord Privy Seal in July 1870 was a shrewd move, creating a buffer between Queen and Prime Minister and taking some of the weight off the overworked Granville), and the support of the Whigs in the Lords was all the Liberals had. Disaffection among the leading Whigs would therefore bring rapid disaster; disaffection among some Whigs there certainly was, as will be shown below, but at Cabinet level the Whigs co-operated sufficiently to maintain the unity of the ministry. It is a moot point whether Russell outside the Cabinet was more trouble than he would have been inside it; Gladstone went to considerable lengths, especially in 1869–70, to keep him in touch, but he came to regard Russell's supposedly failing powers as irremediable.

At the other end of the Cabinet stood John Bright, ill, ineffective in administration, perhaps rather idle, but still a dominant force in non-official Liberalism, or at least regarded as such by Gladstone. Bright represented in Cabinet the old Liberalism of the Anti-Corn Law League but also something of the new Liberalism of the 1860s, the complex clutch of reforming urges round which Radicalism had clustered in the constituencies. To lose Bright, especially before the Education Bill was passed, would be to isolate official Liberalism, that body of men which formed the executive, still essentially the Aberdonian coalition of Whigs and Peelites, from the new enthusiasts.

Gladstone's letters to Bright testify to his persistence and, on the whole, to his success. He encouraged Bright by offering 'early friendly and confidential communication on subjects of great public interest'; he flattered him by praising his 'Herculean efforts'; he arranged for Bright to remain a Cabinet member though unable to attend for several months; he succeeded in delaying Bright's resignation, promised for late 1870, until January 1871, when the worst of the crisis of the Franco-Prussian war was over. In October 1871 Gladstone returned to the pursuit with flattery ('those who have official responsibility must ever feel a natural anxiety to arm themselves with the best assistance and advice'), arranging a visit by Bright to Hawarden, informing him of Cabinet details once he had ceased to be a member, and eventually succeeding in bringing him back into the Cabinet in September 1873 to strengthen the government after the sundry crises of the spring and summer of that year.

Next to the Queen, no one was more cossetted than John Bright. Whereas Lowe received a very sharp analysis of the attributes of his character, Bright's executive deficiencies passed without hostile comment, evoking merely sympathetic understanding. Gladstone began his brutally frank comments on Lowe's political failings by observing that 'I always hold that politicians are the men whom as a rule it is most difficult to understand i.e. understand completely; and for my own part, I never have thus understood or thought I understood above one or two, though here and there I may get hold of an isolated idea about others.' Gladstone's handling of Bright shows he had understood a good deal of the sentimental side of Victorian Radicalism.

In cossetting Bright, Gladstone cosetted Nonconformity; he was much more successful with the particular than the general. He ended with Bright back in the Cabinet but with Nonconformity at best apathetic, at worst openly hostile. Cabinet cohesion was a window-dressing which was intended to mask disintegration in the constituencies. Bright balanced the Cabinet, allowed Gladstone to appear in a more central and less exposed position than would have been the case with Bright absent: Bright had therefore a function *vis-à-vis* the Whigs and the Court as well as *vis-à-vis* the Nonconformists and constituency Radicals.

It was Court and Whig departmental business which formed the first course of the Cabinet's staple diet. Discussion of foreign and colonial business—especially the former—was the regular business of the Cabinet, and was often discussed as the first or second item of the agenda. The second regular function of the Cabinet was agreement on and supervision of the legislative programme. Third, particularly at certain times of the year, the Cabinet discussed finance and the Estimates. It also, naturally, dealt with miscellaneous problems as and when they occurred.

It is hard to disentangle the activities of a Prime Minister from the work of his ministry as a whole, but it is the aim of this and the next chapter to examine the part which Gladstone played in that administration, and to discuss those issues in which he involved himself, or was necessarily particularly involved by the nature of his office. Of course, as Prime Minister and Leader of the Commons, papers dealing with every aspect of the ministry's activities came before him, as they also came before the Queen. But some subjects, of importance for the ministry and its subsequent fate, such as legislation on the drink trade, largely passed him by, and are thus not discussed here.

It will be convenient to discuss Gladstone's involvement as Prime Minister under the headings outlined above: foreign and colonial policy; the legislative programme; the Court; the economy.

Foreign Policy: united Germany and reunited United States

Gladstone had not previously been directly and persistently involved in the making of foreign policy, though he had been Colonial Secretary in 1845–6. However, as Chancellor of the Exchequer, he had seen many Foreign Office dispatches, and he had of course been in Cabinet during both the Crimean and Schleswig-Holstein crises, and throughout the American Civil War. He had therefore been privy in general to the making of much of British foreign policy since 1852, and the Anglo-French Cobden Treaty of 1860 had been more his achievement than that of any other member of Palmerston's government.

For a Utopian and out-and-out free trader, foreign policy might seem in principle unnecessary: international free trade was to lead to international harmony which would replace the need for bargains between governments. But the way that British free trade had developed had not in fact been that of unilateral tariff abolition. Britain by the late 1860s was related to most European countries by a complex series of trade treaties, most of them most-favoured-nation treaties, a process which was still not completed. It was not until the Continental abrogation of freer trade in the 1870s that

British free trade existed quite independently of Continental attitudes. By the late 1860s the framework of the free trade treaty structure was built. Gladstone, as one of its architects, now looked to its defence; while happy to extend the system, he did not come to office with any intention of fundamentally changing it. His objective in the long negotiations over the renewal of the French Commercial Treaty after the 1870 war was essentially to save what he could of the 1860 Treaty; he stressed his 'unchanged adherence to the principles and objects of 1860 whatever force there may be in the consideration that the application of such principles must be subject to considerations of time, place, & circumstance'.

The same can be said of Gladstone's attitude to foreign policy generally. His acute sense of organic and historicist nationality exemplified in *The State in its Relations with the Church* meant that the acceptance of nationality was his starting-point. Foreign policy was not, as it was for the Radicals, corrupt dealings between landed castes,* but rather the means by which European nations communicated for the public good. It was, therefore, desirable and potentially beneficial. Amongst these nations Gladstone discerned a developing awareness of civil progress, based on the acknowledgement of mutual interests, through 'treaties of mutual benefit with every nation of earth; treaties not written on parchment, but based on the permanent wants and interests of man, kept alive and confirmed by the constant play of the motives which govern his daily life'.† It was the function of the British 'to found a moral empire upon the confidence of the several peoples'. His article in the *Edinburgh Review*, an extraordinary initiative for a Prime Minister, anonymously written and published at the height of the Franco-Prussian war, was intended to give public airing to views which could not be given an official imprimatur: 'the silence of a Government need not be copied by those who, not invested with authority, aim at assisting the public mind and conscience by discussion'. It concluded with an interesting and optimistic statement which is both retrospective and admonitory:

Certain it is that a new law of nations is gradually taking hold of the mind, and coming to sway the practice, of the world; a law which recognises independence, which frowns on aggression, which favours the pacific, not the bloody settlement of disputes, which aims at permanent and not temporary adjustment; above all, which recognises, as a tribunal of paramount authority, the general judgment of civilised mankind. It has censured the aggression of France; it will censure, if need arise, the greed of Germany. '*Securus judicat orbis terrarum*.'‡ It is hard for all nations to go

---

* Gladstone seems to have felt no particular irritation at the exemption of the Foreign Office from entry by competition, and he raised few complaints about the quality of the predominantly Whiggish British envoys abroad.

† 'Germany, France, and England', *Edinburgh Review*, October 1870, reprinted in *Gleanings*, iv, begun on 1 Sept. 70, the day of the battle of Sedan. Attempts to keep authorship 'absolutely secret' fairly quickly failed.

‡ 'The verdict of the whole world is conclusive.'

astray. Their ecumenical council sits above the partial passions of those, who are misled by interest, and disturbed by quarrel. The greatest triumph of our time, a triumph in a region loftier than that of electricity and steam, will be the enthrone-ment of this idea of Public Right, as the governing idea of European policy; as the common and precious inheritance of all lands, but superior to the passing opinion of any. The foremost among the nations will be that one, which by its conduct shall gradually engender in the mind of the others a fixed belief that it is just. In the competition for this prize, the bounty of Providence has given us a place of vantage; and nothing save our own fault or folly can wrest it from our grasp.

This passage exemplifies Gladstone's expectations and hopes for foreign policy. Its tone is certainly not thoroughgoingly Radical: the central quota-tion, St Augustine's famous maxim which drove J. H. Newman to Rome, resurrects the image of a Christian, homogeneous Europe. The comity of nations was to mirror the ecumencial councils of the Church.

This introduction of ecumenism at so vital a point reflects Gladstone's personal religious preoccupations of recent years. It also refers to his major preoccupation in foreign affairs in the first year of his ministry: the preparations for the Vatican Council and for the declaration of Infallibility. Gladstone's case against Infallibility was both personal and general: it ruined ecumenism in England, and it cast in doubt the civic allegiance of all Roman Catholic populations. It was 'civic individuality' which gave European nations the right to claim superiority in world affairs, and it was 'civic individuality' which was the guarantor of liberty both personal and national: 'Nothing can compensate a people for the loss of what we may term civic individuality. Without it, the European type becomes politically debased to the Mahometan and Oriental model.' Ultramontanism struck straight at 'civic individuality'; Gladstone's hope was that 'a combined action of the Governments' would strengthen 'the more moderate & right minded Bishops' and consequently either prevent or moderate a declara-tion of Infallibility; 'there may be an opportunity of helping to do what the Reformation in many things did: to save the Pope and the Roman Church from themselves'.

Gladstone's difficulty was first that Britain had no official diplomatic representation at Rome, thus finding it difficult to take the lead, and second, that the Whiggish and world-weary Clarendon, though thoroughly Erastian and anti-Papal, did not invest the controversy with the same ideological significance or urgency as his Prime Minister. The conscience of Europe stirred twice, in the Bavarian initiative of the spring of 1869, and in the French initiative of March 1870. Britain was not included in the Bavarian initiative, and only marginally in the French initiative. In the latter case, Clarendon persuaded the Cabinet, against Gladstone's wishes, to respond to the French appeal verbally, rather than by a note. The voice of Europe, when it spoke, fell on deaf ears, despite the fulfilment of Gladstone's wish that 'Pope & Ecclesiastics' should not be able 'to say with truth that they never received a friendly warning'.

The appeal of the Concert had been spectacularly unsuccessful in the case of the Roman Catholic Church. Its failure called into question Gladstone's hope that 'the general judgment of civilized mankind' would act as the guarantor of the European order. Gladstone realized this; once the Council was under way he hoped that the French would threaten to withdraw their troops, using the threat of leaving the Papacy at the mercy of the Italian Government as a means of containing the Pope's theological ambitions. He also felt this negative use of troops to be the only way of bringing effective pressure to bear: 'withdrawal of the troops is the only measure within the power of France to take which the Pope and his myrmidons care about . . . it is by threats and threats alone that the Court of Rome, as to its Roman & Church policy, is influenced: its whole policy is based in the rejection of reason'.

The success of ultramontanism seemed to Gladstone to mark a major crisis in the progress of 'civic individuality' in Europe, as well as in its effect on Anglican–Roman relations in England and on the Irish situation. It would be going only just too far to say that he regarded it as a worse blow than the Franco-Prussian war, which ended the Council peremptorily but with the French troops staying in Rome long enough to allow a declaration of Infallibility to be rushed through. He returned to the theme frequently in correspondence and speeches, and his attempt to include in his election manifesto in 1874 a passage admonishing vigilance to prevent the effects of ultramontanism on 'civil rights and equality of all' was only struck out at the last moment by the demands of the other members of the Cabinet. His response to ultramontanism was to be the obsession of his quasi-retirement and the occasion of his return to public dispute with the publication of *The Vatican Decrees* in November 1874.

Gladstone had intervened as enthusiastically as he could to stimulate the Concert to action on ultramontanism. He had been held back partly by Clarendon's reluctance but mainly by Britain's weak position: no official envoy in Rome, the lack of Roman Catholic representation in the official classes, and the unfortunate fact that the leader, whip, and wire-puller of the ultramontanists, 'the madmen of the Council', was his former intimate, the apostate H. E. Manning, Archbishop of Westminster, whose co-operation was thought central to the management of the Irish bishops and Liberal MPs and thus to the success of the government's Irish legislation. In such circumstances Britain was relatively uninfluential: 'I agree with you', Gladstone told Clarendon, 'that Dr. Döllinger expects far too much from anything we could say.'

Was this to be the case with the 'deluge of events' in the second half of 1870, the war between Prussia and France which 'unset, as it were, every joint of the compacted fabric of Continental Europe'? Starting from the assumption that 'the nations of Europe are a family', Gladstone saw British involvement in the quarrel as wholly natural: England's 'hand will not be unready to be lifted up, on every fit and hopeful occasion, in sustaining the general sense of Europe against a disturber of the public peace'.

Here he differed sharply from traditional Mancunian isolationism embodied in the Cabinet by John Bright. In addition to the precept of intervention, he supported a traditional priority of the 'national interest' view of Continental affairs. Right at the start of his ministry, he told Clarendon: 'A war between France and Germany would be sad but the compulsory or fraudulent extinction by annexation of the Free State of Belgium would be worse.' The careful qualifications characteristic of any Gladstonian letter show that he did not at that stage regard Belgium as an absolute commitment, and he soon made it clear that British interest was not in itself sufficient: 'I for one believe, but do not know, that the true public opinion of Belgium is possessed with a sense of nationality, & is resolved to struggle for its maintenance. That is the only possible standing point I apprehend for permanent resistance.' The 'dirt in the sky' which Gladstone saw early in 1869 was in large measure lost sight of as the immediate crisis of the Belgian railways passed.

'What pretext has he [Bismarck] for interfering in Bavaria?', Gladstone asked Clarendon in February 1870. By the summer, Bismarck had his pretext, and Gladstone made no complaint about Prussia's conduct in the outbreak of the war, but blamed France's 'folly, inconsistency, and temerity'. His analysis of French politics shows an understanding of the dynamic and unstable nature of the Second Empire, which the Cobden Treaty, in his view, had been intended, but had had insufficient time, to stabilize. He also showed an understanding of the internal dynamics of German nationalism and Prussian politics but made no direct link between them and the events of the first half of 1870. Gladstone could not object to the formation of 'our Teutonic cousins' into a single political nation. It is striking that he assumed that 'Germany' was what Bismarck made it: that is, 'Germany' for Gladstone meant the *Kleindeutsch* solution, and Prussia's policy was thus in his view teleologically directed and justified: 'the aggrandisement of Germany by consolidation from within her own frontiers, is not a matter of which other countries are entitled to take any hostile cognisance'.

Officially, Gladstone and the British government maintained a strictly neutral position, arranging the guarantee of Belgian neutrality by treaty. Privately, Gladstone acted quickly to make the War Office 'study the means of sending 20,000 men to Antwerp', while strongly resisting the use of the occasion for a general increase in military strength, which was 'the extreme susceptibility, on one side of the case, of some members of the

Cabinet'. Gladstone seems to have had no personal doubt about the maintenance of Belgian and consequently British neutrality, for when Consols fell he bought £2,500 at 90 on 18 July.

The defence of Belgium was achieved without the dual priorities of British national interest and the rights of peoples having to be disentangled by members of the Cabinet. The same was not the case with Alsace and Lorraine. Gladstone differed from his colleagues in the vehemence of his hostility to Bismarck's annexation. He discussed the question simultaneously with his old friend, the French free-trader Michel Chevalier, and with Friedrich Max Müller, the peregrinating philologist and apologist for German nationalism who was in 1870 a professor in Oxford. To Chevalier, he blamed the French for making their case against annexation on the basis of erecting 'the inviolability of soil into an abstract principle'; to Max Müller, he complained at the absence of 'previous proof' that 'the inhabitants generally are favourable' and that annexation was militarily necessary to Germany and that Germany would not use Alsatian fortifications against France. Unilateral annexation and lack of general discussion on the terms of the peace would, Gladstone believed, mean 'that Germany, crowned with glory & confident in her strength, will start on her new career . . . without the sympathies of Europe', a mistake as 'ruinous' in its consequences as 'our going, or Mr. Pitt's going, to war in 1793'.

Gladstone was not opposed to flexibility of boundaries; what he required was legitimation of their change. An advance upon the 'old and cruel practice of treating the population of a civilised European country as mere chattels' had been achieved by references to local opinion in plebiscites or votes of assemblies; Gladstone proposed 'military neutralization' as an alternative to annexation in the case of Alsace-Lorraine, and requested the Cabinet's agreement for an appeal to other neutral nations for support. The Cabinet supported Granville's more anodyne suggestion, and a second attempt was drowned by the Gortchakoff circular on the Black Sea clauses of the 1856 Paris Treaty.

In neither the Vatican question nor the Franco-Prussian war had 'the mind of Europe' been as clearly or as forcefully expressed as Gladstone would have liked. His differences with his Cabinet should not, however, be exaggerated. In neither case was Gladstone suggesting more than verbal initiatives, and in both cases his initiatives were intended as homilies which would inform the Cabinet and, if accepted there, the civilized world, what ought to be done, rather than as policies which Gladstone believed had any real chance of success. He did not think that either the Papacy or Bismarck would change course; he felt that neither should be allowed to go against what he saw as the standards of civilization without remonstrances which might act as precedents for the future.

In both these great crises of the mind and shape of Europe, Britain's intervention depended on the attitude of other members of 'the family'. In neither case were the relatives likely to be co-operative, and in the Franco-Prussian war Russia showed that she at any rate would use a family row to take what she could get. In the case of British–American relations, however, only America and the British Empire were involved, and it was thus easier for Gladstone to stiffen the will of his Cabinet at the vital moment.

The problem of the *Alabama* claims involved not only questions immediately arising from damage done to Northern shipping during the American Civil War by the *Alabama* and similar ships, but also the 'indirect claims' (i.e. the claim that the United States should be compensated not only for damage done directly by ships sold to the South during the war by British shipbuilders, but also for the indirect losses suffered—at their most extreme, all the losses caused by the delay in the ending of the war) in settlement of which the United States at one stage suggested the cession of Canada—it had just bought Alaska. The 'claims' also raised the question of security of the Canadian border and the Fenian raids across it, and outstanding Canadian–American disputes on tariffs and fisheries.

Gladstone was also personally involved, in the sense that his notorious Newcastle speech of October 1862, which could be easily and most obviously construed as a recognition of Confederate right to secede, was a severe embarrassment to him and to the government. For most of 1869, following the rejection of arbitration by the Senate in the form proposed in the Johnson–Clarendon treaty of January 1869, Gladstone made little attempt to do more than encourage Clarendon on American questions, sometimes complaining at the 'submissiveness' which the weakness of the Canadian frontier forced upon Britain. The appointment of the historian J. L. Motley as American minister in London severely embarrassed Gladstone personally, for Motley had attacked Gladstone's 1862 speech as a 'consummate work of art', comparable to Mark Antony's burial speech. Gladstone's reaction to Motley's appointment was to demand withdrawal of the phrase; elaborate arbitrations followed, successful only by the time that Motley had lost his own government's confidence.

For Gladstone, unlike Radical pro-Northerners in Britain, did not see the developments leading up to the arbitration at Geneva in 1872 as 'righting a wrong'. He saw the process as exemplifying the means by which two civilized nations could settle differences, without either having to admit being in the wrong. In the autumn of 1869 he began to take a more perceptive view than Clarendon of the highly complex position of Hamilton Fish, the American Secretary of State, to defend Fish against Clarendon's scorn, and to suggest that 'the two countries should set about the consideration of a good prospective system, and should thereafter, in the light of principles thus elucidated, reconsider the matter of arbitration, or any other mode of proceeding in the Alabama case'. Even when Fish revived the demand for the annexation of Canada in exchange for the settlement of the Claims, Gladstone counselled maintaining 'our present composed temper'. The proposal of 'a good prospective system' was embodied in the Treaty of Washington of 1871 whose articles' general significance was in Gladstone's view 'to become rules for international law for the future'.

The successful conclusion of the Washington Treaty seemed to mark the end of the affair, bar the settling of the details. But the American claim, made in their 'Case' of December 1871 prepared for submission to the arbitration tribunal, that the question of the 'indirect claims' was still open, astonished and appalled the British. Gladstone responded with a vigorous denunciation in the Commons of American behaviour, which was both genuinely felt and politically convenient. He then short-circuited the cumbersome channels of communication, by which his own views reached the Americans only via Granville, the Foreign Office, and Thornton, the ambassador in Washington. He proposed to Granville that direct communication between himself and Schenck, the new American minister, should be the first means of negotiation. As Gladstone was already on terms with Schenck, this would give him more personal control and initiative. His first use of this direct access to Schenck was to be the delivering of a vast letter justifying his own record during the Civil War, and replying to the sections of the American 'Case' which seemed to impugn it. In this, he was overruled by the Cabinet, led by Granville. His urge for self-justification was linked to a strong intention to make the negotiation succeed within the terms of the Treaty of Washington and to show that its terms were not ambiguous.

In the extraordinary contortions through which, between March and June 1872, both British and Americans eventually contrived to make the Treaty work, Gladstone's role was to push forward negotiations whenever possible and, when a breaking-point seemed almost to have occurred, to rally his Cabinet, especially Halifax, Kimberley, and Cardwell, the chief dissenters, behind the larger view. 'My determination upon it is now firmly rooted & tested by all the mental effort I can apply.' The strategy prevailed and, greatly assisted by the common sense of Charles Adams, the American arbitrator, the arbitration proceeded without consideration of the 'indirect claims'. Both the Treaty of Washington and the arbitration could be offered to the world as the path for the future. So also, eventually, could Gladstone's self-justification. His vast letter to Schenck —really a political pamphlet—was eventually sent, against Granville's advice, in November 1872 and was published in *Harper's New Monthly Magazine* in the United States in 1876. Gladstone had felt throughout that he and the British position during the Civil War had subsequently been hard done by. He had urged Clarendon to get someone to publish a defence of it.* His letter to Schenck was his version of that defence and marked the start of that assiduous cultivation of American liberal opinion which was to be so marked a characteristic of the rest of his life.

Gladstone's initiatives in some areas of foreign policy thus found him on occasion in disagreement with his Cabinet, and, on the whole, the Cabinet prevailed. Gladstone's concept of an 'ecumenical council' of civilized opinion appealed neither to the Whigs, who preferred the discreet bargains of the closet, nor to the Radicals, who saw in it sinister implications of Continental involvement.

The Colonies, Old and New: free trade, retrenchment, and expansion

Allied to foreign policy, in that it was traditionally a Whig preserve and the subject of routine Cabinet discussion occasioned by the arrival of dispatches, was colonial policy. Of India, the Cabinet heard little. Gladstone's letters to Argyll, the Secretary for India, were largely about British questions. Gladstone's own 'desires' for India's future were that 'nothing may bring about a sudden, violent, or discreditable severance; that we may labour steadily to promote the political training of our fellow-subjects; & that when we go, if we are to go, we may leave a clear bill of accounts behind us'. This vision would have startled many of his contemporaries, but he made no moves to encourage its realization. Indian security was a more immediate problem. On the question of Russian expansion in Turkestan, he followed Granville in a policy of issuing general cautions combined with concessions.

'Colonial policy' for the most part meant the relationship of Britain to her colonies of European descent. Granville's Colonial Secretaryship in 1869 and 1870 was marked by the withdrawal of British troops from New Zealand and preparations for their withdrawal from Canada. This was part of a long-standing and systematic attempt on the one hand to force the colonists to act responsibly, on the other to help to reduce defence costs at home, which accounted for about a third of the British budget. As Colonial Secretary in 1845–6, Gladstone had moved towards self-government in New Zealand as quickly as possible and, as he reminded Granville in 1869, one of his first actions as Peel's colonial secretary had been to instruct the new Canadian Governor-General 'that we did not *impose* British connection upon the Colony, but regarded its goodwill and desire as an essential condition of the connection'.

Even before the 1867 Canada Act, Gladstone had been most reluctant to accept a Vote for Canadian fortifications. As Palmerston's Chancellor, he

---

* Gladstone also felt that his proposal 'early in the war' for rules to govern prospective cases such as the *Alabama* had been neglected, by implication by Russell; but he could make no allusion publicly to this, for Russell was already very touchy on the question of his record as Foreign Secretary.

had played a leading role in the 'Conferences on Canadian Defence' with Canadian politicians which had negotiated the agreement essential to the making of the 1867 Canada Act. Gladstone's readiness to support troop withdrawal was therefore consistent with his position over many years. Considering army reform in 1870, at the height of the Franco-Prussian war, he anticipated getting 'rid of all drafts upon the regular army for Colonial purposes, in ordinary circumstances, except in the four cases of Malta–Gibraltar–Halifax–Bermuda'. But these withdrawals were only to continue in peacetime conditions: where Britain was 'satisfied as to the cause whether Canada were independent of us or not, such [armed] assistance . . . would only be limited by our means'. The 'whole power of the Empire' should be used to sustain 'a political connection' as long as Canada wanted one.

Gladstone thus assumed that the 'union of heart and character' would continue as long as it was desired by both sides, and that it would be a union supported by arms if necessary. How little he anticipated unilateral action by colonies is shown by his astonished reaction to the Australian demand for differential tariffs in 1871. 'Do I understand . . . that New Zealand (for instance) may admit free shoes made in Sydney and tax at any rate she pleases shoes made in Northampton?' He thought this 'advance . . . brings us near the *reductio ad absurdum* of colonial connection, & the people of this country should have an opportunity of passing an opinion on it'. 'Astounding' though this might seem, the British Cabinet was forced to acknowledge there was little they could do about it, despite the fact that it upset all the delicately balanced trade treaties which Britain had concluded with European states in the name of the British Empire as a whole. Reserved powers of commercial treaty-making turned out, to Gladstone's regret more than Kimberley's, to be non-existent, the pass being finally sold by Lord Lisgar, the Governor-General of Canada (formerly known as Young, whose confusions in Ionia Gladstone had been sent out to right in 1858), who without consultation with London gave the Royal Assent to a Canadian Bill establishing differential tea and coffee duties with America.

The movement towards an Empire less formally integrated constitutionally and administratively was thus significant, but it was a movement based on localized fiscal and protectionist priorities, unencouraged and reluctantly conceded by London. The speed with which colonies made use of the legislative freedom which the previous twenty years of imperial policy-making had given them, clearly came as a shock to Gladstone, who seems to have thought that responsible government and support for free trade would go hand in hand. The enthusiasm for colonial development which he had shown in the 1840s was absent; a co-founder of the Canterbury settlement in New Zealand, he gave no encouragement to the various lobbies of similar feeling in the 1870s. Undoubtedly this was a mistake from the point of view of domestic politics: failure to present the positive side of the emotional 'kin beyond the sea' view of colonial relationships and a readiness to rely on an understanding by the electorate of the technical details of long-established policies, made it all the easier for the opposition to link patriotism with Conservatism and claim, as Disraeli did at the Crystal Palace in 1872, that 'there has been no effort so continuous, so subtle, supported by so much energy, and carried on with so much ability and acumen, as the attempts of Liberalism to effect the disintegration of the Empire of England'.

In Cabinet, Gladstone had found himself more cautious than Granville on imperial questions, and differing with Kimberley on the importance of the colonial tariff question. On questions of colonial expansion, he found himself on the defensive. A long rearguard action on the annexation of Fiji, conducted with Gladstone's usual resourcefulness, succeeded in delaying a decision, despite powerful pressures from the anti-slavery lobby, but in the Gold Coast, Gladstone was reluctantly persuaded by the combined action of the Colonial Office and the War Office, to concede the sending of a military force under Sir Garnet Wolseley in the autumn of 1873. He threatened Kimberley with a recall of Parliament, the implied revolt of Bright, the refusal of the Cabinet to defend the expedition in the Session expected in 1874, but it was all to no avail. 'I am not master of the facts', Gladstone told Kimberley, and the War Office saw to it that this remained the case; Gladstone had to rely on newspaper reports for information about the preparation of Wolseley's force, and understandings about Cabinet supervision of the stages of its progress were simply ignored. 'The pressure of the three Departments, with a view to military preparations', Gladstone told Bright, 'has gone beyond what I feel competent to deal with & beyond the mere execution of the orders of the Cabinet.' The Gold Coast question illustrated the weakness both of Gladstone as Prime Minister, and of the office as such. Cardwell and Kimberley effectively prepared and dispatched the expedition on their own authority; the Prime Minister had no constitutional way of stopping them. By the time the Cabinet met, the expedition was on its way. However, the military conduct of the expedition, once launched, on the whole met with Gladstone's approval. It was well organized, cheap and quick, and stood out favourably in all respects in comparison to the Tories' Abyssinian adventure of 1867–8. Gladstone lauded Wolseley's conduct in a flattering letter which may represent, in part, an attempt to repair the generally poor relations between Liberal party and the army.

The discovery of the diamond field at Kimberley in 1869 and the anarchic allegiances of uncontrolled prospectors threatened British informal control of the non-colonized areas of southern Africa. The Cabinet decided in principle to annex the 'Cape Diamond Fields' in May 1871, and the stresses within southern Africa thus provoked prepared the way for the decision to give 'a general encouragement' to 'South African Federation'. However, in the complex maze of southern African relationships and the difficulties of communication with London, the Governor of the Cape, Barkly, on his 'own Act', annexed the Diamond Fields to Cape Colony, regardless of the federation plans—a classic example of action by 'the man on the spot'. Gladstone had warned Kimberley 'that in opening the door to the re-incorporation of the Boer States in the Empire you will (as is your wont) take due precautions against extension of the responsibility of the H[ome] Government'. However, he made no attempt to influence in detail the development of an area which, when he returned to power in 1880, was to prove one of his chief external preoccupations. Neither the Cabinet nor the Prime Minister had any consistent control over imperial expansion, nor, except in the case of Fiji, did Gladstone attempt to intervene decisively in it. 'No objection taken' was the laconic record in the Cabinet minutes of Barkly's initiative.

The Upas Tree: the Irish Church

The second of the chief areas of concern within which it is convenient to discuss Gladstone's Cabinet's preoccupations was its co-ordination and supervision of the form and content of the Government's legislative programme. In Gladstone's first ministry this was a major task, for the programme was exceptionally dense, partly because of the Prime Minister's predilection, partly because of the great volume of bills promoted by the various government departments, and partly, as has been suggested above, because the expectations of the ministry's supporters—to call them a 'party' is to suggest too coherent a description—required that they be kept sweet, or at least supportive, by legislative proposals whether expected to pass or not.

Each legislative proposal must have its own history, its own relationship to government departments and to pressure groups, and will be shaped within the context of a long series of precedents, legal conventions, and departmental preparations. Normally, by the time the proposal reaches the Cabinet, the room for manœuvre is severely constricted. That elaborate and often impenetrable process by which certain measures emerge as the questions of the day can hardly be dealt with in general here. The history of government departments is usually the key to the analysis of this process; but Gladstone had no department, nor did he, except on very rare occasions, deal with departments save through their Cabinet representatives. He did on several occasions, however, act as a one-man department in the sponsorship of legislation, and it will be convenient first to discuss those bills in which he took a particular personal or leading interest.

The Sessions of 1869 and 1870 had Irish legislation as their centre-piece. The Irish Church Bill of 1869 was, and the Irish Land Bill of 1870 became, very much Gladstone's own bill. The Irish Church Bill he prepared himself, in consultation with selected advisers and Thring, the parliamentary draftsman. The Land Bill was prepared in a partnership of varying balance between the Prime Minister and Chichester Fortescue, the Irish Secretary and author of the failed Irish Land Bill of 1866. Not since Peel's Bank Act of 1844 had the Prime Minister been seen as the almost single-handed architect of a major piece of legislation, apart from the unique circumstances of the Reform Bills.

Ireland was for Gladstone a preoccupation, not an interest, an embarrassment, not an intellectual attraction. Clearly, Ireland had not progressed, but Gladstone showed little intellectual curiosity about this anomalous corner of the 'workshop of the world'. His aim in his Irish policy was simply stated: 'our purpose & duty is to endeavour to draw a line between the Fenians & the people of Ireland, & to make the people of Ireland indisposed to cross it'.* Institutional reform (the Irish Church Bill) and social and economic reform (the Land Bill) were intended to have a political effect. Gladstone seems to have believed that if the Irish were shown the Westminster Parliament redressing their grievances by spectacular acts of legislation, then this would encourage their adherence to the existing political structure, both as to institutions and political parties.

The disestablishment of a part of the Anglican Church was, naturally, a formidable political and technical undertaking, an assault on the formal structure of the Establishment as dramatic in principle as anything achieved between 1689 and the present day. Gladstone felt that he had sufficient political impetus to maintain his bill in principle in the Commons despite 'a possible development of *minor* schism in the Liberal body' over details of the Bill affecting Roman Catholics, and indeed this proved correct. In the crisis over the bill in June and July 1869, he was able to use the Liberal majority in the Commons against both the Lords and opponents of his approach in the Cabinet. Almost from the start, he saw the Lords as 'the most formidable stumbling block'.

His bill was predominantly negative in tone: that is, it concentrated on disestablishment, and did not attempt to use the occasion for the more positive incorporating approach which the policy of concurrent endowment implied.† As he told Archbishop Tait, in the Commons 'there is not

---

* A letter to General C. Grey, the Queen's secretary (and husband of Caroline Farquhar) discussing the release of Fenian prisoners. He admitted, under pressure from Earl Grey, that Fenians in Ireland and England 'have had a very important influence on the question of the time for moving upon great questions of policy for Ireland'.

† i.e. the distribution of the assets of the Anglican Church in Ireland between the three chief Irish denominations, Anglican, Roman Catholic, and Presbyterian; the Roman Catholics and the Presbyterians up to disestablishment received State subsistence through the Maynooth Grant and the Regium Donum respectively. These grants were ended with compensation from the Anglican endowments, though they had been a charge on the Imperial Exchequer, not on the Irish establishment.

that distinction between the question of disestablishment and disendowment which exists in Your Grace's mind', and, he might have added, in the
minds of many Erastians, both Conservative and Whig. Concurrent
endowment (i.e. the endowment of the Roman Catholic Church in Ireland
side by side with the Anglican) went against all Gladstone's principles. If
an established church could not represent 'religious nationality', he
favoured the opposite extreme of voluntaryism. The notion of the State
being involved in the support of various denominations which were doc-
trinally irreconcilable he profoundly abhorred, and the ending of the
Maynooth grant in 1869 was probably one of the most satisfactory consequences of disestablishment for him personally. Gladstone successfully
warded off concurrent endowment, favoured by Lord John Russell in his
pamphlets of 1868–9, and by some other Whigs, as well as by many Conservatives. It is hardly likely that the Roman Catholic hierarchy would have
accepted it if it had been offered.

The bill was rapidly drawn up at Hawarden with the advice of Archdeacon Stopford, and with Granville and Acton in attendance. Gladstone
returned to London on 1 February 1869 and by 9 February the Cabinet
'completed the heads of the Irish Church measure to my great satisfaction'.
Complex negotiations, 'conclaves', and discussions changed some of the
details of the bill, but its substance emerged unscathed, and the bill was
given a first reading on 1 March 1869.

Gladstone had made one major change from the plan he drew up in
December 1868: originally, the disestablished Church was to have kept its
glebe houses, and some of their 'immediately annexed lands'. Under
pressure from Roman Catholics, Presbyterians, and John Bright, this continuation of the endowment was drastically reduced. The concession
proved fortuitous for, when the clash with the Lords came in July 1869, the
dispute centred on three chief questions: concurrent endowment; the glebe
lands and other property, and the related question of compensation for
curates; and the threat to delay the date of operation of the Act. Gladstone
absolutely ruled out any concession on the first, and on 26 June 1869 carried
the Cabinet with him: 'Discussion on concurrent Endowment. Govt. do
not entertain it.' The Tories might try to keep the issue alive, but, with the
Queen wanting a settlement, the issue came down to cash, a bargain to be
struck between the two Houses: 'All that remains is to say to the majority of
the H. of C. *such and such a sum* is not worth the quarrel and the postpone-
ment. This sum must be moderate.' Gladstone's low offer on the glebe
lands gave room for manœuvre: Disraeli wanted one sum, Tait a second,
Cairns a third and highest.*

Under the strain and excitement of the negotiations, not least for him,

---

* The glebe (church) lands were sold off by Commissioners, mostly to small proprietors, thus
offering an interesting precedent for land purchase schemes in the 1880s.

Gladstone had the first of those short illnesses which often punctuated all his ministries at times of major crisis. Clearly something more than what today would be called a 'diplomatic illness'—nervous exhaustion would seem to have been the cause—it was none the less extremely convenient, for, rather than the slightly frenetic, Tractarian Prime Minister, it left the composed Erastian Granville to conduct the final negotiations, in which the Opposition's hostility swiftly collapsed and a compromise unexpectedly favourable to the Liberals' demands was reached. The favourable issue left Gladstone, upstairs on his sofa, 'almost unmanned, in the reaction from a sharp and stern tension of mind'.

Gladstone believed Ireland had provided the momentum for the party in 1868 and 1869, and his policy of disestablishment without concurrent endowment had satisfied not only himself, but his Roman Catholic and Nonconformist supporters. This policy had been 'the basis on which the late remarkable co-operation of the Liberal majority has been founded . . . the question whether any other basis would be abstractedly better is a question, at this moment, for Debating Societies'.

The Upas Tree: Irish Land

On the question of Irish land, Gladstone was at first cautious—'the Church is enough for today'—but, following Bright's outright commitment to a major land bill at the end of April, Gladstone—at least from May 1869—had come to see the pace set by the drafting and passing of the Irish Church Bill as being matched by a Land Bill, although this would involve 'both more difficulty and less support', for 'if we succeed with the Church, & fail with the Land, we shall have done less than half our work'; 'we must lay our first parallel the moment we are out of the Church'. Irish land had little of the mandate which it was hard to deny the electorate had conferred upon Irish disestablishment; within the Liberal party it alarmed the Whigs, not only those with Irish land or connections, like Clarendon, but also great Scottish magnates like the Duke of Argyll; it raised by implication exactly that attack on property generally of which opponents of the household suffrage had warned.

On the other hand, Irish land reform was supported by Irish middle-class opinion represented by the *Freeman's Journal* and Sir John Gray, and by the Irish Liberal MPs in the Commons, opinion which, since the start of Fenianism and the Ribbon Men, had come to be regarded in England as relatively respectable and moderate, limited in its aims to a type of demand which the imperial Parliament might feel itself able to go some way to meeting. The Tenant League, which embodied these demands, already called for the 'Three Fs' (fixity of tenure, freedom of sale, fair rent) which were eventually granted in the 1881 Land Act.

Just as Gladstone had declined to see Irish disestablishment as necessarily implying English, Scottish, or Welsh disestablishment, so he tried to isolate the Irish land question from the general question of British social and economic relationships. A simple change in the law of contract was therefore undesirable, as was the intervention of 'a public authority' to determine prices and consequently rent, for this would be a 'principle essentially imperial', 'no less applicable to England & Scotland, than it is to Ireland'. The solution offered by George Campbell, an ex-Indian judge, had in this context an immediate appeal for Gladstone. Campbell's solution, read by Gladstone on 11 August 1869, was, crudely stated, to use the tradition of the Ulster tenant right—the right to bestow or to sell the right of occupancy—as a way to recognize customary rather than contractual land relationships in Ireland generally. Campbell's solution, if it could be carried through into law, fitted splendidly into Gladstone's political pre-occupations. Because its intention was to recognize customary relationships, it could be presented as a conservative measure; because it used a particularly Irish form of customary tenure as its basis, its 'imperial' implications would be much reduced.

It was clearly not the 'Three Fs', but it could be offered to the Irish as reform on indigenous principles, offering both security and compensation to the tenant, ending 'wanton eviction' and, consequently, also ending 'demands for *unjust* augmentations of rent'. The problem was that the simplicity of the 'Three Fs' could not be matched by the bill: 'the circuitous road is really the only one practicable, & is to be much preferred to scaling and descending precipices'. But that depended on how quickly the travellers were determined to reach their destination, particularly if they were not worried about injuries on the way.

For Gladstone as Cabinet coachman, the responsibility was to reach the end of the road; when he tried to take what his passengers saw as the dangerous short cut via the generalization of Ulster tenant right, he was forced to change course. The Whigs led by Fortescue would not stand for so bold a measure, which implied an end of landlord initiative. Fortescue's solution—compensation for disturbance—implied that disturbance, that is, eviction, was to continue, eased by a legislative mechanism. Ironically, this made the question of a precedent for England the more likely. By December 1869 Gladstone found himself faced with the fact that a Land Bill supported by his present Cabinet could not be a tenant-right bill; rather than abandon the bill altogether, he fell back on tenant right for Ulster, compensation for disturbance for the rest.

The Irish Land Act was conceived and passed in the light of what Gladstone saw to be the requirements in Ireland for social and consequently political stability. The plan for some form of State purchase or sponsorship of Irish railways, which he originally intended to accompany the Land Bill to assist in the economic development of this stabilized peasantry, was not pressed. The immediate political objectives of the legislation can be seen in the acute interest Gladstone showed in the reception of the bill in Ireland, and by his attempt to accompany it by the liberation of Fenian prisoners, which the Whigs prevented throughout 1869 until late in 1870, when Gladstone wore down Dublin Castle and obtained 'the very early liberation of all those who can be regarded as purely political offenders'.

The Irish Church Act and the Land Act were intended to stabilize Ireland as it was, not to restructure Ireland for the future. The latter would have involved incorporation of the largely hostile Irish Roman Catholic clergy by concurrent endowment, wholesale evictions, and forced emigration of surplus tenantry, and an agricultural tariff; in other words it would have required the British government to live out of its time, to treat Ireland as the norm and the rest of the United Kingdom as an anomaly.* In the British context, Ireland was an anomaly,† but, in political terms, anomalous treatment could not be taken far; the best that could be done was to hope that marginal social adjustment could produce political tranquillity. 'Right relations' between landlord and tenant might also, in time, encourage economic growth.

Politically, the Land Bill was in trouble from the start. As soon as it was known that a government measure was in the making, expectations and demonstrations rose in Ireland. By November 1869 it was clear that the bill could not meet these expectations. Gladstone attempted to douse them with a letter to Sir John Gray. The Cabinet would not allow the release of Fenian prisoners, and the Prime Minister was unable to avoid having to accompany his Land Bill with a Coercion Bill. In March 1870, Roman Catholic bishops came out for the 'Three Fs', and, in the Irish context, the Land Bill emphasized the inability of the Imperial Parliament to meet Irish demands, rather than the political integration for which Gladstone had initially hoped. Publicly, the Land Bill was marked by alarm among the propertied classes, privately it was one of the two great defeats of Gladstone by the Whigs in Cabinet, the other being the defeat over Alsace-Lorraine a year later.

Irish affairs of Church and land had thus dominated Gladstone's attention in 1869 and early 1870: 'until it is disposed of, it seems to engross and swallow up my whole personal existence', he told Manning, and certainly

---

* Dr Barbara Solow argues that the Act was 'well designed to cure the evils it assumed', i.e. deter evictions and deter landlords from raising rents on tenant improvements, but that it attacked the wrong problems: 'The real problem in Ireland was not the division of a given pie, but the provision of a larger one.' But this is merely to highlight the anomalous position of Ireland in a United Kingdom where growth was spontaneous, considerable, and completely independent of direct government stimulus. B. Solow, *The Land Question, and the Irish Economy, 1870—1903* (1971), 50, 88.

† Bright's demand for simultaneous bills for English and Scottish land, though considered reluctantly by the Cabinet, came to nothing in practice.

no legislative topic, except perhaps the Irish university question, so engaged his attention between 1871 and 1874.

Gladstone had drawn up the Church and Land Bills, and especially the former, as if he were still a department minister. But at the same time, in addition to being First Lord, he was also Leader of the House of Commons. As such, he had responsibility for the details as well as the general strategy of the government's legislative programme, and as such he was expected to be in the Commons to supervise the smooth running of the daily, and nightly, progress of the legislation. It was in this capacity that he was remembered by many backbenchers as responsible in the débâcle of 1865–6, when a large government majority disintegrated over parliamentary reform. Gladstone had, not surprisingly, an acute memory of that crisis in which his political career came near to foundering. The Irish Church Bill held the party together: 'the House has moved like an army', he told Manning, but adding with ominous implication, 'an army where every private is his own general'. The Irish Land Bill passed the Commons, but only after major amendments from Radicals (W. Fowler), and Peelites (Palmer) had been avoided with difficulty, and in the face of the outright opposition of a number of Irish MPs, including Sir John Gray. However, Gladstone's personal authority, and the assumption amongst Liberals outside the Cabinet that the contents of the bill were his, prevented disastrous disruptions on Irish land.

The Upas Tree: Irish education

This was not to be the case with Irish education, 'the redemption of our last Irish *pledge*', to which Gladstone in August 1870 moved after the Land Bill, though without the same insistent urgency as he had moved in 1869 from Church to land. He prodded Fortescue into action without 'violent hurry' and implied to him that he could expect much the same prime ministerial involvement in the preparation of the measure as he had suffered with respect to the Land Bill: 'It seems to me that in the main we *know* what we ought to give them whether they will take it or not.'

The lack of haste and the didacticism were deliberate. The subject was fraught with complexity and possible disaster from the start: 'a difficult & probably a dangerous one for the Government, as there is no more doubtful point in the composition & tendencies of the Liberal party than its disposition to extremes in the matter of unsectarianism as it is called'. A solution could not be reached by negotiation or general discussion. The problem was compounded by events within Ireland, and within Europe. In Ireland, the Keogh judgement of June 1872* infuriated the Roman Catholics, and

* Judge Keogh's judgement, in the Galway by-election petition, powerfully condemned clerical excesses in the election campaign.

the O'Keeffe* case seemed to confirm fears of the civic consequences of ultramontanism. In Europe, the 1870 Vatican Council encouraged a general wave of anti-Popery. Added to this was the great debate about science, religion, and the future role of Christianity in schools and universities. As Broad Church empiricism conquered the English universities, many, and not only Roman Catholics, looked to the Irish experiment as a chance for a fresh start through what to others was an anti-intellectual reaction. All these elements worked together to raise the exceptionally intricate details of the Irish university arrangements to the highest level of political significance. Nothing illustrates the tone and central concerns of Victorian politics more clearly than that the government of the British Empire should resign after a narrow defeat on what to the twentieth-century mind might seem, at least at first glance, to be a mere bill about a provincial university.

Some consideration of the details of this complex problem is therefore necessary.

Experience had shown that no plan of general educational reform in Ireland could succeed until disputes about the apex of the system—the university—had been resolved, and it appears to have been assumed from the start by ministers that Irish university legislation would be both first and separate in Irish educational legislation.

Gladstone, through his work on the 1854 Oxford University Bill, was an experienced legislator in such matters, and his view of the question was in part founded on this experience. But an additional precedent for the Irish University Bill was the Scottish Universities Bill of 1858, which he had, though not in office, successfully amended to permit future unification of the various Scottish universities into one national university, the existing universities becoming its colleges. This proposal had not been popular in Scotland, and had cost him the chancellorship of Edinburgh University in 1868.

The problem in Ireland was religious and financial. The Roman Catholics had set up their own, poorly endowed, Catholic university; the Queen's University, with its 'godless' colleges, set up by Peel and Graham in 1845, had been largely ignored by Roman Catholics; Trinity College, Dublin, was well endowed but Anglican. Thus 'the R.C. grievance . . . is held to consist in this, that an R.C. educated in a college or place where his religion is taught cannot by virtue of that education obtain a degree in Ireland. . . . I think we desire that a portion of the public endowments should be thrown open, under the auspices of a neutral University, to the whole Irish people.' A 'neutral University' was an answer to the Irish demands for

* Father Robert O'Keeffe's suspension for taking successful civil action against other Roman Catholic clergy was upheld by the Commissioners of National Education; O'Keeffe then brought a series of civil actions, winning one against Cardinal Cullen.

a separate, concurrently endowed, Roman Catholic university, existing side-by-side with Trinity College. In the circumstances of the day, quite apart from Gladstone's own antipathy to concurrent endowment, it was probably the only solution with a chance of success, even though Hartington, who reluctantly replaced Fortescue as Irish Secretary in December 1870 under the full weight of Gladstone's moral suasion, pushed his hostility to the 'central university' plan almost to the point of resignation. But a 'neutral University' which incorporated colleges with ancient traditions was hard to translate into a statute. Gladstone drew up the bill with Thring much as he had the Irish Church Bill, at Hawarden, in touch with colleagues only by letter, with only scant reference to the Irish officers in his government, advised on the affairs of Protestant Ireland by a Trinity don, J. K. Ingram, who came over for the purpose. The bill was thus as much his own as the Irish Church Bill had been.

Gladstone's solution was characteristically neat and Burkean, in the sense of restorative conservatism. He made a clear distinction between the University of Dublin, which he showed had existed since the fourteenth century, and Trinity College which had existed since the sixteenth century and had since then effectively subsumed the University within the College. Gladstone proposed to restore the University to its original status, and to allow it to have as colleges Trinity College, the Belfast and Cork Colleges of the Queen's University (which would itself be wound up along with its third college of Galway), and such of the 'voluntary' colleges—Newman's Roman Catholic College in Dublin and the Presbyterian Magee College—as wished to join. Many problems sprang from the restrictive details (which had good Colonial precedents) thought necessary to allow the plan a chance to work: no theology, philosophy, or modern history chairs were to be founded, a professor was to 'be punished or reprimanded' for wilfully offending 'the conscientious scruples of those whom he instructs in the exercise of his office', and the legislature was in the early years to exercise much patronage by nominating the members of the University Council.

The comprehensiveness of the plan offered a bold means of solving this vexed question, which was, as Gladstone pointed out, the first stage towards a general plan of Irish education. It was also a frank recognition of sacrifices which would have to be made if partition in education was to be avoided.

Gladstone made it clear in the first sentence of his speech introducing the bill that the proposals were 'vital to the honour and existence of the Government'—that is, it was from its introduction a matter of confidence, a caveat aimed by Gladstone probably more at the 'secularist' English Liberals than at the Irish. That it was a matter of confidence seems to have been largely the result of Gladstone's identification with the bill: Lord Halifax commented dryly, 'Gladstone had to deal with the third branch of the Upas tree, and therefore made a great deal of the University Bill, not in itself a measure of such vital importance.' But once this was the case, clearly the government had to back the second reading absolutely. Thus the ten 'English and Scotch' Liberals, the thirty-five Irish who voted against the bill, and the twenty-two Irish Liberals who abstained, acted in full knowledge of the consequences. Only twelve 'Irishmen' voted with the government, as opposed to sixty-nine against. The government was defeated on 11 March 1873 by three votes and, after considering dissolution in the context of Gladstone's poor health and the generally poor state of the party, resigned, only to be forced back into office by Disraeli in one of the coolest and boldest calculations of British politics—the last occasion on which the Opposition declined to take office when it was offered.

Not for the first time in Irish affairs, the appeal to reason and concilia-tion came to nought. The earlier Irish legislation of the government had not brought Irish trust in the ability of the Westminster Parliament to act in 'Irish interests'. Indeed, the opposite had happened. Since the 1870 Land Act, the Home Rule Association had made rapid strides, and Irish Liberal Members feared for their seats. Thus when Archbishop Cullen denounced the bill, the game was up. The foundations for the maintenance of the Liberal party in Ireland were already eroded. The University Bill stated what the 1874 general election confirmed: Liberal Ireland was soon to be dead and gone.

Despite the run of home rule successes in by-elections, little of this fundamental shift in Irish politics seems to have been perceived by Glad-stone and those around him. During the making of the University Bill, Gladstone had dealt with the Irish hierarchy—as far as he dealt with it at all—through the agency of Manning. Though from the start there had been doubts and caveats, both seem to have expected the bill to pass. Even as late as 1 March, Gladstone assumed that the bishops' Resolutions, which were 'really War to the knife', were the result of mistaken tactics—'how is it possible this should not have been perceived?'—rather than outright hostility. Gladstone saw the defeat first as a stupid rejection of 'boons' offered to the Irish, secondly as a stab in the back by treacherous, ultra-montane bishops: he told Manning, 'Your Irish Brethren have received in the late vote of Parlt. the most extravagant compliment ever paid them. *They* have destroyed the measure; which otherwise was safe enough.'

Gladstone's Irish measures had been conceived in the spirit of Edmund Burke. Irish land and the University Bill had been profoundly conservative in presentation—the first based on the Ulster tenant right, a prescriptive right by definition ('founded on the original grants to the [Ulster] settlers in the seventeenth century'), the second the resurrection of an ancient univer-sity, a prescriptive right in effect. The disestablishment of the Irish Church by the author of *The State in its Relations with the Church* had been the acknowledgement of a pluralism which was self-consciously a second best. 'There is nothing that Ireland has asked and which this country and this Parliament have refused', Gladstone said at Aberdeen in 1871, going on to acknowledge the remaining 'single grievance' of university education. By 1873 the Irish themselves were registering their disagreement with this view at by-elections. English 'boons' were not enough. 'I have looked in vain for the setting forth of any practical scheme of policy which the Imperial Parliament is not equal to deal with, or which it refuses to deal with, and which is to be brought about by Home Rule.' The endowed Catholic university was exactly such a scheme, and its Gladstonian alternative of 1873 provided the occasion for the cutting of what Gladstone had called in 1871 'the silken cords of love', to the weaving of which much of his and his ministry's time had been devoted.

Education in Scotland and England, 1869–1870

The man who disestablished the Irish Church could carry a Land Bill despite the fact that his supporters almost all thought it too little or too much; the essential struggle had been with Cabinet colleagues. The Anglican Tractarian, the former member of the National Society for the Education of the Poor in the Principles of the Established Church, found himself more personally and politically engaged in the great struggle over English education.

The education question had its roots in two royal commissions and two developments of the 1860s; first, the realization that a combination of voluntaryism and the Established Church could no longer realistically aspire to offer an adequate elementary education in the cities; second, the early stirrings of awareness of the achievements of Continental nations in educational and industrial development. It is, of course, a hoary schoolboy myth that the Franco-Prussian war 'caused' the 1870 Education Act—the chronology of 1870 would have to be reversed to allow that—but awareness of the Prussian model certainly existed as a result of Mark Pattison's report for the Duke of Newcastle's Royal Commission in the 1860s. Once the 1870 war began, Gladstone's *Edinburgh Review* article quickly made the connection: 'Undoubtedly the conduct of the campaign, on the German side, has given a marked triumph to the cause of systematic popular education.'

Gladstone had shown little interest in education in the 1850s and 1860s, save for reform of the universities and public schools. In this context, he was personally an unrepentant advocate of the classical curriculum, which many of his essays and books, including *Juventus Mundi* (1869), were intended to justify, and he deplored the fact that the '*low* utilitarian argument . . . for giving it [education] what is termed a practical direction, is so plausible' that it was winning by default. He and the Cabinet declined to give a government grant to Owen's College in Manchester, and Gladstone later used this decision as a precedent for declining aid for the founding of Aberystwyth. Despite the general concern about the strength of technical education in Germany, the Liberal Cabinet, for reasons both of religion and political economy, refused to be drawn into the direct funding of British universities.

Of the Cabinet, Bruce, Forster, and de Grey were well known protagonists of popular education. A bill dealing with England could not fail to be controversial, and the Cabinet dealt first with Scottish education in 1869. Discussion in Scotland on education had progressed further than in England, and in Scotland only two interests, the Established Church and the Free Church, were taken into account—the vast spectrum of denominational concern characteristic of the English debate was absent.* None the less, Argyll's Scottish bill, introduced into the Lords in February 1869, was soon in difficulties. The Lords treated it as a precedent for England, where they already disliked the important Endowed Schools Bill, also of 1869, a measure in whose preparation Gladstone seems to have played no part. The Lords amended the Scottish bill so as to destroy the notion of a 'national system', and leave denominationalism as firmly entrenched as possible. By the time the bill reached the Commons in the summer, it had become enmeshed in the crisis of the Irish Church Bill. Gladstone seems to have given no attention to it outside the Cabinet; concessions were made to keep the bill alive, but there was no real prospect of it passing, and it foundered, eventually succeeding in a revised form in 1872. In October 1869 Gladstone encouraged de Grey and Forster to meet with him 'to lay the foundation stone of our Education measure in England'. This suggests that a vague opinion that there would be an English bill was already forming (Gladstone in early September already assumed the predominance of 'the two large subjects of Irish Land and Education in England'), but Gladstone's letter clearly had a stimulating effect, for no preparations seem to have been made hitherto. Why Gladstone encouraged the question is unclear. Certainly, popular pressure for an English bill was already considerable. Gladstone may have hoped it would prevent Irish land becoming overdominant and contentious. The two issues fed on each other: in Cabinet, land predominated to the extent that education was discussed only once before the full bill was approved in Cabinet on 4 February 1870, without any controversy being noted by Gladstone. In the Commons, Irish land was to some extent subordinated to the great debates on English education.

The Scottish bill had made it clear that the path of a successful English bill would require careful planning: that the route lay through a minefield was not immediately apparent. From Gladstone's point of view, Forster and de Grey's proposals, that the existing system of denominational schools be supplemented where necessary by school boards locally elected, was in

---

* The interests of Roman Catholics and Episcopalians were virtually ignored in Scotland.

general satisfactory. He was characteristic of his times in showing little interest in the bill's proposals apart from the religious dimension. He never made any attempt to modify the general structure of their plan. This was not surprising as it was the only plan likely to survive the Lords, and it was one which he could, in general, support. Not only Anglican but Roman Catholic interests were at stake, as Gladstone recognized in putting Manning in touch with de Grey at a very early stage.

Following the position that his friend, the High-Churchman Dean Hook, had championed since the late 1830s, Gladstone focused at once on the aspect of the bill which particularly concerned him personally: 'the proposal to found the State schools on the system of the British and Foreign Society would I think hardly do';* he made clear what was to be, with some modification, his consistent preference throughout the ministry: 'Why not adopt frankly the principle that the State or the local community should provide the secular teaching, & either leave the option to the Ratepayer to go beyond this *sine quâ non*, if they think fit, within the limits of the conscience clause, or else simply leave the parties themselves to find Bible & other religious education from voluntary sources.' As he told Bright retrospectively, 'the application of the Rate to be confined by law to secular teaching only' was the only 'solid and stable ground'.

On this issue, Gladstone found he had the Cabinet, the Anglican Church, and the Dissenters against him. If restriction to secular teaching could not be achieved, Gladstone went to the other extreme. In a long memorandum written on 29 May 1870, after meeting several Nonconformist deputations, he made as strong a case as he could against 'the plan that the Bible be read & explained, while formularies are to be forbidden', though admitting that the proposal had some advantages. The absence of formularies (i.e. of an understanding of the dogma, structure, and teaching of the apostolic church) would be a surrender to latitudinarianism and Nonconformity.

However, the absence of formularies was exactly the solution reached through the Cowper–Temple amendment, agreed by the Cabinet on 14 June 1870. As Gladstone's memorandum of 29 May 1870 recognized, 'the concord of opinion' behind this solution was 'due to a great anxiety to maintain a direct connection between religion and popular education', and in practical political terms it was the only way of reconciling the two. The acceptance of this was a major personal blow for Gladstone. It was not exactly a defeat, in that he had not associated himself systematically with the bill and his usual persistence had not been placed behind his own preference. But it was a personal concession which rankled more deeply than any of the many concessions Gladstone made to hold his ministry together.

* The Nonconformist British and Foreign School Society had from 1833 distributed an Exchequer grant and provided non-denominational religious teaching.

The Education Bill was the largest of the government's legislative measures in whose preparation Gladstone did not involve himself intimately at every stage, though, as we have seen, his interventions and encouragement were at certain moments extremely important. It ran side by side with his Land Bill, and once it was in the Commons Gladstone, the most formidable of the Liberal front bench in procedural manipulation, took over much of the responsibility for its safe passage. Together, the Land and Education Bills brought to a dramatic close the Session of 1870—the last occasion until 1911 when two major, highly controversial bills were run together in a single Session.

CHAPTER VIII

The First Government: Distintegration and Downfall

The Declining Efficiency of Parliament: the legislative log-jam—The Crown and 'the Classes': the Queen, republicanism, army purchase—Patronage, from the Garter to the Church—The Economy: the working classes and their unions, the propertied classes and their rates—Fiscal Policy: the Budget, the Estimates, and the 'scandals'—Chancellor Again: the downfall of the government and resignation as party leader—Constituencies, Public Speaking, and the Press in the early 1870s

1. To engage now [March 1874] is to engage for the term of Opposition, & the succeeding term of a Liberal Government. These two cannot probably embrace less than a considerable term of years. (1830–41. 1841–52. 1866–74.)
This is not consistent with my views for the close of my life.
2. Failure of 1866–8.
3. My views on the question of Education in particular are I fear irrecon-cileable with those of a considerable portion of it. Into any interim contract I cannot enter.
4. In no case has the head of a Govt. considerable in character & duration, on receiving what may be called an emphatic dismissal, become Leader of Opposition.
5. The condition of the Liberal party requires consideration.
   a. It has no present public *cause* upon which it is agreed.
   b. It has serious & conscientious divisions of opinion, which are also pressing, e.g. on Education.
   c. The habit of making a career by & upon constant active opposition to the bulk of the party, & its leaders, has acquired a dangerous predominance among a portion of its members. This habit is not checked by the action of the great majority, who do not indulge or approve it: & it has become dangerous to the credit & efficiency of the party.

The Declining Efficiency of Parliament: the legislative log-jam

The disestablishment of the Irish Church, the Irish Land Act, and the Education Act of 1870, three of the triumphs of the century, were bought at a high legislative price. In June 1869 the Cabinet for the first time considered 'Bills Abandoned', and the midsummer purge of bills proposed but not passed became a distinctive feature of the ministry. The policy of 'filling up the cup', of starting bills which were certain to run into difficulties and then of not allowing enough time for the resolution of those difficulties, might keep the fissiparous elements within the majority occupied, but it would not necessarily keep them happy.* The use of the 'clôture' (or the guillotine as it is called today) was considered, but it was not introduced.

The problem was circular: the bringing forward of legislation was a form of party discipline, but an undisciplined party would not support the means by which such legislation might pass the Commons, namely a readiness to subordinate the interests of particular groups to the success of the government legislative programme. That programme was, of course, impeded by the wrecking tactics of the Lords. But since members of the majority in the Commons were often equally vocal in their hostility to aspects of government bills, the Lords could claim to be doing no more than playing their natural role in the constitution. In fact, government homogeneity barely existed outside the government's early Irish legislation. The whips could never be sure when the spirit of 1866 would arise again, and the large majority obtained at the 1868 election had always been expected to produce problems of management.

Gladstone did not blame Glyn, the chief whip. He thought that 'there is something of a tide in politics. At the Election we had an immense impetus & we came back with more than a natural or nominal majority'; by 1871 he saw the tide as turning, and by 1872 he thought 'that our hold over the Constituencies is weakened, & that the Conservatives may begin soon to think of another advent to power'. Disraeli saw the same pattern. He waited until the 'immense impetus' had spent itself, and in 1872 he pounced. Disraeli's strategy was to let the Liberals discredit themselves. Their vast and unprecedented flood of legislation, whether passed or not, was in itself discrediting; the Conservatives appeared conservative simply by sitting silent on their benches.

Despite his position as First Lord and Leader of the House, there was little Gladstone could do. Several of the proposals were personally repugnant to him; he was reluctant to admit that the preservation of Oxford and Cambridge as national universities required the abolition of religious

---

* Gladstone described the process to his constituents: 'such was the state of public expectation and demand with regard to every one of those subjects [Scottish education, licensing, local taxation, mines regulation in 1871], that it was not in our choice to refuse to place our views before Parliament in the form of a bill laid upon the table; and I believe I am within the mark in saying that if we had attempted to avoid incurring that responsibility, either other members of Parliament would themselves have endeavoured to procure—not legislation upon the subject, but at least the production of measures of their own ...' or resolutions would have been passed demanding government bills.

tests,* and he had little enthusiasm for the ballot, necessary corollary of parliamentary reform though he might admit it to be. The Cabinet did not prove to be a suitable body to redeem the situation. Though it oversaw the details of parliamentary business, it does not seem at all to have acted as a body for developing a coherent party strategy. This may well have been an impossible objective, but Cabinet members do not seem to have thought in terms of a party structure of electoral management. The Cabinet continued to act chiefly as an executive body, distanced and often estranged from the political structure which had placed it in power.

The Crown and 'the Classes': the Queen, republicanism, army purchase

Cabinet members received their seals from the Queen, and relationships with the Court were one of their chief preoccupations. Gladstone's daily journal testifies to the vast amount of time, in letter-writing, visits, and negotiations, that the leader of a government, and especially of a reforming government, had to spend on the monarchy. Both the Queen and the Prince of Wales seemed major problems. In the heady enthusiasm of post-reform Britain, the relationship of the Court and 'the democracy' was very uncertain.

The absenteeism of the Queen and the blatant profligacy of the Prince created the conditions for the only moment in the history of industrial Britain when it seemed as if republicanism might become a serious political issue. Gladstone took the view that the risk was not worth taking, and that the monarchy must be strengthened by positive action on the part of its members and defenders. He believed that to meet republicanism, Bradlaugh and Dilke, by repression 'would tend to establish rather than end the controversy. What is needed is that we should if possible do or cause something to be done of a nature likely to remove the dissatisfaction, of which the absurd republican cry is an external symptom'.

From the first Cabinet of the ministry, he brought forward a plan to associate the monarchy more closely with Ireland, more particularly suggesting that the Irish Office should be reformed, and that the Prince of Wales should become Lord-Lieutenant, presiding as a constitutional monarch in that country. He urged this pertinaciously, especially after the Prince's involvement in the Mordaunt divorce case. From late in 1870 Gladstone pursued his plan with spasmodic assistance from Granville and Halifax. But the Queen was a match for them, and would not give an inch. Gladstone persistently tried to overcome her refusal to appear in public; when she said she would not open a bridge, he demanded she name a substitute. Gladstone's moment came with the Prince's near-fatal illness in

* Gladstone hoped for what the Queen's Speech of 1870 called a 'legislative settlement'—i.e. a compromise saving some of the entrenched Anglicanism of Oxford and Cambridge. He worked to head off 'absolute secularisation'.

December 1871. He insisted that the Queen should capitalize on the swelling sympathy for the Prince by a public appearance at a thanksgiving service at St Paul's. He met every argument with a prepared position, and at the crisis of the discussion, when the Queen 'contracted her objection to the length of the service', he trumped her by quoting the '*Annual Register* of 1789 (from which it appears that the Commons set out at 8 a.m., the King and Queen at 10, and their Majesties only returned to the Palace at half past three.)' The Queen gave way, and the service was a great success, especially for Disraeli, who was loudly cheered outside the cathedral.

Gladstone and his Cabinet's battle with the Queen had to be kept a secret within the Establishment. The Cabinet could not say what pains they took to save the Queen from herself and from the Radical wing of their own supporters. What had in bygone years been stock patriotic Whig criticism of the Civil List, now, in the context of post-reform politics, could easily be made by the Tories to seem, and in a few cases actually was, open republicanism. Gladstone himself gave away a trick in trying to win over his constituents at Greenwich by quoting an egalitarian parody of the National Anthem from the *Secularist Hymn Book*, and calling it 'a questionable book [with] verses which I think contain much good sense'. Gurdon, Gladstone's secretary, issued a denial that the book as a whole had his approval, but it was too late. It was to this sort of incident that Disraeli could refer when he accused Gladstone of alternating 'between a menace and a sigh'. The Whigs were of little help, except individually and behind the scenes. Palmerston and Russell had dissipated the legacy of Melbourne, and Gladstone had failed to capitalize on the resemblance of high-principled earnestness between himself and Prince Albert which in the early 1860s had looked as if it could bear substantial fruit.

Undoubtedly Gladstone's overbearing, moralizing manner did no good. We have seen in the case of John Bright that he knew how to flatter; in the case of the Queen, he never took up the trowel. In his persistent advocacy of the Prince of Wales's potential usefulness, and in his meetings with the Prince, there are some signs of a Liberal–Marlborough House alliance being formed, but this would have conflicted too much with Gladstone's plans for the public rehabilitation of Victoria for it to emerge as a serious element in politics.

Personal emollience might have helped, but behind the growing private friction lay great public issues. The abolition of purchase in the army—the ability of army officers to buy promotion rather than, as in the navy, earn it by merit—seemed an assault as brutal as disestablishment on the internal traditions of the landed class and the Court. First raised by Cardwell in Cabinet in March 1870, the question became, for Gladstone, part of a general plan of reconstruction of the mores of that 'vast leisured and wealthy class'. Prompted by the Franco-Prussian war, and particularly by the 'mechanical perfection' of the Prussians, whose 'most consummate army' was 'put into the field with the greatest expedition, and at the smallest cost ever known', Gladstone wanted 'complete and definite' army reform involving India, the Colonies, the militia, and the training of officers by 'making all our young cadets learn a soldier's business in the ranks', and a complete overhaul of the activities of the peacetime army: 'the greatest difficulty of all in truth is this: to redeem the officer's life from idleness in time of peace'. He consistently urged Cardwell to go beyond abolition of the purchase of commissions, but Cardwell's Army Regulation Bill was primarily a purchase abolition and compensation bill, together with the centralization of control of the militia.

The bill appeared therefore as an attack on the privileges of a caste, without offering, as Gladstone had wanted, the prospect of its reconstruction in the national interest. That caste constituted the heart of the most privileged section of Victorian society, and its exclusiveness was emphasized by its leader, the Queen's cousin, the Duke of Cambridge, commander-in-chief and colonel of the Horse Guards. The struggle through the summer of 1871 was long and bitter—much more so than that over Irish land or Church. Back-benchers on both sides of the House defended their interests with a fanatical resolution which the Duke of Cambridge did nothing to moderate. With immense difficulty the Queen, who had in the first instance supported the abolition of purchase, was brought to suggest to her cousin that he should support her government's bill in the House of Lords, but the best he would do was to abstain.

The bill wrecked the government's programme in the Commons and was summarily dismissed in the Lords. Although the proposal was supported in principle by both front benches, the organs of representative government proved unable to abolish the purchase system by legislation. The executive then did what it could have done at any time, effected abolition by Royal Warrant. This was possible because purchase had been made illegal by an Act of 1809, except in those cases in which a Royal Warrant allowed an exception (the 'regulation' price purchase). The Cabinet's Royal Warrant withdrew these exceptions which in fact had spread to cover almost all commissions. This left the officers of the army with the prospect of purchase being ended without the financial compensation which Cardwell's bill provided, and the Lords therefore hastened to pass it. The complexities of the constitutional wrangle about purchase made the government's position difficult to explain popularly. Its use of the Warrant when blocked in Parliament was seen as high-handed, and the fact that a chief need for the bill had been to give compensation to the officers was soon forgotten. To some, Gladstone seemed a bit of a bully. He could equally be seen as resolute and resourceful in a way that few progressive Prime Ministers are.

In Gladstone's view, the defence of purchase represented the failure of the landed class to justify its existence in the modern industrial world. He approved in principle of wealth, the Court, and an hereditary aristocracy. He was cautious about the absorption of the middle class into the aristocracy, despite his own record, telling the citizens of Liverpool in 1872, 'I know not why commerce should not have its old families rejoicing to be connected with commerce from generation to generation. . . . I think it is a subject of sorrow, and almost a scandal, when those families which have either acquired or received station and opulence from commerce turn their backs upon it and seem to be ashamed of it. (Great applause.) It is not so with my brother [Robertson] or with me. (Applause.)' He saw the aristocracy as a separate class with its own duties. His views on army reform centred not on the opening of the army to middle-class entry, but on efficient promotion and training within the traditional military caste. But he wanted Court and County to follow the middle-class values of efficiency, application, and economy. He believed that obsession with wealth was coming to dominate the aristocracy at the expense of duty, especially 'in the Clubs, and in the army'. 'Ploutocracy' he commented in the aftermath of the purchase crisis, produced 'a bastard aristocracy & aristocracy shows too much disposition, in Parliament especially, to join hands with this bastard.'

Gladstone's problems were therefore not confined to the Queen and the Duke of Cambridge; rather, his relationship with the upper echelons of the Court was symptomatic of a general distrust felt for him by landed property, Whigs as well as Tories.

Patronage, from the Garter to the Church

As First Lord, Gladstone was responsible for the exercise of the vast range of Crown patronage, from awarding Garters to filling Regius chairs, bishoprics, deaneries, and rectories. Civil Service reform might have reduced the whips' source of patronage but that of the First Lord was by no means diminished. The response to Gladstone's exercise of patronage strikingly illustrates the extent to which landed society was reluctant to associate itself with his administration.

Offers of honours such as the Garter and posts of influence and significance in the localities, such as lord-lieutenancies, were rejected on political grounds by erstwhile supporters of Whig–Liberal governments. The Garter was declined on political grounds by the Duke of Leinster in 1869 and the Duke of Norfolk in 1870, the latter despite Gladstone's assurance that 'the public would consider your acceptance of the Garter as implying not by any means a permanent pledge but a present inclination *towards* the party & the Govt.: as indeed they may already have thought from so slight a circumstance as your doing me the favour to drive with me on the celebration of the Queen's birthday'. The failure to secure Norfolk, the youthful leader of the English Roman Catholics, was a particular blow, given the lengths to which Gladstone went to solicit that denomination's support. The Lord-Lieutenancy of Staffordshire was offered to Wrottesley, who refused it, to Gladstone's Peelite friend and, in the Oak Farm days, his creditor, Dudley, who refused it, and to Hatherton, who refused it. Wrottesley was eventually persuaded to accept it. Hostility to the ministry and to Gladstone personally was not as marked as it became in the 1880–5 government, but the steady drift of the landed classes away from the Liberal party had clearly begun, as surely as the Court was finding itself the agent of the Tory party.

The exercise of Church patronage the First Lord shared with the Lord Chancellor; Gladstone tried to ease the demand for parish livings, 'which throw me to despair', by informally linking his patronage lists with those of the Lord Chancellor, and he also sent Hatherley a list of those deserving cathedral preferment. Sharp attention was paid to the politics of priests receiving promotion, more so than to their position in the theological spectrum. 'No talents, no learning, no piety, can advance the fortunes of a clergyman whose political opinions are adverse to those of the governing party', wrote Lord John Russell in a dictum generally true of the nineteenth century, and true in some measure of Gladstone's patronage, at least in so far as Liberal bishops could be found.* He asked the ex-Tory MP, Sir William Heathcote, a prominent Tractarian, to report to him on 'eminently good' clergymen, but with the significant proviso that Heathcote should include information about their attitude to Irish disestablishment.

The unexpected recovery of Tait from an illness in 1869 removed the excitement of an archiepiscopal appointment. There was a clutch of appointments of bishops in September 1869—Wilberforce from Oxford to Winchester, Temple to Exeter, Hervey to Bath and Wells, Mackarness to Oxford. These were not appointments of mere ecclesiastical significance—each of them was subsequently circularized by Gladstone with an appeal to vote for the Irish Land Bill in the Lords. He also canvassed episcopal support for the Army Bill abolishing purchase in 1871, and for other measures. Liberalism would certainly seem to be the reason for the appointment of Temple to Exeter. Temple was one of the contributors to *Essays and Reviews* (1860), the modernists' manifesto, and his promotion caused outrage in Tractarian circles. Gladstone re-read Temple's essay after appointing him, finding it 'on reperusal . . . crude and unbalanced, but neither heretical nor sceptical'. The episcopal appointment which caused much the most difficulty was the comparatively minor one of St Asaph, that see whose separate preservation Gladstone had tried to make a condition when first invited to join the Cabinet by Peel in 1843: here Gladstone

* Earl Russell, *An essay in the history of the English government and constitution* (1865 edn.), 309.

wished to appoint a Welsh-speaking bishop so as to moderate the appearance of the Anglican Church as an alien element in Welsh culture. Though previously unimpressed by the Welsh language, Gladstone evidently thought that such appointments could affect what he called the 'singularly susceptible population' of the Principality. Joshua Hughes was nominated after a 'very laborious though interesting search'. Gladstone's speech to the Eisteddfod at Mold in 1873 emphasized the seriousness with which he had begun to take Welsh affairs.

The Economy: the working classes and their unions, the propertied classes and their rates

The last of the areas of routine business with which the First Lord and the Cabinet were necessarily involved was government finance and the economy. By the 1870s, 'finance' appeared to have little to do with the state of the economy. It would not be true to say that the Cabinet had no interest in the working of the economy, but it would be true to say that it took no direct responsibility for it. When Daniel Jones, a miner from Newcastle-under-Lyme, wrote to tell him of his unemployment and to complain of low wages, Gladstone made the classic mid-Victorian reply:

The only means which have been placed in my power of 'raising the wages of colliers' has been by endeavouring to beat down all those restrictions upon trade which tend to reduce the price to be obtained for the product of their labour, & to lower as much as may be the taxes on the commodities which they may require for use or for consumption. Beyond this I look to the forethought not yet so widely diffused in this country as in Scotland, & in some foreign lands; & I need not remind you that in order to facilitate its exercise the Government have been empowered by Legislation to become through the Dept. of the P.O. the receivers & guardians of savings.

Gladstone was becoming uneasily aware, as were other perceptive observers of the Victorian economy, that the economy worked with a chronic 'enormous mass of paupers', and that: 'Again, and yet more at large, what is human life, but, in the great majority of cases, a struggle for existence? and if the means of carrying on that struggle are somewhat better than they were, yet the standard of wants rises with the standard of means, and sometimes more rapidly. . . .'* He was moreover aware that 'great vicissitudes mark the industrial condition of society; and we pass rapidly in a series of cycles from periods of great prosperity to periods of sharp distress'. He suggested to Lowe that what would have amounted to a primitive cost of living index should be drawn up, so that the condition of the working

* Budget speech of 1864, in W. E. Gladstone, *Financial Statements* (1864), 519. What exactly Gladstone said on this topic in the 1863 budget is the subject of dispute; see the *résumé* of quotations by Engels in his preface to the fourth German edition of the first volume of *Das Kapital* (1890).

classes in 1832, 1852, and 1872 could be compared, but nothing seems to have come of this. The items Gladstone suggested for the index are an interesting reflection of Victorian priorities: the price of lodging, fuel, clothing, food, travel, books, and newspapers.

Gladstone was fortunate in that, in general terms, his first ministry witnessed the emergence of the nation from a period of 'sharp distress' (the beginnings of which occurred in his later years at the Exchequer in the 1860s) into an upward cycle, largely though not wholly stifling the first widely-based murmurings against free trade since the early 1850s. In 1867 and 1868 during Disraeli's Chancellorship, *per capita* net national income had actually fallen slightly to £21.9, but by 1874 it had reached £27.4 at 1900 prices, or risen from £27.2 to £34.6 at current prices.* Gladstone saw this spectacular rise as a vindication of the fiscal and institutional reforms of the previous twenty years and of the principle that the maximum freedom of the market and the minimum absorption of its funds by the Government was the best guarantee of the creation of wealth.

This dramatic increase in national prosperity was, of course, not necessarily fully apparent to contemporaries, nor did it benefit all groups or classes equally. Its immediate political consequences are uncertain. Gladstone's administration had to deal with two political problems whose origins lay deep in social reactions to economic change: the problem of trade unions and their status, and the problem of the propertied classes' reaction to taxation. It is hard to judge how much the political expression of these problems was occasioned by economic change: first, change in the form of the uncertainties of the 1866 and 1873 disruptions of the money-market; second, in the end of the gradual inflation which had underpinned growth in the 1850s and 1860s, and which gave way at the end of 1873 to the start of the long deflation of the 1870s, 1880s, and 1890s; third, in both downswings and upswings of certain sectors of the economy. A further underlying factor was the political opportunity and alarm which the household suffrage encouraged in the working and propertied classes respectively.

The economic problems of the working classes came before the Cabinet in the form of the trade unions. The Trades Union Congress, which first met in 1868, characterized with a new urgency a problem which had been recognized but not solved in the early 1860s: the legal status of unions and their funds. The Gladstone Cabinet offered the first tentative legislative solution to a series of questions which, a century later, remain contentious. It recognized the legal existence of trade unions and secured their

* Feinstein's calculations in B. R. Mitchell and P. Deane, *Abstract of British Historical Statistics* (1962), 367; any such estimates have their difficulties, but all indices for 1868–74 show the same trend; e.g. GNP at constant factor cost (1913 = 100) rose from 43.7 in 1870 to 48.9 in 1874; C. H. Feinstein, *National Income Expenditure and Output of the United Kingdom* (1972), table 7.

property by allowing them to register their rules with the Registrar of Friendly Societies, and sought to ameliorate those areas of the criminal law specifically affecting the actions of trade union members. This legislation took the form of two Acts, both passed in 1871, the Trade Union Act and the Criminal Law Amendment Act. This simple statement disguises a complex narrative in 1869, when a bill introduced by Thomas Hughes and A. J. Mundella was withdrawn in the light of government promises of legislation, and prolonged pressure in 1871 when the government's original single bill finally passed as two separate Acts. The Cabinet's principles were 'to prevent violence; and in all economic matters the law to take no part'. The first phrase revealed the Cabinet's intention to allow peaceful collective bargaining, the second its unwillingness to circumscribe the activities of trade unions on the grounds merely of their alleged violation of the canons of orthodox political economy by combining 'in restraint of trade'.* The bills' drafters, however, underestimated the ingenuity of the bench, for the directions to the jury of Mr Justice Brett in the Gas Stokers' Case of December 1872 revealed that the statute had insufficiently protected trade unionists from the operation of the common law of conspiracy,† whilst local Justices of the Peace tended to interpret the provisions of the Criminal Law Amendment Act affecting picketing in a more restrictive manner than its originators had intended. As a result, the hostility of a labour movement, swelled both in numbers and in confidence by the exceptional prosperity of the early 1870s, was directed towards the Gladstone government.

The TUC campaign for amendment of the labour laws led Robert Lowe, the new Home Secretary, to suggest the possibility of some concession and, on the prompting of Bright, Gladstone encouraged Lowe in September 1873 to bring proposals before the Cabinet following 'some rather careful inquiry'. Under Lowe's guidance the Cabinet, with dissensions from Selborne the Lord Chancellor, moved towards fresh legislation which would restore the position in which the Acts of 1871 had sought to place the unions. The Cabinet in November 1873 seems to have agreed to the heads of a bill which would have done much of what Disraeli's Cabinet eventually did in the Conspiracy and Protection of Property and the Employers and Workmen Acts of 1875.

Gladstone did not set out directly to involve himself in trade union questions, and the legislation seems to have been largely departmental in inspiration. His role in September 1873 was as co-ordinator rather than

---

* Clause 2 of the Trade Union Act 1871 attempted to place unions and their members beyond charges of conspiracy; it was intended that the Criminal Law Amendment Act would do this.

† 'It is clear, therefore, that in 1871 the Legislature was passing a statute regulating all the relations between masters and servants; and by those provisions they practically say that there shall be no other offences as between master and servant but the offences detailed in the preceding part of this section'; Mr Straight's argument defending the Gas Stokers, E. W. Cox, *Reports of cases in criminal law* (1875), xii. 331.

initiator. There is a hint that he played some role in getting the Gas Stokers' sentences reduced. He discouraged the use of troops in the particular case of a farmer who persuaded the army to take over the harvesting to enable him to dismiss unionized labour, but in general Gladstone was characteristic of the ambivalence of the propertied classes towards unions: he recognized their existence and their usefulness in producing order and coherence in industrial relations, but he would not give them the tools they thought they needed to do the job. Thus he encouraged 'the employment of the spare time of soldiers in useful civilian occupations', thinking 'there is always a risk, lest the labouring classes should like other classes be led to exaggerate their own rights in such a matter, so deep does the principle of monopoly lie in human nature'.

As a Flintshire land- and coal-owner he became involved in a bitter controversy over the closed shop, discussed in the next chapter. As Prime Minister, he did not encourage a swift restoration of the intentions of his own government's legislation, and he paid for this politically. The extent of Cabinet agreement in November 1873 was insufficiently wide, or Gladstone was insufficiently interested in the question, for the loss of trust on the part of the unions to be reduced. The snap dissolution of January 1874 occurred during considerable union anger with the Liberals; the election manifesto promised much to the middle classes, but nothing specific to the unions—the plans for restorative union legislation being only hinted at. Not surprisingly some unions and unionists worked for the Tories at the general election, or ran their own candidates.

The reaction of urban ratepayers against government—not necessarily only Liberal governments—was a marked feature of these years. The State in normal circumstances raised its revenue by two quite separate means: national taxation, requested in the budget and granted in the Finance Bill, raising in 1868 £67,800,000, and local taxation, assessed and raised locally mainly from the taxation of owners and occupiers of rateable property, raising in 1868 £19,800,000. But the total expenditure of local authorities (the difference being made up by loans, government subventions, and rents and sales of locally owned property) was £30,140,000—nearly half the figure for the national government's income, a total which Goschen described as 'astounding'.

The difficulties involved were various; in the counties the rates were administered by the non-elected Quarter Sessions, in the towns by the corporations elected on the 1835 local franchise; the Tories had argued since the later 1840s that where local administration had to deal with questions which were essentially national, the cost should be borne by the Exchequer and raised by national not local taxation. This was the line of attack which the Tories returned to in 1869 when at the very start of the first Session Sir Massey Lopes called for a royal commission.

Lopes repeated his demands for an amelioration of the rate-payers' burdens at intervals throughout the government, and with considerable success. G. J. Goschen's two bills of 1871 (which offered an ambitious attempt to consolidate and standardize, 'to make all hereditaments, both corporeal and incorporeal' liable to rates, while at the same time surrendering the house tax to the relief of local rates) were withdrawn virtually without discussion; they were condemned as being overfavourable to urban dwellers. In April 1872, having previously forced the ministry to withdraw by the device of moving the previous question, Lopes defeated in 259:159 a conciliatory amendment moved by the Liberal Sir Thomas Acland and carried his own resolution that 'it is expedient to remedy the injustice of imposing Taxation for National objects on one description of property only'. The Cabinet's decision had been to 'oppose Lopez [sic] and stand on things already agreed'.

The problem was that the Cabinet could not agree. Gladstone deplored any concession on the part of the Exchequer: 'my judgment is very hostile to taxing the Exchequer for local purposes. Even Sir R. Peel went too far in that direction.' When the Cabinet tried to agree on legislation following Lopes's resolution, he told Goschen: 'I seem but very little to see my way towards doing the thing that the H. of C. wants us to do.' The Cabinet had a 'much prolonged . . . general conversation introduced by W.E.G. on the question of Local Taxation'. Some agreement was reached on a bill to standardize assessment and valuation, consolidate the rates, and abolish exemptions—that is, to set the existing system on a more regularized basis—but in 1873, despite Tory taunts, no local government bill was introduced, Stansfeld, the new president of the Local Government Board, falling back on a select committee on parish boundaries. The solution that Gladstone had proposed to Goschen in 1869, 'to occupy the ground' by 'a measure for County Boards on the elective principle' was then returned to. At Gladstone's suggestion, Stansfeld drew up plans in November 1873 for county boards; the Cabinet's reaction was uncertain, in general favourable to mixed county boards (i.e. made up partly of elected representatives, partly of JPs), but with ominous reservations from Goschen.

Before the Cabinet could meet to discuss a bill, Gladstone had decided on dissolution. In his election address he pointed out that the government 'have been unable to meet the views of those who appear to have thought that, provided only a large amount of public money could be had in any form to relieve the rates, no great heed need be paid to anything else'. But he recognized the 'very general desire that some new assistance should be afforded to the ratepayers of the country from funds at present under the command of the State', and he promised 'a thorough and comprehensive, not a partial, handling of the question . . . relief coupled with reform of local taxation'; there would be 'relief of rates and other property'.

Gladstone was 'rather uncomfortable' about local taxation, and remained so. He loathed the gradual conflation of imperial and local finance implied by grants-in-aid—'doles' as he called them—but this was a conflation hard to avoid and one which was steadily increasing even before his own government's Education Act gave to grants-in-aid what was in the long run to be their greatest fillip.*

In its dealings with economic questions as manifested by trade unions and the local taxation movement, the Gladstone Cabinet cannot be said to have had much success. Both ran as festering sores throughout the Parliament, and neither was healed by the time of its dissolution.

Fiscal Policy: the Budget, the Estimates, and the 'Scandals'

The Cabinet also dealt with the economy more directly, through the Estimates, the budget, and the Finance Bill, all recurring items with an accepted timetable in the Cabinet's year, the Estimates being drawn up in the autumn, the budget in the spring.

Competence in fiscal management was the long, strong suit which the Liberals had played throughout the 1860s, and it was the card Gladstone's defenders could play when he was accused of erratic behaviour in other areas of policy. It was therefore a major blow to the reputation and self-respect of the government when, in 1871, Lowe's budget had to be withdrawn (following powerful opposition to the Estimates and to his proposals for a match tax balanced by change in the succession duties)—the first time this had happened to an established administration since Wood's budget of 1851.

Gladstone had, on the whole, let Lowe have his head. He had sent him a list of measures which he saw as still outstanding from his long chancellorship, but he had not tried to exercise as close a supervision of the preparation of Lowe's budget as his own experience might have warranted, though the two were, naturally, in very frequent correspondence. Lowe was quite an inventive chancellor, though without raising any major threat to the framework of fiscal behaviour which Gladstone had established. Gladstone only saw the 1871 budget shortly before it was due to be presented to the Commons. The match tax might be thought to have offended against orthodox Gladstonianism, in that it broadened the basis of indirect taxation, but Gladstone does not seem to have objected to it on that score; nor does he seem to have seen soon enough the political dangers involved, though he advised Lowe to discuss the point with Glyn, the Chief Whip. His main reservations were on the political difficulties of reforming the death duties, though even here he showed no real alarm.

Gladstone's 'list of remnants' sent to Lowe at the start of the government

---

* Gladstone supported the proposal of Lowe for the change made mid-way through the Education Bill debates, by which the Exchequer grant to denominational schools was increased.

referred mainly to minor adjustments and improvements to his own work as chancellor; no major constructive measures remained, though many of the adjustments were controversial. Gladstone's remnants were: abolition of remaining corn duty, abolition of tea licences, change in probate duty, abolition of conveyance duties save railways, commutation of fire insurance duty, reduction of income tax, reform of malt duty. In his budget of 1869, Lowe dealt with many of these; he abolished the corn duty, repealed the tea duty, abolished the fire insurance duty altogether, against Gladstone's judgement, reduced conveyance duties, and reduced income tax by a penny. Much more of a problem was the question of retrenchment, without whose continuance the whole carefully balanced compromise which Gladstone reached on taxation in the 1850s and 1860s was likely to collapse. Gladstone found Lowe an ineffective ally in his battles with the spending departments.

The government came into office pledged to further retrenchment, and made much in the electoral campaign of Disraeli's profligacy in his financing of the Abyssinian expedition of 1867–8. Gladstone had spent much of the 1860s in conflict with Palmerston on the question of retrenchment, and especially on the War Office and Admiralty expenditure, which accounted for about a third of government expenditure. Now Prime Minister, with control of appointments, he should have been in a good position to achieve his ends. After the débâcle of Lowe's budget in 1871, and as it became clear that in legislative terms it was going to be very hard to follow the success of the 1869 and 1870 Sessions, he began to look to finance as the unifying element of the domestic programme, as it had been in the 1860s under his own chancellorship. The routine item of the Estimates was seen as central, 'bearing upon the position of the country, the party and the Government'. Gladstone told Cardwell in 1871:

They will be the *key* to our position at the outset of the session. We may announce Bills, but nobody will believe in them (unreasonable as the unbelief will be), except the Ballot; and that is discounted. On the Estimates will depend our chance of a fair start.

Expenditure on defence fell dramatically through retrenchment and reorganization in both army and navy in April 1869 and April 1870, but army expansion following the Franco-Prussian war spoilt the graph, and the abolition of purchase was also expensive, varying from year to year, but around £800,000 per annum. Gladstone hoped to get the figure back as nearly as possible to that of the pre-war Estimates, but, despite considerable savings by Cardwell by the end of 1872, the situation was gloomy: 'we have upon the last Estimates taken back all but some 300,000 of the £2,200,000 saving or thereabouts which in Feb. 71 we had made upon the Estimates of our predecessors'. This was particularly reprehensible in view of the fact that for Gladstone the defeat of France in 1870 had had one great advantage—the disabling by land and sea of 'the only country in Europe that has the power of being formidable to us'.*

Gladstone's view of France had been that she was a potential danger that could be slowly neutralized by commercial ties: her neutralization had now been more decisively achieved by Bismarck. In this sense, the result of the war of 1870 had been a bonus for Britain. The consequence thus ought to be, according to the maxim that 'policy determines expenditure', that naval and military retrenchment should be the easier. But this was not the view of the War Office or the Admiralty, where forces for expansion operated almost independently of the cabinet ministers responsible for those departments, forces to which historians have as yet paid slight attention. 'Policy determines expenditure' seemed to mean to those departments that policy demanded greater expenditure.

The problem of the Estimates was compounded by inflation, which reached its peak at the end of 1873, and was recognized particularly to affect the Navy. But inflation, and the marked rise in national wealth, also benefited the Exchequer: the yield from indirect and direct taxes markedly increased, and splendid surpluses occurred in 1872 and 1873. The opportunity for spectacular budgets was thus created.

In 1873 the major weakening of the government from its resignation and then resumption of office in March was emphasized by further blows to its fiscal record, when irregularities in the use of the Post Office Savings Bank's funds and in the contract for the telegraph to southern Africa were revealed.

The 'scandals' (as Gladstone called them) of the summer of 1873 highlighted a general failing of the administration explicable in part perhaps by Gladstone's absorption in legislation and the legislative process. The falling away of the popularity of the government was in part the result of a dislike for its tone. For all its administrative achievements, especially in the defence departments, it had become associated with departmental mismanagement and even, in the summer of 1873, with a want of probity.

Keen as he was on administrative efficiency in his own department, when he had one, Gladstone rather assumed efficiency in others, and had poor intelligence for gaining early knowledge of when things were going astray. His absence of interest in gossip, written or spoken, and in the small change of politics, perhaps intimidated colleagues and subordinates from keeping him in touch with those small details which signal danger to the acute political eye.† Small incidents that go wrong tend to be as much

---

* This contrasted markedly with Disraeli's conclusion: 'The balance of power has been entirely destroyed, and the country which suffers most, and feels the effect of this great change most, is England.'

† Gladstone's reliance on Granville meant that he was well up on potential crises in foreign policy, but much less so for domestic matters.

remembered as great legislative achievements that go right. An Opposition leader as witty as Disraeli was well placed to exploit this weakness; he waited for the legislative achievements of 1869–71 to run their course and then moved into the attack in 1872, capitalized upon the unpopularity of aspects of the legislation, set the tone for subsequent Toryism by pillorying the patriotism of the government, and, in the government's embarrassment at the 'scandals', reaped the reward for abstaining from accepting office.

By July 1873 Gladstone found himself the leader of a demoralized government which was almost at the point of breakdown. Only the end of the Session offered some respite. In attempting to come to terms with the situation, Gladstone implied that, individual failings and muddle apart, Lowe's suzerainty of the Treasury was too weak: the implication was that he had failed to see that the Permanent Secretary and the Financial Secretary knew the whole business of their department, and it was, of course, the duty of the Treasury to oversee all such financial details throughout the administration. The canons of Victorian public life put the responsibility for 'the scandals' on the head of the department; however much his subordinates had let him down, Lowe was the man responsible for the fiscal probity of the nation. 'Cardwell broke to Lowe the necessity of his changing his office' and he had, in effect, to resign as chancellor, being shifted to the Home Office. After a day off at Chislehurst, and 'a very anxious day of constant conversation and reflection', Gladstone wrote to the Queen on 5 August to submit details of the reshuffle, as a result of which he became Chancellor of the Exchequer: 'he submits this recommendation with extreme reluctance, and greatly in deference to the wish of his most experienced colleagues'.

Chancellor Again: the downfall of the Government and resignation as party leader

Thus it was that on 9 August 1873 Gladstone 'received a third time the Seals of my old office', and became Chancellor of the Exchequer as well as First Lord of the Treasury. He did so with his government in rare and sustained disarray, and by doing so he opened a Pandora's box of constitutional precedents, as to whether he would have to stand at the by-election obligatory to those taking an office of profit under the Crown. He may have accepted the chancellorship with 'extreme reluctance' but he immediately plunged into its work with enthusiasm and apparent forethought. Two days—a Sunday intervening—after taking the seals, he revealed a daring and dramatic plan, and then left for Hawarden:

Saw . . . Mr Cardwell: to whom at the W.O. I told in deep secrecy my ideas of the *possible* finance of next year: based upon abolition of Income Tax & Sugar Duties with partial compensation from Spirits and Death Duties. This *only* might give a chance.

The last sentence of this passage revealed the political motivation which was a central element of the plan—a bold attempt to regain the initiative within his own party and in the country generally. Coupled with the plan outlined to Cardwell, though apparently not mentioned to him, was a substantial relief of local taxation—in the order of £800,000 per annum. This was to be done not through further grants-in-aid, which he so much disliked, but by relieving localities in proportion as they paid national taxes such as the house tax and licensing fees. Gladstone had always looked to the house tax as preferable to the income tax, but in a budget which set out to relieve local taxation, which was largely raised on property, the house tax could hardly be expected to bear all the burden. Gladstone therefore turned also to the death duties in the form of the legacy and succession duties, though these would have constituted something of a 'tit-for-tat' for the local taxation reforms.

The abolition of the income tax was not, of course, a new idea. Gladstone had always disliked the tax as such and when considered purely on its own terms and not in comparison to other taxes. He disliked it first because of the inequities inherent in it; second, because in the 1860s he had come to see it as encouraging rather than discouraging expenditure because of the ease with which it brought in revenue. In the mid-1860s, looking for ways of encouraging retrenchment, he had considered income-tax abolition before deciding that the enfranchisement of artisans would strengthen the retrenching arm of the Commons.

Abolition rather than reduction of the income tax had not been one of the 'remnants' he had left to Lowe, but in the spring of 1873, that is, well before he had resumed the chancellorship, he returned to the subject, when Childers raised it with reference to Lowe's budget preparations. 'The idea of abolishing Income Tax is to me highly attractive, both on other grounds & because it tends to public economy. . . .'

The problem, as it had always been since the 1840s for the Peelites, was that the income tax could not be treated in isolation, or considered on its own terms only. It was, as we have seen, a central feature of the great compromise between direct and indirect taxation which was the distinguished, and in contemporary European terms, distinguishing achievement of mid-nineteenth-century Britain. Before the 1867 Reform Act Gladstone had seen direct taxation as falling upon those with the vote, indirect upon those without it: the direct tax payers had thus been the 'virtual representatives' of the indirect. After 1867 this was changed: the indirect taxpayers, or some proportion of them, now had the vote—the days of virtual representation in the British political system were thought to be ending, save for women and, as yet, farm labourers. 1867 was widely expected to inaugurate a bid for booty from the working classes, but what in fact it marked was a relaxation of the need for responsibility on the part of the propertied classes.

Before 1867, direct taxation had been an act of self-sacrifice on the part of the propertied classes, for they alone paid it and they alone elected the representatives to the Parliament which imposed it. After 1867, however, direct taxation, unless altered, was thought to be the servant of the extended franchise. This alarmed Gladstone just as it alarmed Lord Salisbury, though for different reasons. Gladstone always feared the ease with which the income tax, in particular, raised revenue and consequently encouraged expenditure; Salisbury feared it as a weapon of class vengeance. Abolition of the tax in the new circumstances thus took on a new urgency for Gladstone as a means of maintaining the minimalist State. On the other hand, he retained, as it behoved him as leader of the Liberal party to retain, a strong concern for balance in the incidence of national taxation: income tax might go, but not at the expense of a shifting of the burden on to the non-propertied classes who, despite 1867, could hardly be said to be exerting significant pressure upon the structure of British politics in the 1870s. 'You cannot provide for the means for abolishing Income Tax, either in whole or in part, out of new indirect taxation', he told Childers, and he wanted 'to go a little beyond this & say that when the Inc. Tax is abolished *some part* of the means must be got out of some new impost touching property'. Thus the plan included the reform of and an increase in the death duties, although this was not mentioned in Gladstone's election address.* Death duties might, in Salisbury's terms, wreak great havoc, but they were difficult to use to produce great revenues quickly.

The 1874 budget was intended to ensure retrenchment without upsetting class relationships. But its presentation in Gladstone's election address of January 1874 looked like a bid for the middle-class vote. In the short or even medium term this can be seen as a shrewd enough move, for the battle in British politics in the 1870s and 1880s was a contest for the support of the middle class.

The budget plan was therefore a bold and comprehensive scheme. The 1853 and 1860 budgets had launched great governments; the 1874 plan was intended to end one by crowning it in fiscal triumph. But despite the balancing element of alternative sources of direct taxation, and of some concessions towards the 'Free Breakfast Table' being demanded by the Free Trade League, the 1874 budget plans put their main emphasis on the relief of taxation in the two areas of principal concern to the propertied classes, income tax and local rates: the budget would therefore have lacked the wide social vision which had distinguished the great budgets of 1853 and 1860. In those years, interlocking plans of vast complexity had been presented to the nation as major contributions to the solution of the mid-Victorian problems of political and social integration and order. The 1874

---

* The address reserved the position by mentioning 'judicious adjustments to existing taxes', *The Times*, 24 January 1874, 8.

budget would have been narrower in conception and probably highly divisive within the Liberal party in the country. Moreover, the abolition of income tax would have placed so inelastic a corset around government spending that it would certainly have quickly snapped. Either the income tax would have been swiftly restored, or the Liberal party would have found itself defending a fiscal system in which indirect taxation was given an ever-increasing role, and this would have brought to a much earlier burial its attempt at the creation of a non-class-based popular party.

That those developments were anticipated and that the abolition would have been politically controversial within the party is shown by the reaction of both the Radical *Bee Hive* and Bagehot's *Economist* to Gladstone's election address of January 1874 which outlined his budgetary intentions. The *Bee Hive* argued that the proposal was socially unjust, the *Economist* that it was socially dangerous. James Aytoun in the *Bee Hive* stated that 'To this, as the old consistent advocate of the rights of the working classes we are altogether opposed',* and Bagehot, always a moderate direct taxer, argued in the *Economist* that an intense effort ought to be made by 'the best persons of all parties to retain it', for, in addition to the income tax's valuable elasticity, 'there is . . . much more than mere money in this tax. We want in our taxation not only real equality but apparent equality. . . .'† That tribune of provincial Radicalism, the people's Joseph, retrospectively drove the point home with characteristic, uncompromising hyperbole: Gladstone's proposals in his election address constituted 'the meanest public document that has ever, in like circumstances, proceeded from a statesman of the first rank. His manifesto was simply an appeal to the selfishness of the middle classes.'‡

Reaction on the Tory side tended to express alarm that post-1867 British politics was indeed becoming an auction in which the two parties bid for the prize of democratic support. Lord Carnarvon, an extreme case in the sense that he had resigned with Salisbury in protest at the Derby–Disraeli Reform Bill, but none the less rather typical of High Tory reaction, noted in his diary:

All Engd runs in a state of excitement. In a few days the election will begin. I do not like either Gladstone's or Disraeli's addresses. G. offers a bribe of £5,000,000 in the shape of the remission of taxn & D at once caps it. It is what we said at the passing of the last Reform bill that the constitution wd be put up to auction on each genl election.

But for Gladstone, the plan was the best that could be offered to answer the political problem which had been so clearly defined at the time of the

---

* *Bee Hive*, 31 January 1874. E. S. Beesly in the same issue argued: 'Mr Gladstone has sacrificed the lower classes, who worshipped him, to the richer classes, who disliked him', but concluded that 'on his past record . . . I do not expect that we shall find him proposing any financial scheme which, as a whole, will amount to relieving the rich at the expense of the poor'.

† *The Economist*, 31 January 1874.

‡ J. Chamberlain, *Fortnightly Review*, xxii. 412 (October 1874).

defeat in March 1873 on the Irish University Bill: 'There is now no *cause*. No great public object on wh. the Liberal party are agreed & combined.' His difficulty was that, despite a surplus of about £5 million, and about £2 million anticipated from 'new sources of revenue', in order to abolish the income tax, relieve local taxation, and make remissions on the sugar duties, he still needed about £600,000 more. He wanted the sum to come from retrenchment in the army and navy estimates, especially the latter. Details of the budget proposals were linked with a general statement on 'the pledges of [18]68', and 'the principles of economy'. But Cardwell and Goschen, the two ministers concerned, could not find the economies. Warning shots were fired in the correspondences of the Recess, intermingled with tart exchanges about the purposes and expenses of the Gold Coast expedition. But Gladstone, rightly believing that the long inflation which had lasted since the early 1850s was ended and that prices and therefore government costs were now falling, saw no immediate reason to bring the issue to a decision, and he suggested that the question of the Estimates be put off until his return to London early in January. He does not seem to have revealed to Cardwell or Goschen the extent of his demand for further retrenchment in the Estimates.

The legislative programme for the Session of 1874 was agreed upon, as was the custom, at the Cabinets before Christmas in 1873. The Cabinet decided '*Not* to take Co. Suffrage, *not* to take Land Laws'. The county franchise, on which Ripon had resigned though without public fuss in the midst of 'the scandals' in July, and to which Gladstone had given, via Forster, general personal approval, was too divisive a topic for the Cabinet to tackle: it threatened a rapid return to the fissures of 1866. Local taxation relief was necessary, but not an adequate basis for party rehabilitation: 'the Tories are completely beforehand with us, secondly they will outbid us if we enter into a competition'.

In Gladstone's view, this left only 'Finance', i.e. the budget, as a focal point round which the party could rally. The November Cabinets thus confirmed the view that Gladstone had held since 'the scandals' of the summer: only the budget could restore the party to something like a coherent and companionable body. He spelt out his arguments in a gloomy letter to Granville on 8 January 1874: he considered the subject of dissolution at this time, in the context of the general weakness of the party and the government, but concluded: 'Dissolution means either immediate death, or at the best Death a little postponed, and the party either way shattered for the time.'

On 16 January 1874 Gladstone returned to London. Cardwell had been sent a copy of the letter to Granville, and the extent of its demands for reduction of the defence estimates had taken him by surprise: 'I have not received from Gladstone any intimation that he considers a further reduction of establishment possible or proper: & I do not see the way of effecting it', he told Granville, with a clear hint of possible resignation. After a conference with Granville and Wolverton, Gladstone found 'the prospects of agreement with the two Depts on Estimates are for the present bad'. Next day, a Sunday, Gladstone returned to thoughts of dissolution:

This day I thought of dissolution. Told Bright of it. In evening at dinner told Granville and Wolverton. All seemed to approve. My first thought of it was as escape from a difficulty. I soon saw on reflection that it was the best thing in itself.

The 'escape from a difficulty' probably meant the Estimates; Gladstone listed the first reason for a dissolution as being 'we gain time, & avoid for the moment a ministerial crisis'; the only other subject for a crisis at that time was the county franchise, on which Gladstone reaffirmed his general and personal support to a deputation on 21 January, but it would have taken some time for a ministerial crisis to have developed on that subject, as the Cabinet had already agreed not to introduce a bill. The large amount of reduction in defence estimates that Gladstone wanted—between £1 million and £600,000—would need much more than marginal adjustments and was bound to produce a major row. Gladstone tried to get Goschen and Cardwell to sign a paper to agree to keep the Estimates question open. The dispute could not be mentioned during the election campaign; but if the government were returned to office Gladstone could bring further pressures of retrenchment and the pledge to abolish income tax to bear upon the Admiralty and the War Office to return to something like the expenditure levels of February 1870. Further, if a dissolution was to be had within the next three months, it was necessary, because of the constraints of the parliamentary timetable for financial questions, that it be done immediately.

The dissolution was therefore essentially a dissolution against the defence departments. Even combining the offices of First Lord and Chancellor of the Exchequer had not allowed Gladstone to prevail against them. First, their expedition to West Africa was on a scale which Gladstone believed was excessive, second, they were behaving, and seemed likely to behave successfully, as if Palmerston had never died. Only an election victory on the general principles of retrenchment, and the specific pledges to remove the most elastic variable of the government's revenue, the income tax, and to make remissions of local taxation by central government help, would suffice to crush them.

The disastrous election bore out Gladstone's earlier forecast of the party 'shattered for the time' rather than the tentative optimism of his notes for the Cabinet: 'I think our victory is as likely in an immediate as in a postponed Dissolution. While we run fewer chances of a crushing defeat.' The long run of by-election losses in 1873 proved no false guide: the 1874 general election ended the pattern of British elections since 1847, that whoever it was that made up the majority in the Commons, it was not the Tories.

Thus ended Gladstone's first administration; he resigned on 17 February 1874 without meeting Parliament. On 19 February he drafted a letter to the chief whip stating 'it is not my intention to assume the functions of leader of a Parliamentary Opposition in the House of Commons to the new Government'. This letter, clearly intended for publication had it been sent, disclaimed difficulties with the party as a reason, but Gladstone's personal views became clearer in a series of notes made in March: the electorate had rejected his view about retrenchment, a significant section of the party differed irreconcilably from him on education; the 'failure of 1866–8' boded ill for his future shadow leadership, especially given the tendency of back-benchers 'of making a career by & upon constant active opposition to the bulk of the party' even when the party was in office. But the first reason was personal: to accept leadership meant to accept the future presumption of office as well, i.e. a Tory Parliament followed by a Liberal Parliament, the two of which could amount to fourteen years: 'this is not consistent with my views for the close of my life'. Pressed by alarmed colleagues, he accepted a compromise, that he should remain as nominal but inactive leader in the Commons, the position to be reconsidered before the start of the Session of 1875.

Gladstone had spent much of his administration in conflict with his colleagues and with groups in his party both 'left' and 'right', but when it came to the point, they could not let him go. The Liberal party aspired to classlessness, but it was riddled with class; it hoped for interdenominationalism but it divided between Erastianism, sectarianism, and secularism; it tried to offer justice to the three kingdoms but it satisfied none. Gladstone stood outside the Cabinet and the party; his class was indefinable, his religion exceptional; he was an extreme Radical on some questions, an unreconstructed Conservative on others; he was at the same time a chief architect of the mid-nineteenth-century settlement and seen as one of the chief threats to its continuation. Disraeli was self-evidently exotic, but viewed from the perspective of any one of the groups that constituted the Liberal party, so was Gladstone.

In the decades after the start of household suffrage, British political parties slowly, surprisingly slowly, and in the case of the Liberals only in part, took on those attributes characteristic of a modern party: bureaucracy and caution. But during the transitional phase, exceptional demands were made of their leaders and especially of the leader of the Liberal party as it struggled to preserve its identity caught between the certainty of a property-based Conservative party and the uncertainty of developments 'to the left'. The position resulting from the defeat of 1874 was, of course, only the start of a long-drawn-out and ultimately unsuccessful attempt by the Liberals to meet the problem of 'the squeeze', but one thing was already clear: no available Whig could successfully appeal over the horizon of his own constituency to the disparate groups beyond. Much as they were coming to fear Gladstone, the Whigs feared isolation more.

Constituencies, Public Speaking, and the Press in the early 1870s

The abrupt dissolution in January 1874 caught the party as well as the country by surprise. Since the abortive resignation of March 1873, dissolution had been, in general terms, a probability, but the speed with which events moved in January and February 1874 was unusual; there had not been a dissolution in the Recess without prior announcement since that of 1780. It found Gladstone in considerable embarrassment with respect to his own seat. His election address was written for 'an unnamed constituency', and the decision to stand again for one of the two Greenwich seats was taken at the last moment. The doubts were justified when he came second to 'Boord the distiller . . . more like a defeat than a victory, though it places me in Parliament again'.

Gladstone's relationship with Greenwich had been neither intimate nor amiable. The 'constituency was a kaleidoscope of advanced Liberals, Republicans, and naval dockyard workers, many of whom were Tories. Retrenchment by both Tory and Liberal governments had borne heavily on the dockyards, but Gladstone had dealt with the various delegations which waited upon him with homilies on the national need for reduction of government establishments. None of the interest in the unemployed which he had shown in Lancashire in the 1860s was bestowed on the dockyard workers who had lost their jobs. Gladstone's contact with the constituency had been mainly through his colleague as MP, Alderman Salomons, but Salomons had died in 1873, and the Tories captured his seat at the by-election.

Despite the weakness of the local Liberal organization and its obvious need for leadership, Gladstone went to very considerable lengths to avoid speaking in the constituency. 'You cannot treat Birmingham as I am able to treat Greenwich, & you are I believe to address your constituents shortly', observed Gladstone to Bright at the end of 1869. 'No-one had had so little to do with my now being member for Greenwich as I have myself' he told the chief whip, but he did little to remedy this situation.

He spoke, after prolonged stalling, at the great meeting at Blackheath in October 1871,* but even then chiefly because speeches in his son's marginal constituency of Whitby, and in receiving the Freedom of Aberdeen, meant that Greenwich could no longer be ignored. He did not speak there again until the general election, and considered in the meantime other

* For such meetings, see the illustration in this volume.

possibilities for a seat, especially his old constituency of Newark, which he had held between 1832 and 1845.* The rapid dissolution in January 1874 thus found Gladstone almost as much a stranger to his constituents as when he first met them; it allowed no time for a change of seat, and little time for campaigning—only three election speeches were made.

The prototype of a new style of popular executive politician which Gladstone had so carefully developed in the 1860s was thus to some considerable extent set aside. There were no great set-piece addresses other than the few mentioned above. Appearances at the annual Lord Mayor's banquet were resented and resisted when possible. A half-hearted attempt to rally popular support behind the Irish University Bill was made in March 1873, the odd gathering at railway stations or outside the gates of great houses received a few words, but of 'The People's William' there was little sign.

Of course, there were some good reasons for this. After 1870, any speech was likely to be either evasive or divisive, and Gladstone speechifying would license his opponents within the Cabinet to do likewise—the contents of the Blackheath speech were a matter for Cabinet discussion: 'WEG invited contributions, or cautions.' Even so, Gladstone forfeited one of his major assets, and allowed the shades of the Cabinet and the party in the Commons to crowd closely around him; it was strange to see an England with Disraeli as the leading demagogue.

Gladstone's strategy of wooing the votes of the propertied classes—exemplified especially in the relief of local taxation proposals—showed the acuteness of his perception of the real implications of the household suffrage, and it may be that this encouraged him to avoid giving hostages to the Tory press in the form of speeches to great crowds. But the nature of much of the rank-and-file following of the Liberal party was such that deference was no longer enough. Commenting on Gladstone's speech at Whitby attacking the bias of the metropolitan press, Lord Houghton told Gladstone shrewdly: 'there is a Demon not of Demogogism but of Demophilism, that is tempting [you]'. It may be that there was, but Demos personally saw little of it during this government, and was offended.

Gladstone's appearance in the 1860s as a new kind of executive politician had been, as we have seen, buttressed by his shrewd use of the press, and especially of the Liberal *Daily Telegraph*. He retained his press contacts, but used them much less frequently and more formally. His contacts were mainly with editors, whereas previously they had been mainly with reporters. Thornton Hunt, the *Telegraph* reporter whom he had seen sometimes almost daily when at the Exchequer and during the Reform Bill

---

* He also declined an invitation to stand at a by-election in Kincardineshire, a safe Liberal seat, primarily for 'the family reason'—i.e. his brother Tom's Toryism, Fasque, the family home, being in the constituency; to have resigned his Greenwich seat in mid-Parliament would have been an extraordinary manœuvre. There were various other offers, including Chester.

debates, barely appears in the journal after December 1868; he died in 1873. Contacts with Levy, the owner and editor of the *Telegraph*, were irregular and seem to have been limited to announcements for formal developments, such as the order of government business, the dates of state visits, and the like. Gladstone showed himself willing to use his *Telegraph* contacts to get a 'special' reporter sent to investigate a scandal in Shetland, but he does not seem to have used the *Telegraph*, as he had in 1866, to ventilate his views on Irish policy.

The Times replaced the *Daily Telegraph* as the focus of Gladstone's attentions. Delane, its editor, was kept in touch with the developments of the Irish Church Bill, and to some extent with the preparation of the Irish Land Bill. He was summoned for consultations during the crisis with the Lords in July 1869. When the 1871 Session ran into difficulties, with ballot and army bills being dismembered in the Lords after long struggles in the Commons—both reforms which when passed seemed to general consent both necessary and just—Gladstone singled out the metropolitan press for particular blame in his speech at Whitby in September 1871:

A considerable section of the Metropolitan Press had discussed with greater severity the proceedings of Parliament during the last Session than had been the case with the Provincial Press. He was bound to say that he could find reason for that difference in this fact,—the present Government had not hesitated when it thought the public interest required it to make proposals which had been highly offensive to powerful classes in this country (cheers) . . . the effect of that bias was most felt where wealth was concentrated, as in the metropolis, and where . . . the opinions of the Clubs, rather than the opinion of this great nation, were reflected in a considerable portion of the Metropolitan Press.

In this speech Gladstone indicated the extent to which Liberalism was ceasing, despite its majority in the Commons and its hold over certain sections of the civil service, to be the party of 'the establishment'. Whereas in the 1850s the Tories had found themselves bereft of metropolitan newspaper support, the Liberals in the 1870s found the balance shifting in the other direction. These developments caused the Liberals considerable anxiety. Gladstone suggested to Glyn, the chief whip, that Liberal weakness among the London evening papers might be countered by *The Echo* having a second edition which would serve as an evening edition, but he does not seem to have taken a sustained interest in regaining the initiative for the Liberals. His outburst at Whitby initiated a tradition of complaint within Radical circles which was to prove enduring; that he did little behind the scenes to find a remedy was to be equally characteristic of the Radical leadership.

This indifference may in part have been because the most popular and the most influential of the London papers, the *Daily Telegraph* and *The Times* respectively, remained loyal to Gladstone, if not to the Liberal party.

Both papers supported the return of the government, and especially of Gladstone, at the election of 1874. The *Telegraph* did so in its capacity as still almost a party paper, though already with qualifications; *The Times* with some reservation after an initially very favourable reaction to the financial proposals ('the coloured lights on the stage soon fade'), but none the less quite emphatically:

... there are good chances for a Government which has given proofs of energy and capacity, and has a magnificent programme ready for the Session. After all, no one can do Mr Gladstone's work as well as Mr Gladstone and it is Mr Gladstone's work which the Conservative Party has now proffered itself to do [by agreeing to income tax abolition]. . . . On the last occasion the watchword was Gladstone and the disestablishment of the Irish Church; now it is Gladstone alone.

Both papers were soon to be lost not only to the Liberal party but to Gladstone also.

Gladstone did pay attention to publications designed to win the argument at the highest level. His own article on the Franco-Prussian war has been discussed above. In 1872 he encouraged, without success, Cardwell to publish 'in a Pamphlet a full but *popular* account of our army system as it now is . . . it would help to stereotype a state of opinion you have well earned'. More successfully, he told Goschen 'I should like to see the whole substance of your Report . . . put out in the best form, as a great document upon the subject.' This resulted in Goschen's *Local Taxation* (1872), a work which exemplified the rationalistic approach to public opinion pursued by the Liberals.

Gladstone's first government petered out, never recovering from the abortive resignation of March 1873. In this it followed the Liberal stereotype: every Liberal government between 1830 and 1895 ended by the disintegration of its own support in the Commons; only the Asquith Cabinet bucked the trend. The Liberal Party's strength was its ability to regroup on a basis of compromise and reconciliation during the intervening period of Tory rule. Gladstone felt, as the quotation of March 1874 at the head of this chapter shows, that he had little to offer to that process.

CHAPTER IX

A Prime Minister's Private Life

*The Daily Round: fitness, correspondence, the Commons, weekends, and
reading—Laura Thistlethwayte: 'duty and evil temptation', 'like a story from the
Arabian Nights'—Family Affairs in the Early 1870s—A Public Man and his
Money—Religion in Retirement: 'Vaticanism' the end of a career?*

Finished my additions to the Article for the Q.R. and the correction of
the proof. Read . . . Middlemarch.

On this my 65th birthday I find myself in lieu of the mental repose I
had hoped engaged in a controversy, which cannot be mild, & which
presses upon both mind & body. But I do not regret anything except my
insufficiency: and my unworthiness in this & in all things: yet I would
wish that the rest of my life were as worthy as my public life, in its nature
& intent, to be made an offering to the Lord Most High.

The Daily Round: fitness, correspondence, the Commons, weekends, and reading

Few politicians in peacetime can have been more fully stretched than
Gladstone in his first ministry. The description of the previous two
chapters has tried to indicate the main areas of government activity in
which he involved himself. Any reader of this survey could not but be
puzzled by Lord Houghton's view, that Gladstone had a 'one idea at a time
faculty', a view which has had an eminent following since. It may be that
Gladstone sometimes presented himself as having one idea at a time, and it
is certainly the case that a departmental minister, trying to cope with a line
of policy in which the Prime Minister was interesting himself, must have
felt that he was Gladstone's sole object of attention. But the first ministry
shows Gladstone at the height of political awareness, sensitive to the
implications of every phrase in every letter on a vast range of topics.
Certainly he was more interested in some topics than in others, and he was
completely identified with three of the government's main bills. But even
his speeches in the House show the extent of his mastery of the work of the
ministry as a whole—indeed he increasingly found himself not merely con-
ducting the orchestra from the piano, but playing most of the other instruments as well.

In a man prone to tension, it is not surprising that this experience was
wearing. In January 1874 he had been in office continually since 1859, with

the exception of July 1866 to December 1868. The administration was punctuated by Gladstone's illnesses, many of them occurring at moments of crisis. 'Tightness in the chest', fever and diarrhoea removed him from direct political leadership during the crisis over the Irish Church negotiations in 1869, the 'scandals' crisis in July 1873, and the negotiations about the Estimates and dissolution in January 1874. His physician, Andrew Clark, played an important though not quite clearly definable role in the attempted resignation of March 1873. Gladstone also suffered at less politically sensitive moments.

These bouts of illness do not seem, however, to have had any lasting effect. He recovered from them with persistent resilience. His handling of the correspondence of both Chancellor and First Lord in the months at the end of the government certainly does not suggest that he was exhausted either physically or mentally. His walk of thirty-three miles in the rain across the Grampians from Balmoral through Glen Feshie to Drumguish and Kingussie does not suggest a body enfeebled by illness—indeed it recalled his habit as an undergraduate of walking from Oxford to Leamington Spa at the start of the University Vacation. Reviewing himself on his sixty-fourth birthday, Gladstone found it was inward 'strain and tossing of the spirit' which troubled him—outwardly 'a weaker heart, stiffened muscles, thin hairs: other strength still remains in my frame'.

Resilience was one of Gladstone's most notable features as an executive politician. A minor example, though a telling one, was his regular evening entry in the journal. The entries for the first administration are slightly longer than for the earlier years of the 1860s. There may be some link here with Gladstone's decision no longer to write 'political memoranda' recording the course of important events, save for royal interviews and the occasional crisis. Certainly, the recording of the day's activities, however briefly, was important to him: when he left the little volume behind at Hawarden during a visit to Spencer at Althorp, he immediately asked for it to be forwarded, keeping up with the entries on writing-paper and sticking it into the volume once regained.

The journal was preserved partly to record a schedule which was, at the least, exacting. Compared to some Presidents and Prime Ministers in the second half of the twentieth century, Gladstone's level of activity, especially if the Recess is included, was not especially severe. But it must be remembered that a Prime Minister before the First World War prepared all his speeches and answers to questions himself, conducted much of his correspondence personally, and had, comparatively, very little in the way of supporting staff. It was for Gladstone himself to check that Cabinet decisions were carried out, and to complain when returns and tables were not produced as requested.

On top of this was the priority given to the affairs of the House of

Commons. As Prime Minister, Gladstone regularly sat on the Treasury bench in the Commons for seven hours a day, and attendances of over nine hours occur quite frequently. Hours of attendance in the Commons, together with church services, are always recorded in the diary. Gladstone usually began sitting in the Commons about 2.15 p.m. and often sat, with an hour off for dinner, until after midnight. He did not find these long sittings particularly stressful, for, commenting on a rare bout of insomnia prompted by an evening of unsuccessful attempts to persuade John Bright to rejoin the Cabinet, he noted: 'My brain assumes in the evening a feminine susceptibility, and resents any unusual strain: tho' strange to say, it will stand a debate in the House of Commons.' The morning and, sometimes in the Recess, part of the afternoon also, was given over to correspondence, for Gladstone's inclination was always to proceed by written argument, whether his colleague was out of London or on his doorstep. The development of policy by social intercourse was not Gladstone's method: in the whole of his first premiership he does not record entering a political club.*

This personal isolation should not of course be exaggerated. Gladstone saw a very great deal of his colleagues. Political dinners were regularly held at his house in Carlton House Terrace. During the Session, he rarely dined at home. If not entertaining, he dined out, sometimes with members of his government and party, sometimes with old Tractarian friends like Sir Walter James and Sir Robert Phillimore, quite frequently with one of his secretaries (often Algernon West), and quite frequently also with Mrs Thistlethwayte. Gladstone is almost always careful to note in the journal whom his host or hostess was for the dinner, which in the Session was usually an hour long at most. He very rarely notes a political discussion at these dinners. Compared with the Palmerstonian years, Glastone used the country house weekend sparingly, usually visiting aristocratic relatives, such as the Cavendishes at Chislehurst, rather than touring the great Whig houses. Next to Chislehurst and Granville's refuge at Walmer Castle, Lord Salisbury's Hatfield was, surprisingly, his most frequent weekend visiting place.

Gladstone's outpouring of correspondence was huge and his writing methods merit description. When the post was opened, certain letters were set aside to be answered by the private secretaries. These were usually letters about deputations, invitations to speak, begging letters, and the like. Gladstone personally answered the important letters, often at great length. Copies of these letters, save those on family affairs, or to Mrs Thistlethwayte, were then made by the private secretaries. Gladstone indicated on the holograph how the letter was to be recorded—one tick in the bottom left-hand corner meant that it was to be copied into the letter-book, two

* He joined the Reform under strong pressure from Glyn, the chief whip, and resigned in 1874.

ticks that it was to be copied on to a separate sheet of paper and filed separately. This recording process operated, unfortunately, only while Gladstone was in office: systematic recording in the letter-book ceased at the end of February 1874 and on 5 March 1874 Gladstone noted 'tomorrow I encounter my own correspondence single-handed'. While out of office, he had no secretary, though copies of letters were sometimes made for him by his wife or children.

Gladstone thus ran an embryonic 'cabinet office', probably more formally organized and certainly more fully recorded than that of his predecessors. This went some way to compensating for the absence of a Prime Minister's department, but the want of any permanent staff meant that there was no necessary continuity of this practice when a change of office occurred. The records of his premiership are much more systematic than those of any of his predecessors, and the care and attention to recording and filing by both the secretaries and Gladstone himself reflect not only his awareness of the importance of records for the smooth running of business, but also his awareness of his own role as an historical phenomenon. The Peelites were unusually conscious of the use to which private papers might be put—viz. the rapid and unusual printing in 1856 by Cardwell and Stanhope of Peel's memoranda of 1845-6, and of the private printing of Lord Aberdeen's papers by his son, Gladstone's erstwhile secretary, Arthur Gordon, to which endeavour Gladstone as Prime Minister gave very considerable attention. Gladstone's awareness of his own historical role, and the part that his letters were to play in it, was heightened by the death of his close friend of the 1830s and 1840s, James Hope (-Scott) in 1873. A lengthy appraisal of Hope-Scott and a sorting of Gladstone's collected papers followed. Gladstone had reached that stage in his life when his archives were becoming one of the chief sources for British political and religious life from the 1830s onwards. He was soon to reach that strange position—starting perhaps with the biography of Samuel Wilberforce (1879)—of seeing himself as a chief actor in the published biographies of the day, and watching the intimate personal and religious crises of his youth replayed before his own and the public's gaze.

Correspondence was, then, together with sitting in the Commons during the Session, the main business of his day; it was the lifeblood of his ministry and the process by which the Cabinet maintained its identity and the Prime Minister his suzerainty. This was particularly the case given Gladstone's quite frequent absences from London, especially in autumn and winter. In 1872, for example, he was away from London between 5 August and 10 October, and between 16 October and 14 November, as well as for many other short absences. These spells of absence were rarely used for directly political purposes. Attendance at Balmoral was unavoidable, but Gladstone did not otherwise devote much time to political week-ending. As already mentioned, most of his weekends away were spent with Lord Frederick Cavendish and his wife (Catherine Gladstone's niece) at Chislehurst, without a house party. Weekends away were, in fact, for relaxation.

There were of course exceptions. Two visits to Chatsworth were clearly politically important, as were several visits to Lord Salisbury at Hatfield. Salisbury and Gladstone shared a quasi-Tractarian High-Churchmanship and a contempt for Disraeli, but they shared little more. Gladstone felt that these visits, which were not reciprocated, went well ('There are no kinder hosts than here'), and he approved of what he found: 'In few Chapels is all so well and heartily done.' Their shared dislike of Disraeli reflected the intense moral and religious language in which both men expressed their view of politics, but this certainly offered no basis for co-operation, and Salisbury remained one of the ministry's most persistent and effective critics. The two visits to Salisbury's young nephew Arthur Balfour, at his shooting lodge and at his Scottish home, Whittinghame (in 1872 and 1874 respectively), and Balfour's strong friendship—quite how strong is not clear—for Catherine Gladstone's niece, May Lyttelton, had obvious political overtones for both families. But most of Gladstone's visits were to old cronies such as Wolverton, Milnes Gaskell, Edward Ellice, and his undergraduate friend Walter Sneyd. Of course, no act by a Prime Minister is without political implications—Gladstone's visit to the Roman Catholic convert Ambrose Phillipps de Lisle at Garendon had implications well beyond the mere observation of de Lisle's monastery—but it is fair to say that Gladstone did not primarily intend these visits to be political in tone, and that his use of them differed from his rather assiduous use of the political weekend in the 1860s.

This readiness to distance himself physically from his colleagues—especially in the Recess—while remaining in touch with them by letter to the extent that he wished to do so, clearly allowed Gladstone to give himself periods of rest and regeneration which his tendency to nervous illness at times of stress and crisis suggests was essential. Most of his creative work—the three Irish bills, and the budget planned in the autumn of 1873—was done at Hawarden, and he returned to London from the country the more eager and the more resourceful politically.

Although Gladstone was throughout these years an intensely active Prime Minister—much more so than Disraeli in the government which succeeded him—it should not be thought that his energies were wholly devoted to the process and policy-making of government. Gladstone organized his routine in such a way as to permit—in all but exceptional crises—a continuation of his habit of extensive reading in an eclectic range of subjects—from a biography of Schleiermacher, through Trollope, Disraeli, and George Eliot to a vast range of pamphlets, periodicals, and tracts, ecclesiastical, classical, and secular. His very demanding attendance at the Commons naturally reduced his reading during the Session, though even then it is rare for a day to pass without some record of reading outside government papers. But in the Recess and on Sundays, the level of reading differs little from that in earlier decades of the diary. The reading may be said to be rather more practically directed, in that much of it was intended to provide background information to governmental questions—for example, the first three months of 1869 not surprisingly find Gladstone deep in literature and ephemera on the Irish Church. But he also found time in those same months to read, *inter alia*, Bagehot on money, Baxter on taxation, Giffen's essay on his own finance, Matthew Arnold's *Culture and Anarchy*, Cobbett's *Reformation*, Sedgwick's 'charming book on Cowgill Chapel', Coleridge's *Life of Keble*, J. E. Morgan's 'Town life among the poorest', and the Duke of Argyll's *Primeval Man*, as well as various works on the preparations for the Vatican Council. In those months we also find him correcting the proofs of *Juventus Mundi*, a short version of his Homeric views, which was published in August 1869. An important example of Gladstone's reading influencing his views on policy is his study of works on Irish land in 1869, in particular his reading of George Campbell's pamphlet, 'The Irish Land'.

On the whole, Gladstone recalled his reading accurately. The books in his library, now preserved at St Deiniol's Library at Hawarden, show him to have been a careful, if rapid, reader. He annotated his books with lines, ticks, and crosses, and wrote the odd comment in the margin, writing 'ma' (the Italian for 'but') when he disagreed with the author. He often compiled a short index on the back inside cover, books in those days rarely having a printed index.

His parliamentary speeches show a mind hardly ever at a loss for a fact or a reference. Gladstone had nothing of the contemporary trend which he discerned and roundly condemned in a speech at Liverpool College in December 1872—a trend towards 'a scepticism in the public mind, of old as well as young, respecting the value of learning and of culture, and a consequent slackness in seeking their attainment'. This speech, which caused much controversy, including a public exchange with Herbert Spencer, offers an interesting insight into the conclusions Gladstone was drawing from his eclectic gleanings from the contemporary scene, for in it he adumbrated, at a very early stage, what was to become in the hands of others a general critique of Britain's relative economic and cultural decline:

In the ulterior prosecution of almost any branch of inquiry, it is to Germany and to the works of Germans that the British student must look for assistance . . . a far greater number of her educated class are really in earnest about their education; and they have not yet learned, as we, I fear, have learned, to undervalue, or even to despise, in a great measure, simplicity of life.

Gladstone was alarmed at the 'corroding pest of idleness—that special temptation to a wealthy country'. Yet admire German achievement as he did, he deplored its most prominent ideological trend even more, denouncing the materialism of D. F. Strauss's *The old faith and the new* and with it both those in England who promulgated such opinions theologically, and those who—almost all of them in his own party—argued for secularism in education.

His reflections on the spirit of the age thus showed alarm at the corrosive consequences of wealth, and fear that the 'reconciliation between Christianity and the conditions of modern thought, modern life and modern society' which it had been his life's mission to accomplish, might after all be a sham reconciliation dependent on the surrender of traditional Christianity to scientific materialism. Gladstone's hopes for the Christian future rested first on ecumenism between the apostolic churches, Anglicans, Roman Catholics, and Orthodox (with the Nonconformists following in an ill-defined theological relationship)—an ecumenism he worked to promote even when Prime Minister and which he now saw failing—and second, on the refutation of ideas of the Straussian sort through the methodology of Joseph Butler, the eighteenth-century Anglican divine and philosopher, whose '*method of handling* . . . is the only one known to me that is fitted to guide life, and thought bearing upon life, in the face of the nineteenth century'. The Vatican Council set the first back by a century, and the onward progress of secular Darwinism rendered victory over the second at best a very long haul.

Laura Thistlethwayte: 'duty and evil temptation', 'like a story from the Arabian Nights'

Correspondence, relaxation, reading, the stress of public life, religion, the conversion of prostitutes, all come together in Gladstone's relationship with Laura Thistlethwayte, the evangelical ex-courtesan whom we have already met and who had, by the time he became Prime Minister, already established a degree of friendship with Gladstone, originally through the Duke of Newcastle.* This friendship consisted of an occasional dinner at her house in Grosvenor Square, and an intermittent correspondence, mostly on religious topics.

However, Gladstone told her in November 1869, 'I have only known you in an inner sense within the last two months.' This was true, for in September 1869, Laura Thistlethwayte made a move towards great intimacy with the Prime Minister, accusing him of misunderstanding and mockery. In response Gladstone wrote describing their relationship since 1864:

In my ragged letter of yesterday, I did not get *through* my answer to your question 'had you knowledge of all this when you came to see me'? Yet it may be short—No!

* See above, pp. 157–8.

I told you some things I did perceive; and I proceed. The modesty (so to call it) struck me, with which, when I rather thrust open your door (I fear) after one friend's death [i.e. the Duke of Newcastle in 1864], you did not hasten to call me in; it struck and pleased me. With regard to myself afterwards, I thought you interpreted me too favourably, and in all things seemed to dress me (so to speak) in colours agreeable to yourself. But I did not dream that, as among your *friends*, I was drawn into any inner circle. I have not a good opinion of myself. And, if I see kindness from any one gushing out upon me, it mainly strikes me what a fund of it they must have, to spend so liberally. Again, you ask did kindness (in, not to, me) draw me to see you? There was enough in what all knew of you, to draw me, without kindness: a sheep, or a lamb rather, that had been astray; (I omit what you do not wish to be mentioned but what, I do not deny, enhances interest—), and that had come back to the Shepherd's Fold, and to the Father's arms. . . . I fretted, as oftentimes I have done, at my want of time and free mind for the cultivation of friendship; but there was no period at which I should not have been very sorry to think I was seeing you for the last time.

Yet I did not then know you as I know you now through your tale, and what accompanies the tale.

The 'tale' referred to was Laura Thistlethwayte's autobiography, now lost, which she sent to the Prime Minister in at least twenty-three batches during September and October 1869. It was accompanied by an outpouring of undated letters written on exotic paper with Eastern symbols in a vast and illegible hand; the scent on the paper still wafts, at least metaphorically, upwards to the reader. The manuscript and letters taken together 'astonished', tantalized, and perhaps titillated Gladstone: 'duty and evil temptation are there before me, on the right and left'. He was clearly deeply attracted to her, and when a joke in one of his letters was taken as a slight, he was mortified and profoundly disturbed until all was set right.

This tiff—almost a lover's tiff—on paper brought the affair to a crisis. Laura Thistlethwayte wrote 'a great, deep, weighty word' which Gladstone in his reply could not bring himself to repeat—apparently 'love'—and she suggested they burn their letters to each other. Gladstone drew back: was she sure the word should be used?—burning letters was 'dangerous. It removes a bridle: it encourages levity in thought.' On the other hand, he admitted she had 'got within my guard'—with Gladstone something achieved perhaps only by his wife and, years before, Arthur Hallam and James Hope.*

In Mrs Thistlethwayte Gladstone had found an ideal object of fascination: educated enough to understand something of his mind, young enough to offer beauty, religious enough to seem redeemed, but exotic enough to

---

* After October 1869, he began his letters to her 'Dear Spirit', though ending 'Ever yours, W.E.G.' He wore a ring she had given him: 'I will have it engraved "L.T. to W.E.G." ' She, with more circumspection, insisted on a mere 'L'. The ring can be seen on Gladstone's right hand in many of his later portraits and photographs.

stand outside the ring of society women with whom he usually corresponded on religion. 'It is like a story from the Arabian Nights, with much
added to it' was his comment on her autobiography.

The dramatic but apparently resolved nature of Mrs Thistlethwayte's
life and religion called forth a response from Gladstone:

There is a *region* beyond that of interest in your tale, beyond bewilderment, beyond
gratitude for an open-hearted confidence: but the first step into that region
prompts me to remember as a sacred trust what is for your peace and weal. If in
speaking thus I seem mysterious and strange it is because I am so. My life is a battle
between inclination and duty. Inclination calls me to repose, duty leads me into
conflict: I have high aspirations, and mean tendencies. But a voice above the din
orders me to study your peace and your weal.

Her bid for attention had come at a timely moment; Gladstone needed the
friendship and attention of a woman outside his family circle. In the 1860s
this role was fulfilled occasionally by Lady Waldegrave, but chiefly by the
dowager Duchess of Sutherland, to whom Gladstone wrote very regularly
when they were apart, letters usually on literature, with some politics
added. The dowager duchess died in October 1868; Gladstone was one of
her pall-bearers.

Mrs Thistlethwayte was hardly the dowager duchess, but Gladstone saw
her in the same context: 'You were never to me simply a common acquaintance. Friendships with women have contributed no small portion of my
existence. I know the meaning of the words "weakness is power": apparent
weakness is real power.' And again: 'what could lead you to tell me I was
made much of by women. I fear only my own declaration, that valued and
precious friendships with women had formed no small part of my life. That
is true. In every principal case they were women older than myself. To be
prized by women in general is in my opinion a great glory, because of their
gift of judging character: but it is a glory I cannot claim and do not deserve.'

The questions her exotic tale raised, the state of her soul, and the relationship between them could only be resolved by a lengthy meeting. This
took place over a weekend at the Thistlethwaytes' house at Boveridge
whither went Gladstone and Arthur Kinnaird, the Whig MP who, with
Newcastle, had introduced the couple. At Boveridge 'Mrs. Th. came to my
rooms aft[ernoon] and at night.'

After this meeting, the affair—for such it must be called—reached a more
balanced state. Letters and meetings, especially the former—sent in
specially marked envelopes to avoid the private secretaries—continued to
be frequent, but without the extreme excitement and intensity of the
months of October to December 1869.

Much of this correspondence reflects the curious ambivalence of the
religious mind. Gladstone's stated urgings were all towards morality. He
accepted Laura Thistlethwayte's protestations of virtue and defended her

against traducers. He urged her towards restoring relations of every sort with her husband, and suggested to her that her 'vocation' should be to 'act upon the bitter wintry frosts which originally cast your wifehood in a mould of ice'. Yet Gladstone's relationship with her was clearly fraught with danger for him, as is shown in his correspondence with her and by his frequent use of 'X' (the sign usually used after a morally dangerous meeting with a prostitute) as a comment on his meetings with her. That willingness to be tempted, to 'court evil' while doing good, which had played so important a part in his early rescue work, that feeling that he must expose his soul and body to spiritual danger, clearly in the case of Laura Thistlethwayte led Gladstone on, for a time, to a point not far short of infatuation.

However, that point *was* short of infatuation. Gladstone did not use 'the weighty word' back to Laura Thistlethwayte, and despite all, he maintained some sort of balance. Though Mrs Thistlethwayte took up much time in letters and meetings, especially in 1869–70, Gladstone never reached the degree of dependence of H. H. Asquith on Venetia Stanley.

The affair was, like Gladstone's work with prostitutes, carried on in the full knowledge of the political élite, amongst whom Laura Thistlethwayte was notorious. It occurred at the height of the Cabinet bargaining about the contents of the Irish Land Bill, and of Tory speculation about the balance of power within the Cabinet. The fifteenth Earl of Derby noted in his journal on 11 December 1869:

Strange story of Gladstone frequenting the company of a Mrs. Thistlethwaite, a kept woman in her youth, who induced a foolish person with a large fortune to marry her. She has since her marriage taken to religion, and preaches or lectures. This, with her beauty, is the attraction to G and it is characteristic of him to be indifferent to scandal. But I can scarcely believe the report that he is going to pass a week with her and her husband at their country house—she not being visited or received in society.*

The episode thus added to Gladstone's reputation amongst leading Whigs and Tories for eccentricity and 'madness'† and contributed to their underestimation of his self-control and resilience.

Generosity and naïvety characterized Gladstone's behaviour. He persistently saw the best—'a sheep or a lamb rather, that had been astray . . . and that had come back to the Shepherd's Fold'‡—where others had seen mere chicanery, and he largely ignored the dangers to himself, both as to

---

* J. Vincent, ed., *Disraeli, Derby and the Conservative Party* (1978), 346.

† Carnarvon had earlier reached this view: 'Gladstone seems to be going out of his mind. Northcote has just told me that Gladstone's last passion is Mrs Thistlethwayte. He goes to dinner with her and she in return in her preachments to her congregation exhorts them to put up their prayers on behalf of Mr G's reform bill.'

‡ Laura Thistlethwayte's feelings are hard to determine from the jumbled state of her letters to Gladstone—several hundred, undated and virtually unsortable—but they seem to be genuine enough: 'Oh how madly I love', she docketed Gladstone's letter of 16 March 1871.

the effect all this might have on his relationship with Catherine Gladstone, and as to the public. He several times reassured Laura Thistlethwayte about the security arrangements for safeguarding her letters and manuscript—'Were it to fall into the hands of some rogue'—but he assumed security and confidentiality on her part.

His confidence was justified. Mrs Thistlethwayte seems to have made little attempt to capitalize on her new respectability, save to send Gladstone frequent invitations to dinner, which were quite regularly accepted, and she seems to have had few political ambitions, unlike Olga Novikoff, 'the M.P. for Russia', who emerges in 1873 as something of an alternative to Mrs Thistlethwayte as a female correspondent outside the family, though the intensity of the relationship is in no sense comparable.

'Mrs. Th's' non-political nature may have been part of her appeal (though her Irish origins seem to have played some part in conditioning the tone of Gladstone's expressions about Ireland during the preparation of the Land Act), but her religiosity, constant expressions of suffering and pathetic concern with respectability would seem, in addition to her 'signal soul clad in a beautiful body', to have aroused in Gladstone a powerful fellow-feeling and sympathy. Her youthful sufferings had coincided with his great crisis of 1850–1, his 'saddest' year which 'well nigh tore me to pieces'—the height of his self-flagellation at the time of the Gorham Judgement, the apostasy of Manning and James Hope, and the crisis of his rescue work. With Laura Thistlethwayte in the 1870s he felt he could share, at least in retrospect, something of the crisis of the Victorian soul which his wife's serenity could not begin to comprehend: that Tennysonian mixture of religion, sex, and patriotism, each element both stimulating and moderating the others to produce a soul in great tension but in balance*—a mixture whose balance Gladstone only just maintained, and which conditioned all his public and private actions and thoughts. The pregnant image of his repeated phrase, 'my country is my first wife', was no convenient or casual platitude; it reflected the emotional and in some ways sexual involvement of Gladstone with his nation.

The Thistlethwayte affair seems to have siphoned off a good deal of the nervous energy which usually accompanied Gladstone's work with prostitutes. This certainly continued regularly while he was Prime Minister, and several of his encounters are marked by the sign 'X', denoting temptation on his part. But the sign is also used after some of his meetings with Mrs Thistlethwayte, a fact which in itself testified to the ambiguity of her position in Gladstone's mind. Was she friend, or rescue case? When she left for Egypt on doctor's advice in 1872, he noted in his diary: 'It is well for me that she goes.' She was not away for long, and no rescue case took her place as the focal point of Gladstone's extra-marital fixation.

* Gladstone gave Mrs Thistlethwayte his annotated copy of Tennyson.

Laura Thistlethwayte was not Gladstone's mistress in the physical sense—the reader may here be reminded of Gladstone's solemn declaration in 1896 that he had 'never been guilty of the act which is known as that of infidelity to the marriage bed'. But she fulfilled the other functions of that office.

'It embarrasses' was Gladstone's comment on her 'extraordinary claim for sympathy'; the reader may well feel the same about the correspondence which Gladstone's children, with a commendable sense of responsibility to posterity, decided not to destroy, but to preserve, side-by-side with their father's daily journal.

Not surprisingly, rescue work exposed Gladstone to danger: there is at least one suggestion reaching the stage of discussion with solicitors of what seems to be a paternity suit—'a "plant" as it is called'—though nothing came of it.

Family Affairs in the Early 1870s

What Catherine Gladstone thought of the Thistlethwayte affair, of the rescue work in this period, or of the meeting with the solicitors can only be guessed at. With respect to the 'plant', Gladstone told Freshfield, the solicitor, that his wife 'was wiser than I & said "You are too credulous"'. She may well have thought the same about her husband's relationship with Mrs Thistlethwayte. Self-reliant though Catherine Gladstone was, it is hard to believe that she was not wounded—though she may have become inured.

Certainly the family life of the Gladstones continued happy, though the closeness of the family was necessarily diminished by the dispersal of the children—Henry Neville to India, Herbert to University College, Oxford, and a Third in Mods, Agnes to be married. But Willy worked closely and now more easily with his father politically, and Stephen became rector of Hawarden on the death of Henry Glynne, Catherine Gladstone's brother.

Much the saddest family event of the early 1870s was the death of Sir Stephen Glynne, Catherine's other brother, the shy bachelor whose gentle antiquarianism had charmed away alarm at his financial incompetence. His funeral was a great Hawarden occasion, honoured with a full description in the diary. The mourning was intertwined in classic Gladstonian and Victorian fashion with the resettlement of the estate, as Gladstone gave his children 'a sketch of the romance, for such it is, of the financial history', and Willy entered into an inheritance he can hardly have felt was his own.

Stephen Glynne's death also provoked intense conversation on the future between the diarist and his wife: 'the future seemed to clear a little before her. But how greedy I am—not satisfied with the last 22 years, or the last 35!' Immediately after this, the death of his niece Ida, Sir Thomas Gladstone's daughter, required a visit to Fasque, the family house in

Kincardineshire, and brought about something of a reconciliation between William and his fiercely Tory elder brother. For William Gladstone it was understandably a nostalgic occasion, this visit to his father's house with its 'old and still dear details'. Ida's coffin was placed in the family vault next to that of his cherished daughter Jessy, and Gladstone's thoughts returned, as so often, to the dreadful, shattering year of 1850–1.

A Public Man and his Money

Defeat in the general election in January 1874 and retirement from active leadership of his party placed Gladstone in an unwonted situation. For nearly fifteen years, since 1859, he had been in office or expecting imminently to be in office. Now he was, at his own insistence as well as that of the electorate, responsible largely if not solely to himself. Difficulties at once arose. The first of these was money. 'Expulsion from office' brought to a point of crisis Gladstone's personal finances. The salary of £5000 which he drew as First Lord of the Treasury (he had received the same amount as chancellor from 1859 to 1866) had provided the chief element of the income necessary for his day-to-day living. With this assured, he had been able to make substantial capital purchases while in public office by borrowing, usually from his bankers, S. Scotts. In terms of his total assets, he was a wealthy man. At the end of his period of office, his accounts stood thus:

Class I	Property in Hawarden Parish	153,000
	Seaforth Estate	37,000
	Lease of 11 Carlton House Terrace	23,500
	Mortgage on Trinity College [Glenalmond]	2,500
	Outstanding rents etc.	4,000
		220,000
Class II	£8000 5% Preference Metropolitan District Railway at £62½	5,000
	£57,500 Ordinary Metropolitan District Railway at £30	17,000
	£5000 Philadelphia & Reading Mortgage Bonds	5,000
		247,000
Class III	Furniture, books, porcelain etc.	22,100
		£269,100

Against these assets were to be counted debts of £39,000, which included mortgages on 11 Carlton House Terrace (£4,500), on the 'Chester block' Saltney purchase at Hawarden (£9,000), the Aston estate purchase (£12,000), and the loss by Robertson Gladstone of about £6,000 of his brother William's share of the Seaforth estate near Liverpool. The Aston Hall purchase, which was made in October 1869 for £57,000, contained two collieries, and was a substantial addition to the Hawarden estate, but it only produced £2069. 10s. 1½d. net income in 1873. The net income on Gladstone's Flintshire estates for 1873 was £2695. 8s. 5d. (gross £5703. 18s. 8d.), a return on his assets there of two per cent.

Gladstone's purchases of land in Flintshire were less risky than his holdings of railway stocks and shares. As the above table shows, he was heavily, and in terms of his portfolio, narrowly involved in the Metropolitan District Railway. He had held shares in it for some time, but had increased his holdings at the end of the 1860s, and in 1869, after selling some of its stock, he bought £10,000 more. Unfortunately for him, the company fell into difficulties. Its dividend was passed and its shares fell. It is hard to calculate from Gladstone's records exactly what his losses on this railway were, but they appear to amount to about 50 per cent on about £50,000.

Gladstone's activities in the stock market, both as Chancellor and Prime Minister, were therefore, over a period of a decade, considerable, and known to be so. As mentioned above, he had no qualms about buying Consols when they fell to a favourable 90 when Bismarck invaded France. The *Chester Chronicle* found it necessary to point out that this was not money-making at the public expense and that 'the world of gossip . . . ringing with stories of Mr. Gladstone's pecuniary difficulties' was proved wrong.

The *Chronicle*'s report referred to the Aston Hall purchase, but gossip of this sort about Gladstone's share purchases seems to have been quite widely circulated, encouraged, apparently, surprisingly, unjustifiably, and perhaps for personal political ends, by his own stockbroker, James Watson, Lord Provost of Glasgow, whom he knighted in 1874. Lord Derby noted in his diary: 'In singular confirmation of the stories we had heard at Minard, the Lord Provost [i.e. Watson the stockbroker] told Pender, who repeated it to me not an hour afterward, that the Premier had been very active in stock exchange speculations, and had lately employed him (Watson). Very strange—but what motive had he to invent the story if not true?'* This sort of story was a clear exaggeration, and represented that expectation of hyperbole which Gladstone already encouraged among Tories. Gladstone had not been 'very active'; he had made purchases in the Metropolitan District Railway Company over a period of several years which had not paid off. He was at no time in financial difficulty and, with money as cheap as it was in 1869–72, short-term borrowing backed by the sort of assets Gladstone commanded was in no way imprudent.

---

* Watson's implication that his employment by Gladstone was unusual was quite misleading— they had been in regular correspondence and dealings since 1851. Nothing in the summer of 1872 in the Hawarden account books seems to bear out Watson's tale; there were no changes in the MDR holdings; £3,600 Pennsylvanian and Reading stock was bought.

None the less, Gladstone was short of ready cash, and in 1872 he drew the state of affairs to his wife's attention: 'why and how more pinched'. In 1873 he anticipated having to give up his house in Carlton House Terrace 'at or about the expiry of the present Government'. When his salary ended in February 1874, his immediate position became dramatically worse. He calculated in June 1874 that after 'necessary allowances' for his wife and five of his children, and his usual charitable donations, he had only £1000 'for all general expenditure whatsoever'. The death of his brother-in-law Sir Stephen Glynne, the owner of Hawarden, just after these calculations were made, made little difference for by the arrangement of 1865 the Glynne estates went to Willy Gladstone and anyway produced little net income. The way was thus pointed to the sale of 11 Carlton House Terrace and of some of his art collections as the best means of raising his income, and preparations were made in the last months of 1874 for the sales of these assets in 1875.

The second difficulty about the life of 'mental repose' which Gladstone intended for himself was that, still an MP, his activities were necessarily subject to persistent scrutiny. Thus his support for the manager of the Aston Hall Colliery in opposing attempts by the miners to impose a closed shop had national as well as local implications: even the life of the country squire exposed him to national attention and controversy.

The Aston Hall controversy was symptomatic of the sort of class tension which Liberalism could never avoid at the constituency level, however integrative its national ideology aspired to be. But far more dramatically national in implication were to be the religious thoughts which Gladstone retired to Hawarden to contemplate.

Religion in Retirement: 'Vaticanism' *the end of a career?*

Gladstone's religion had always been a complex and indivisible blend of the national and the personal. Intense personal experience related in his personality intimately and inseparably to intense feeling about 'National Religion'. A similar synchronous purpose pervaded his study of Homer which was always justified in terms of his religious view of world history rather than by antiquarianism. Thus his contemplation in his retirement of things of the spirit necessarily led rapidly to public involvement in ecclesiastical controversy. He found both the Anglican Church and Christian Europe threatened—the first by Archbishop Tait, Disraeli, and the anti-ritualists in both parties, and the second by the Papacy. Partly as a reward to what had been a powerful element in their support in the elections, the Conservatives made ecclesiastical bills—the Public Worship Regulation Bill for England and Wales and the Church Patronage Bill for Scotland—the first chief legislative business for their large majority.

In a manner reminiscent of his opposition to Palmerston's Divorce Bill in 1857, Gladstone moved Resolutions intended to transform the Public Worship Regulation Bill, and had to withdraw them a week later.* His ill-temper shows even through the flatness of the columns of Hansard. But whereas in 1857 he had acted on his own with a few friends to maintain the 'Catholic' position, in 1874 he was still nominally leader of the Liberal party, which contained a significant body of opinion, exemplified by Sir William Harcourt, hostile to 'Puseyism' and in favour of the bill. The isolation of the Tractarian Liberals within the party, evident in the controversy over education during the government, thus became confirmed in opposition.

The problem of the Vatican Council, and the issues of civil liberty and allegiance which it seemed to raise, had, as has been shown earlier, greatly exercised Gladstone's administration, both in its foreign and in its British policy. For Gladstone there was an added element—his longstanding and intense ambivalence about Roman Catholicism. He was drawn by its internationalism and majestic tradition, but repelled by what he saw as its authoritarianism, anti-liberalism, and refusal to acknowledge a distinction between secular, civil allegiance on the one hand, and spiritual obedience on the other. 'Temporal power' was the phrase by which Gladstone summed up these deficiencies; he saw the Vatican Decrees of 1870 as the climax of an attempt by the Papacy to regain by ultramontane authoritarianism what it had lost to nationalism. The apostasy of his sister in 1842 and of several of his friends in 1851 had provoked, as we have seen, the most intense crisis of his married life, a disturbance in the balance between religion, sex, and patriotism causing a reaction in all three elements of his personality. Recollecting this, he told Samuel Wilberforce on the occasion of the apostasy of his brother Robert Wilberforce in 1854:

For could I, with reference to my own precious children, think that one of them might possibly live to strike, though in sincerity and thinking he did God service, such a blow, how far rather would I that he had never been born.

It was not merely prudential politics, important though those certainly were, which caused Gladstone to make, on the occasion of her conversion to Roman Catholicism, a 'termination of any literary relations' between himself and his cousin, Mrs Bennett, his assistant when he translated Farini's *Lo Stato Romano* in the 1850s. Gladstone's public role had involved him in attempts to frustrate the success of the Infallibilists, led by Manning; his private religious contacts had led to links with the Old Catholic movement through his old friend J. J. I. von Döllinger, now excommunicated for his opposition to the decisions of the 1870 Council.

* He also powerfully opposed the Scottish Patronage Bill, but in this he had a substantial part of the Liberal party with him.

Just after leaving office, he dropped a hint that public expostulation might be on the way.

Hostility to developments in both Anglicanism and Roman Catholicism were expressed in Gladstone's signed article, 'Ritualism and Ritual', published in the *Contemporary Review*, and begun in August 1874 when the passing of the Public Worship Regulation Bill was completed. Alarmed by the barriers to Catholic ecumenicalism being erected by both sides, disturbed by the conversion to Roman Catholicism of Lord Ripon, his recent Cabinet colleague, moved by Charlotte Yonge's life of the Tractarian bishop J. C. Patteson which he was reviewing, impressed by the arguments and conferences of the Old Catholics, and stimulated by the appeals for help from Döllinger, whom he was visiting in Munich, Gladstone inserted into the proofs of his article on ritualism a fierce denunciation of British Roman Catholics for their supine reaction to the Vatican Decrees. After further consideration of the Old Catholic position, and with initial encouragement from the anti-Infallibilist Lord Acton, Gladstone 'Wrote on the Papal questions', writing which blossomed into his pamphlet *The Vatican Decrees in their bearing on civil allegiance: a political expostulation*, published on 7 November 1874. Acton, Ambrose Phillipps de Lisle, and Arthur Gordon who were at Hawarden during its preparation were alarmed by its intemperance: 'They all show me that I must act mainly for myself.'

Act for himself Gladstone certainly did. The pamphlet was a remarkable blend of political theory, Protestant anti-Popery, and Tractarian *angst*. Beneath the historical and ecclesiastical argument, important in itself and in its political implications, lay a profound sense of anger and betrayal— anger with the 'direct influence' of the Irish Roman Catholic bishops, anger with the Papacy from which much had never been expected, betrayal by Manning who should have known better, and by Newman who should have done more.

The Vatican Decrees showed Gladstone's extraordinary capacity to change direction. He had gone out of office at the start of 1874 after a spirited initiative in national finance; he ended the year as the protagonist of a vast controversy on Church and State whose pamphlets poured as voluminously from presses in America and Europe as they did from those in Britain. But he also confirmed the political direction which he had taken after the defeat of the general election by his informal retirement, for on the last day of 1874 he prepared for transmission his letters to Granville formally resigning as leader of the Liberal party. The Vatican controversy showed Gladstone's inability to leave the world of affairs; his resignation of even the title of party leader showed his refusal to accept that world's conventional limitations.

The day before revising his letters of resignation, Gladstone finished

Middlemarch: 'It is an extraordinary, to me a very jarring book.' 'Every limit is a beginning as well as an ending' remarks George Eliot in her 'Finale', and such a 'limit' was 1874 for Gladstone. What George Eliot called 'the home epic—the gradual conquest or irremediable loss of that complete union which makes the advancing years a climax, and age the harvest of sweet memories in common' was for Gladstone an epic written on a national as well as a domestic scale. From his country, his 'first wife', he found himself estranged, rejected by the political nation, at odds with most of the Protestant element of his own party on Anglican religion and education, and with almost all the Roman Catholic element on the Papacy. Gladstone's career was an extraordinary public epic, and 1874 was an important caesura in it—a break before a further twenty years at the forefront of British public life. That it was not the intended conclusion but a caesura before a long finale was not, and could not be, apparent to Gladstone.

References

CHAPTERS I AND II are new; notes to them will be found below. Chapters III to IX are already in print, and full references will be found in their footnotes in the relevant volume of *The Gladstone Diaries*: I have retained for this book only those footnotes of general interest. The following is the correlation between the chapters in this book and the printed Introductions: chapters III and IV are the Introduction (1840–1854) printed in Volume III (1974); chapters V and VI are the Introduction (1855–1868) printed in Volume V (1978); chapters VII, VIII, and IX are the Introduction (1869–1874) printed in Volume VII (1982).

In the preparation of these Introductions for incorporation in this book I have been very grateful for the assistance of Jean Gilliland, Fiona Griffiths, and Francis Phillips, and to Deryck Schreuder for reading the proofs.

Notes to Chapter I

1. S. G. Checkland, *The Gladstones. A family biography 1764–1851* (1971) contains an exhaustive account of the making of the family's finances, based on the huge family archive, now at St Deiniol's Library. See Checkland's Appendix II for a summary of the fortune.
2. 19 Apr. 60; all references to Gladstone's *Diaries* are in this form. In the references below, 'Add MS' refers to Additional Manuscripts in the British Library, among which are the Gladstone Papers, and 'Hawn P' to the manuscripts in St Deiniol's Library, Hawarden.
3. Gladstone's recollection in 1892, quoted in J. Brooke and M. Sorensen, eds., *The Prime Minister's Papers: W. E. Gladstone. i. Autobiographical memoranda* (1971), 16; henceforth *Autobiographica*.
4. Checkland, op. cit., 233–4.
5. G. W. E. Russell, *Mr. Gladstone's religious development. A paper read in Christ Church, May 5, 1899* (1899), 7, quoted in P. Butler, *Gladstone: church state and tractarianism. A study of his religious ideas and attitudes, 1809–1859* (1982), 12. Russell's evidence was a letter (not now extant) from Mrs Gladstone in 1818 or 1819, 'communicated' by J. Macdonald of Edinburgh. I have benefited from discussions with Perry Butler and from teaching a class on 'Church and State' for many years with John Walsh, to whom I am also grateful for his comments on this and the next chapter. I am similarly obliged to Marilyn Butler.
6. *Autobiographica*, ii. 61.
7. R. I. and S. Wilberforce, *The life of William Wilberforce* (1838), iv. 83 (Wilberforce was a friend of Gladstone's mother, see *Autobiographica*, i. 15); 29 Dec. 31.
8. *Autobiographica*, i. 140; see Butler, op. cit., 14.
9. W. E. Gladstone, 'The Evangelical movement: its parentage, progress and issue' (1879), in *Gleanings of past years* (1879), vii. 219. Applied to John Gladstone, this was a slightly unfair remark, as he built up a good collection of paintings. For the guns, see J. Morley, *The life of William Ewart Gladstone* (1903), i. 10–11.

10. *Autobiographica*, i. 13.

11. Ibid., 21. See also Butler, op. cit., 14.

12. See Add MSS 44715–8.

13. Gladstone to A. C. Benson, 26 August 1897, in A. C. Benson, *Fasti Etones* (1899), 501, 505.

14. Printed list of membership in Add MS 44717, f. 105.

15. Gladstone to his father, 25 June 1826, Hawn P 222.

16. See Gladstone to his father, 7 July 1826, in *Etoniana* (1938), 340; *Etoniana* reprinted accurately extracts from a number of Gladstone's letters home from Eton, the originals of which are at St Deiniol's. Extracts from the selection were reprinted in P. S. H. Lawrence, *The encouragement of learning* (1980). For Gladstone's later recollection, see C. Milnes Gaskell, *An Eton Boy* (1939), xvi.

17. Benson, *Fasti Etones*, 502; Gaskell, though of Unitarian background, was also a strong Canningite; he was a Tory MP 1832–68, holding office as a whip during Peel's government 1841–6.

18. See below, p. 177.

19. Benson, *Fasti Etones*, 502.

20. J. Kolb, ed., *The letters of Arthur Henry Hallam* (1981), 49. This splendid edition contains Hallam's copious letters to Gladstone; unfortunately few of Gladstone's to Hallam have survived. Gladstone's recollections in old age are in his 'Personal recollections of Arthur H. Hallam', *Daily Telegraph*, 5 January 1898, 9.

21. Kolb, *Hallam*, 77 (13–14 September 1826).

22. Ibid., 220.

23. See T. H. Vail Motter, *The writings of Arthur Hallam* (1943) and Henry Hallam's in this respect very candid memoir of his son in *Remains in verse and prose of Arthur Henry Hallam* (1834).

24. Vail Motter, op. cit., 45; the probable attribution of Gladstone as the subject seems quite right, especially given the date of composition—May 1829—and the poem's slightly nostalgic tone, reflecting the chronology of disintegration of intimacy quoted above. Vail Motter is clearly right in stating (p. 35) that the subject of the poem 'My bosom-friend' must be Gaskell and not Gladstone.

25. 1 July 26; 4 July 26; 10 Feb. 27.

26. F. H. Doyle, *Miscellaneous Verses* (1840), 25.

27. 2 Mar. 27; see also Checkland, op. cit., 114.

28. 26 Nov. 25.

29. 18 Dec. 26; 12 Mar., 14 June 27. Epitomes of Gibbon and of Hume are in Add MSS 44717, 44724, and 44792.

30. 3 June 27.

31. 4 May 26 and Kolb, *Hallam*, 108, 169.

32. Begun on 14 January 1827, just before his Confirmation. Doyly and Mant may have been used at the school's suggestion: in Newman's novel, *Loss and Gain* (1848), 3, Charles Reding at Eton fell 'into the hands of an excellent tutor, who, while he instructed him in the old Church-of-England principles of Mant and Doyley, gave his mind a religious impression . . .'. In Gladstone's annotated

copy, 'St. Saviour's College', where Reding goes after Eton, is noted as 'Ch.Ch.'.

33. 4 Feb. 27. The five volumes of Blair's *Sermons* (Gladstone had the 1822 edition) begun on 23 October 1825 were read together with Sumner on Sundays throughout 1826 and later. Blair's influential *Rhetoric* (1783) was read on weekdays. For him, see R. B. Sher, *Church and University in the Scottish Enlightenment* (1985).

34. 24 Sept., 1 Oct. 26.

35. 1 Feb. 27.

36. C. Milnes Gaskell, *Records of an Eton schoolboy* (1883), 85.

37. 2 Dec. 27.

38. Recollections of C. J. Canning in Gaskell, *Records of an Eton schoolboy*, 100.

39. Gladstone to his father, 3 November 1824; Hawn P 222; on the timing of his entry to Christ Church probably as a Commoner, rather than as a Gentleman Commoner.

40. Gladstone to his sister Anne, 17 November 1828, Hawn P 745.

41. Gladstone, 'Classical Education' [1835], Add MS 44725, f. 70; J. H. Newman, 'The Tamworth Reading Room' (1841) in *Discussions and arguments* (1872), 275.

42. See 24 Jan.–11 Apr. 28; the character of the Turner household is suggested by the presence of Miss Sumner, J. B. Sumner's sister. On the other hand, Turner introduced Gladstone to Edward Craig, a high Calvinist preaching in Edinburgh, whom Gladstone visited almost daily during a stay in Edinburgh in April–May 1828; see Butler, op. cit., 20–1.

43. Gaskell, *Records of an Eton schoolboy*, 140.

44. Add MS 44719, f. 246; n.d.

45. Gladstone to his father, 15 September [1831], Hawn P 222.

46. *Letters to M.G. & H.G. by John Ruskin with a preface by . . . G. Wyndham* (1903), 15.

47. Add MS 44808.

48. C. R. L. F[letcher], *Mr. Gladstone at Oxford 1890* (1908), 16.

49. Gladstone to his father, 27 September 1829, Hawn P 222; 'It was Hallam's communication concerning the Cambridge Society that first gave me the idea of going about to different people here with the idea of getting one similar to it set on foot among ourselves.'

50. Gladstone to his mother, 20 January 1830, Hawn P 394.

51. Gladstone to his mother, 19 February 1830, Hawn P 394.

52. See 21 Mar. 36 and Morley, i. 161.

53. Gladstone to his father, 31 May 1831, Hawn P 222.

Notes to Chapter II

1. 16 Aug. 40.

2. Correspondence in Hawn P 223 and 637; possibly with a view to keeping the seat open for Tom Gladstone, whom he praised later in the letter, John Gladstone (while leaving the decision open to William) told the Duke that William 'will complete his 23rd year in December and altho' his mind is matured beyond his years, yet I doubt if his experience is sufficient to justify his thus early entering upon such serious and responsible duties as Your Grace holds

out to him'; William, however, accepted by return of post from Italy. For this defence of pocket boroughs, see W. E. Gladstone, 'The County Franchise and Mr. Lowe thereon' (1877), reprinted in *Gleanings of Past Years* (1879), i. 136.

3. Gladstone to his sister Helen, 23 October 1831; to his father, 7 May [1831], Hawn P 222.

4. Gladstone to his mother, 7 April 1835, Hawn P 394 f. 214; Butler, 53n.

5. *Autobiographica*, i. 37.

6. Meeting of 12 June 1830, Add MS 44804, f. 42.

7. 'Report and proceedings of the opening of the Liverpool Collegiate Institution' (1843), 13. For the Reform Bill, see his notes for his Oxford Union speech and his 'Letter to Mr. Grant' (unpublished) in Add MS 44721, ff. 28, 86.

8. Memorandum of March 1829, now in Hawn P, printed in D. C. Lathbury, *Correspondence on Church and Religion of William Ewart Gladstone* (1910), i. 2–3.

9. Butler, 26–7; 3–4 Aug. 30.

10. 12 Aug. 30; letters of August 1830 printed in Morley, i. 635; the originals are in Hawn P 222.

11. Add MS 44719, f. 216. The authorities Gladstone quotes in this memorandum are Mant and Paley.

12. Letter of 7 January 1832 in *Autobiographica*, i, App. 2.

13. See the important thesis by Richard Brent, 'The emergence of Liberal Anglican Politics: the Whigs and the Church 1830–1841' (Oxford, 1984).

14. Section on Church and State in Gladstone's Oxford Union speech on the Reform Bill, 16 May 1831; notes in Add MS 44721, f. 23.

15. 'Report . . . of the Liverpool Collegiate Institution' (1843), 10.

16. For the continental dimension, see A. Vidler, *Prophecy and Papacy* (1954), ch. 4 and W. G. Roe, *Lamennais and England* (1966), ch. 4.

17. Add MS 44722–8. A. F. Robbins, *The early public life of . . . Gladstone* (1894) has much well-researched detail on Gladstone's constituency and parliamentary activities.

18. *Nottingham Journal*, 22 December 1832; 3 and 5 June 32.

19. 19 Feb. 35; Add MS 44724, f. 4 and *Autobiographica*, ii. 21.

20. 20 Nov. 35. See his reading lists set out following 28 Feb. 38, and Owen Chadwick, 'Young Gladstone and Italy' in P. Jagger, ed., *Gladstone, Politics and Religion* (1985). Aristotle's *Politics* was begun in the previous Recess, in August 1834.

21. Paper of 26 October 1835, Add MS 44724, f. 203; 4 Mar. 38; 'Speech on Irish Church Temporalities Bill, 31 March 1835' (extracted from 'The Mirror of Parliament'); 31 Mar. 35.

22. Add MS 44719, f. 115; the essay continues with many other similarly balanced comparisons. *Phaedo* was the main Platonic text read as an undergraduate. For Plato and Aristotle in Oxford, see D. Newsome, *Two Classes of Men. Platonism and English Romantic Thought* (1974). I am obliged to Dr Julia Annas for her comments on Gladstone's essay.

23. 'On the Principle of Government', begun on 24 May 31; Add MS 44721, f. 3.

24. 'Of the law of social obligation', of 16 December 1835, Add MS 44725, f. 183.

25. Notes on Aristotle's *Politics*, 1835, Add MS 44723, f. 125ᵛ. Gladstone repeated this comparison, with a slightly more Aristotelian leaning, to his son in 1860,

Lathbury, op. cit., ii. 164, quoted in Newsome, op. cit., 74. See also Agatha Ramm, 'Gladstone's Religion', *Historical Journal* (1985) and R. J. Helmstadter, 'Conscience and Politics: Gladstone's First Book' in B. L. Kinzer, ed., *The Gladstonian Turn of Mind* (1985), both published after this chapter was written; I do not go the whole way with Professor Helmstadter's views on Gladstone's Aristotelianism, but he has written a powerful essay on the basis of the published sources.

26. 8 Feb. 32.

27. For an interesting gloss on this, see O. Chadwick, op. cit., 69. For his Oxford notes on Roman Catholicism, see Add MS 44719, f. 191.

28. 29 and 31 Mar. 32; 8 Oct. 38.

29. 15 Apr. 32.

30. 13 May 32; it is important to note that Gladstone went to the Prayer Book to look into 'the details of the system'; he was *not*, as Magnus thought, 'idly examining the *Occasional Offices*' (see Magnus, 12).

31. W. E. Gladstone, 'Speech on Irish Church Temporalities Bill, 31 March 1835' (extracted from 'The Mirror of Parliament'). See also his speech of 29 June 1840, published in pamphlet form as 'Speech of W. E. Gladstone, esq., M.P., in the House of Commons, Monday, June 29, 1840' (1840); inadequately reported in *Hansard*.

32. See H. C. G. Matthew, 'Gladstone, Vaticanism, and the Question of the East', in D. Baker, ed., *Studies in Church History*, xv. 417 (1978).

33. Gladstone's annotated copy of Arnold's pamphlet, dated 'January 1833' (the month of publication) is in St Deiniol's Library, as is his annotated copy of Arnold's important 'Postscript'.

34. Note of 27 October 1837, Add MS 44727, f. 178. See 20, 27 Aug., 29–31 Oct. 37. See also 24–6 Feb. 36. Gladstone's copy of Coleridge's *Church and State*, with marginal annotations, proof corrections and an added quotation, is in St Deiniol's Library.

35. 24 Mar. 34 (fly leaf).

36. *The State* (1838), 6, 17–18.

37. *Church Principles*, 3.

38. *The State* (1838), 312.

39. 'Speech on Irish Church Temporalities Bill, 31 March 1835' (extracted from 'The Mirror of Parliament'), 8.

40. Notes of 1838 on Palmer (e.g. criticizing his over-confident demarcation between which Churches' members can be saved) in Add MS 44728, f. 138ff.

41. *The State* (1838), 312.

42. *Church Principles*, as quoted in D. Nicholls, 'Gladstone and the Anglican Critics of Newman', in J. D. Bastable, *Newman and Gladstone* (1978), 121–4.

43. Paper of 25 February 1836, Add MS 44726, f. 21.

44. For an interesting exposition of Butler's influential arguments on this point, see J. R. Lucas, 'Butler's Philosophy of Religion Vindicated' (1978), 8. For the passage on politics of 11 December 1835, see Add MS 44725, ff. 108–9.

45. For the Scottish Church, see note of 25 August 1838, Add MS 44728, f. 141; see also *The State* (1838), ch. 3. For the Irish Union, see 'Speech on Irish Church

Temporalities Bill, 31 March 1835' (extracted from 'The Mirror of Parliament'), 9.

46. 19 Apr. 39 and letter to Russell, 12 April 1870 in *Diaries*, vii. 275; quoted in Morley, i. 130.

47. Butler, op. cit., 68–9.

48. 1 May 38. See also Gladstone's strong defence of the cathedrals on Puseyite lines in his 'Speech ... in the House of Commons, Monday, June 29, 1840' (1840) on the Ecclesiastical Duties and Revenues Bill, reprinted from *The Mirror of Parliament*. For this aspect of Pusey, see H. C. G. Matthew, 'Edward Bouverie Pusey: from Scholar to Tractarian', *Journal of Theological Studies* (1981).

49. J. S. Mill to G. d'Eichthal, 27 December 1839, in F. E. Mineka, ed., *The Earlier Letters of John Stuart Mill 1812–1848* (1963), ii. 416.

50. Notes on Aristotle, 1835, Add MS 44723, f. 120. Speech on disfranchisement of Liverpool freemen, 1 March 1833, *H* xxii. 474.

51. Article intended for *Dublin University Magazine*, written in May 1834, Add MS 44681, f. 12. On 17 May 34, Gladstone noted: 'finished my paper: a sorry affair'; doubtless he therefore did not submit it for publication.

52. 18 June 34.

53. Add MS 44728, f. 28 and Lathbury ii. 433.

54. Letter of 18 December 1835, in Magnus, 27, which gives a good description of the affair.

55. Verses written in September 1837, Add MS 44727, f. 175, partly quoted in Richard Shannon, *Gladstone* (1982), i. 63.

56. 14 Nov. 37; 31 Jan. 38; and Magnus, 30.

57. M. R. D. Foot's translation of Gladstone's Italian diary entry, 28 Apr. 38.

58. 23 May and 4 June 38.

59. 3 Dec. 35ff.

60. 23 July 38; 29 Jan. 38.

61. 30 Jan.–1 Feb. 36.

62. In Magnus, 38–9.

63. 6 Feb. 39.

64. 8–15 June 39.

65. 14 June 39.

66. 15, 27 July 39.

67. 'Report of the Liverpool Collegiate Institution' (1843); John Gladstone was a chief contributor to the Institution.

68. This, and subsequent figures, are taken from the 'Secret Account Book' and from the 'Rough Books' in the Hawarden Papers.

69. Memorandum of 18 September 1836, Add MS 44726, f. 147.

70. Add MSS 44779–81.

71. Note of 25 March 1838, Add MS 44728, f. 36.

72. Paper dated 5 May 1839, Add MS 44728, f. 254.

73. Letter of 4 September 1826, the third of his *Liverpool Courier* letters, Add MS 44718, f. 74; *Nottingham Journal*, 11 August 1832; pamphlet dated 21 November 1834, Add MS 44723, f. 306; see 20–1 Nov. 34. There are notes made in 1835 on

'Free Trade and Toryism', but these are on the legislation of the 17th and 18th centuries; Add MS 44724, f. 205.

74. Correspondence of January 1841 in Add MS 44135, f. 1ff. and part in Morley, i. 232, 239; it is unclear on the MS whether the italicization is Gladstone's or Cobden's.

75. W. E. Gladstone, 'Course of commercial policy at home and abroad', *Foreign and Colonial Review* (January 1843), 264.

76. Undated paper, probably 1839; Add MS 44728, f. 336; 24 Mar. 34.

Further Reading

GLADSTONE'S huge archive is preserved in three parts: first, in the British Library, whither Tilney Bassett, the family archivist, sent what he regarded as the public section of the papers; second, deposited in St Deiniol's Library, Hawarden, and produced by the Clwyd Record Office next door, is the family section of the papers, together with a good deal of minor political correspondence not sent by Bassett to London, and the papers of Sir John, Catherine, Thomas, Helen Jane, and other Gladstones and Glynnes; third, in Lambeth Palace Library and owned by the Archbishop of Canterbury, are the diaries, their ancillary papers, and the Thistlethwayte correspondence (these become available progressively as they are published in the *Diaries*). Letters *from* Gladstone are to be found in virtually all nineteenth-century collections.

A career as vast as Gladstone's has spawned a huge literature, not yet gathered together in a bibliography. The following books and articles, relevant to this volume, are only a selection.

The various contemporary lives of Gladstone, and especially those by R. Masheder (1865) and G. Barnett Smith, 2 vols. (1879) are mostly well-informed and well-illustrated. W. Bagehot, 'Gladstone', *National Review* (1860), reprinted in *Biographical Studies*, ed. R. H. Hutton (various editions) is the most interesting contemporary interpretation. A. F. Robbins, *The early public life of W. E. Gladstone* (1894) is very well-researched as is Sir T. Wemyss Reid, ed., *The Life of... Gladstone* (1899) with excellent illustrations. Sir E. W. Hamilton, *Mr. Gladstone. A monograph* (1898) is an important memoir by one of Gladstone's secretaries; two other secretaries' works are also useful: Lord Kilbracken, *Reminiscences* (1931) and Sir A. West, *Recollections 1832–1886*, 2 vols. (1899). Two autobiographical works by Cabinet colleagues sometimes have difficulty in avoiding becoming biographies of Gladstone: Lord Selborne's *Memorials*, 4 vols. (1896–8) and the Duke of Argyll's *Autobiography and memoirs*, 2 vols. (1908). The many Punch cartoons of Gladstone are collected in *The political life of... Gladstone... illustrated from Punch*, 3 vols. (n.d.), with a well-informed commentary; the cartoons are more illuminating than most monographs.

But the starting point of all works on Gladstone will always be John Morley's finely researched biography, 3 vols. (1903). Robert Blake memorably quoted the *DNB*'s remark, that Monypenny and Buckle's *Disraeli* is a 'quarry and a classic'; Morley's life is both of those, and a living interpretation also. How often the modern scholar thinks he has found a startling quotation or a new idea, only to have to admit it is already 'in Morley'! Morley worked quickly and made some slips; he also purposely omitted much on Gladstone's private life, in the way that Harrod did with Keynes. This does not, in my view, greatly vitiate his treatment of the public career, including Gladstone's views on public Christianity which Morley, despite his agnosticism, treats generously. Morley's omissions do, however, seriously limit our all-round understanding of Gladstone's character and of the preoccupations of his age; as with many Victorian biographies—Liddon's

Pusey is a notable exception—the masking of 'frailties' makes the subject less sympathetic to the modern reader than need be the case. None the less, though I have by no means offered an interpretation similar to Morley's, my respect for him has grown each time I have used him. Morley's shortcomings are discussed in M. R. D. Foot, 'Morley's Gladstone: a reappraisal', *Bulletin of the John Ryland's Library* (1969).

Gladstone is now fairly well served by editions of his papers and works. The chief are: *The Gladstone Diaries with Cabinet Minutes and Prime-Ministerial Correspondence*, eds. M. R. D. Foot and H. C. G. Matthew, nine volumes (1968–86) now having been published to reach 1880 (the first includes a notable Introduction by M. R. D. Foot); D. C. Lathbury, *Correspondence on church and religion*, 2 vols. (1910), an under-used work; P. Guedalla, *The Palmerston Papers, Gladstone and Palmerston, 1851–1865* (1928) and *The Queen and Mr. Gladstone*, 2 vols. (1933); Agatha Ramm, *The political correspondence of Mr. Gladstone and Lord Granville*, 4 vols. (1952–62); J. Brooke and M. Sorensen, *The Prime Minister's Papers: W. E. Gladstone*, 4 vols. (1971–81) includes many of his 'autobiographical' memoranda; A. Tilney Bassett, *Gladstone to his wife* (1936); his edition of *Gladstone's Speeches* (1916), has a useful bibliography; W. E. Gladstone, *Gleanings of past years*, 7 vols. (1879) and *Later gleanings* (1897, 2nd edn. 1898) are Gladstone's own selection from his reviews, pamphlets, and articles.

Morley was followed by J. L. Hammond's moving book, *Gladstone and the Irish Nation* (1938, reprinted with an introduction by M. R. D. Foot 1964), a salute from a liberal generation that had lost its base and perhaps its way, which is *a fortiori* the case with Erich Eyck, *Gladstone*, tr. (1938). Alec Vidler, *The Orb and the Cross: a normative study in the relations of church and state, with reference to Gladstone's early writings* (1945) anticipated by a generation the revival of interest in early Victorian religion. Philip Magnus, *Gladstone* (1954) used the private family papers, but not the diary and its ancillary documents; the book makes Gladstone accessible but rather quaint; the *Diaries* have rendered out-of-date some of Magnus's sections on the private life. S. G. Checkland, *The Gladstones. A family biography 1764–1851* (1971) is a fine account very largely based on the family papers. Several older studies of aspects of the career remain valuable: F. W. Hirst, *Gladstone as financier and economist* (1931), commissioned by H. N. Gladstone to remind Liberals of their duty; P. Knaplund, *Gladstone and Britain's imperial policy* (1927) and *Gladstone's foreign policy* (1935); F. E. Hyde, *Gladstone at the Board of Trade* (1934); D. H. MacGregor, *Public aspects of finance* (1939) and J. A. Schumpeter, *History of economic analysis* (1954) have important sections on Gladstone; A. F. Thompson, 'Gladstone's whips and the General Election of 1868', *English Historical Review* (1948) and his lapidary 'Gladstone' in *British Prime Ministers* (1953); J. L. Hammond and M. R. D. Foot, *Gladstone and liberalism* (1952); G. M. Young, 'The Schoolman in Downing Street', *Victorian Essays* (1962). Some more recent studies are J. B. Conacher, *The Aberdeen Coalition 1852–1855* (1968); Maurice Cowling, *1867: Disraeli, Gladstone and revolution* (1967); Richard Deacon, *The private life of Mr. Gladstone* (1965), a curious amalgam of error and inside information; D. A. Hamer, *Liberal politics in the age of Gladstone and Rosebery* (1972); David Nicholls, 'Gladstone on liberty and democracy', *Review of Politics* (1961); John Prest, 'Gladstone and Russell', *Transactions of the Royal Historical Society* (1966); F. B. Smith, *The making of the Second Reform Bill* (1966); John

Vincent, *The formation of the British Liberal Party 1857—68* (1966); Maurice Wright, *Treasury control of the civil service 1854—1874* (1969).

Gladstone has naturally figured prominently in the great boom in Victorian studies since the 1960s. Recent books and articles dealing with the part of his career covered in this volume—some of them using the *Diaries* and their Introductions extensively—include: B. Baysinger and R. Tollison, 'Chaining Leviathan: the case of Gladstonian finance', *History of Political Economy* (1980); D. E. D. Beales, 'History and biography' (1981); Perry Butler, *Gladstone: Church, State and Tractarianism* (1982); L. Goldman, 'The Social Science Association 1851–1886: a context for mid-Victorian liberalism', *English Historical Review* (1986); D. Hamer, 'Gladstone: the making of a political myth', *Victorian Studies* (1978); A. B. Hawkins, 'A forgotten crisis: Gladstone and the politics of finance during the 1850s', *Victorian Studies* (1983); Boyd Hilton, 'Gladstone's theological politics' in M. Bentley and J. Stevenson, *High and low politics in modern Britain*; H. Lloyd Jones, 'Gladstone on Homer', in *Blood for the Ghosts* (1982); M. J. Lynch, 'Was Gladstone a Tractarian?', *Journal of Religious History* (1975); G. I. T. Machin, 'Gladstone and nonconformity in the 1860s', *Historical Journal* (1974); H. C. G. Matthew, 'Disraeli, Gladstone and the politics of mid-Victorian budgets', *Historical Journal* (1979) and 'Gladstone, Vaticanism and the Question of the East' in *Studies in Church History*, vol. 15 (1978); David Nicholls, 'Gladstone and the Anglican critics of Newman' in J. Bastable, *Newman and Gladstone* (1978); J. P. Parry, 'Religion and the collapse of Gladstone's first government, 1870–74', *Historical Journal* (1982); Marcia Pointon, 'Gladstone as an art patron and collector', *Victorian Studies* (1975); Agatha Ramm, 'Gladstone as Man of Letters' (1981) and 'Gladstone's Religion', *Historical Journal* (1985); Deryck Schreuder, 'Gladstone and Italian unification: the making of a Liberal?', *English Historical Review* (1970), 'Gladstone and the conscience of the state' in P. T. Marsh, ed., *The Conscience of the Victorian State* (1979), and 'Gladstone as trouble-maker', *Journal of British Studies* (1978); David Steele, *Irish Land and British Politics* (1974); and there is a crop of recent biographies: E. J. Feuchtwanger, *Gladstone* (1975); Joyce Marlow, *Mr. and Mrs. Gladstone: an intimate biography* (1977); Richard Shannon, *Gladstone*, i (1982); Peter Stansky, *Gladstone* (1979).

B. Kinzer, ed., *The Gladstonian turn of mind* (1985) and P. J. Jagger, ed., *Gladstone, politics and religion* (1985) are collections of essays many of which are of value. Two series of reviews of the *Diaries* are of interest in themselves: Agatha Ramm in the *English Historical Review* (1970, 1976, 1979, 1984) and Derek Beales in the *Historical Journal* (1982, 1983).

Brief Chronology, 1809–1874

1847	August	Elected for Oxford University (two seats): Inglis, 1700; Gladstone, 997; Round, 824
	December	Oak Farm bankruptcy
1848	April	Serves as special constable during Chartist meetings
1849	July–August	In Italy, following Lady Lincoln
1850	April	Death of Catherine Jessy
	June	*Remarks on the Royal Supremacy* (on the Gorham case)
	October	In Naples
1851	February	Back in Britain. Intense rescue work
	April	Hope and Manning apostasize
	April, July	*First* and *Second Letter to Aberdeen*
	December	Death of Sir J. Gladstone 'On the functions of laymen in the Church' and translation of Farini, *The Roman State*, 4 vols.
1852	January	*An examination of the official reply of the Neapolitan government*
	July	Re-elected for Oxford University: Inglis, 1369; Gladstone, 1108; Marsham, 758.
	December	Speeches on free trade, Disraeli's budget Chancellor of the Exchequer
1853	January	Re-elected for Oxford University: Gladstone, 1022; Perceval, 898
	April	First budget
1854	March	Second budget
	April	Oxford University Bill
	May	War Budget
1855	February	Out of office
1856	September	'The declining efficiency of Parliament' in *Quarterly*
1857	August	Opposes Divorce Bill
1858	March	*Studies on Homer and the Homeric Age*, 3 vols.
	November	Lord High Commissioner Extraordinary for Ionian Islands
1859	February	Returned unopposed for Oxford University
	March	Back in Britain
	April	Returned unopposed for Oxford University
	June	Chancellor of the Exchequer
	July	Re-elected for Oxford University: Gladstone, 1050; Chandos, 859
	November	Elected Lord Rector of Edinburgh University
1860	February	Budget and Cobden Treaty
1861	February	Post Office Savings Bill
1862	October	Newcastle speech on American Civil War
1864	March	Government Annuity Bill
	May	'Pale of the Constitution' speech Start of contact with Laura Thistlethwayte

1865	July	Defeated at Oxford University: Heathcote, 3236; Gathorne Hardy, 1904; Gladstone, 1724
		Elected for S. Lancashire, three seats: Egerton, 9171; Turner, 8806; Gladstone, 8786; Leigh, 8476; Thompson, 7703; Heywood, 7653
	October	Death of Palmerston: Russell Prime Minister
1866	March	Reform Bill
	June	Out of office on resignation of Russell's government Exchequer and Audit Act
	October	In Rome
1867	February	Back in Britain
	December	Speeches in Lancashire
1868	March	Supports Compulsory Church Rates Abolition Bill Moves resolutions for Irish Church disestablishment
	November	Elected for Greenwich, two seats: Salomons, 6684; Gladstone, 6386; Parker, 4704; Mahon, 4372
		A Chapter of Autobiography
		Defeated in S.W. Lancashire: Cross, 7729; Turner, 7676; Gladstone, 7415; Grenfell, 6939
	December	Prime Minister
1869	March	Irish Church Disestablishment Bill
	August	*Juventus Mundi*
	October	Intense correspondence with Laura Thistlethwayte
1870	February	Irish Land Bill
	March	Elementary Education Bill
	October	'Germany, France and England', on Franco-Prussian War, anon. In *Edinburgh Review*
1871	July	Abolition of purchase by royal warrant
1872	September	Alabama claims arbitration award
1873	February	Irish Universities Bill
	March	Unsuccessfully offers resignation of government
	June–July	Government rocked by scandals
	August	Chancellor of Exchequer as well as Prime Minister
1874	January	Dissolves Parliament
	February	Re-elected for Greenwich: Boord, 6193; Gladstone, 5968 (Liberal); Liardet, 5561; Langley, 5525 (Liberal)
		Resignation as Prime Minister and quasi-resignation as Liberal leader
	June	Death of Sir S. Glynne
	July	Resolutions on Public Worship Regulation Bill
	September	In Germany with Döllinger
	November	*The Vatican Decrees*
	December	Writes letter formally resigning as Liberal leader

Index